The Four Graces

Queen Victoria's Hessian Granddaughters

By Ilana D. Miller

Second Edition – 2014

EUROHISTORY.COM

ISBN 978-0-9771961-9-7
Copyright © 2011 Ilana D. Miller
First Edition – April 2011
Second Edition – September 2014

Published by:

Kensington House Books
a division of Eurohistory
6300 Kensington Avenue
East Richmond Heights, CA 94805 USA
Telephone: (510) 236-1730
Fax: (510) 778-8465
Email: books@eurohistory.com
URL: http://www.eurohistory.com

Cover design by Arturo E. Beéche and David W. Higdon
Editing by Arturo E. Beéche & David W. Higdon
Layout & Design by Arturo E. Beéche
A proud product of the USA

To Countess Mountbatten of Burma, CBE, with affection and in memory of her beloved Grandmother, the eldest of the Four Graces...

Table of Contents

*(*) All illustrations provided by the Eurohistory
Royal Photographic Archive and Dr. Mary Houck*

Acknowledgements

*I*would like to acknowledge the gracious permission of Her Majesty Queen Elizabeth II in allowing me to examine letters, documents, and photos in the Royal Archives and to quote portions of those documents. I wish also to thank Pamela Clark, the Registrar, Frances Dimond, the Curator of the Photograph Collection, now retired, and all the staff at the archives for their hard work, patience, and help, as well as the wonderful supply of tea and cookies that were essential for any kind of research.

For the valuable insights he provided, I would like to thank HRH The Duke of Edinburgh for graciously taking the time to answer questions about his grandmother, Princess Victoria of Hesse and by Rhine.

I am also grateful to Lord Brabourne and the Broadlands Archives for permitting me to read and quote from documents there. Dr. Christopher Woolgar and his staff at the Hartley Library Archive & Special Collection, Southampton University, were unfailingly courteous and helpful.

With the permission of Landgraf Moritz of Hesse, the Hessisches Staatsarchiv, comprised of Dr. Prof. E. G. Franz and his staff, were accommodating not only to me, but to my fellow researchers, Katrina Warne and Sue Woolmans, who were both indefatigable and incredibly generous with their time for this endeavor.

I want to thank Alexander von Solodkoff as well as Duchess Donata and Duchess Edwina of Mecklenburg for giving me access to letters from their great-grandmother, Princess Irène of Hesse and by Rhine, from Hemmelmark Archives.

The Hoover Institute went above and beyond the call of duty, providing me with a copy of all the correspondence consequent of Princess Victoria's effort to arrange transport for the coffin of Grand Duchess Elisabeth to Jerusalem for burial. I would like to thank the archivist Ronald M. Bulatoff for answering questions about Mikhal de Giers.

I am grateful to Prince David Chavchavadze and Professor Will Lee for providing me with material about a visit that the Grand Duke Dimitri Pavlovich made to Princess Victoria and for permission to use that material.

I would also like to thank Philip Goodman for giving me permission by email to use comments of his wife, Sonia Goodman, about Baroness von Buxhoeveden.

Both the photo collections of Eurohistory and Dr. Mary Houck have granted me unrestricted use of their materials. I am extremely thankful for their generosity.

I am enormously appreciative that Mr. Robin Piguet wrote the letter that introduced me to The Countess Mountbatten of Burma, CBE, and for my subsequent correspondence with that lady. She and her late husband, Lord Brabourne, were kind enough to invite me to lunch, and besides tasting my first partridge, I was regaled with interesting tidbits about Lady Brabourne's mother, Edwina Mountbatten and grandmother, Princess Victoria of Hesse and by Rhine. She has graciously answered questions and patiently read chapters and her comments have been invaluable. It is to Patricia, that I fondly dedicate this volume.

A book like this requires much time, research, and travel, and is a true collaborative effort. I would like to thank and acknowledge as many people as possible knowing that I will forget some, and hope that they will forgive me for the inadvertent omission.

Hugo Vickers kindly gave me some parts of his research that speeded the development of this project. He never hesitated to answer any of my questions. I would like to mention the late Theo Aronson, who showed me and many others "how it's done" – he was a very dear man. Christopher Warwick and I had many lively email sessions discussing our theories about Princess Elisabeth of Hesse and by Rhine and Grand Duke Serge Alexandrovich. Greg King shared his extensive knowledge about the Hesses and the Romanovs with me, never failing to respond to all queries. John Van der Kiste generously answered any questions put to him.

I would like to thank Arturo Beéche for his enduring faith in this subject and his constant encouragement and enthusiasm. I appreciate David Higdon, Henry Wong and Seth Leonard for providing their expertise in preparing this second edition for publication.

I would like to thank Gloria T. Miller for her technical reading and Katrina Warne and Sue Woolmans who generously read the chapters over and over again, making suggestions and catching any factual errors that might have occurred. However, any technical or factual errors are mine and mine alone.

I would like to most especially thank my late dear Dad for his constant badgering; I would like to think that somewhere he is seeing this volume in its final form.

The following friends have been steadfast cheerleaders, Xeroxing or emailing letters, documents, and photographs, of places, people and things, in case they might be of some help for this project; I hope that they will be gratified with the results: Kevin Brady for his extensive knowledge of Irène; Ricardo Mateos Sainz de Medrano, for his suggestions and interesting letters from the Madrid Archives; Diana de Courcy-Ireland for her encouragement and the lovely lunches at Fortnum's as well as our wonderful day on the Isle of Wight, and Marion Wynn, also for her encouragement; Margaret Guyver for keeping me company in Romsey; Ian Shapiro for his constant support, cups of tea and interesting letters; Robert Golden for his unique look at Kensington Palace; Colin and Janice Parrish for the fascinating day in Bray and Cliveden; Charlotte Zeepvat for answering any and all questions and Coryne Hall for being so helpful; Margaret and Pamela Davis for their enthusiasm and making suggestions about where I might find additional material; Marlene Eilers Koenig for answering questions very early on as well as her impeccable resource *Queen Victoria's Descendents*; and, Lisa Davidson and Charles Stewart, for our monthly lunches and analytical discussions at the Farmers Market.

And also to my friends and relatives, who have been patient with me during this long journey: Liz Freedman, Soozi Parker Levin, Judy O'Brien, Georgia Taylor, Christina Wright, Lisa and Tom Miller, Steve Fisch, Sheri de Borchgrave, Frances Heller, Scott, Lisa, Spencer, Erika, Sydney, Zachary Samuel, Adam and Corey Miller, Rebecca, Ana and Aaron Schilleci, all the Karpels, the Goulds, Mike Woolmans and Steve Mothersdale for his constant emails at a tough time.

Lastly, as always, to my wonderful parents.

Prologue

December 1947

Kensington Palace sits quietly amid the grass, the wind-swept trees, and the honking Canadian geese, in Kensington Gardens. Though the park is virtually in the center of London, it is a serene, wooded respite in the middle of a noisy crowded city. Children play, mothers wheel their infants up and down the gravel paths, and young men organize soccer games on the grass of this sanctuary from the raucous world around. The palace, located at the side of the park, conveys a quiet, solid dignity. If one stands and gazes at it for a few minutes, the noise and confusion seem to disappear.

The tumultuous story of Princess Victoria of Hesse and by Rhine, favorite granddaughter of Queen Victoria, wife of the First Sea Lord of the Admiralty, and, now in her waning years, the Dowager Marchioness of Milford Haven, and her three younger sisters, begins at Kensington Palace, a few years after the end of the Second World War. The palace was used as a domicile of many royal relatives. Mostly princesses and duchesses, they used "KP," as they affectionately called it, as a sort of pied-a-terre in town. Others, including several widowed daughters of Queen Victoria, found the palace a kind of dower house. Because of its unique residents, it was called the 'Aunt Heap' by, amongst others, the Duke of Windsor.

Princess Victoria and her younger sisters, Elisabeth, Irène, and Alix, had been an integral part of a unique family group their grandmother had half-lovingly and half-wryly called 'The Royal Mob'. This mob included Queen Victoria's nine children and her forty-two grandchildren. Some of them became sovereigns and sat on various European thrones. In turn, this led to the Queen being called 'Grandmama of Europe.' This group of Kings, Tsars, Kaisers, Empresses, Queens, Princes, Princesses, Grand Dukes, and some otherwise Lords and Ladies, converged on the Queen during wars, natural disasters, and family disagreements in order to celebrate weddings, mourn deaths, commemorate reigns and otherwise forgather.

Unlike many of her cousins and even her sisters, Princess Victoria, the eldest of the Hessian Grand Ducal children, had elected not to ride the wave of glory, or grand tragedy. She had neither throne nor magnificent marriage. Instead, she had chosen to remain the bedrock foundation of her immediate family. She was a person that in the maelstrom of wars, grotesque murders and infamous scandals, pervasive of the century, remained a solid and abiding lynch-pin for her Hessian siblings. Their personal collective fates were perhaps the most consistently tragic of Queen Victoria's numerous and extended family.

By early fall 1947, with Britain in its postwar austerity period, many of those children and grandchildren were gone – and along with them, much of the 'Sturm und Drang'. Princess Victoria's Aunt Beatrice, the Queen's last remaining child, had died during the war, leaving just scattered relations – some separated by the bitterness of two bloody wars, and others by time, distance, and indifference. Nevertheless, the 'Mob' was reviving for a tiny instant in order to attend a royal wedding. Having gone to countless royal weddings, christenings, coronations, jubilees and funerals, it is hard to imagine any such occasion being unique, special, or even interesting to the eighty-four-year-old princess. Nevertheless, this one surely was – and not just because it was a gathering of the remnants of those bygone days. No doubt, the Princess smiled to herself as she fingered the velum envelope turning it around in her hands. She assuredly felt vindication for herself, her late husband, his brothers and sister, and, indeed, her entire family.

****

Though Victoria's sisters did unimaginably well in the dynastic marriage sweepstakes, Victoria's marriage to Prince Louis of Battenberg, himself the product of a morganatic union, had been considered a marriage beneath a granddaughter of Queen Victoria – something of which to be ashamed. It was a marriage that would face severe discrimination by many of the leading Royal Families of Europe. Foremost among the detractors was her first cousin, Kaiser Wilhelm. He was joined by Tsar Alexander III of Russia, also a cousin, who disliked Victoria's husband and his family, for political reasons and because they were not quite 'of the blood'.

Or, perhaps the dislike was simply jealousy, that Louis and his brothers, a family of ambitious princes, were called the handsomest in Europe by one of their staunchest enemies, German Chancellor Prince Otto von Bismarck.

Victoria's grandmother, Queen Victoria, surprisingly enlightened, never entertained these prejudices. While Wilhelm and Alexander scoffed, the Queen was indignant since Victoria was, beyond question, her most beloved granddaughter. What, she would ask, were they talking about? Horses? Cattle? The Queen, in fact, loved quoting Lord Granville, who said that if the Queen approved of such marriages, what had other people got to say about them? It certainly improved the Princess's cause when the Queen's own youngest daughter, Victoria's Aunt Beatrice, married into the same family.

In addition to the dynastic skepticism expressed by the then future Kaiser and the Tsar, there were others that nursed a long-term dislike of Victoria's husband. Many in the Royal Navy harbored enmity toward him during his extensive service, only because he was a German prince, who, in their opinion, was getting preferential treatment because of his close relationship to the British Royal Family. It was true that he had never been a man who espoused the particular male bonhomie that is so prevalent in the various branches of military service. He never seemed to enjoy the drinking and general carousing in which the other officers indulged. Furthermore, he was too intellectual. His interests lay in discussing books and music rather than the less cerebral matters which interested many of the other naval officers.

Yet, despite all of this, he was adored by his men.

****

In the end, however, the story of Victoria and her sisters had always been a tale only half told. Alix, the youngest, was the most often profiled in connection with the downfall of the Romanovs and Imperial Russia, as was, to a lesser extent, Ella, called the most beautiful princess in Europe. Victoria and Irène were thrust into the background since Victoria's life was so private, and Irène's was so fraught with unhappiness, being on the opposing side to her other sisters in two tragic wars. Therefore, telling the story of the four Princesses together recounts a somewhat different tale, where the illumination of the eldest and strongest,

Victoria, and the more malleable Irène, provide context and a greater understanding of their more famous sisters.

Therefore, on this particular fall day, as the life of Princess Victoria was very slowly coming to its conclusion, she opened the vellum envelope. Its contents took on a particular significance for the old lady that was especially sweet. With deep satisfaction and perhaps even a glimmer of triumph, she read:

> *The Lord Chamberlain is commanded by*
> *Their Majesties*
> *to invite The Dowager Marchioness of Milford Haven*
> *to the Ceremony of the Marriage of*
> *Her Royal Highness The Princess Elizabeth,*
> *with*
> *Lieutenant Philip Mountbatten, Royal Navy*
> *in Westminster Abbey,*
> *on Thursday, 20th November, 1947, at 11.30 o'clock, a.m.1*

Her grandson, Prince Philip of Greece and Denmark, now just plain Philip Mountbatten, RN*, was marrying Princess Elizabeth of Great Britain and Northern Ireland, the woman who would one day become Her Majesty The Queen.

(*) *Prince Philip was made Duke of Edinburgh on his wedding day.*

Part I

June 1860 – April 1884

Chapter I

June 1860 – April 1863

Though it was a place where she spent a great deal of time, Queen Victoria did not really like Windsor Castle and called it *"poor sad old Windsor."*[1] The Queen said it had been the scene of a very unpleasant incident in a youth full of unpleasant incidents and domestic power struggles. She especially hated the Tapestry Room since, as a young girl, she had been roundly scolded there. The young Princess had been accused by her mother Princess Victoria, Duchess of Kent, of *"making up to King William IV* [her uncle] *at the dinner he had given for her birthday when he had drunk her health and had insulted"*[2] her mother. No doubt the room reminded her of her own stifled and contentious childhood.

Nonetheless, on that particular April 5, the Queen had spent a long and exhausting night in that room, sitting with her second eldest daughter, Alice, Princess Ludwig of Hesse and by Rhine, for the entire length of her labor. The Tapestry Room had a view of the Long Walk, along with a sizeable park with lawn, trees, and wildlife, which seemed to stretch for miles. Doubtless Queen Victoria often looked wearily out onto the park as the long night dragged on and on.

At four thirty-five in the morning, after an exhausting labor, a baby girl was born. She was the first of Queen Victoria's grandchildren to be born in England, and was called Victoria Alberta Elisabeth Mathilde Marie. The Queen had long ago decided that all her grandchildren would have either "Victoria" or "Albert" in their names. Victoria of Hesse, however, was the first of the Queen's granddaughters to actually be called "Victoria." She was, as well, probably the only one to have no diminutives and no strange or obscure nicknames for which the royal family was justly famous. Victoria for her entire life remained Victoria.

The family's relief at Alice's coming through the birth so well completely offset the usual disappointment that the child had not been a male. Indeed, the Queen received many congratulatory letters from her relations, including her uncle and mentor, King Leopold I of the Belgians. In a letter from Alice's eldest sister and the Queen's first child, Victoria ("Vicky"), Princess Friedrich Wilhelm of Prussia, she wrote feelingly:

> *My heart is filled with joy and thankfulness that dear Alice has got over her troubles and that the evil hour is past – The dear little girl – what a little darling it must be...It will become your favorite of all your Grandchildren now – I do not doubt as you were present when it came into the world.*[3]

Her tone was wistful since her Prussian "in-laws" were not nearly as accommodating as Alice's Hessians – there would be no question where Vicky's Prussian children would be born – certainly not near Vicky's mother. Nonetheless, she was extremely pleased when she was asked to be godmother to her niece. Queen Victoria was not perhaps so tactful when she wrote back to her daughter "[The child] *will be called Victoria, – the 1st of our g[ran]d children that will be called after either of us. This I know was not your fault – but it grieved me."*[4] Vicky was unquestionably grieved as well.

It must be said that the Queen, however relieved as she was at her daughter's safe delivery of a child, was no more enamored of babies than she had ever been. She wrote to Vicky: "*Of course I shall take great interest in our dear little grand-daughter, born at... Windsor in the very bed in which you all were born, and poor, dear Alice had the same night shift on which I had on when you all were born! I wish you could have worn it too.*" She couldn't resist adding, "*I don't admire babies a bit the more or think them attractive.*"[5]

June 1862

The oppressive atmosphere of the wedding at Osborne House, on the Isle of Wight, could best be described as depressingly funereal.

The bride's father, the Prince Consort, Prince Albert of Saxe-Coburg and Gotha, had died just months before, plunging the entire court into deep mourning, and her mother, Queen Victoria of Great Britain and Ireland, was now in a lifelong purdah from which she seldom emerged. The bride was Princess Alice, the oldest daughter still home at the time, and the groom, a young man from the Hessian Grand Ducal Family and the presumptive heir to the Grand Dukedom, Prince Ludwig. Though the court was prostrate with grief, it was Prince Albert's wish that the marriage take place. Certainly, at that point, it was the view of the Queen and therefore her entire family that nothing in the physical world could countermand any of the late Prince's desires.

Princess Alice Maud Mary was born on April 25, 1843, at Buckingham Palace. She was the third child and second daughter of Queen Victoria. As she grew, she was considered by those who knew her, an extremely intelligent, artistic and deeply empathetic person. She grew up largely in the shadow of her brilliant older sister, Vicky. The favorite of her father, Vicky would eventually become, first, Crown Princess of Prussia and, later, German Empress. Had Vicky not been her sister, Alice, with her intellect, her questioning, her deeply spiritual nature and well-developed social conscience, would have been the shining light of the family.

Growing up in a family of nine children, Alice was particularly close to her father, her older brother Prince Albert Edward, the future Edward VII, and her younger brother, Prince Leopold. Their childhood was a happy one, as their father, only slowly being given official duties by his wife, was completely in charge of the well-being and education of his large family. But childhood ended quickly for Alice, when her beloved older sister, Vicky, at the age of fifteen, was engaged to the future Crown Prince Friedrich Wilhelm ("Fritz") of Prussia and was married at seventeen. Now, Alice became the oldest girl at home, though herself only fifteen. It was just a matter of time before she, too, would leave the safe haven of her family to fulfill her destiny.

Alice's courtship with Prince Ludwig of Hesse and by Rhine began the summer of 1860 during Ascot week. Other princes had danced before Queen Victoria's second daughter, including the Prince of Orange, also known as the "Orange Boy." However, in his case, it was thought that he was not quite right for the Princess, being a rather dissolute young man. Later events would prove this to be correct. Prince Ludwig, by no means dissolute, was judged to be a far more worthy contender.

In June 1860, Queen Victoria invited the two sons of Prince Karl, the brother of the childless Grand Duke Ludwig III of Hesse and by Rhine, to accompany her and her family to Ascot. Ludwig was not the son of the Grand Duke but rather his nephew. The Grand Duke's first marriage to Princess Mathilde of Bavaria was unfortunately childless.

At her death, the Grand Duke married again. However, this union was entirely unsuitable since he married his house maid, Magdalene Appel, created Baroness von Hochstädten. The odd couple was no doubt quite content together, as his wife continually referred to him as *"Der gute Herr."** In these circumstances, it was a relief that there were no children from this union. Since he had brothers and nephews, the problem was soon solved as it became clear that his brother, Prince Karl, would be his heir, and thereafter Prince Karl's son, Ludwig.

It was obvious that week at Ascot that Ludwig and Alice were attracted to one another. Such happenings were eagerly remarked upon when a presentable young prince was in the company of one of the Queen's unmarried daughters. Usually, the Queen was not receptive, and in some cases downright resistant, to courting and romances. She was never very comfortable with the aforesaid courting, romance or, indeed, anything that might mean that one of her daughters might be taken from her.

Ludwig, possibly out of fear, but more probably of shyness, did not approach the Queen and the Prince Consort during that first visit. Perhaps he was intimidated by the fact that he could not, at present, offer Alice anywhere near the standard of living she was currently enjoying. Certainly, it would have been a coup for the Hessian Family to capture the hand of the second daughter of the Queen, who was considered the doyenne of monarchs.

But it was all the more puzzling since Ludwig left before anything was settled. Albert had actually hoped for and expected the Prince's addresses to their daughter.[6]

Six months later, the young suitor was invited once again to Windsor with more felicitous results. He and Alice were left alone in a room and, more emboldened than before, Ludwig quickly proposed. He was accepted though Alice promptly went to her mother to ask if this was all right.

"Certainly," the Queen was said to have replied, and continued to crochet furiously, since she was at least as agitated as the now successful suitor.[7]

However, all would be arranged to suit the Queen, of course, and not the engaged couple. For one, they would have to wait at least a year, due to the immaturity of the bride. Thus, the delay was more likely so that the Queen could get used to losing another daughter to marriage. Next, she envisioned that the couple, who, at present, had no pressing duties or obligations at the Hessian Court, would naturally spend most of their year attending on herself. The Queen was of the mind that her unmarried daughters were there to wait upon her personal desires as unpaid secretaries, companions, and maids. Were they to marry heirs to kingdoms, such as did Alice's eldest sister, Vicky, then she could understand that they must go there to live and their first allegiances would be to their new homes (except, of course when it came to childbirth, when it was understood that English physicians, nurses and nannies were unquestionably a must). Nonetheless, if this was not the case, then, they were to be nearly as much at their Mama's disposal as they had before their marriages. Ludwig, whom Victoria described as *"honest, modest, warm-hearted"*[8] was above all unassuming. The Queen felt that she would not have any problems convincing the couple of the efficacy of her plan.

It was only the previous December 1861, over a year after the engagement was announced, that the Prince Consort lay dying. During Albert's last illness, Alice's mind focused completely on nursing her father, and acting as his confidant. Although it was tragic that a daughter was nursing her own father on his deathbed, Alice found the work

---

(*) *"The Good Sir."*

deeply satisfying. Despite the love and care, the Prince quickly succumbed to typhoid, no doubt weakened by worry and over-work. Alice vowed afterward that she would honor his memory in word and deed as faithfully as did her mother. Alice immediately moved into the bedroom next to her mother's and was put "in charge" of her. She, though herself in the throes of grief, would take her mother's orders, convey messages between the Queen and her ministers and *"altogether acted with great presence of mind, zeal and intelligence where all was consternation and confusion."*[9]

An ideal "stay-at-home" daughter though she was proving, it had been Albert's wish that Alice should marry. As the weeks went by, the Queen came slightly and most reluctantly back to herself, and the wishes of her beloved Albert became paramount. She was, therefore, determined that this wedding would be made to happen as soon as possible. The date was set for July 1, 1862. Nevertheless, the months leading up to the ceremony continued to be full of sadness. Grand Duke Ludwig III's first wife, the Grand Duchess Mathilde, died in May of that year, and Queen Victoria commented that the *"Angel of Death still follows us...*[N]*ow Alice's marriage will be even more gloomy."*[10]

The wish being, perhaps, father to the thought, the day, though sunny and warm, was, indeed, full of weeping and sadness. Ludwig's brothers and father were present as well as "dear" Albert's brother, Ernest, Duke of Saxe-Coburg and Gotha, who gave the bride away. Drowning in her nearly fanatical grief, Queen Victoria thought nothing of weeping during the entire ceremony. She thoughtfully sat away from the attendees so that her face would not be seen.

"It was a terrible moment for me,"[11] the Queen wrote in her journal entry for that day. She commented on how tall and beautiful Alice looked and commended her for her dignity and self possession. Further, she marveled at how both the bride and groom answered distinctly and clearly to the Archbishop who performed the service. *"I restrained my tears, and had a great struggle all through, but remained calm."*[12] As a result of the Queen's "restraint" Alice's siblings, especially her younger brother Prince Alfred, were weeping copiously.

While the couple spent their honeymoon at St. Clare, Springfield near Ryde, on the Isle of Wight, the Queen was making her plans. Alice would have all her children in England, since she, the Queen, did not quite trust German physicians or midwives. She happily contemplated the future in which Alice and Ludwig would continue to keep her company, joined in appropriate intervals by little Hessians. This, however, was not quite how things were to be.

****

Darmstadt, the capital of Hesse and by Rhine, is located in the western part of Germany, near to the Rhine and the city of Frankfurt. The town is nestled in the lush mists and blue-green rolling hills of the river valley between the Rhine and the Main. The Grand Ducal Family of Hesse was said to be the oldest Protestant ruling dynasty of Europe and counted Charlemagne as one of their ancestors. Another illustrious ancestor was St. Elisabeth of Hungary. As a very young girl, in 1220, she had been married to Prince Ludwig, heir to the Crown of Thuringia. She led a solemn and saintly life, and as a follower of St. Francis of Assisi, she was completely devoted to the poor. After her death, she was buried in Marburg and quickly canonized.

More recently, the Duchy's fortunes were more secular than saintly. The Hessian land had been divided into four parts: Rheinfels, Marburg, Kassel, and Darmstadt. The Duke of Hesse-Darmstadt decided, in 1806, with princely expediency, to throw in his lot with Napoleon. As a result, Hesse-Darmstadt became a Grand Duchy with the additions of Mainz and Worms. A few years after joining the Emperor of the French, Hesse was given a new constitution and Ludwig X became Grand Duke Ludwig I of Hesse and by Rhine.[13] When Alice arrived in Hesse, Frankfurt and Hesse-Homburg had been added to the Grand Duchy, making it the largest since the earlier divisions. Later on, those new territories, as well as Hesse herself, would be absorbed into Prussia and the Second German Reich.

Becoming a Grand Duchy gave Hesse and by Rhine a little more status in the world. As a result, in the early 1840's, when the Tsarevitch of Russia was looking for a bride, he looked no further than Darmstadt and the daughter of Grand Duke Ludwig II. Ludwig was married to Wilhelmine of Bavaria. Although they had a substantial family, they were not an entirely happy couple. The Grand Duchess bought a house outside of Hesse called the Heiligenberg, and spent most of her time there. It was said that she lived quite openly with Baron Augustus Senarclens von Grancy, a senior court official. The Baron was a Swiss in the service of the Grand Duke and the Equerry of the Grand Duchess. Other children of the marriage were born while the Grand Duchess was spending most of her time at the Heiligenberg, meaning that perhaps these youngest children were not fathered by the Grand Duke, or more precisely that they were fathered by Baron Augustus. Later, their great-granddaughter Princess Victoria addressed these rumors about her great-grandparents in her memoirs written in 1942. She commented simply: *"*[H]*oni soit qui mal y pense!"*[*][14] Apparently, the young Tsarevich was not much deterred by such innuendo. He married the youngest daughter of the house, Marie, in 1841.

Ludwig II died in 1848, and was succeeded by his son, a third Ludwig. When it became apparent that he would never have heirs, he named his brother Karl as his successor, and thereafter, young Ludwig. Prince Karl and his wife, Princess Elisabeth of Prussia, were an extremely close couple. Since Prince Karl was not always in the most vigorous of health, Elisabeth watched over him devotedly. In the future, she would watch over her many grandchildren with similar devotion. Princess Elisabeth was, according to her granddaughter, Princess Victoria, the most broad-minded of women. Although, religious, good, and a little shy, she was extremely tolerant of the views of the young and idealistic. Indeed, Victoria remembered *"her listening with an amused smile at my lecture on Home Rule for Ireland and the advantages of socialism when I was about 16."*[15]

Darmstadt had the enviable reputation of being a town of great culture. Its rulers and later its Grand Dukes encouraged arts, literature, music, architecture, and theater. Although small in size, it had a most impressive opera house. The most famous singers of the day often performed there. This included the incomparable Jenny Lind. The Grand Ducal Family also befriended and encouraged the great German writers, Schiller, Goethe, and the brothers Grimm. Alice, happily, continued this tradition receiving and encouraging the philosopher and theologian, David Strauss, and playing piano duets with the great Romantic composer, Johannes Brahms.[16]

Darmstadt, as a city, was an unusually appealing place. It was a typical medieval market town, sitting on flatlands. As it developed through the years, its layout became formalized and attractive, with some older narrow roads remaining alongside cobbled streets, more modern wide avenues, large squares, Rococo buildings and fountains. Nearly

---

(*) *"Shame on him who thinks this evil."*

every house had a garden and the streets were a profusion of *"chestnut trees, lime trees and acacias."*[17] The woods that surrounded the town were filled with *"beechwoods where violets and lilies-of-the-valley grew...there were green fields of cowslips and buttercups, [and] there were great pine forests."*[18] An idyllic, quiet background, with tree-covered hills nearby, and other charming towns and villages to visit; the town was, in fact, the perfect place in which to grow up.

****

When Alice and Ludwig arrived after their short honeymoon, Darmstadt was in a state of great excitement to welcome the new bride. The buildings were decorated, the young girls wore flowers, there were *"fluttering flags..., ringing of bells,"*[19] and crowds of people, numbering in thousands, who lined the streets to see the young Princess, daughter of the great Queen Victoria, who would someday be their Grand Duchess. Though her welcome from the town was warm, her reception by the officials and members of the government was less so. Alice would never feel quite comfortable with the upper classes of the capital* and mostly socialized with the English people and the artists, musicians and philosophers living there who would frequently visit. Such associations made her rather unpopular with the old guard. Nevertheless, Alice never seemed to let this bother her.

I often felt sorry for her, her cousin by marriage, Princess Marie of Battenberg, wrote, *she was so kind and so congenial to us, more so than our Hesse relations, and in a different way...For me, Alice was a most attractive and arresting personality...It interested me also to hear people speaking of the complete absence of Court usages in her house, and of her intercourse with people of the middle classes, who were 'not eligible' for presentation...*[20]

Marie's father, Prince Alexander of Hesse, also approved of Alice, and the traits that made her different, and interesting. He wrote to his sister, the Tsarina, saying that she would also like Alice. He described her as a woman full of charm *"very cultured...and talented."*[21]

Alice, and later, her children, would always feel most comfortable with the Battenberg family. It was a family that would play a large part in their lives. The Battenbergs had a town residence called the Alexanderpalais, but lived during the summers at the Heiligenberg, the home that Prince Alexander had inherited from his mother, Grand Duchess Wilhelmine. Here the Hesses spent many of their summers, not only with their Battenberg relations, but also with their Romanov cousins.

As Alice settled into her new duties, she found much about small German Court life that was different and unnerving. Perhaps most strange to the new bride was the unusual meal schedule kept by her in-laws. It was very different from that which Alice was accustomed to, and like her sister, Vicky of Prussia, Alice found it difficult to adjust to the odd hours. Dinner time, which was at four o'clock in the afternoon, and during which everyone was arrayed in formal evening dress, was an extremely awkward and doubtless unappetizing hour for Alice. Accustomed to the hours favored by her mother, the Princess, when she felt more confident, simply rebelled and contrived to eat at home at the hours she preferred. Though it was never her intention to anger him, her insistence on her English schedule seemed to have *"vexed the Grand Duke."*[22]

Alice, demonstrated in this and many other ways, that she was an independent soul, and did not conform easily to the Court of Darmstadt. That, however, never prevented her from being a well-beloved member of the family and a *"landsmütter"** to her people. She pursued her interests in social work, founding the Alice Frauen Verein. The so-called "Women's Union" devoted itself to building a home for unmarried mothers, a vocational school for women and girls, an orphanage and the Alice Hospital. Indeed, she was an avid follower of Florence Nightingale, and endeavored to adhere strictly to her Notes on Nursing. Alice believed, as did Miss Nightingale, that nursing was a noble profession for a woman, an alternative to being a governess or other such pursuits. Considering all these projects, it can come as no surprise that she was deeply interested in women's rights as well.

Initially, the couple had no official residence and spent the first three years of their marriage in a relatively modest house in the Upper Wilhelminestrasse. This area was then a part of the Village of Bessungen, though it was just steps away from Darmstadt. As Alice began to settle into her new role, she considered of prime importance the construction of a home for herself and her soon to be growing family. With the dowry of £30,000 granted to her by the British Parliament, Alice and Ludwig began work on what would be called the Neues Palais, or the New Palace. There were all sorts of exciting plans for the dwelling that would be fit for the future Grand Duke. The construction itself would take three years, and like most such projects, go over the proposed budget. However, the end result would be the one dwelling in a city of many palaces, which Alice could decorate as she wished and call her own.

In addition to the Neues Palais, the family owned a hunting lodge in the forest retreat of Kranichstein. The lodge an *"old, grey palace, whose walls were mirrored in the still waters of the pond, like the palace of the Sleeping Beauty, dreaming in the silence of the autumn woods,"*[23] was, indeed, an enchanted castle, and within easy reach of Darmstadt. The dwelling, recently refurbished, was the oldest building in the area dating back to 1329. Inside, the walls were filled with antlers and other hunting trophies. The windows looked out on the mysterious green forests and misty, crystal lake. In a custom that continues to the present day, various guests scratched their initials or names on those windows, including Queen Victoria, who had gladly indulged in this custom on one of her visits. Her Majesty had also decided that the dining room ceiling was not high enough for her comfort, so she paid for the roof to be raised, and it became the largest room in the house.

The building of the Neues Palais commenced as the young couple settled into their lives in Darmstadt. However, beginning in the autumn following their marriage, in November of 1862, they began their round of visits to England. Indeed, the Hessians' first visit extended for nearly eight months.

During that first visit, two events of importance took place. Alice's brother, Prince Albert Edward of Wales ("Bertie"), was married on March 10, 1863 to Princess Alexandra of Denmark. Alexandra, who was known in the family as "Alix," was an extremely attractive young lady, and it was hoped that this marriage would put a damper on Bertie's profligate ways. Though it was, in many ways, a successful marriage, its success did not extend to putting a damper on anything that Bertie desired to do during his very long tenure as Prince of Wales. Nevertheless, the day was one to celebrate, though the Queen later wrote in her journal that she had quite overlooked, yet still managed to notice, that Alice looked *"extremely well in a violet dress, covered with her wedding lace...[and]... [Ludwig] in the Garter robes leading her."*[24]

(*) *Literally, "Mother of the Land," in this case, "Mother of the people."*

Dresses, such as were the fashion in those days, with their huge bell-shaped crinolines, hid a myriad of figure-faults. In Alice's case, the dress successfully obscured the fact that she was over eight months pregnant. The Queen was particularly elated that Alice would give birth while in England.

At Windsor, less than a month later, Alice went into labor.

****

The christening ceremony took place on April 27, 1863, in the Green Drawing Room. The new baby was christened in the Queen's arms, standing over a table with a white cloth and an altar plate. The font, the same font in which all of Queen Victoria's children were christened, was placed on the front of the table. The sponsors were the Queen herself, Prince Alexander of Hesse, there representing the Grand Duke Ludwig III, the new Uncles, Bertie, and Ludwig's brother Henry. Prince Alexander received, as a souvenir of the ceremony, a set of three pearl studs mounted in emeralds and diamonds,[25] that would, ironically, later go to little Victoria's own children. The baby wore a lace robe over white satin and a lace wrap that had been worn by all of her father's Hessian siblings.

She was, according to her grandmother Victoria, very much admired, looked at, and much was made of her. She was, after all, an attractive baby with downy blonde fuzz on her head, large heavy-lidded blue eyes – very much the eyes of her Uncle Bertie, her grandmother, and many of the Hanoverian Royal Family before her. The best thing, however, that the Queen could say about Victoria was that she had been very good and not cried during the sprinkling by the clergyman. After that, they all went to lunch, but the Queen, who, for reasons she didn't explain, dined alone with her youngest child, Beatrice – the new baby's aunt.[26]

Chapter II

May 1863 – November 1878

*I*n May 1863, the young couple, and their new baby, returned home to Darmstadt. Motherhood was a constant source of delight and excitement to Alice and she reveled in writing progress reports to her mother. The Queen maintained a copious correspondence with all her relations. However, between her married daughters, and later several of her grandchildren, there exists volumes and volumes of letters. Queen Victoria insisted on being completely current on all aspects of each child or grandchild's life and thence to offer advice for every situation. She was a woman of tremendous commonsense so that the advice was rarely irksome – besides, since she rarely held back her feelings and opinions from her family, everyone knew her views on myriad subjects.

Not surprisingly, unremitting letters traveled back and forth from Darmstadt to Windsor, Balmoral, Osborne, or Buckingham Palace, detailing what little Victoria did, how she behaved, or how she looked, and certainly the state of her health. All the clothes that the Queen had given Baby had been much admired, Alice wrote[1]; she was, according to her mother, endlessly adored – she was good, strong, could sit up, laugh, and had a loud shriek, *"she does not cry very much, but she is passionate."*[2] She recounted all the things that would be of interest only to a doting grandparent, which at that point, the Queen was most certainly not. Despite the fact that she had warned everyone that she didn't like babies very much, she would, nevertheless, have been disappointed and disapproving if the letters and anecdotes did not come at regular intervals.

That same summer, another palace became a favorite of Alice and her family. For the first time, little Victoria visited the Heiligenberg, a beautiful and relatively simple palace, belonging to her Great-Uncle, Prince Alexander of Hesse. Located just ten miles south of Darmstadt, it was here that the families came together for holidays in the spring and summer. These respites were a welcome break from all the duties and responsibilities. It was here that everyone could relax and be themselves. It was also at the Heiligenberg that Victoria, and later her siblings, as previously mentioned, became acquainted with her Battenberg and Romanov cousins. The year 1863 was the beginning of an annual 'invasion' of the Russian Imperial Family, which continued in various forms until just before the First World War.[3]

Alexander of Hesse was the youngest son of Grand Duke Ludwig II and Grand Duchess Wilhelmine. When his sister, Marie, was married to the Tsarevitch in April of 1841, Alexander was invited to accompany her to Russia. Handsome, charming, and extremely eligible, Prince Alexander became a favorite member of the Russian Court. After much matrimonial maneuvering and rejections, Alexander became attracted to Countess Julie von Hauke, his sister's lady-in-waiting. The Prince *"had grown more and more interested in [Julie]... who was now filled with a consuming passion for him."*[4] In the beginning, Julie's love for him was quite one-sided. However, her devotion was immensely appealing to the young man, with the added attraction of no parents and obstacles.

Julie Therese von Hauke was born in Warsaw, November 12, 1825. She was short in stature with brown hair and eyes and said to be extremely clever. Julie and her siblings were orphaned at an early age and were taken to St. Petersburg to be raised and educated at the Tsar's expense. Several of the von Hauke girls grew up at court and eventually became ladies-in-waiting to Alexander's sister.

Finally her persistence (and availability) was rewarded and Julie received a proposal of marriage from Alexander, which was happily accepted. The couple was married on October 28, 1851, but they were forced to leave Russia quickly after their marriage since the Tsar strongly disapproved of the alliance. A week after the wedding, Julie was made Countess Battenberg by her new and more tolerant brother-in-law, Grand Duke Ludwig III of Hesse and by Rhine. Some years later, in 1858, the couple settled in Darmstadt where Countess Battenberg was, in time, elevated by the Grand Duke to Princess of Battenberg – the title she handed onto her four sons and one daughter. Julie first gave birth to a daughter, Marie in 1852, and thereafter to four sons: Louis, 1853, Alexander, 1857, Henry, 1858 and Franz Joseph, 1861 – all the Hessian children's first cousins once removed.

In the winter, the Battenberg family lived in the Alexanderpalais or Alexander Palace in Darmstadt. However, in the spring and summer, their home was the Heiligenberg. The region was hilly, deeply forested and made up of small towns, fields, and vineyards. The road leading to the palace was narrow, steep, and winding, lushly lined with green ivy-covered trees. Below the property, there were mock ruins of a medieval abbey. Built in the nineteenth century, it was used for games or meditation. Past the abbey was a mausoleum dedicated to the Battenbergs. From here one enjoyed an amazing view of the Rhine Valley and the tiny village of Jugenheim.

The relatively modest palace, with its two towers, gardens, bathhouse, and ballroom, (added in 1873) was by far their favorite home. The building exuded an uncanny calm and serenity that made it a novelty, particularly for the Romanov visitors. The house, though close enough to Darmstadt, could not be more isolated from the outside world. It had a picturesque view from its perch near Seeheim and above Jugenheim.

Alice and her family attended these spring and summer visits with the Battenbergs where they often met Aunt Marie, Empress of Russia, and her children. Paul and Serge, her youngest sons, were favorite playmates of the Hessian and Battenberg children. Marie's older children, Alexander, Marie, Alexei, and Vladimir, were uninterested in the Hessian babies, though Marie Alexandrovna was a close friend of Princess Marie of Battenberg.

The summers were idyllic in those far off childhood days. They all enjoyed each other's company, climbing trees, running and playing together. Their routine was hardly strenuous, but scrupulously followed and fondly remembered years later. After a formal dinner at one o'clock, the adults loosened their corsets and took a very welcome siesta. The children, not needing a nap, enjoyed some kind of excursion. They often piled into the dog carts with various nannies and attendants, and rode down into Jugenheim, where the townspeople knew the little ones well. They would buy cakes and candies, and then return to the Heiligenberg just as tea was being served.

At eight in the evening, the adults had supper, then, afterward, cards or dancing. The children after a light supper went to bed. They would often fall asleep to the strains of the orchestra, as their parents and attendants danced downstairs. They loved to listen to the music floating up to their rooms and the echoing of laughing voices.

These visits were, for Alice and her family, a welcome change from her obligations in Darmstadt. For the Empress Marie, they were a godsend. At the Heiligenberg, Marie, who was never in the best of health, had no need to exhaust herself as she often did in Russia. Since life at the Heiligenberg was very much a relatively middle-class existence, the immense, nearly unimaginable grandeur of the Russian Imperial Court – the processions, ceremonies, and social engagements – seemed very far away.

Interestingly, Alice got on extremely well with the Romanovs, an issue which worried and often irritated her mother. Queen Victoria had a deep-seated suspicion of Russians, certainly easy enough to understand after the vicious fighting that took place between the two countries in the Crimean War. However, since the cessation of hostilities and for the remainder of her reign, Queen Victoria saw little necessity to change her mind about Russia or the Russians. In the Queen's opinion, Russia was a country with a terrible society, a bad climate, and an autocratic government. In a letter to one of her granddaughters, she called it *"villainous and atrocious."* Never one to leave anything unsaid, she told Alice that she was a little annoyed that she was so taken with the Russian Imperial family.[5] Though individual Russians were bearable and in some cases, as time went on, even nice – as a whole, the country, socially and politically was never redeemable in the eyes of Queen Victoria.

* * * * * * * *

It was apparent even in the early months of her life that Victoria was an exceptionally bright and intelligent child. She could talk at the age of nine months and seemed in all other ways advanced for her age. By the age of two, her mother complained that she was very wild, and that she was jabbering more in German than in English[6], and at three, Alice was able to begin teaching her to read. The little girl had a fertile and active imagination. An early manifestation of this was the monsters she created who resided in dark, concealed places in their first house in Bessungen. The house, which had the look of a banker's mansion, had a large garden in the front which reached down to the Heidelberger-strasse. There was a hidden, but also, in Victoria's mind, frightening, staircase that fascinated her, and she, again, imagined all sorts of strange creatures lurking around that scary place.[7]

By autumn 1863, the family had returned once again to England, to stay with the Queen. Early on, these visits were becoming a bone of contention between Alice and her mother. Quite simply, Alice and Ludwig lacked the necessary funds to travel with their retinue to England on a constant basis. More importantly, Alice was now not only a wife, but also a mother, and no matter what the Queen thought, had pressing duties and responsibilities to the Grand Duchy despite not yet being the Grand Duchess. Indeed, there was no Grand Duchess and she was for all intents and purposes the first lady of Hesse and by Rhine. Consequently, she chafed at being at the constant beck and call of her own mother. Though the Queen was gently confronted with the first reason, she ignored such practical matters as money, and began to feel that Alice was simply not being a good daughter. Luckily for Alice, John Brown, the Queen's personal attendant and well-beloved servant, came into the picture. Through his good offices, a full-blown family controversy was avoided and Alice's services were not required.

By the following year, Alice's family again increased with the birth of a second daughter, Elisabeth Alexandra Louise Alice. Known in the family as "Ella," she was born in their little home in Bessungen. The new baby was described as *"the most lovely child one has ever looked upon,"*[8] and her reputation as being one of the most beautiful women in Europe would continue throughout her entire life. Alice was proud to be nursing little Ella herself, and never neglected to say so. The Queen, however, looked upon the 'animalistic' practice of breast feeding with extreme distaste, and went so far as to name one of her cows,

"Princess Alice."[9]

Ella, the nearest sister to Victoria in age, with whom she shared a bedroom, was also her dearest sibling. They were destined to remain close all their lives. In some ways, they were very much alike, but in others, quite different. For example, Ella was always the more lady-like of the two, wanting to be dressed properly, act properly, wear her hair just right, and was demonstrative in her likes and dislikes. Victoria, on the other hand, was always up to some mischief. Being such a tomboy, she was always ruining her clothes, climbing trees, running about, and careless in her appearance. She was also, by far, the most intellectual of all her siblings, yet the least able to show emotion in public. Even as a small child, the things closest to Victoria's heart were the hardest to express in public.

Victoria and Ella were a sweet little pair, their mother wrote, though full of mischief (most probably at Victoria's instigation) *"they can be such friends to each other,"*[10] and they were – together, apace, during the rest of their childhood, and afterward.

****

In 1865, Alice and her mother became temporarily estranged over the matter of the marriage of Alice's younger sister, Helena. It was arranged that Helena was to marry the impecunious Prince Christian of Schleswig-Holstein-Sonderburg-Augustenburg. Alice strongly disapproved of the match for several reasons not the least of which was that Prince Christian, being fifteen years the nineteen-year-old Princess's senior, was simply too old for her. This contention was in addition to the Queen's annoyance that Alice wasn't visiting England as often as her mother required. Though relations were temporarily strained between them, Alice was still the one to persuade others to forget their own negative feelings and support the marriage when it appeared to be a fait accompli.[11]

While letters flew across the channel over these controversial issues, Alice and her family prepared to move into the Grand Ducal Neues Palais in March 1866. The edifice, which had been under construction for the past three years, was criticized as being in the style of a *"Victorian Piccadilly mansion, and completely unsuited to its surroundings."*[12] However, Alice built it to her own specifications and it suited her admirably. The house was composed of a ground floor and three stories used by the family. Inside, Alice created rooms of *"real luxury,"*[13] though, to her, they were just in the style reminiscent of Osborne and her youth. All the furniture was acquired from Maples of London, and included her beloved chintz fabrics for upholstery and drapery. The rooms were filled with family photographs and portraits, particularly those of her parents. Now, happily settled, the Hessian family had plenty of room to expand. This was just as well since Alice was carrying her third child and, needless to say, they were quickly growing out of the Bessungen House.

However all was not harmony. Just a few months later, in June, a critical political crisis occurred. The Prussian Prime Minister, Chancellor Otto von Bismarck, decided the time was at last ripe to challenge the Austrians and Southern Germans for leadership of all the Germanic peoples and thereby form a Second Reich. To this end, he instigated a war between Austria and Prussia ostensibly over violations of the Schleswig-Holstein Treaty. The Austro-Prussian War began on June 16, 1866, and continued for seven bloody weeks. However, ten days after hostilities started, the Austrians were defeated decisively at the Battle of Sadowa in Bohemia. Though the war dragged on for weeks more, the Prussians triumphed because their military machine was far more modern and efficient than those of the Austrians and their allies.[14]

The Hessians, who had sided with the Austrians, signed the armistice, but could only wait with dread to see what would occur next. Queen Victoria was very disturbed that Vicky and Alice would so obviously have to be at odds at this time. There was no question that the two younger women were also deeply disturbed by this turn of events. Vicky wrote to her mother that there was simply nothing she could do about this.[15] Alice, who was about to give birth any moment, had prudently sent Victoria and Ella to their Grandmama at Windsor, and the two little ones attended Helena's still hotly contested wedding.

On July 11, alone, and in the confusing midst of war, Alice gave birth to Princess Irène Louise Maria Anna. Irène was the Greek word for peace, but the family put off actually calling the baby Irène until they were certain that the armistice would take place and be ratified in August. Alice, in what had become her typical manner, went about visiting hospitals, and doing all she could to alleviate the suffering of the sick and the wounded. But, like her father, the Princess had a tendency to overwork, and her health was easily undermined. To make matters more difficult, Ludwig was gone at this crucial time, since his place was at the head of the Hessian Regiments.

As August arrived, the Hessians were starving and Alice, her newborn baby, and the servants had little food. The Prussians began swarming over Darmstadt, eating, drinking, and looting. What was worse, the Prussian commander forbade any communication with the Hessians in the field, so there was no way for Alice to send word to Ludwig of their plight. Then, of course, the worst possible thing happened – there was a case of cholera in the Prussian camp.[16] Indeed, there would be cases of both cholera and smallpox in Darmstadt courtesy of unsanitary conditions and the Prussian soldiers.

Finally, in September of that year, a peace was concluded. The Hessians were assessed a devastating indemnity of three million florins and, quite naturally, such a large and humiliating sum took years to pay. Financially, the Grand Duchy was at its very lowest ebb. Along with the indemnity, there were other revenues and lands which the treaty entitled the Prussians to appropriate. Those lands included parts of the Hessian Grand Duchy proper: Hesse Homburg and Frankfurt. The only good news for the Hessians was that they were to endure a short occupation of only six weeks, and the looting was eventually curbed.

For Alice, the most joyous part of the cessation of hostilities was that her two little girls returned home from England. Since the two children were no longer infants, Queen Victoria appeared to enjoy them more. Becoming more like regular human beings to her, she wrote approvingly of the little Hessian Princesses in her journal: *"Took leave with much regret of darling little Victoria & Ella, who are such little loves. They have been quite like my own*, during these last 2 months & are really 2 as handsome, clever, & engaging Children, as it is possible to see."*[17]

Paying the Prussian indemnity was a devastating financial burden that would color their lives for years to come. The family, however, was all together again, and settled into a pleasant routine in their new home. In 1867, Mrs. Mary Anne Orchard ("Orchie") arrived at the Hessian Household to serve as head of the nurseries and would stay until the last child was married. With a German and English maid to help with menial tasks, she quickly organized the three little girls into the schedule that would be henceforth typical of their childhood. She would awaken and dress the girls, give them Bible lessons, and at bedtime, tell them stories. Their days were highly regimented since it was thought that the

---

(*) *The Queen often underlined for emphais, and henceforth, in letters of Queen Victoria's the uderlining is hers.*

best way to raise children was to set strict limits and be firm about those limits.

They rose at six o'clock and began lessons at seven. Their breakfast at nine was extremely simple, usually consisting of porridge and sausage. After eating, they would leave the house and go riding or walking, and, of course, breathing deeply for an hour. Afterwards, lessons went on until two in the afternoon, when the family would get together for luncheon. After luncheon, the children went out again no matter the weather. They were encouraged to exercise and take long walks. At five, they ate a large tea and then were put to bed by seven. The Hessian children were adhering to a diet set by Queen Victoria and the hours that Alice preferred. In this, as so many other things, the Princess showed that she was not a typical aristocratic parent of the day – for she spent far more time with her children than many other mothers of her class. Nursing them, teaching them to read, paying close attention to their lessons, exercise and general routine – this close scrutiny of her children was not characteristic of royalty.

While the children grew, Alice began to organize her Women's Union which would later be called the Alice Frauen Verein. The chief emphasis of the Union was the training of Red Cross Nurses. However, there were many other auxiliary branches that reached into other areas. As mentioned, not only did she found an orphanage, but she also founded a girls school for training as clerks and the making of handicrafts, a home for unwed mothers, and also an insane asylum.[18] Being greatly interested in the Women's Movement, she chaired the 'Frauentag' (or Ladies Assembly), for the purpose of discussing further employment for women, the sale of women's handiwork, nursing, better schools for girls and how all of these issues had been handled in England. The conference was held in Darmstadt in 1872.[19]

It appears that her philanthropic works satisfied Alice's soul far more than her relationship with Ludwig. Though a devoted couple, they were somewhat mismatched – they seemed rather more comfortable than passionate. Ludwig was a hale and hearty soul who was happiest outdoors stalking in the woods with a British-style Norfolk jacket and a gun in hand. Alice, on the other hand, was a far more complex individual. She was intellectual, artistic, and loved music, theater, and art. In addition, she often questioned those constants all around her, and delved into her spirituality in a way that inevitably caused the Queen to disapprove. *"I would earnestly warn you against trying to find out the reason for & explanation of everything... [for] in the end [it will make you] miserable."*[20] Though this letter was actually written some time later, to Princess Victoria, it not only reflects the Queen's attitude towards any sort of profound and therefore uncomfortable query into that which is not easily known, but also to the spiritual journey that Alice undertook at that time. Later, Victoria, too, would constantly quest to understand and question everything. Alice, the Queen told her granddaughter, perhaps wishfully, had once looked for answers in Science and Philosophy, but came back, finally, to faith.

****

Alice and her mother continued their estrangement through Victoria's early years. Though they did visit occasionally, these visits were strained. As a result, the Queen usually wrote complaining letters about her second daughter to Vicky, Crown Princess of Prussia, her eldest one. As an example, after the Hessian family paid a visit to Berlin in 1867, the Queen hastened to write Vicky that she was annoyed that so much was made over Alice in Berlin, since that was certainly not done when she was in England.[21] That same month, it appeared that Alice had the nerve to ask that the Queen send her girls pearls for their birthdays. *"Pearls of any good size,"* she wrote to Vicky in something of a huff, *"cost nearly £30 to £40 a piece now, and two for them to each child each year would be far more than I could give to all her children."*[22]

Vicky, nevertheless, was pained by the alienation of her mother and her closest sister. Since the two families visited back and forth regularly, the Hessian children were well-acquainted with the Prussian cousins. After another such visit, Vicky wrote to the Queen,

> *Alice and I pass very pleasant hours together. Indeed you need not dread her visit. She is so gentle and amiable and so delighted at the thought of going to England as she looks forward to meeting you so much; I am sure you would not wish to throw a chill or a damp on that feeling... [S]he is so graceful and elegant, dresses so well and with her lovely complexion is allowed by all to be a charming personality. I am sure you like to hear that.*[23]

That Vicky felt the need to 'sell' her sister to the Queen, shows just how difficult the relationship had become between mother and daughter.

Victoria, at the age of four, came to the rescue. She wrote in pencil to her grandmother, with a very clear and legible handwriting, a precocious thank-you note for gifts that the Queen had sent, thus beginning a long and satisfying correspondence between them that was to last until the Queen's death in 1901. Possibly, it also encouraged a kind of rapprochement between the Queen and Victoria's mother.

The Hessian family spent June and July 1868 with the Queen. It had been a few years since they had been together for a long visit and it turned out more pleasantly than the Queen had expected. *"Alice is not strong,"* she wrote to Vicky, *"– but most kind, amiable and discrete. I never saw her so amiable, gentle and sensible since the summer of '63!"*[24] And about the children, *"Alice's two eldest girls are indeed quite lovely and Victoria most engaging. Irene is very plain."*[25] Thankfully, now all seemed to be forgiven between mother and daughter. Indeed, Alice was moved to write to her mother about little Victoria: *"The child born under your roof and your care is of course your particular one, and later, if you wish to keep her at any time when we have been paying you a visit, we shall gladly leave her."*[26]

Meanwhile, as visits to England became more regular, the Hessian and Battenberg families continued to get together not just at the Heiligenberg, but also in town. The eldest Battenberg boy, Louis, tall and handsome with brown hair and brown eyes, was becoming quite taken with the English Royal Navy. In turn, Victoria's maternal Uncle, Prince Alfred, Duke of Edinburgh, was impressed by young Louis' interest, as was Princess Alice. Indeed, they both encouraged him to join the navy. The young Prince was *"spellbound by the sight of Lieutenant Prince Alfred in his glittering naval uniform, and the stories he told of life in the Royal Navy – unquestionably the world's finest."*[27]

There was, naturally, much discussion about this issue in the Battenberg family. Alexander and Julie were very aware of all the moves that their children made. Though relatively poor, they were extremely ambitious for their sons, and knew that they would have to make their way in the world completely on their own initiative. Actually, they would have preferred that young Louis join one of the many German or Austrian regiments, and tried to persuade him, but the youngster remained firm. In 1868, at the age of fourteen, his parents finally acceded to his wishes and permitted him to join the Royal Navy. In his memoirs, Prince Louis credits Alice for her help and encouragement and wrote that they often discussed his plans.[28] His first ship was *HMS Minotaur* – a flagship of the channel fleet. The boy passed his exams and Prince Louis of Battenberg became a naturalized British citizen with Princess Alice as one of his sponsors.

In fall 1868, a most exciting event happened in the Royal Hessian Household. On November 25, fulfilling the expectations of the Grand Duchy, Alice was delivered of the much desired boy. He was called Ernst Ludwig, and was born at the Neues Palais in Darmstadt. Victoria was five years old, and had only practical concerns. She wanted to know why more guns were fired for him than had been fired for her and her sisters, and she expressed quite vocally her disappointment that little Ernie, as he was forever called in the family, was not another sister. *"Ernie's double name of Ernst Ludwig,"* she explained in her memoirs, *"was borne by a landgrave in the 17th century."*[29]

While all this excitement was taking place, Victoria, who was a rapid learner, began to have what her mother called a *"little lesson"* every other day from a Mr. Geyer, whom Alice assured her mother, *"teaches little girls particularly well."*[30] Alice was immensely pleased with the little girl's progress and wrote to her mother that her *"facility in learning is wonderful, and her lessons are a delight."*[31] Under the strictures of her father, Prince Albert, who thought that education and opening up the minds of young children was tremendously important, there were many teaching masters employed in the Hessian household. In their school room, the children were exposed to the rigors of reading, writing, languages, dancing, gymnastics, drawing, religious studies, and everything that it was thought proper for children to learn. Ernie, of course, would later have a tutor, Herr Müther, and also a military and university education, but until then, he would be part of the nursery routine.

By the age of seven, Victoria had learned to read in German and became an avid 'book worm.' She was interested in virtually every subject, and therefore wanted to read nearly any book she could obtain. She kept little notebooks delineating the books she had read almost until the end of her life. Her tastes were varied and catholic. Books on history, philosophy, biography, geology, as well as mysteries, children's books, and novels, were 'devoured' at an incredible pace. In her notebooks, she would often jot down her critique of the books. She would re-read the ones she liked, usually out loud to family and friends. They were her constant companions and she was well-known in the family for a good recommendation and always having a book at hand.[32] Because the children were very popular in the Duchy, their photographs, in various poses and settings, were always in demand. Victoria wiled away the time during the long process of sitting for photographs by reading her beloved books.

As the eldest, as well as the tomboy of the group, she ordered all the children about as much as she wished and was quite a little tyrant. She ruled the younger children *"with a rod of iron, though...Ella being nearest [in]...age, would rebel sometimes against too much ruling. So [they]...ended by dividing the authority over the younger ones between [them]."*[33] In addition, Victoria and her siblings were well known for their boisterousness. When they played with the properly brought up little girls of Darmstadt society, the Hessian children encouraged them to such rowdyism that they became *"almost as wild as [the Hessian children] were."*[34] However, they were not as stout-hearted as Victoria and her siblings and when they got hurt, they cried. Naturally, Victoria heartily despised them for that.[35]

The parents of these little girls, apparently not impressed with the dubious honor, were not particularly interested in their progeny playing with the Grand Ducal children. But, that mattered little to the children since they loved their own company best, and did not really need outside playmates. They would spend endless hours amusing each other by playing games and telling stories. They would amble along on their afternoon exercise spinning thrilling tales to one another, Victoria's about knights and outlaws, while, Ella's, very typically, were about nice little girls. Little Irène, who was not as quick as her older sisters, was a willing listener and a devoted follower.

Another favorite abode for the family was at Kranichstein, the old Hessian hunting lodge. During summers at the lodge, Alice would spend hours playing with her children. The children, in turn, would also amuse themselves by rowing about the lake, playing with the dogs and horses, and even tagging after the men on a hunt. This they did with some trepidation, always terrified that a wild boar might make an appearance. Victoria learned to ride during those summers at the hunting lodge. Her little pony, "Dread," a gift from her Aunt Beatrice, was named after a character in *Uncle Tom's Cabin*.

Every other summer, being chronically short of money, they traveled to a Belgian seaside resort, often Blankenberghe, and stayed in a modest hotel. Bathing in those days consisted of using bathing machines which were placed right next to the water. The bather would enter the machine, which looked like a small dressing room on wheels, change into a bathing costume and then the machine would be pulled right up to the water. The bather would then emerge on the other side where, it was hoped, there would be a much smaller group of spectators, and plunge into the water. Victoria remembered entering into the sea in a horse-drawn bathing machine which bumped and rocked, and as the driver shouted *"'hue' to his horse, encouraged it to enter the water."*[36] Nevertheless, the sight of such machines must have appeared comical to the children. They often preferred to spend their time on the shore building sand castles, playing croquet and other games as well as taking donkey rides.

Summers in Darmstadt were often spent with members of Alice's family who were visiting from England. Princess Marie Louise of Schleswig-Holstein, Aunt Helena's daughter, fondly remembered the times in Hesse. They visited the theater and opera and Marie Louise remembered seeing her very first opera there.[37] All the family, Hessian and English cousins alike, loved these performances. The great actress Eleanore Duse actually came to perform in an Ibsen play in Darmstadt, while Victoria remembered vividly seeing and hearing Jenny Lind sing. The great diva was already an old lady; nevertheless, Victoria was struck by her *"clear and beautiful voice..."*[38]

During the last winter before the Franco-Prussian War, Vicky, Alice and their families spent several months in Cannes together. The sisters' husbands, Fritz and Ludwig, went together on a Grand Tour of sorts, traveling through the exotic Levant, while leaving their wives and families at home in Europe. Cannes was a far more luxurious resort than that to which the Hessians were used and they loved it. While the two men went through Italy, Turkey, Egypt, and Palestine, Vicky and Alice reveled in being close once more.

January 1870 brought serious illness to the family – scarlet fever. Alice, as usual, nursed her husband, Victoria, and little Ernie through this dangerous disease, bringing her to a state of near exhaustion. However, unfortunately, this episode was just a prelude to that which would later prove far worse.

When the Franco-Prussian War broke out that summer, Alice plunged into her nursing with an almost fanatical zeal. Once again the Princess worked herself mercilessly, not only in body but in mind, organizing nursing and undertaking Red Cross work. She, along with her mother-in-law, Princess Elisabeth, were the heads of all the charitable institutions in Hesse. In that capacity, they visited four hospitals in addition to the newer ones that Alice had quickly set up. Being dedicated and compassionate, Alice nursed the wounded without regard to whether they were German or French.

Victoria, who was old enough, at seven, to understand what was happening, went with her mother to soup kitchens, helping her to carry the hot bowls of soup. Accompanied by her sisters, Victoria would learn the importance of public service from her mother. This, however, was the first time that she actually saw, at close quarters, her mother's good works. Indeed, there were even some wounded who were housed in the Neues Palais. Victoria remembered that her mother had two wounded officers at the palace, one who was suffering from typhoid and the other whose leg was completely shattered. Victoria recalled that the officer with the shattered leg, *"liked to show us bits of bone he kept in a pill box."*[39] The little tomboy, no doubt, delighted in this bit of gore.

Alice permitted herself little rest during this time. Naturally it undermined her health more than usual since she was, once again, pregnant. However, Hesse was fighting on the side of Prussia in this war and the tension which had existed between her and her sister Vicky just a few short years ago, was not a problem. Nevertheless, being pregnant weakened Alice and the constant work and stress took a toll on her delicate psyche and health. Vicky and the Queen worried constantly about Alice, her tendency to disregard her health when work was to be done, and her disposition to ignore emotional strain. The Queen wrote to Vicky, *"[p]oor Alice makes us all very anxious, and she seems anxious not to leave Darmstadt. I have no doubt that you will both advise her for the best."*[40]

As summer turned into fall, Prussia had its first and decisive victory at the Battle of Sedan. Though Prussia early triumphed in this adventure, Ludwig was away most of the time with the Hessian Troops and wasn't home again for Christmas or hardly at all until the following year. Hesse having joined the Prussian Empire, which was consolidating itself during these months, was given a mere two votes on the Imperial Council. Closer to home, on October 7, 1870, Alice gave birth to a boy, Friedrich Wilhelm, called "Frittie." The little fellow was, as Victoria recalled, a very pretty and winsome child. He would also exhibit definite signs, quite early, of what had become the family curse – hemophilia.

That winter 1870-71, was a particularly cold one and little Victoria had her first case of chilblains, an inflammation of the hands and feet resulting from exposure to extreme cold. The little girl had strong memories of the ensuing pain but would assign the blame partially to poor circulation. She endured chilblains during her entire life, and whenever her handwriting was shaky, she would apologize to the recipient of the letter and explain her condition.

In February 1871, a preliminary peace treaty between France and Prussia was signed at Versailles. One of the provisions of the treaty was that France would give up its eastern provinces known as Alsace-Lorraine. Though Hesse was now on the winning side, this did nothing to negate the fact that they still owed Prussia much of the indemnity that had been levied after the Austro-Prussian War. Hesse was, therefore, continually pinched for money, and Ludwig and Alice were no exception. They were forced to retrench even more stringently, than previously, and regretfully had to dismiss some of their staff.

Meanwhile, Victoria dutifully wrote letters to her grandmother thanking her for birthday gifts of pearls, (despite the Queen's complaints about the cost of pearls, she did send them out to her granddaughters for birthdays and Christmas) reporting that she had a new governess, Fräulein Kilz, and that Papa has gone away with the army again. Little Ernie had such a funny sense of humor, she wrote some days later, that Frittie laughed loud enough at a joke to astonish the entire family, but Papa was still not home.[41] Victoria's letters to her grandmother, which were rather frequent for a seven year old, had the same plaintive refrain ... Papa was not home, he was away. This was because a state of war continued to exist between Prussia and France until May 1871. All were looking forward to his return and the promise of a visit to England again that fall.

In September, the family went to Balmoral and from there to Sandringham. However, hopes for a restful visit were doomed to failure since Victoria's Uncle Bertie, the Prince of Wales, contracted typhoid, and was extremely ill. Alice and Aunt Alix, the Princess of Wales, anxiously nursed the patient. To complicate matters, the children were at Buckingham Palace, having contracted whooping cough. The youngsters, however, got over the disease quickly and were transferred to Windsor Castle where they played in the old nurseries and enjoyed their aunts and uncle's toys and books. Queen Victoria, who remained with them at Windsor, would not tolerate the well-known disorderliness and noise of the Hessian children, especially when their Aunt Beatrice joined in (who was, after all, only thirteen years old at the time). Pages were frequently sent up to the nurseries to request that the children 'settle down,' but they found it difficult to obey. The crowd of youngsters, which also included the Wales cousins, loved playing in the wide corridors of Windsor, hiding behind curtains, in corners, or under the large pieces of furniture. When one child was discovered by the others, the inevitable bursts of laughter and shouting ensued. The most delicious part was a table with lemonade and biscuits which was outside the Queen's room and the cousins contrived to steal these on a constant basis.[42]

Victoria, the oldest of the 'gang,' missed her mother dreadfully. Alice and Aunt Alix continued to nurse Uncle Bertie, who had come dangerously close to death, neither leaving his side until he was quite well. This necessitated a much longer stay than they had anticipated and a much longer time for Alice away from her children. Victoria wrote wistful and longing letters from Windsor in English, telling her mother all about her life with Grandmama and what she and the other children were doing.

Due to the serious illnesses, it wasn't until January 1872 that the family returned to Darmstadt. Their days passed in their familiar pattern and Alice was pregnant once again. On June 6, the Princess was delivered of a girl, whom they called Princess Victoria Alix Helena Louise Beatrice. She was, nevertheless, always called Alix or Alicky, in the family. Alice said that she called the little girl "Alix" because *they murder my name here...*[43] pronouncing it horribly. The baby was blue-eyed, with golden hair. As a small child she was of such a sunny and happy disposition, so that one of her nick-names was "Sunny." Alice thought she was very much like Ella in appearance, except, perhaps a little smaller. Little Alix adored Victoria from the beginning. She always looked up to her and thought her very clever.

While Alice, never strong these days, was recovering from the birth, Victoria and Ella were sent to the Heiligenberg to be with the Battenberg family. Their oldest Battenberg boy cousin, Louis, was away in the Royal Navy and so their playmates were Henry, whom they called "Liko,"* who was fourteen, and the youngest Battenberg boy, Franz Joseph, called in the family, "Franzjos," who was just eleven. Victoria loved playing with Liko, who was not above getting into trouble with his younger cousin. Franzjos, however, was delicate and studious, and like the little girls in Darmstadt, had an aversion to Victoria and Ella's loud and rambunctious ways. His only recourse was to send them off on constant errands so that he could read in peace. Not much deterred, Victoria climbed trees, got into scraps, and, as usual, was continually ruining her clothes. Ella, while she frequently joined in the fun, was a model of decorum, and always careful of her appearance.

(*) *Henry's Italian nurse called him "Enrico," and "Rico" for short. The children, like many little ones pronounced ther "rs" well, and the name evolved into "Liko."*

After the birth of Alix, it seemed that Alice was never quite well. She appeared to suffer consistently from something or other, whether it was headaches, fever, extreme fatigue, or other complaints. Victoria, who kept a close watch on her mother, was sensitive to her moods, and wrote to the Queen: *"Mama returned from Baden yesterday, and is laid up with a feverish attack and rheumatism so that she can not write."*[44] In the letters she wrote to her grandmother, there are many such comments about Mama's not being well and the hope for a quick recovery.

In April 1873, Victoria reached her tenth birthday. Her character, honest, courageous, intelligent, and neglectful of her own appearance, was becoming fixed. She loved being the children's leader and playing with her little brothers and sisters. She would often lament that she should have been the man of the family.[45] Her strength was already noticeable in her constant devotion to her mother, whom she may have sensed as weaker and in need of her stalwart protection. This was never more apparent than in May of that year, when the Hessian family faced a terrible tragedy.

Ernie and Frittie were playing in Alice's bedroom while she was practicing the piano. Strangely, Alice was practicing, among other things, Chopin's Funeral March. The little boys' game took Ernie to an adjacent room. When Frittie saw Ernie in the window from the adjacent room, which was at a right angle from the room in which Frittie was playing, the little boy accidentally ran towards an open window and fell out onto the terrace below. Everyone was horrified since he was a hemophiliac, but for the moment, though unconscious, he seemed all right. However, that evening of May 29, he quickly took a turn for the worse and died of a massive hemorrhage.

Without question, the family was devastated by this death. Alice never really recovered and Victoria was deeply shocked, giving her a fear of the disease that would haunt her for the rest of her life.[46] Little Frittie's death was particularly traumatic for Ernie, whose life would be strongly impacted by this. He is purported to have said to Alice, *"When I die, you must die too, and all the others; why can't we all die together? I don't like to die alone like Frittie."*[47] As a consequence, the older sisters, very naturally, tended to coddle him and encourage his sensitive nature. Even as an adult, they often shielded him from unpleasant realities, and they never seemed to have allowed him to 'harden up' much. The distraught family spent November and December of that year with the Queen in England.

In spite of adversity, the family would go on as it always had. Alice was once again pregnant and Victoria was, as became her habit, very caring of her mother. At the time of her eleventh birthday, she wrote to the Queen, to thank her for presents, but also to report about her mother. *"[Mama] has had a bad sore throat for the last day or two and Sunny [Alix] had one too..."*[48] In this letter, Victoria also expressed her strong desire to follow in her grandmother's and her mother's footsteps in all she did. *"I hope I may be able to become what you wish for I should very much like to be a comfort to Mama."*[49]

As Victoria and Ella progressed from childhood to girlhood, there were many discussions between Alice and her mother concerning what the destiny of a young girl should be. They wrote to each other at length about their disgust at parents raising girls only for marriage. Alice felt that this was far too prominent a feature of raising daughters in England particularly in the upper classes. She wrote: *"I want to strive to bring up the girls without seeking this as the sole object for the future – to feel they can fill up their lives so well otherwise... A marriage for the sake of marriage is surely the greatest mistake a woman can make..."*[50] Alice was as determined not to make this mistake as she was to have her children marry for love. Ludwig readily acquiesced. Theirs was an unusual ambition for that time, and assuredly in that social circle.

In May 1874, Victoria and Ella were sent to visit Prince Alexander and Princess Julie's eldest daughter Marie and her husband Gustav, future Prince of Erbach-Schönberg. Schönberg was another of the charming towns nestled around the Darmstadt area. Here Marie and Gustav lived in a lovely castle on a hill with beautiful misty woods as their garden. A great place to play, of course, but Victoria and Ella's concerns were elsewhere with their mother, who on May 24, gave birth to her last child. Princess Marie Victoria Feodore Leopoldine, known as "May," was born at the Neues Palais. The happiness of this birth could not assuage the grief that had come to the family the previous year. Victoria, always sensitive to her mother's moods and feelings, expressed herself in a poignant piece of poetry which Alice sent along to Queen Victoria, saying: *"Victoria composed this for use for the 29th...this year/ without any aid/ & gave it to me very shyly only for myself. Please read it & return it."*[51] The little poem ended with the stanza:

"Oh, weep not mother I beseach [sic]
thee
For Fritzie is in heaven
In heaven where angels sing
with glee
And sins are all forgiven

1874 Victoria."[52]*

It was a grief her mother could not set aside.

Nevertheless, as in all things, the girls continued to grow, healthy, happy, and at least in Victoria's case, full of mischief. But, as was her nature, she was always keeping a watch on Mama, to make sure she didn't work too hard, wasn't feeling ill, or, at least, was eating properly. She continued to write to her grandmother of the comings and goings at Darmstadt, including the visitors who arrived. Sometimes it was Aunt Vicky's children, the Prussian cousins. The older girls agreed that Heinrich, or as he was called in the family, Henry, the younger brother, was far more pleasant than Willy, the elder. Sometimes it was the English cousins, and sometimes it was their favorite uncle, Prince Leopold – a close friend of Ludwig and a dear brother to Alice. He was, certainly, the children's favorite and a visit from Uncle Leo was a very special occasion.

In the spring of 1875, the family went for another visit to England. Ludwig and Alice stayed with the Queen at Osborne since "Alice is looking pale and worn."[53] As pale and wan as was Alice, *"[Ludwig], on the other hand, is looking blooming and the children are superb. Little Alix is the most lovely child..."*[54] The Queen was extremely pleased with the children. She felt that they were *"strikingly handsome, and so lovable and well brought up. The two eldest Victoria and Ella, a wonderfully pretty girl, are with us here and bring life into the house with their childish merriment. Moreover, they are very obedient."*[55] Though concerned about Alice's health, she was also pleased that the last vestiges of bitterness from the earlier troubles seemed completely gone.

The patterns of their visits to England continued through this decade, spring, or summer in Osborne or Balmoral, and possibly back to Buckingham Palace or Windsor for

---

(*) For the entire poem see: Appendix A

family parties or other occasions. However, it soon began to appear that the Hesses would inherit their Grand Duchy. As early as the summer of 1875, Victoria noticed that not all was well and wrote to the Queen that her great-uncle, Grand Duke Ludwig III, was suffering from poor health, and even having trouble walking and standing. All would be calm for a while. Perhaps Victoria was being a little too concerned about the grown-ups around her.

She and the other children continued their lessons. Soon her mother decided that Victoria was capable of doing the Oxford Examinations for Young Girls, a difficult set of tests. Victoria's clear advantage was that she was a constant reader, and because of her correspondence with her grandmother, was already becoming a very capable writer – skills very important for the examinations. She was proud of her letter-writing ability and often commented to her mother how Ella and Irène had to bite their pens agonizing over what to say, while all her thoughts just flowed out of her pen.[56]

During these years, she and Ella also indulged in reading about their Cousin Louis Battenberg and his exploits in the Royal Navy. He accompanied the Prince of Wales to India and at the last moment had to replace the official illustrator who fell ill. The two girls giggled over Louis' drawing of some sailors desperately trying to load an ostrich onto their ship. He was quite talented and many of his drawings found their way into The Illustrated London News. It is easy to imagine Victoria wishing she could join him on his travels and adventures, and chaffing at her silly dance classes, which she considered a waste of time.

On their next trip to Balmoral in 1876, all noticed that Victoria, at thirteen, was becoming quite a young lady. She was growing tall, with blond hair turning into strawberry blond and blue grey eyes. Her brother thought she had *"very aristocratic features and resemble[d] mother more closely than any of the rest of us."*[57] She was extremely talkative; in fact, Queen Victoria called her a 'gasbag' since she adored debating and controversy. The young girl eagerly espoused causes, and followed her mother's footsteps as a progressive. She was one of those pragmatic people who always wanted to know why a thing was so. Her mother commented: *"Victoria is immensely grown, and her figure is forming. She is changing so much – beginning to leave the child and grow into the girl. I hear she has been good and desirous of doing what is right; and she has more to contend with than Ella, therefore double merit in any little thing she overcomes, and any self-sacrifice she makes."*[58] Apparently being good was a lot more difficult for Victoria than it was for Ella.

She continued to take some notice of her Cousin Louis, who seemed a very glamorous figure, looking so smart in his Royal Navy uniform. Prince Louis was now tall and slim, just over six feet, with wavy dark brown hair, liquid brown eyes, and a full navy-style beard. The beard made him look older and more authoritative, though he was in his early twenties. He had obviously inherited a great deal of his father's charm. He had been promoted to Lieutenant, and was a great favorite of Uncle Bertie. As time went on, he was encouraged to join in the social life of the Marlborough Set.* What the Hessian girls didn't know about Louis was that he was getting quite a reputation for being something of a Lothario, with a girl in every port.

Little dreams and girlish fancies were put aside, however, as other more important events claimed their attention. In March 1877, their beloved Grandfather, Prince Karl of Hesse died, and then, three months later, their Uncle, Grand Duke Ludwig III of Hesse and by Rhine died, leaving their father, Prince Ludwig, as the Grand Duke Ludwig IV of Hesse. With this change of circumstances, the family, thankfully, no longer had money worries.

(*) *Marlborough House was the town residence of the Prince and Princess of Wales. Their social circle was called the "Marlnborough Set."*

Nevertheless, they were overwhelmed with functions, ceremonies, and obligations. Alice's vitality, which had become even worse after the death of Frittie, was being sapped by the ever larger responsibilities. Nevertheless, she faced them stoically. To be helpful, the family tried to take small breaks from responsibilities so that Alice might recover her strength. The problem remained that the holidays never seemed long enough, and Alice never seemed to fully recover. *"Mama is very tired & looks very white."*[59]

In July 1878, the family went to Eastbourne in Sussex for a holiday, staying in Highcliffe House, Grand Parade, which overlooked the sea.[60] They were constantly mobbed by people. Though Alice was not in the best of health, she was happy meeting some of her old friends as well as the constant flow of relatives. That summer, a significant addition was made to the family in the person of Miss Margaret Hardcastle Jackson ("Madgie") who, like Mrs. Orchard, stayed until the children were grown. She was an Englishwoman of modern ideas, which in those days meant she was broad-minded and felt that little girls, as well as little boys, could do anything. She hated dishonesty and lack of responsibility as well as gossip, malicious or otherwise, and truly instilled this dislike into her charges. She also reinforced that which their mother had already rooted into their beings – a deep social conscience.[61] The children were taught that their position was *"nothing, save what their personal worth can make it,"*[62] and that they should be modest and unselfish. This point was stressed by Alice, who, in turn had been taught this by her own parents. To her, perhaps, this was the most important lesson of all.

While in Eastbourne, Alice could not help but get involved in the charities *"and even [visited] a home for reformed prostitutes..."*[63] She was forever remembered in that community for her good works that summer, which had taken the place of her much needed rest. The children had a wonderful time at the seaside, but also loved visiting London. They stayed at Buckingham Palace and were able to tour London, visiting museums, the House of Lords, and many of their relatives. A most exciting event for fifteen-year-old Victoria, and fourteen-year-old Ella, was being invited to a large garden party at Uncle Bertie's Marlborough House. There, they met their Cousin Louis, looking splendid, as usual, in his naval uniform. They left the party without permission so that Louis could row the two young ladies around the artificial lake at Buckingham Palace. They were reprimanded by Miss Jackson for this infraction, but, they, no doubt, felt that it had all been worth it. Indeed, it was a halcyon summer and too soon ended.

****

One evening at the beginning of November 1878, the family sat around the fireplace at the Neues Palais while Victoria read *Alice's Adventures in Wonderland* out loud. Alice noticed that as the girl read, Victoria's voice was becoming hoarse and that her face was looked flushed and feverish. Alice sent her straight to bed with a hot-water bottle. Soon enough Victoria was diagnosed with diphtheria and telegrams were sent fast and furious from the Neues Palais to Windsor Castle as, one by one, all the family, excepting Alice and Ella, fell ill with the highly contagious disease. Ella was sent away to her paternal grandmother, and the Queen wrote in her journal: *"Alice telegraphs: 'Alicky tolerable; darling May very ill, fever so high; Irene has got it too. I am miserable, such fear for the sweet little one.' ... Poor dear Alice, and she so delicate herself."*[64] Alice's delicacy did not prevent her from throwing herself into the most important nursing she would do in her life. She was going from sick room to sick room soothing fevered brows while the family physicians tried to match her twelve hour schedules.

Soon, however, things began to improve. Victoria, the first to come down with the disease, was the first to be on the road to recovery. The good bulletins from Darmstadt caused *The Times* of London to speculate about where the family had acquired the disease. According to the Berlin Clinical Weekly *"the physicians arrive at the conclusion that the infection has been communicated by kissing."* This because no one else in the household but the family caught the disease and the sanitation of the Palace was pronounced *"perfect."*[65]

Indeed, the other children, one by one, began to recuperate except little May. The youngest of the Hessian family, weakened by a terrifically high fever, died tragically on November 16, at the age of four. The Queen was notified immediately and wrote, stricken, in her journal: *"A very dreadful day...precious little May was gone! This is too dreadful. How my darling child adored that little angel! Alice terribly grieved but brave. [Ludwig] better, Ernie less satisfactory, and the others better, especially Alicky."*[66]

As horrible as May's death was, the rest of the family continued to rally. Ernie, who was not told of his sister's death, constantly asked for his little playmate. Alice allowed the children to write to one another during their illness and Irène tried to comfort her little brother and possibly keep his mind off of May saying, *"I hear your throat hurts you very much... If you try not to think of the pain so much it will not hurt you quite so much."*[67] Ernie persisted and eventually, Alice decided to tell him that his little sister had died. She put her arms around him, to comfort him and kissed his brow. The disease, insidious and contagious, struck. Alice, being worn out from all the nursing and all the tragedy, could not, or would not, fight the illness.

She had been, in fact, in a compromised state for quite some time. It seemed inevitable that she, among her immediate family, would not improve and that the disease would ultimately claim her. Because her fever was so high, from the beginning it was thought to be a hopeless case. The Queen, desperate to do something to save her daughter, sent her personal physician, the eminent Sir William Jenner, to look after the convalescents and Alice. Victoria wrote to her grandmother to thank her for this consideration and to report: *"Dear Mama is so dreadfully ill, & the news to day is very bad, we are so anxious & miserable. May God here* [sic] *our prayers..."*[68]

On December 14, the fateful day when Prince Albert had died in 1861, the Queen wrote in her journal: *"This terrible day come round again! Slept tolerably, but woke very often, constantly seeing darling Alice before me...When dressed, I went into my sitting-room for breakfast, and met Brown* coming in with* [a] *telegram ... from [Ludwig], which I did not at first take in, saying: 'Poor Mama, poor me, my happiness gone, dear, dear, Alice, God's will be done.'"*[69] The evening before, Alice had been conscious, and had visits from her mother-in-law, and Sir William Jenner. Afterwards, Ludwig came to wish her goodnight. Alice, the last of the family to come down with the disease, became the first of Queen Victoria's nine children to die. She did so in her sleep, on that significant day, December 14, at 7:35 in the morning.

The Queen wrote in her journal: *"That this dear, talented, distinguished, tender-hearted, noble-minded, sweet child, who behaved so admirably during her father's illness, and afterwards, in supporting me, and helping me in every possible way, should be called back to her father on this very anniversary, seems almost incredible, and most mysterious."*[70]

(*) *John Brown, Queen Victoria's personal attendant.*

Chapter III

December 1878 – April 1884

The Hessian family was devastated by the loss of Alice. Indeed, it was an unimaginable bereavement coupled with the loss of little May. As reaction to the tragedy quickly set in, letters arrived from all branches of the extended family. Some had a tendency to dwell on the terrible misfortunes associated with death. Queen Victoria was, naturally, one such person. She commiserated with Victoria saying:

Time seems to make our dreadful loss only greater, and you will feel day after day more and more the irreparable dreadful loss your darling Mama is to you! ...who was so devoted to you all, ...& gave her precious life for you all! –...It is a great privilege to be her Child – but it is also a great responsibility to become really worthy of her – to walk in her footsteps...& to try & do all you can for others as she did! –...[1]

This was hardly something that any fifteen-year-old could live up to. Nevertheless, Victoria had already made up her mind to try, as best she could, to take her mother's place in the family. She was determined to be the main source of support for the other children and for her father, as well, so bereft as they were and without the center of their existence.

It is too dreadful, she wrote to her grandmother, that after we all had recovered our own darling Mama should fall sick too...without her & little May it does not seem like home anymore. If you had seen how she went about from seven o'clock & earlier in the morning, till late at night...always with one or the other of us, you would understand how we feel now, that we can never see her again in this world.[2]

Having returned home from her grandmother's, the Princess Karl, Ella, too, wrote to the Queen lamenting her mother's death. It was strange, she told her grandmother, to see her Papa again, after she returned home. Ernie did not yet realize it, and all of them, she continued, felt as though they were in an awful dream.[3]

As horrible as Alice's death was for Victoria and Ella, it was even more difficult for their younger siblings. Irène, who probably felt outshone in beauty and intelligence by her elder sisters, was lost without her mother's guidance and encouragement. She became shy and was considered extremely backward by her eldest sister and her grandmother. Alix, the youngest daughter, was devastated. It was thought that this death was most influential in the molding of her character since all that was 'sunny' about her seemed to disappear. As an example, her cousin Marie Louise of Schleswig-Holstein observed, some years later, that Alix loved to go about being perennially doleful, wondering what would happen when another real sorrow would assail her. It was, perhaps, an unfair observation since she had sustained the loss of a parent and close sibling. Then, of course, there was Ernie, just ten years old, living with the clear memory of tragically losing his little brother. His morbid fear of dying alone was stronger than ever. In fact, he was terrified of death, disease, and desertion.

Victoria, however, was absolutely determined to fill the void. She would pull herself together and would emulate her mother, *"the mistress of the house, a wise and loving wife and mother whom we respected as much as we loved."*[4] Ella too, was determined to make *"Mama's life our example."*[5] And, between them, they grew up quickly.

While Ella completely surpassed her older sister in beauty and gentleness, Victoria was intellectual, bossy, a voracious reader and garrulous. Her bossiness held her in good stead even now as she took over the family, though she often reverted to her hoydenish ways. She did, as usual, have a temper, and the Queen urged her to moderate herself – be gentle and not judge others too harshly. However, she sweetened this criticism by telling her that she had never found Victoria *"the least difficult to manage."*[6]

Victoria's weekly letters from the Queen were supportive, helpful, and always full of advice. Though the older woman encouraged her to wallow in the deep mourning into which she, herself, had descended, Victoria saw no purpose in this. As a teenager, she asserted her pragmatism and independence. She refused to be mired in gloom. Not only was she the strongest and most mature of the children, but also, as her mother before her had charge of the Queen after her beloved husband's death, Victoria, in effect, now had charge of her father, the Grand Duke. She became the de facto head of the family and wrote: *"My childhood ended with her death for I became the eldest and most responsible of her orphaned children."*[7]

Happily, Victoria, with the support of Ella, had the inner resources to cope quite well. Even Queen Victoria managed to bestir herself from her terrible grief and wrote *"...think of me as your mama..."* And, from that moment forward, the Queen would carefully monitor their lessons, their days, what they wore, what they ate, what they read, their confirmation studies, whom they met, and indeed, everything she could about their lives. Being as far away as she was, she was, nevertheless, able to accomplish this end through constant communications and frequent visits back and forth in England or in Hesse. The Hessian grandchildren would be the closest to her, save the ones that actually lived with her in later years. Perhaps the very shy Irène said it best when she wrote: *"I am sure your wish to replace dear Mama has been fully fulfilled, for I feel more and more that you are like a second mother to me."*[8]

After Alice's death, Kranichstein, the enchanted hunting lodge, where she spent so many summers, was closed. The lodge on the misty lake was so much associated with her, that people thought they could see her face in the windows calling to her children at play. It was too painful for the family to return there. For some time, it would also be too painful to return to the Neues Palais and any of the other homes, all of which were strongly associated with Alice. Instead, the family began to spend their summers at another of their hunting lodges, originally built in 1721[9], and called "Wolfsgarten." Located between Frankfurt and Darmstadt, it was there where the family slowly recovered from its loss, and began once again to prosper.

Wolfsgarten stood in a deeply wooded area just a few miles outside of Darmstadt. It was built around a shady grass-grown courtyard with a stone fountain and pergolas in the center. Aunt Helena's daughter, Princess Marie Louise of Schleswig-Holstein, recalled that Wolfsgarten was her favorite of the Hessian residences. She remembered, in particular, the beautiful fountain in the middle of the square around which were built the resident buildings and stables. She and the other children used to *"dabble* [their] *hands and try to catch the goldfish."*[10] Opposite the large rose-red colored brick palace where the Hessian family and any royal visitors stayed, were the stables *"with their clock tower and green painted doors."*[11] On either side of the courtyard stood small one-story houses occupied by the retainers and any visitors who might be there. According to one visitor, "[p]*eople had breakfast in their own little houses, but for lunch and dinner, everybody went across to the big palace, and on rainy days wooden planks were laid down from house to house to enable people to go to and fro without getting their feet wet.*"[12] It was no hardship for the Aunts and Uncles and their various cousins to pay long visits to the beautiful house. They rode, played tennis, had picnics, and took long jaunts into the woods that surrounded the house. When they weren't at Wolfsgarten or the Neues Palais, the Hesses were at Osborne, Balmoral, or Windsor. To Victoria and Ella, members of Alice's family were filled with small and poignant reminders: Aunt Louise moved like mother and Aunt Vicky sounded like mother.[13]

Though they saw less of Aunt Vicky than of the other British relations, they did see something of her eldest son and their cousin, Willy, who would later become the troublesome Kaiser Wilhelm II. He was attending university at Bonn. Even as a university student, his younger cousins considered him pompous and bossy. He would visit the older girls frequently and take Victoria and Ella on rides or walks around the country. He would often insist that they sit down while he read passages from the Bible. Worse, he was the culprit who taught sixteen-year-old Victoria to smoke, which became a lifelong addiction. "*I remember secretly smoking up chimneys and out of the windows at the hotels. Though my father did not object to my smoking Miss Jackson did, authorised thereto by Grandmama.*"[14]

Queen Victoria, herself, hated the habit of smoking, and no one was allowed to smoke in her presence. She was only grudgingly persuaded that rooms in her various residences ought to be set aside for smokers. Even her favorite grandchild, Victoria, was never, in any circumstances, allowed to smoke in her presence. There was one exception. Once, when Victoria was staying with the Queen at Balmoral, they were both sitting outside. The midges were particularly awful, and since the Queen had heard that tobacco smoke kept them away, she encouraged Victoria to light up. She even asked to try a cigarette, but hated it.

It was almost immediately after Alice's death that the family went to Osborne. Many of the Aunts and Uncles were also visiting. Victoria was sensitive to her grandmother's sorrow and wrote to her: "*I know how sad it will be for you to see us arrive! but please take comfort that it is just what dear Mama would like best – to know us with You –*"[15]

Uncle Leopold, of course, was always amusing, and though often laid up for weeks with his hemophilia, he would also visit Darmstadt every year until his marriage. These visits provided a great deal of comfort to the entire family as he had always been considered a particular friend as well as the favorite Uncle. He was, Victoria wrote, "*a delightful uncle to us all, only ten years older than myself.*"[16] He was also very much like an elder brother to the older pair, but one who would also guide them in their intellectual and cultural pursuits. Victoria wrote that he was the most cultivated of the Queen's sons and "*influenced our growing taste in art and literature and got on well with Papa.*"[17]

Many of the other Aunts and Uncles, Alice's siblings, would later take turns making visits and helping to raise the children. The Queen would, at intervals, send several 'helpers' to stay with the family in Darmstadt, which included Uncle Leopold, as well as Aunt Helena and another of Alice's younger sisters, Aunt Louise. So, at one time or another, all of the Queen's children came to visit and care for the Hessian family.

After a long and therapeutic visit to Osborne, the Hesses traveled back home where they could resume their daily lives. The Queen thought this the best course of action, feeling it imperative to return to some kind of normal existence immediately. Since she saw weddings as solemn occasions and not moments for hilarity, the marriage of her son Prince

Arthur to Princess Louise Margarete of Prussia took place, as had been scheduled, in March 1879, just a few short months after Alice's death.

The Hesses returned to the Neues Palais in spring 1879 for the first time since that terrible November. Victoria wrote that it was *"sad going over it again."*[18] However, they had the company of Uncle Leopold, which was doubly welcome since Victoria's birthday came just a few days later. Irène wrote to her grandmother that she took her uncle around their mother's rooms, and that they looked so desolate and dreary. At the time, Alix was still weak and only just beginning to convalesce from her terrible bout of diphtheria. It was a glum homecoming.

Victoria wrote of feeling quite bereft when her Uncle Leopold left at the end of April, telling Queen Victoria: *"When Uncle was here there was someone for Papa & us to go to in free time, someone who went out with us like Mama did so that we did not notice how different everything was, so much, then."*[19] However, as a close friend, Uncle Leopold had a continued interest in the family and their news, writing to Irène: *"I hear good accounts of you from Louis Battenberg, whom I saw yesterday."*[20]

Much had changed, though, in the household, Victoria wrote to the Queen, and everyone still felt a certain amount of dread going into the various rooms of their family home. Papa was using another bedroom, actually, the rooms that the Queen had used when she visited; the children had their breakfast and lunches with Papa, but the other meals were, as usual, in the school room. The worst was coming to breakfast and passing Alice's room and not being able to say good morning. Now it was quiet and empty. They all still felt a horrible dread going into the house and the rooms. Nevertheless, they all took a deep breath, and led ably by Victoria, and to a lesser extent by Ella, went on.

After returning home, Victoria wrote even more frequently to her grandmother. Her letters now showed the maturity of one woman sharing news, feelings, and items of interest with another. In May of that year, she wrote to congratulate the Queen on becoming a great-grandmother. *"We were delighted to hear Cousin Charlotte* [Princess Charlotte of Prussia] *has a child; it is so funny to think that you are a great grandmother & Aunt Vicky is a grandmother."*[21]* A few months later, she wrote to the Queen to commiserate with her on the funeral of the Prince Imperial, son of Emperor Napoleon III, who was killed in the Zulu War of 1879. Now, she noted, the exiled Empress Eugenie, a great friend of Queen Victoria's, would be quite alone. There were also harmless bits of gossip (Miss Jackson would countenance nothing more), such as: *"We were so surprised to hear of Cousin Stephanie of Belgium's engagement**, when we saw her two years ago she seemed so young still; but I hope she will be very happy."*[22]

Victoria was an avid reader of newspapers, as well as such of her father's papers as she was permitted to see. When she wrote to her grandmother, she never hesitated to give her opinions on world events. In September 1879, at Kabul in Afghanistan, there was a valiant defense and a resultant slaughter of British Embassy personnel by a mob of Afghani soldiers and townspeople: *"We were so shocked to hear of the treacherous way in which your embassy was massacred. Papa has been away shooting & I therefore opened the tellegram* [sic]. *Did the Ameer* [sic] *order the massacre, or was it the people who revolted, the papers we have seen say the latter! Anyhow, it proves how little such eastern nations can be relied upon."*[23]

In November 1880, commenting on problems in South Africa, Victoria wrote:

(*) *Princess Charlotte of Prussia married Hereditary Prince Bernhard of Saxe-Meiningen. The baby, their only child, was Princess Feodora of Saxe-Meiningen.*
(**) *Princess Stéphanie of Belgium became engaged to Crown Prince Rudolf of Austria.*

"You must be very vexed at the new disturbances that have broken out once more in the Cape – it is dreadful that as soon as one war is over another seems always to come – & they must be very expensive, though good practice, I should think for the soldiers."[24] There were also many comments about politics in Victoria's correspondence. It appeared that the Queen encouraged the older girls to give their views and discuss important issues in their letters.

Victoria continued to keep her grandmother appraised of her siblings' progress and the fact that their paternal grandmother Elisabeth often came for lunch and to listen to their lessons. In a bit of an 'about-face', she now lamented that she was terrible at expressing herself, *"I am affraid [sic] that my letters are very stupid, & I always envy people who can say nicely what they think, somehow I never do it properly."*[25] She complained that she was careless with her letters because she was always in a hurry. She also expressed a great deal of her own and her siblings' loneliness. It seemed that her father was always out somewhere shooting – in fact, that became a somewhat plaintive refrain, Ella writing, *"Papa is nearly always away..."*[26] However, in all this, the girls took one phrase the Queen wrote much to heart: *"You must try & write what you feel & think too as you get older."*[27]

As Victoria, Ella and Irène, grew, when taken as a threesome, they embodied beauty, intelligence, and style and were much admired. The Queen offered them copious amounts of counsel about marriage and related subjects. She worried especially about Ella who had a tremendous 'crush' on one of her Heiligenberg playmates, her cousin Grand Duke Serge Alexandrovich, son of Aunt Marie and Uncle Alexander II of Russia. This did not bode well for the obnoxious Cousin Willy, since it was about this time, during his university days, that he fell in love with the already spectacularly beautiful Ella, and wanted to make her his wife. *"Willy of Prussia stayed two days."* Victoria told her grandmother, *"He rode out with us all once, & read us a very amusing book called 'Midshipman Easy.'"*[28] No doubt it was more diverting than his Bible lessons. When Willy pushed his suit with Ella, who had thoughts only for Serge, she refused him. According to her brother, Ernie, *"[n] either his mother nor mine wanted anything of it because of their close relationship."*[29] Willy never spoke to her again, and, according to Ernie, hated Serge and *"went after him in every possible way."*[30]

The Queen, who knew that marriage with Willy might prove very difficult for Ella, was nevertheless disappointed that she would not be dissuaded from her preference for Serge. Serge was, of course, a Russian and the Queen had a well known aversion to everything Russian. She wrote to Victoria: *"I hope you will not get at all Russian from the visits to Jugenheim! Dear Mama tho' loving the language had such a horror of Russia & Russians!"*[31] This last was, perhaps, wishful thinking on the Queen's part since Alice already had an excellent relationship with her aunt-in-law, the Empress Marie, and her Romanov family.

Truthfully, Queen Victoria was worried that one of her precious Hessian granddaughters would go to Russia and this she dreaded. Besides her obvious prejudices, she very prudently felt that none of them were equipped to handle such a difficult position, except, perhaps, Victoria, who had never shown any inclination in that direction. She had hoped that Victoria would persuade Ella not to go to that 'horrible place' and to accept Willy's suit. However, because of his bombastic personality, Victoria agreed with Ella's rejection of Willy's proposal.

Victoria, nonetheless, protested her own innocence in 'going all Russian.' It is interesting to note that both older sisters were not the least in awe of their grandmother, although they always addressed her with love and respect. Irène, however, seemed to tiptoe around subjects with her grandmother, afraid of incurring her wrath either against herself or her loved ones. Victoria frequently took the 'bull by the horns' and responding forcefully to the Queen's letter, she wrote that truthfully, she really didn't think much of the Russian cousins.

Every body has always been very kind, but I do not believe if they were a hundred times more kind they would make us a bit Russian, they have such odd manners & say such odd things to each other & even once about the English that it made one quite angry, they seem to think themselves perfect too...The cousins are very tall & lazy & never seem to know how to amuse themselves, they talk very little & don't seem to know what to say, so that after we have talked about the weather & the roads, they generally are silent or talk among themselves.[32]

Victoria's sensible assessment of the Romanov young men should have satisfied the Queen. It did not, however, since Victoria was not the granddaughter about whom she was concerned. She continued, unabated, to fret about her Hessian granddaughters and their penchant for Russian suitors. Through the next few years she would do all she could to discourage the matches that nonetheless came.

****

The inevitable first anniversary of Alice's tragic death came in December 1879. It was a sad day for the family and Darmstadt – there were the wreaths laid at the mausoleum, telegrams from most of the family, and a bust of the Grand Duchess, dedicated at the Alice Hospital. However, the most difficult thing was the strange feelings experienced by the family without its mother. Victoria continued to brood about this and all the events of that previous year. Her strongest impression was that of the tremendous isolation she felt during that awful month, and the fact that she saw little of her mother, particularly during her own recuperation.

A year had passed before Victoria even began to sort out her feelings about that trying time. She finally wrote a long and difficult letter to her grandmother. It was only when she was feeling better, she wrote, that her mother had told her about little May's dying: *"Poor little May, I never guessed what had happened till dear Mama told me, & now I am rather glad, because you see she was still so small & would not have remembered dear Mama & we would not have known what to do for her – but now she will always be with dear Mama."*[33]

As the numbness of shock was wearing off, the memories of that time continually filled Victoria with unease. She was still very confused by her loss and felt conflicting emotions during that sad month. Perhaps, she was most upset about the feelings of selfishness that she had experienced. She was convinced that her mother thought she took May's death lightly because when Alice told her what had happened, Victoria was so lonely for her mother, *"that I did not understand it properly & felt as if somehow I did not belong to the others, who had had Mama all the time, & when we were together again in the Schloss & Ella had been with the grown up people & I with Alix in the nursery, it seemed all wrong."*[34] She acknowledged some jealousy and possible guilt that she had felt during the illnesses, although she was too practical to chastise herself for having given the disease to her family. However, since she was the first to recover, she felt her mother did not give her the same attention that her other sick siblings received. In all fairness, she would have only been vaguely aware of her mother's presence during the most serious times of her illness.

Letters like these, which enabled her to express her thoughts and emotions, did help Victoria to reconcile herself to her loss. Sometimes it felt almost natural to her that her mother was gone, and at others it seemed strange and awful. The Queen, always a receptive listener, would not allow Victoria to immerse herself in any of the many emotions that inevitably were omnipresent during the anniversary. Though she, herself, often wallowed in grief, she, nevertheless, encouraged her granddaughter to get on with the care of her family since, "[s]*o much depends on you darling Victoria as the eldest.*"[35]

****

In March 1880, Victoria and Ella were confirmed together. At such an important event in their lives, both girls sorely missed their mother. Those feelings, however, were mitigated very much by the presence of their grandmother, Queen Victoria. There was, according to the Queen's journal of that date, a great deal of excitement, along with the inevitable hustle and bustle. "*Victoria & Ella,*" she wrote were "*all in white, both looking nervous.*"[36] They both walked together into the chapel and the Queen took Victoria's hand. The service was long and solemn and both Victoria and Ella stood up and "*in a clear audible voice recited the Apostle's Creed, followed by Luther's explanation of it, from the Catechism, which they repeated alternately. It was very long, but they answered so well.*"[37] Though this was certainly considered a rite of passage to adulthood, the two girls didn't officially 'come out' until the following year. Victoria had delayed her own celebration so that the two of them could come out together.

As was her wont, the Queen continued to offer Ella and, especially, Victoria advice about their deportment and manners. A few days after the confirmation, when taking her leave from Darmstadt to travel on to Baden-Baden, she cautioned Victoria: "*You must learn to be posée* [level-headed]*, not talk too much or too loud – but take your place as your beloved Father's eldest daughter deprived of your beloved mother!*"[38] She didn't approve of Victoria's voracious reading, nor did she like her riding spirited horses or even shooting, which she was learning to enjoy with her father. She felt that these activities made Victoria 'fast,' though the Queen was probably not aware of the definition of that word. "[I]*t is not lady like to kill animals & go out shooting – & I hope that you will never do that. It might do you g[rea]t harm if that was known as only fast ladies do such things.*"[39] It has to be said that this was probably one of the few bits of advice which Victoria ignored.

There were more serious issues that the Queen discussed with her granddaughters. They talked about the nature of Victoria and Ella's relationships in Darmstadt. Because they were both still young and did not have a mother's guidance, they were wary about being in Darmstadt society. Indeed, Victoria was convinced that they were not ready for it quite yet.

Papa is going to begin inviting a few people to dinner now & then as he must see them sometimes & it is quite nice for us. I have begged him not to have any real parties yet – & I am sure you will not wish it as Ella is only 16 & I not so very much older. I know too that dear Mama was never very anxious about our knowing & seeing all the people here, as they are rather second rate & have often no very good manners.[40] If this sounded snobbish, it should be remembered that Alice never got along well with Hessian nobility or high society.

Victoria, however, had one very natural concern. As a royal princess, she was never sure if people liked her for herself or because of her position. In the same letter she wrote,

> *As we are so many, we never feel the want of acquaintances as single girls would & these here generally behave as if we were a sort of demi-god, or are rather vulgar...Papa has much to do & of course does not know much about them & leaves it to us so I thought it would be right to ask you – as dear Mama is not there – & I am sure you think as she did.*[41]

The Queen responded addressing the issue of friends, but also other important matters such as table deportment and marriage.

> *You are right to be civil & friendly to the young girls you may occasionally meet, & to see them sometimes – <u>but</u> never make <u>friendships</u>; girls' friendships & intimacies are very bad & often lead to great mischief – Grandpapa & I never allowed it, & dear Mama was quite of the same opinion. ... And at the dinners remember <u>not</u> to talk too much & especially not too loud & not <u>across the table</u>...*

> *There is another <u>most important</u> thing wh[ich] you are <u>quite old</u> enough for me to speak or write to you about. Dear Papa will, I know, be teazed [sic] & pressed to make you marry, & I have told him you were far too young to think of it, & that your 1st duty was to stay with <u>him</u>, & to be as it were the Mistress of the House...I know full well that <u>you</u> have no ideas of this sort & that you (unlike, I am sorry to say, so many <u>Princesses</u> abroad) – don't wish <u>to be married</u> for <u>marrying's sake</u> & to have a <u>position</u>.*[42]

This letter, while seeming to gently argue the point to Victoria, nevertheless, reflected Alice and Ludwig's wish that none of the children marry where they did not love.

> *"Your dear kind answer to my last letter,"* Victoria responded, *"has made me very happy & I will try always to remember your advice & to follow it – & not be like so many German Princesses."*[43]

Even at the age of seventeen, when many girls would at least be starting to wonder what life might hold in store for them, thinking about a possible match, or just simply what was next, Victoria was interested in none of this. Her primary responsibility, with some reinforcement from the Queen, was the care of her motherless family. Her father seemed content to leave much to her since he was, as she told her grandmother on many occasions, constantly out shooting.

Another project which was important to Victoria and Ella was the education of their brother, Ernie. During a rather lengthy visit that Victoria made to the Queen, she wrote often to her little brother. In one letter, she admonished him and advised him to inform his tutor, Herr Müther, to write to the Queen on a frequent basis in order to give his progress reports. Nevertheless, she wasn't just trying to manage him, though she would often do this as the years went on. She also made efforts to write about things that she knew would amuse him.

> *We play the turning-piano very often & I wanted to play it on Sunday only Brown & Co would have fainted. Grandmama has been riding several times when we walked & her pony will stop at all the bushes to eat & once the wind blew her cloak over her parasol which she shut up, so she was all covered up in it [;] we laughed dreadfully.*[44]

However, it wasn't only Ernie that Victoria and Ella had to watch, but the other children as well. Ella told her Grandmother that Uncle Leopold and Aunt Beatrice helped Irène and Alix with their lessons. Nevertheless, she sorrowfully reported that Fraülein Textor complained about Alix, though she was working harder now. That the Queen was interested in this minutia was obvious when she wrote back that she expected the two girls to make sure that the young ones were *"very punctual ab[ou]t their lessons – for I am sorry to say all 3 tried to evade them when they were here..."*[45]

It seemed an unfair load to put on the young pair. Nevertheless, they both were well able to carry it, and did so without hesitation. "I will try to show you how grateful I am," Victoria wrote, *"for all your love & kindness by trying to please you in all I do & by teaching the others the same. & by looking up to you as I would to dear Mama were she still with us & I feel sure Ella will do the same."*[46] But, along with the responsibilities, Victoria was also trusted with the privileges of an adult. In October 1880, she wrote the Queen a letter full of excitement and pride as she was to represent her grandmother at the christening of Princess Marie of Erbach-Schönberg's son, Victor, of whom the Queen was the godmother. *"Papa has let me know that you wish me to represent you at the christening of the Erbach baby on the 26th. I am so pleased & thank you very much for having chosen me."*[47]

Not only was she able to attend this function, but her father was now treating her and Ella as adults, taking them to the theater and to the opera and inviting people of interest to the Neues Palais. One such person, Victoria wrote to her grandmother, was a mesmerist who came to show them his techniques. Victoria told the Queen that she found this very curious and most interesting.[48]

Christmas 1880 was spent at their Hessian grandmother's. During the two years that followed Alice's unfortunate death, the family could not reconcile themselves to the loss long enough to stay home at the Neues Palais and open their presents. However, things did improve soon after. In the beginning of 1881, Grand Duke Ludwig held his first formal dinner since Alice's death. Victoria, naturally, wrote her grandmother an account of this first real adult social occasion which she and Ella attended. The party, she related, was made up mostly of men, with few ladies, which relieved Victoria, since she felt that women were so much more critical about things than men – an obvious point, but nevertheless insecurity on her part. Dealing with adult women without her mother was trying for her.

The evening began as her father presented her to all the guests and initially it seemed that all the men had to do was pay her compliments. Victoria was never comfortable with flattery and told her grandmother quite categorically that she hated *"such stuff."*[49]

In these and other occasions, however, she certainly understood the importance of making a good impression on the people her father, the Grand Duke, entertained. Irène was able to write a glowing report about Victoria and her demeanor at such times to the Queen saying that *"Miss Jackson says everybody was much pleased with her nice manners and she did not seem at all shy."*[50] Irène, who told her grandmother she envied Ernie's lack of shyness, continued to be extremely diffident so this observation was all the more poignant.

Thankful to leave social subjects behind, Victoria began another political discussion about Britain's intention of pulling out of Afghanistan, though something far more portentous would happen just a few months later. The Tsar of Russia, Alexander II, was assassinated in St. Petersburg. *"The murder of the poor Emperor of Russia has been so dreadful that I am sure it must have moved you very much. It must have been horrible for poor Aunt Marie* who was his favourite child. Papa left us yesterday morning for St. Petersburg &*

(*) *Grand Duchess Marie Alexandrovna, Duchess of Edinburgh, the only surviving daughter of Tsar Alexansder II.*

will only arrive there late in the afternoon on Sunday. It is a long & tiring journey."[51]

One can only imagine what the Queen thought of this. Certainly, she would have felt uneasy that her son-in-law had traveled to the funeral of the Tsar in such a climate. However, she was not the only person who felt uneasy. A few days later, Ella wrote, ironically as things turned out, *"[t]he death of the Emperor of Russia is too dreadful. How I pitty [sic] poor Aunt Marie & the present Czar who can never feel sure of his life. ... I will be so pleased when [Papa] is back again from this dreadful Petersburg."*[52]

In the young life of Princess Victoria, things closer to home were to become of greater interest. She was becoming more aware of her Cousin Louis Battenberg, who was now a Lieutenant in the Royal Navy. He continued to be a favorite cousin of Victoria's Uncle Bertie, and was encouraged to stay at Marlborough House, where he met fascinating people such as Sarah Bernhardt, and the opera singer, Madame Adelina Patti. In 1880, he had an affair with the Prince of Wales' former mistress, the famous actress and professional beauty, Lillie Langtry. The affair was short, but passionate, and culminated with the birth of Langtry's only child, Jeanne Marie, in May 1881. Louis was persuaded by his parents to continue his career in the navy and to tarry no longer at Marlborough House.

Victoria and Ella spent June and July with the Queen in England. Because of their mourning, Victoria only attended some dinners and very low-key social events. However, she did attend a ball, possibly her first, and she wrote about it to Ernie. She had danced with Uncle Bertie and some other gentlemen and it all went off very well, she told Ernie, excepting that her gloves were spoiled by sweaty palms and her dress was torn.[53] She was less amusing and more candid in her memoirs as she remembered the ball years later. She had not been, she wrote, a great success *"for what with the heat, the strong scented flowers ... which filled the fireplace before which we stood and the giddiness which overcame me when waltzing in the crowd, – I felt quite faint."*[54]

After their visit to England, they were off to Belgium, staying with the King Leopold II and Queen Marie-Henriette at Laeken. The Belgian Royal couple were relatives whom they often visited. *"Cousin Leopold ... was a tall thin man, with a nose nearly as long as Cyrano de Bergerac's and his slow, drawling voice seemed to proceed from it."*[55] They returned home with the summer soon coming to an end after more visits from the English Aunts and Uncles.

Victoria continued to be primarily concerned with Ernie and his failure to take his lessons seriously. She felt responsible for his lack of discipline, and wrote the Queen endlessly about these problems. She told her grandmother that Ernie had a habit of dreaming over his lessons and neglecting his concentration. He seemed to lack pride in his work and was not ashamed when he did poorly. Interestingly, she also wrote that he was far more respectful of their Uncle Leopold than of his own father. However, this was probably due to the fact that his father was, perhaps, out shooting a little too much, and not paying the attention to Ernie that he needed. The Queen was completely aware of the situation and had written to Victoria, *"Herr Müther has given me an acc[oun]t of the studies & I must say – Ernie's g[rea]t absence, inattention & backwardness are becoming serious in his position & at his age."*[56] The fact was, no matter how much of a sergeant-major Victoria tried to be, she was usually contrite about her treatment of her brother saying how much she scolded and dictated to him. The Queen, however, wiser in this instance, would have none of this, answering crisply: *"You should speak to Herr Müther & then to dear Papa & we must all urge something being done."*[57]

Irène was showing definite signs of improvement as she was growing up. She was not as backward and shy as she had been, especially after her mother's death. As a matter of fact, the Queen's wish to replace their mother was completely fulfilled in Irène's estimation. Victoria wrote a letter to her grandmother thanking her for having Irène at Balmoral and said, *"I think you will find her improved, but she is very silent, partly from shyness partly from the sense that she is slow, I mean in thinking. Ernie & Alicky are much quicker & I think she feels it. I am sure the change & being with older people will do her good & make her more independent."*[58]

A few months later, the family had reason to rejoice in another event. Uncle Leopold was engaged to Princess Helene of Waldeck-Pyrmont. The Queen was shocked and upset that her invalid son was marrying, but consoled herself with the thought that *"Victoria and Ella like her very much."*[59] Victoria was eminently pleased about this as she knew how much her uncle wanted his own home and family. *"Though I hope to tell you myself tomorrow how pleased I am to hear that everything is settled at last & that you are really engaged to be married, I must send you these lines, or you may think I have no feelings. Ella joins with me in wishing you every possible happiness..."*[60] Leopold and Helene were married on April 27, 1882. The Hessian family attended the wedding, and then returned to Darmstadt with the exception of Ella and Irène, who stayed behind with their Grandmama.[61]

In fall and winter of 1882, Victoria, Ella, and Irène went to Italy. The journey started in Lucerne, and then went on to Milan, Florence, Venice, and Modena. Victoria told her Grandmother that she liked Florence the best, though she ventured the opinion that the present day Italians were not worthy of their heritage. Though she evidently had no respect for the Italians, she thought their country and towns were more picturesque than Hesse. Darmstadt appeared bare, she thought, after Italy. Irène, however, was far more impressed. In a letter to Ernie she catalogued every sight the trio had seen and like a typical tourist remarked that they saw *"something new & beautiful"* everyday.[62]

More interesting, Cousin Louis of Battenberg was on a long leave that winter and was spending time with his parents. Louis and Victoria began to see quite a lot of each other and even danced together at balls. Perhaps, Victoria, now, no longer considered her dance lessons a waste of time. The girls called Louis *"Our English Cousin,"* and Ella and Victoria remembered his kindness rowing them around the lake at Buckingham Palace. They never forgot that though he was a very smart man about town, he had always found time for them. Victoria's letters to the Queen began to mention him. *"Poor Louis Battenberg, who came over with [Papa,] is still very lame tho' he pretends to make light of it."*[63]

While Victoria began to dream about Louis Battenberg, the Queen was determined on a course that would steer her precious Ella clear of Serge Alexandrovich, the brother of the new Tsar Alexander III of Russia. At the beginning of January 1883, she asked Victoria her opinion of a possible match between Prince Friedrich of Baden and Ella. The Queen felt that Ella, who was nearing eighteen *"sh[oul]d not marry for a year or 2 – but it w[oul]d be a v[er]y nice &comfortable position for her. Russia, I c[oul]d not wish for any of you and & dear Mama always said she would never hear of it."*[64] However, Victoria quickly wrote back telling the Queen that Prince Friedrich had visited, and Ella thought he was nice, though

Ella & I never talk about those sort of things – but she seems neither to like or dislike [Friedrich] in any way – she laughs at his oddities & says he is good natured & nice – but I do not think cares at all for him yet – though I think Papa told her that he came here because of her – I am not sure. I do not think either that she cares for one of the Russians cousins.[65] Whether this was a sop to the Queen, it is hard to say, though it must also be said that Victoria would never have purposely misled her. It was most probable that she and Ella never discussed such matters.

Quickly enough, however, Friedrich proposed and was rejected. Since "[Papa] *would [never] oblige any of us to marry against our inclination and Ella told Papa that she found Friedrich much too good and solemn a person for her taste. Friedrich took the refusal well –... "*[66], for there was little doubt in Ella's mind that she would marry no one but Serge Alexandrovich. Queen Victoria was less sanguine:

> *Oh! Dear! How very unfortunate it is of Ella to refuse good* [Friedrich] *of Baden so good & steady, with such a safe, happy position, & for a Russian. I do deeply regret it.*

> *Ella's health will never stand the climate wh[ich] killed your poor Aunt & has ruined the healths of almost all the German P[rince]sses who went there; besides the dreadful state Russia is in, & the very depressed bad state of Society. You told me, only quite lately darling Child, that you thought Ella cared for no one? What does this all mean?*[67]

Again, Victoria was most certainly not lying; she was simply trying to soothe her grandmother. Possibly, she was trying to prepare her gently for the inevitable and hated Russian match. Oddly enough, she had a very brief flirtation of her own at this point with a Russian – Grand Duke Michael Mikhailovich, known in his family as 'Miche-Miche.' She would meet the Grand Duke again much later on.

Another Battenberg came into the forefront of the Hessian Princesses' life that spring 1883. Louis' younger brother, Alexander, whom the family called "Sandro," was having difficulties of his own. In 1879, he had been elected Prince of Bulgaria by the Bulgarian National Assembly and Sandro, though only twenty-two, had accepted the crown. The crown had first been offered to Prince Alexander of Hesse, and then to his son, Louis, however, in the end, it was Sandro who accepted the challenge. Support for his position, guaranteed by Chancellor von Bismarck of Prussia and Tsar Alexander II of Russia. However, things began to prove problematic when it became obvious that Sandro was not a puppet of the Russians or the Prussians. Added to that was the fact that Sandro was courting Princess Victoria of Prussia, Aunt Vicky's second daughter – a slap in the face to Prussia because of Sandro's parents morganatic status. Ultimately the Prussians didn't want to anger Russia, who, more and more, felt that Sandro was not a ruler with whom they could deal or control.

Victoria, who had a firm grasp of the situation, discussed it with her grandmother.

> *Sandro ... tied his hands by a promise to the late emperor* [the assassinated Tsar Alexander II], *to try & work in concert with the Russians sent there ... – while really the Russians were anything but pleased at the other powers forcing the Bulgarian independence on them, & the Bulgarians themselves are now very jealous & angry at all this interference...*

> *If he throws up his work, however, I think it will be the sign of a very weak spirit. If he would cease fearing these Russians, the Bulgarians would like him all the better, & after all, the Russians can not openly do anything to harm him, as the other powers are much too careful to let their influence in the Balkans peninsula grow stronger.*[68]

Sandro, however, had good reason to fear the Russians. Because of his support of the Bulgarian Parliament, the Russian Secret police made a botched attempt to kidnap him in

1883, and remove him from the country. Tsar Alexander III, his cousin, who particularly hated Sandro, and his henchmen were unsuccessful, but, nevertheless, Sandro and his supporters had been nervous ever since. It was a difficult situation incurring the wrath of both the Russians and the Prussians.

In another letter, Victoria continued discussing the debacle in Bulgaria. She said that the Russians had hoped that Sandro would be a tool in their hands so they petted and flattered him, but when it was seen that he wasn't, they put their favor towards others. However, Victoria felt, that if the Prince *"sticks to his post & feels that the other powers will back him up he has enough basis to hold his own for a long time to come..."*[69] Before its resolution, further unpleasant events would take place. Alexander and his brothers would suffer greatly at the hands of their cousin.

****

"Time seems to me to go very fast. It sometimes seems as if it were only yesterday that we were all romping about with May in Mama's room after tea – & now we are big girls & even Alix is serious & sensible & the house is often very quiet."[70]

Victoria was in a reflective mood and her life, as spring wore on in 1883, was about to radically change. Victoria and Ella had been invited to Scotland. However, something important kept Victoria from accepting the invitation. Ella, of course, understood. She told her father: *"If Victoria does not go with me to Scotland she will become engaged to Louis Battenberg."*[71] Instead, Victoria elected to spend some time at Seeheim, their hunting lodge near Jugenheim and in close proximity to the Heiligenberg. The house was hot, she wrote the Queen, but the woods around were pleasant and cool. Besides, she had not visited the lodge since Frittie died.[72]

Louis Battenberg made frequent visits to the lodge. They would drive together in Louis' pony cart or walk in the cool woods, go down to the pond at the front of the property and have discussions. It is possible that Louis told her something of his life in the navy. No doubt Victoria, with her fertile imagination, had already imagined Louis' life – sleeping in hammocks on deck, swaying in the balmy sea breezes, idealized at best. Louis told her about the maggot derbies the men had on deck, how they shook them out of their rations and actually trained them for racing.

It was not all as romantic as Victoria probably supposed and there was a darker side to his adventures. At the time, the British Navy had an anti-intellectual and anti-foreigner streak that made his life extremely difficult. As a result, Louis was often misunderstood by his fellow officers. They could not comprehend why he would rather read or draw than spend time in the mess halls drinking with them. Perhaps Louis was unwise in that regard. He probably should have choked down his protests and done as the others did - however, it was simply not in his character. He suffered for it then – with all the bullying that he endured – and, later on, with far more serious consequences.

Nevertheless, the pair got to know each other well during those visits. Louis proposed to Victoria in June of that year. He was thrilled when Victoria accepted him and wrote to his cousin, George, later King George V:

I have a great piece of news to tell you. Our mutual cousin Victoria has promised to be my wife! I can't tell you how happy I am. She is such a lovely darling girl, as you know, and I am nearly off my chump altogether with feeling so jolly...Everybody here is pleased about it and your Grandmother [Queen Victoria] *has been so kind about it. She has written to offer me the yacht.* Isn't it grand?*[73]

The engagement was officially announced in July 1883. Reaction from the Hessian Parliament about their Princess becoming only a Serene Highness was negative, since they refused to grant the couple any *"form of financial reward in the event of their marriage."*[74] Initially, both the Grand Duke and the Queen were not particularly pleased. It meant that Victoria would be leaving home and not taking care of the children. However, the other Hessian children were excited about having their first brother-in-law. Irène wrote to her grandmother that *"[w]e are all so pleased that dear Victoria is going to marry L[ouis] Battenberg. He will be such a kind elder Brother to us."*[75] Ernie, too, was happy with this new brother, writing later: *"We loved him so much as he was so good-natured and calm."*[76] Indeed, they were so happy and affectionate toward Louis that he and Victoria didn't have much time alone together.

Louis appealed to Victoria on many different levels. Not only was he intelligent, cultured, and kind, but she loved the fact that he was 'lower' than she on the social scale. A mere Serene Highness surely gratified her liberal leanings. The Queen's secretary Sir Henry Ponsonby penned an interesting description of Victoria and her new, and what might be depicted in royal terms as penurious, situation.

The bride Victoria [is] *'bright, lively but full of strange ideas. She locks herself up with her mother's books and papers and has imbibed Kant. Some say that she has shown her condemnation of princely titles by insisting on marrying a semi-Prince, going as low as she could in the scale of Princes without hurting susceptibilities. They will have no money from Hessian Parliament as she's not marrying a real Prince.*[77]

These leanings, however, disturbed her grandmother since they were virtually anti-royalist. However, in this, Victoria was very much like her mother. At yet another banquet, Victoria, who seemed to have been happy to share her views with Sir Henry Ponsonby, made remarks, he noted, very similar to what her mother said in a conversation many years before. *"I dare say Royalty is nonsense and it may be better if it is swept away. But as long as it exists, we must have certain rules to guide us."*[78]

Eventually, Queen Victoria gave her whole-hearted approval of the very attractive Prince for her favorite granddaughter, since, among other things, the Queen was susceptible to a handsome face. She wrote: *"[Y]ou have done well to choose only a Husband who is quite of your way of thinking & who in many respects is as English as you are..."*[79] Unquestionably, though Victoria would be spending a good deal of her married life in England, the Queen was still sad to let the child, Victoria, go, *"I suppose you write a g[rea]t deal to Louis Battenberg?,"*[80] she asked wistfully.

The Queen, who, in fact, thought Victoria would not marry at all because she wouldn't want to leave her father, became a great defender and supporter of Prince Louis. She wrote to her friend, and Aunt Vicky's mother-in-law, the Empress Augusta:

With regard to Victoria's engagement, it is precisely because she is so talented that should not have made a conventional marriage with some prince who would have been called

---

(*) *An appointment to the Royal Yacht.*

a good match, but would otherwise have offered no advantages. The English element in Louis Battenberg attracted her very much, since she is herself so very English.[81]

Other family members were a little more pragmatic. The Queen's son, Prince Arthur, Duke of Connaught, wrote to his mother on receipt of the news, *"Let me now say how much surprised I was to hear of Victoria of Hesse's engagement with Louis Battenberg...I have always liked him very much & I think he will make her a good husband, I only wish his rank were a little higher & that they had a little more money between them."*[82] Still more distant members such as Alexander III of Russia completely disapproved of Louis and Victoria's marriage, only a little less than he had wholeheartedly disapproved of Louis' brother, Sandro. The Prussians, at least Chancellor von Bismarck and Cousin Willy, were also offended that Victoria was not marrying a Prince of the Blood, whose remarks, as mentioned, the Queen found entirely offensive.

The Queen did not like lovers or courting much more than she had done in the past, and when Victoria joined her at Osborne that July, she was very specific about when Louis could visit. Her grandmother was rather possessive of her, and expressed displeasure when her own wishes were not considered first and foremost.

Louis Battenberg is coming here tomorrow & I shall be very pleased to see him. But I much regret that what I told Papa nearly a month ago has not been listened to & that he is coming to be at Cowes with Uncle Bertie, for I wished to have you to myself, & as you are, for the last time – how can I avoid asking him, & Uncle Bertie will be constantly wanting you to go with him. This last I do protest against.[83]

Louis obviously noticed the Queen's distaste for courting, and mentioned that he was only allowed to see Victoria *"by stealth, as she did not approve of engaged couples 'spooning'."*[84] Victoria, however, though sensitive to her grandmother's feelings, did not entirely pay heed. *"I hope you were not vexed at Louis Battenberg having once or twice come to see me."*[85] She was, indeed, vexed.

Characteristic of the Queen, she did not hesitate to offer as much marital advice as she could to her granddaughter. She admonished her about running after amusements when she ought to stay home and be a good wife and mother. She knew that Victoria would always find her happiness in her home, but she warned her to *"[b]eware of London & M[arlborough] H[ouse],"*[86] meaning, of course, the evenings and soirees of Victoria's Uncle Bertie and Aunt Alix, of whom the Queen strongly disapproved.

With Victoria nicely settled, however, the Queen was less concerned about what her granddaughter should do and how she should behave after marriage. Instead, she plunged completely in her anxieties about Ella and the almost certainty of her engagement to Serge. This would be the entire tone of her letters to Victoria until nearly the time of Victoria's wedding in spring 1884.

In September 1883, the Queen wrote that she was sure that heaven and earth would be moved to procure Ella, as though she was a bauble of some sort, for Serge Alexandrovich. *"[W]ith Ella's character & health I can see nothing worse than her living in Russia. Believe me when I speak so strongly ag[ain]st it."*[87] In subsequent letters that month, the Queen told Victoria that she would be slightly reconciled if Ella could spend part of every year outside of Russia. However, having said that, she also cautioned that Ella must not expect to spend it with Queen Victoria as she couldn't have a Russian Grand Duke around her for so long. The Queen continued to lament over Ella's probable engagement, *"I have got Ella's letter but I really do not feel quite able to answer her yet... I know how dearest Mama was ag[ain]st the idea, (tho' personally she liked Serge) & I also feel that Ella will be quite lost to me..."*[88] In the same letter she complained that Ella was so changeable and "*unaccountable; she told me how she hated the Russians, she refused Serge 3 weeks ago & now she takes him & forgets all.*"[89]

More important, from Victoria's point of view, was that Louis spent Christmas with the Queen. Louis was extremely touched by the Queen's kindness, she wrote, and then grew reflective: "*This old year is now at an end, & the new one, which is to bring such a change in my life is close but I feel that I know what I am about to do & that you will be as kind & good to me as you have always been & therefor, I can look forward with pleasure.*"[90]

As the New Year passed, Ella and Serge were officially engaged in February. As she did in most things, when faced with a fait accompli, the Queen soldiered on and accepted the inevitable. She wrote a note congratulating the couple, which Ella truly appreciated. "*Serge remains still a week I think, he was very much pleased by your kind message & with the others thank you many times for having thought of them all.*"[91] Even younger sister Irène put her oar in to convince the Queen, that really, Serge wasn't that bad. "*I assure you the more one sees of him the nicer one thinks of him.*"[92]

Without a mother to plan her wedding, Victoria was left to do much of the arrangements of the ceremony, the reception, and rooms for all the guests completely on her own. She was hopeful that Queen Victoria would be able to attend, but she was not optimistic. The wedding had been set for February, and the Queen had mentioned that she would not be able to come at that time. "*It was only a hope that I expressed when I mentioned your being present at our wedding next year & though nothing would have given me more pleasure...*"[93] Ultimately, however, the Princess was destined not to be disappointed, since the Queen did make the effort. The Hessians had changed the date to mid–April 1884, and, in a letter sent in the fall 1883, the Queen made up her mind to attend.[94] This was as exciting for Ella as it was for Victoria since she felt it would be a wonderful opportunity for the Queen to get to know her new fiancé.

Victoria worked long and hard on all the arrangements, without much help from her father, for reasons that soon became clear. She was constantly writing to her grandmother about who would be coming, where they would be staying, and what they would be doing.

However, right before the wedding, a tragic event occurred. Victoria's favorite uncle, Leopold of Albany, died suddenly on March 28, 1884. "*It is so terrible...that I feel... stunned. Dear Uncle was so kind & loving to us all, such a friend to Papa that this sorrow now is very hard to bear.*"[95] Naturally, the wedding was postponed again, while Victoria and her family dealt with yet another wrenching loss.

Part II

April 1884 – January 1901

Chapter IV

April 1884 – February 1885

Queen Victoria and her sensible advice came to the rescue once again. As she had, after the death of Alice, the Queen maintained that weddings were solemn and not frivolous occasions, so that this one need not be put off for long. Since she deemed May weddings unlucky, she determined on a date at the end of April. Arriving with all due pomp, the Queen made her appearance about two weeks before the event in order to help Princess Victoria with the arrangements for the guests and the ceremony.

On April 30, 1884, Princess Victoria and Prince Louis of Battenberg were married. Though the festivities commencing on that sunny April day were called the Wedding of the Decade, most of the excitement emanated from the fact that the Queen of England was attending the ceremony and preceding celebrations. Victoria, herself, made most of the arrangements for the nuptials and provided for the great number of visitors who were invited. It seemed as though everyone in the family was coming to the wedding as the Queen would be there. It would, therefore, become one of the 'Royal Mob' gatherings, as Queen Victoria half affectionately called them. The 'Mob' consisted of many members of the British Royal Family, the Prussians, the Russians, the Scandinavians, and even the Habsburgs. Joining these notables, many others also made their way to Darmstadt to attend. Frankly, it was a strain on the small Grand Duchy, the least of which was the actual monetary cost. It was primarily a great worry for Victoria, who did her best to try to house all the visitors. Foremost on her mind, however, were accommodations for her Grandmama. Therefore, instead of being a completely joyous occasion for the young bride, it was extremely stressful.

The wedding preparations were not the only cause of Victoria and her sisters' anxiety. Some time before, she and her family had become aware that their father was having an affair with Madame Alexandrine de Kolemine. Originally a Polish Countess, Madame de Kolemine had lived in Darmstadt for the past two years. She was the recently divorced wife of the Russian Charge d'affaires, and was said to be extremely beautiful and very accomplished. Far from being unhappy about their father's mistress, Victoria and her sisters actually liked the lady and were glad their father had found companionship. According to Sir Henry Ponsonby, *"Princess Victoria* [was] *always with her and the Grand Duke."*[1]

Perhaps Victoria thought that Madame de Kolemine would help the Grand Duke to miss her less when she married. Certainly she was happy for him at a time when she was so happy herself. Marriage to the lady, however, was out of the question. Victoria herself said that "Dear Papa will never marry again."[2] Undaunted, Grand Duke Ludwig nevertheless decided at that extremely inconvenient time that he must marry Madame de Kolemine immediately. To this end, he wanted Victoria to 'feel out' the Queen and see how she might react to this news. Naturally, Victoria was horrified, not the least over the bad timing.

When Queen Victoria and her youngest daughter, Beatrice arrived at the Darmstadt station, she recorded in her journal that Victoria looked tired and unwell. It was obviously due to the strain of the arrangements as well as having to deal with the de Kolemine affair. It must be added that Victoria was most probably still depressed over the death of her favorite Uncle Leopold.

As her father requested, Victoria had reluctantly related to Queen Victoria such details of her father's affair of which she was aware and the fact of his up-coming marriage. While understanding that Ludwig would want some kind of happiness and companionship in his life, the Queen felt very strongly that she could not have him as near to her as before if he went through the marriage with such a woman. She told Victoria that such a choice did him immense harm and further, that she very much wanted him to pause and reflect on this and the hurt that it would inevitably cause everyone that he loved. Remarriage, she went on, was all right if a proper and suitable lady was selected.* The Queen disapproved of his choice, for several reasons – besides being divorced, Madame de Kolemine was of another religion. She concluded by saying that "[f]*or all our sakes I entreat him to delay <u>at any</u> rate so serious & I must fear, fatal a step*."[3] Victoria duly and painfully conveyed these sentiments to her father.

To add to the young bride's headaches, yet another potentially alarming drama was unfolding. Princess Beatrice, the child the Queen expected to be a lifetime companion and secretary, fell in love. Her mother had done her best, since Beatrice was old enough to notice men, to keep them safely away. No young men were to be in proximity to the shy, somewhat withdrawn princess, and no unsuitable relationships were permitted to be formed. It went so far that the words 'marriage' and 'engagement' were not supposed to be uttered in her presence. Prince Louis related that at the first family dinner he had with Queen Victoria some years before; he had sat between the Queen and Beatrice, who never spoke a word. *"Many years afterwards I heard that the Queen, when I had passed all my Lieutenant's exams sent word to the First Lord of the Admiralty that she wished me to be employed exclusively on foreign stations. She was afraid I might want to marry Aunt Beatrice!"*[4] Evidently, a handsome young man about the place was not to be borne. It would complicate their lives.

While the Queen was assisting Victoria to concentrate as best as she could on her own wedding, such a relationship was forming under her very nose. Beatrice had become acquainted with Louis' extremely attractive younger brother, Prince Henry of Battenberg, called "Liko" in the family. Liko had been one of Victoria's childhood playmates and she knew him and liked him very much. He was a very good-looking young man, an officer in the Garde du Corps, and looked particularly splendid in his uniform. Shy and slightly older, Beatrice was swept off her feet and their courtship commenced during those days just before the wedding.

Victoria, observant as she was, most probably decided that discretion was the better part of valor, and appeared to take no notice of the situation. More importantly, she said nothing to her grandmother.

****

Throughout the planning of the wedding, Queen Victoria did not hesitate to make her own wishes known. While the Queen was still in England, Victoria kept her informed about all the arrangements and did her best to accommodate her grandmother. The Queen was adamant that she did not want the bulk of the visitors to come until about five days before the wedding, even her eldest daughter, Victoria's Aunt Vicky, was only to come a week before. Interesting to note, this was still the time that Louis' brother, Sandro of Bulgaria,

(*) *Odly enough, there was a point after the discussion of the Deceased Wife's Sister Bill of 1883, when there was talk of Queen Victoria's daughter, Beatrice, as a second wife for the Grand Duke Ludwig IV. However, the match and the bill came to naught.*

was courting Aunt Vicky's daughter, Princess Victoria of Prussia, and Victoria wanted to give the couple a chance to be together. *"Aunt Vicky will probably arrive a day before the other relations, I asked her to, for poor Sandro is forced to leave almost immediately after my wedding in order to receive the Crown Prince of Austria's visit."*[5]

Ella was, of course, as helpful to her sister as she could be. However, she was overwhelmingly absorbed with her own upcoming June wedding in St. Petersburg. Moreover, she was vitally interested in making her choice of bridegroom more palatable to her grandmother and wrote: *"I am so glad you will see Serge when you come next month & hope he will make a favourable impression on you, all who know him like him & say he has such a true & noble character."*[6]

A few days before the wedding, Victoria and the Queen, together without any attendants, walked through Alice's rooms. As seemed to be the custom in the family, Ludwig and the older girls had chosen to leave Alice's rooms exactly as she had left them. Arm in arm, Victoria and her grandmother looked at Alice's things: her night dress folded on the bed; her silver brushes and mirrors laid out just so on her dressing table; and, her piano in the sitting room, with its Spanish shawl. The visit was extremely poignant for both the mother and daughter of Alice, and as they slowly made their way around the room, they no doubt felt the eerie affect of someone being away for a few days, not gone forever.

The Queen also took the opportunity to present Victoria with her wedding presents. These gifts along with all of the wedding gifts were displayed in an apartment of the Neues Palais, and made, according to *The Times* of London, a handsome show. Among the beautiful objects Queen Victoria had gathered from all corners of her empire, there included a pair of gold hair-pins, set with diamonds and pearls, five silver table-baskets, Indian shawls, Scottish shawls, Irish poplin and lace, English lace and Welsh materials. The couple had also received many dinner and tea services from various members of the different royal families, and quite interestingly, a brooch in the shape of an anchor from Grand Duke Serge of Russia. Victoria's paternal grandmother, Princess Elisabeth, gave her a fire screen which she had painted herself, while her new 'in-laws,' Prince Alexander and Princess Julie, gave her an exquisite sapphire and diamond diadem.[7]

****

The morning of the wedding finally dawned. Victoria was nervous and feeling ill. According to the Queen's journal, the Princess was unwell and did not come down to breakfast. Unfortunately, she had managed to sprain her ankle the night before. She had heedlessly, and in her typically tomboyish manner, jumped over a coal scuttle. Along with a very sore ankle, Victoria was unquestionably extremely drained from the week's controversies, and doubtless wanted to relax on her sofa and spend some time away from the hordes of family just downstairs. However, the Queen sent her personal physician, Sir James Reid, to tend to her granddaughter, for the bride could not be indisposed. Sir James determined that Victoria had been so engrossed with her wedding preparations, that she had, more or less, forgotten to eat for several days. Then, the night before the wedding, *"she had indulged in a late night feast of lobster which, devoured on an empty stomach ... had caused violent indigestion and sickness."*[8] The ill girl upstairs, however, did not stop the Queen and the rest of the family, Aunt Alix, Uncle Bertie, and the Wales cousins,* from tucking into very

---

(*) Albert Victor, George (King George V), Louise (Duchess of Fife), Victoria and Maud (Queen of Norway).

substantial breakfasts, and later, lunches.

At some point during that day, and with some help from Sir James, Victoria managed to pull herself together and begin the long business of getting dressed for her wedding. She wore her mother's wedding dress with a Honiton point lace pattern veil, in which she was photographed a little before the wedding. In the photograph she looks extremely serious (in part due to the long photographic exposure processes of the day) and contemplative. It is probably one of the few times that Victoria was photographed in formal dress and diadem, and though she was never thought to be the beauty of the family, she was certainly beautiful that day.

The Queen wrote further, "*She came down looking so pretty in her dear Mama's wedding lace over white satin, on her head the veil, [a] ... diadem given her by her Parents-in-law, & a wreath of orange flowers & myrtle, which I had given her. The dress was very long, but she had no train.*"[9] The Queen then described what the other Hesse children wore: "*Ella was in great beauty, wearing some of Serge's beautiful presents, including an enormous cabochon sapphire drop, set in diamonds. Irène looked also very nice, & Alicky lovely in a short white dress. Ernie was quite plainly dressed in an Eton jacket & trousers, with white gloves.*"[10]

Victoria, Grand Duke Ludwig and the Queen drove together in a state coach and pair. The people of Darmstadt lined the streets, not only happy that their princess was getting married, but curious to see all the royalty that would be attending the ceremony. They were, according to *The Times* of London, a very orderly crowd, and behaved in a respectful manner.[11] The Queen was splendid in a "*black silk dress, with a white coiffure of lace, diamond, ornaments, and various orders, including the Garter, the Victoria and Albert, the Star of India, [and] the Red Cross...,*"[12] her usual evening dress made just a little more formal with decorations, diamonds and pearls, but never a diadem or crown – always the widow's cap.

Before the religious ceremony, Victoria and Louis entered into a civil marriage and signed a marriage contract. This was a "*dry, formal, matter of fact proceeding*"[13] performed by Freiherr von Starck, the Minister of State. At about five-twenty in the afternoon, the entire party entered the chapel at the old Schloss, according to rank. Queen Victoria took her seat at the left of the altar. After she was seated, Grand Duke Ludwig followed with little Alix, Uncle Fritz of Prussia with Aunt Alix of Wales, and then Uncle Bertie of Wales with Aunt Vicky of Prussia. They all took their places to the right of the altar. Afterward, the rest of the family moved to their seats: Princess Elisabeth of Hesse, and Louis' family: Prince Alexander and Princess Julie, along with their sons, Sandro, Liko, and the youngest son, Franzjos as well as Louis' only sister, Marie, and her husband Gustav of Erbach-Schönberg.

Victoria entered the Chapel on the arm of her father and Prince Alexander. They were followed by Louis looking splendid in full English naval dress, a superbly cut tail coat, and around his neck the Grand Cross of the Order of Bath and the Star of the Hessian Order of Louis and Chain. The bridegroom walked into the Chapel between his mother, Princess Julie, and Princess Elisabeth, Victoria's paternal grandmother. The Queen continued:

The young couple, who looked very handsome, [moved to] their places in front of the altar, where stood the old Court Chaplain Bender, who performed the service very well. ... The two rings laying on the Bible, were presented to the young couple ...Both, looked deeply impressed. When they rose from their knees, another Hymn was sung, which concluded the service. I went up to dear Victoria & embraced her tenderly, & also kissed L[ouis]...[14]

According to *The Times* the ceremony was only about a half an hour and in fact, quite short, but made a striking impression on all who attended. *"The English residents in Darmstadt were, so far as space permitted, furnished with tickets of admission to the chapel."*[15]

The Wedding Reception and Banquet was held in the Kaisersaal of the Neues Palais at six that evening. The Queen had elected not to attend the banquet, but did see Victoria and Louis off when they left for their honeymoon at the Heiligenberg later that evening. Victoria continued to limp as a result of her adventure of the previous night; however, she managed to get through the proceedings without any visible problem. At their banquet, there were no speeches, but Uncle Fritz of Prussia proposed a toast to the couple's health. All raised their glasses and the Crown Prince of Prussia proclaimed: *"To the health of the newly married couple,"*[16] and after that there was an exhilarating flourish of trumpets.

At about nine o'clock that evening, the newlyweds took leave of the Queen who had been waiting in the library to see them off. Victoria was wearing a very simple traveling costume and hat. As they left, the party, the Queen wrote, we *"followed them to the door... We saw them get into the carriage, amidst a shower of rice & slippers, & drive off to Jugenheim, which it will take them an hour to reach."*[17]

On the morning after the wedding, Louis wrote a touching letter to his parents from the Heiligenberg. For those who wonder about the devotion of royal married couples, this letter is perhaps a confirmation of that commitment:

"My dearest parents,

I want to take this opportunity on the first morning of my married life to say to you what my heart was too full to express yesterday. I thank you with all my heart and soul for the great and endless kindness and love you have shown me all my life. You have given me the opportunity to bring home my beloved Victoria as my wife, and few men can have found such an angel as she is. To my life's end I shall owe you my thanks for that. My happiness is so overwhelming that I cannot yet take it all in, and my heart is full of thankfulness to everyone who has helped me to find it. I can look into the future with confidence, because I am sure that our married happiness will resemble yours – I cannot wish and hope for more, for such perfect domestic happiness as yours must be the rarest that two people on this earth have ever enjoyed.

God bless you and reward you for all you have done for me.

Ever your grateful and loving son,

Louis.[18]

****

While Victoria and Louis contemplated their future happiness at the banquet and later on at the Heiligenberg, the Grand Duke Ludwig had virtually forced the Prime Minister to secretly marry him and Madame Alexandrine de Kolemine. Victoria, who was usually delegated to break bad news to the Queen, was, happily, unavailable to do so. Eventually, it fell to Queen Victoria's lady-in-waiting, Lady Ely, to inform her of the entire unabridged story. It can only be imagined the great trepidation that Lady Ely felt as she revealed the news to the Queen and naturally the whole affair sat poorly with Grand Duke Ludwig's now former mother-in-law. She was extremely displeased, and dispatched the matter swiftly. The Queen decided, plainly and simply, the Grand Duke must annul the marriage at once, principally since the reputation of the lady was such that his younger unmarried daughters could not be put in her care. She resolved that the bride must be informed right away, and that her son, the Prince of Wales, must be the one to tell the Grand Duke. After giving those orders, she settled back, satisfied that the matter was now finished.

Grand Duke Ludwig, oddly, was in utter shock. He, for reasons best known to himself, did not understand the negative reactions of those around him. Following Bismarck's orders, the Prussians left in disgust the following day. They were not, the Chancellor felt, to be thus polluted by morganatic marriages, past, present or future. Quickly, however, the Grand Duke acquiesced to the Queen's wishes, her regard, being in the end, more important to him than a second marriage. Madame de Kolemine was, not to put too fine a point on it, bought off, and the proceedings for the annulment commenced. The lady swiftly decamped to Moscow with love letters and toothless blackmail threats. She subsequently remarried and was quite alive after Ludwig's demise.

Interestingly enough, the Grand Duke did see her, for the last time, the following summer, in order to say goodbye. He then wrote to Victoria about the meeting. She, in her newly found bliss, was full of compassion for her father, and wished that she could have been there to help him with the pain of such an encounter. She wrote "[t]*hat you saw Alex*[andrine] *I find quite natural ... it will have been a sad meeting, but necessary. Do you not think it is also better for the two of you if it does not happen again soon as it must always renew the pain, and I always fear she could give in to new false hopes...?*"[19]

Meanwhile, back in Darmstadt – matters having been settled to her satisfaction – the Queen betook herself, Ella, who was spending her last unmarried days with her grandmother, and her daughter Beatrice, back to England. The Grand Duke was to visit Windsor quite soon afterward, but was, for now, hiding unhappily at the Neues Palais. All the different family branches departed as quickly as possible, and decided amongst themselves that he had brought great disgrace to the fine Hessian Family. Then, just as quickly, it was forgotten.

Being just a ripple in the family, the Grand Duke consoled himself by continuing in the Queen's good graces and by a long visit to Balmoral. Victoria later said: "*The episode was a nine days scandal in the whole of Europe, and a painful one for my father, alas.*"[20]

****

Throughout their married life due to Prince Louis' professional commitments, the couple would move around often and usually live in rented houses so that the Prince could pursue his career. The Heiligenberg, however, would be the place that they most considered home, and where they would spend as much time as possible. As they began their married life, they were certainly not overly endowed with worldly goods, Victoria not having a dowry from the Hessian Parliament, and Louis, with some minor investments, living on his pay. However Louis wrote to a friend, "*She is a regular sailor's wife, and takes an immense interest in all naval matters... We are not blessed* [with] *much ..., and have to live in a small way, though we are all the happier for it, I believe.*"[21]

Before their departure to England and only a few days after the wedding, the Queen along with Beatrice and Alix, drove to the Heiligenberg to see the newlyweds. As they drove from Jugenheim, they were able to see that the town had been specially decorated for Louis and Victoria's wedding and those decorations were still up some days later. In her journal, the Queen noted: *"L[ouis] & Victoria received us at the door of the very large sort of hall... They showed us over the house, which is very pretty & full of recollections of the late Empress [Marie] of Russia, one room being kept, just as it was, when she lived there as a girl ... The young Couple's rooms are upstairs, & very nice & cheerful, quite English looking."*[22]

The Queen and her party departed for England, and Louis and Victoria followed some days later after a week's honeymoon at the Heiligenberg. Actually, they would have only a few weeks in England before they were off once again to St. Petersburg and Ella's wedding. Nevertheless, Victoria was able to accomplish much in a very short time. They rented a home called Sennicotts, located near Chichester. This location was extremely convenient for Portsmouth Harbor where the Royal Yacht, *Victoria and Albert*, Louis' appointment since 1883, was docked. Ella, who visited the couple later in the month wrote to her grandmother, the Queen, that *"[t]his place is quite lovely, the house most comfortable & prettily arranged & the grounds charming. It is a perfect little house but seems so curious it should belong to Louis & Victoria one hardly understands it."*[23]

Those short weeks were full of excursions, pottering about their new home and rambling around the countryside. It would be just a quick taste of what home and navy life would be for Victoria. As would always be her custom, she continued to write to her siblings. She had more or less made a promise that she would always return to Darmstadt whenever Louis was at sea.[24] Doubtless this would comfort her, having left the family for whom she had been caring for more than five years. Now only her father and the three younger children remained at home. The letters, would, therefore, continue with advice and in Ernie's case, gentle chides to do better and work harder at his studies. When she felt she had mothered him perhaps more than she ought, she would endeavor to amuse him with a long account of just what they did during that month.

"We take long drives in my poney-cart [sic] or in the dog cart about the country, which is very pretty. The roads are excellent, smooth & hard & pass through tidy little villages or wind in and out among meadows, for there are very few fields here abouts..."[25] After her bucolic description, Victoria told Ernie about a trip to Portsmouth and to *HMS Royal George* where the officers of *Victoria and Albert*, lived. *"We drank tea with the officers... After that we saw the Inconstant in which Louis served last ... and looked at [his] old cabin, where the blue paint he had it painted was still on the doors & little bits of chintz hanging in the corners at the wall."*[26]

However, those early days ended nearly as soon as they began. At the end of May, Louis and Victoria traveled to Darmstadt, and from there began their journey to St. Petersburg and Ella's wedding. Though depressed about having to say goodbye to so many people, Ella was *"so glad Victoria & Louis arrive this evening it will be a little cheerier then..."*[27] In June 1884, the entire Hessian family as well as many others of the multitudes of royal houses, went to St. Petersburg for Ella's wedding. The obvious 'holdout' was the Queen, whose views on Russia were well-known – particularly to the Russians.

The Queen, however, did not hesitate to give instructions and admonitions. Victoria was to caution Ella never to write anything confidential through regular mails – the fact that the secret police were so pervasive explains this caveat. She also expressed her fervent desire that such grandeur, riches, and being a Grand Duchess would not spoil her. Ella was quick to disabuse her grandmother of these thoughts. *"I hope that when you see* me again you won't find any change in my character for the worse, as I long to be simple in manners & as good as Mama would have wished me to be."[28]

This admonition was to be repeated by the Queen later when Victoria and Ella's youngest sister Alix went to Russia to marry the Tsarevich. Her sister's wedding when Alix was just twelve, was to mark the beginning of the love affair between Nicholas and Alexandra, as she was later called. Nicholas, called "Nicky" in the family, was a handsome boy of seventeen, with clear blue eyes, who took Alix under his wing, and, as a consequence, the young girl blossomed. Alix, who was a shy and quiet adolescent, was carefree and actually laughing – she, who had previously derived so much pleasure in being doleful, was happy. She absolutely adored Russia. Indeed, of all the siblings, she was the one who seemed to have an excellent relationship with Serge, who teased her saying that *"he had seen her bathed"*[29] because they had all known each other for so long.

It was not just her fascination with the exoticism and grandeur of Russia, or her love for the enigmatic Serge, though this was captivating enough to an impressionable and lonely young girl, but also her very real and growing attachment to Nicholas. He took care that she would have a good time at all the events and parties celebrating the marriage. He made her a present of a brooch which she, after some thought, handed back to him the following day. Alix had no idea in what spirit the bauble had been given to her. Nevertheless, she was hurt when Nicky cheerfully offered the brooch to his sister, Xenia. It was all, no doubt, so bewildering to the young girl, but of one thing she was already sure – that she cared for Nicky.

Serge was often described as a true gentleman, extremely cultured, intellectual, and artistic, who also had a certain shyness about him – a real reticence and reserve that made people think that he was cold and stiff. He was tall, slim, and was quite handsome in a stern and austere kind of way. He had a full beard and penetrating gray-green eyes. But, Serge appeared to have no warmth, and whenever he was around Ella, he would constantly and severely criticize her clothes, her deportment, and the things she said. And, all Ella would do is cast her eyes down meekly and say, in the French that the Hesses spoke to their Russian cousins,

"Mais, Serge. . . ."[30]*

The impression of his sternness and austerity was reinforced by the fact that he was a political reactionary who was against any kind of liberalization of Russian politics or life. In addition, he was the Commander of the elite Preobrajensky Guard, the Imperial Guard, and later the Governor General of Moscow. Interestingly enough, reactionary though he was, Victoria came to like him very much, thinking that he was an extremely fine gentleman. Nevertheless, he continued through their marriage, to reprimand Ella like a schoolmaster if she made even the slightest error.

There was no mistaking, however, that there was definitely something appealing about the Grand Duke. Queen Marie of Romania, daughter of the Duchess of Edinburgh who was also Grand Duchess Marie Alexandrovna, and Serge's only sister, wrote: *"I must admit that even at his sweetest moments, there was nothing soft nor particularly encouraging about Uncle Serge; there was a tyrant within him, ready at any moment to burst forth; there was something intolerant, unbending about him ... But for all that we loved him, felt irresistibly attracted to him, hard though he could be."*[31]

Ella and Serge would make their home in, amongst other places, the Sergueivjia

Palace* in St. Petersburg. But perhaps the most 'homey' of their homes was Illyinskoje, which was by the Moskva River, just sixty kilometers west of Moscow. Illyinskoje was a wooded country estate with a large park, cottages, and a farm. It was a two-story oak structure with a facade boasting a pillared portico, and terraces and a long drive bordered by two rows of lime trees. Ella, like her mother Alice, furnished the house in the British way with imported chintzes and furniture. The rear of the house faced the river with broad terraces where they would often eat breakfast or take tea.

****

It took three days to get from Darmstadt to St. Petersburg. It is easy to imagine Victoria, with her boundless imagination and endless curiosity, enjoying the long trip by train. She admired Russia and its vastness, comprehending its breadth only as she spent those days in a train watching its great expanses speed by. For the younger Hesses, it was the excitement and novelty of a protracted journey to an exotic land. There were stops in several Russian villages, as the train drew closer to St. Petersburg. Then there was an escort of Grand Duke Serge's Preobrajensky Guard, joining the Hessian party at the Russian border. They were escorted to St. Petersburg and the palace where they would stay – Peterhof, the royal compound on the Gulf of Finland.

Doubtless, it occurred to Victoria that such a meeting between the Battenbergs, as she now was, and the Tsar, would not necessarily be a harmonious one. Sasha, Tsar Alexander III, had shown such a tremendous dislike for Sandro and such disdain for the Battenbergs, that meetings on these family occasions, even though they were first cousins, were not particularly felicitous. Interestingly enough, Willy of Prussia did not attend. It seemed that he had made a vow never to see Ella again after she refused him, and, was foregoing the pleasure of the family gatherings he loved so much.

Instead, beside Uncle Bertie of Wales, one other of the senior members of the British Royal Family would be in attendance, Victoria's uncle, Prince Alfred of Edinburgh. He was one of Louis' early mentors in the navy. His wife, the Grand Duchess Marie Alexandrovna, delighted in showing her British relations her old home. Since she chafed at having to give Aunt Alix of Wales precedence when she was in England, showing the splendor and utter grandeur of her childhood home must have given her great satisfaction.

The entire Russian Court was at Peterhof and the Hessian party was met at the station by Serge and Sasha. They were all driven away from the train station in gilded coaches. As they left the station, they noticed, to their surprise, crowds cheering as their Tsar and his brother came to meet them. This was rather unusual for Russia, as demonstrations of such a nature were not given as a matter of course to the monarchs. They were mostly feared, not loved and were quite understandably wary of large crowds. Victoria saw soon enough, that despite these demonstrations, which were most probably staged, there was a great deal of security for all the members of the Russian imperial family and their guests – and with good reason.

Grand Duke Ludwig and his unmarried children stayed at the Grand Palace, and Louis and Victoria stayed next door in the Benois Wing. The entire party had arrived a week before the wedding and spent much of their time exploring the fairy tale palace complex.

(*) *Also known as the Belosselsky-Belossersky Palace.*

Peterhof was immense, made up of several residences, beside the main ones. Some were very baroque and ornate, and others, in the Italianate style which was so well beloved. The gardens were beautiful, still green, and blooming with the last of the spring flowers. There were pavilions, beautiful parks, waterfalls, fountains, and beautifully intricate flowerbeds. Victoria wrote to her grandmother that she was *"agreeably surprised with the country here which is exceedingly pretty."*[32] In addition, she told the Queen that Ella had charmed everyone in the family and that the Russian Court, with its jokes, parties and informality, greatly contrasted with the stiffness of the Berlin Court.

Nevertheless, Victoria and her family would soon discover that everything in Russia was on a grand scale. The rooms were huge, the gardens were enormous, and even the people seemed to be taller and broader than Western Europeans. It must have appeared to Victoria, that she and her family lived virtually a middle class existence in comparison to the golden chimera of the Romanovs. Their little palaces in Darmstadt, and even the exquisite summer resort of Wolfsgarten, must have seemed like little guest villas to the visiting Romanov relatives. Quiet and shy Irène, who would not go to Russia as the Queen feared, was overwhelmed, and told her grandmother that being in Russia was like a beautiful dream.

It might have been difficult for Victoria to resist the enormous attraction of all the grandeur and magnificence, and how easily one could get used to such a luxurious life – but in the end it was not. She would see two of her sisters do so, and yet, curiously, as much as she would visit the country, she never felt the same yearning for Russia that had bewitched her sisters. Perhaps, her egalitarian nature was repelled by such unimaginable luxury, set, as it was, against even more unimaginable poverty.

Accompanied by their cousins, the Hesse family went on shopping expeditions to the famous and fashionable Nevsky Prospekt in the city center of St. Petersburg. The impressive and wide boulevard of the Prospekt was thick with carriages and crowded with people in Western and Russian peasant style clothes. Victoria was particularly impressed with the richness and beauty of the scenery. She saw that it deserved its reputation as being one of the most beautiful cities in Europe. The days were sunny, the avenues were broad, and, the river Neva sparkled beautifully in its pink and orange stone banks. She enjoyed the sights and smells of the Russian court, as well, which her cousin, Queen Marie of Romania, wrote, was replete with the scent of sunflower oil, leather, and cigarettes. All in all, there was a Byzantine quality to Russia which made it vastly alluring as well as completely fascinating. Certainly for a first time visitor, the court, the palaces, and the city of St. Petersburg were completely enchanting.

****

On June 15, the morning of her wedding, Ella's sisters, the Empress Marie Feodorovna, who handed the hair dresser the *"hairpins and little combs"*[33] necessary for the elaborate coiffeur, and various maids helped her dress for the long and difficult ceremony ahead. Her dress, which was extremely heavy, was of white and cloth of silver. She wore both a crown and a diamond tiara, along with earrings, and necklace that had belonged to Catherine the Great. The jewelry was tremendously heavy, the earrings being so weighty that they had to be supported by wires that dug into her head. To add to her discomfort, Ella had a ten ruble piece in her right shoe for good luck, which naturally dug into her toes.[34]

The day was rigorous for all the participants. Since Ella had not converted to Russian Orthodoxy, there were two ceremonies – Lutheran and Russian Orthodox. Young Nicky was Serge's best man, and proudly held the crown over his much taller Uncle during the Orthodox ceremony.

After both ceremonies, there was a long, protracted, and stiffly formal wedding breakfast. Victoria certainly felt for Ella, who had to endure an endless day with such oppressive attire. However, she was more concerned that Cousin Sasha, the Tsar, had handed a painful snub to her husband. Prince Louis came into the banquet room with his family after the wedding and was astonished when he was escorted to where officers of *HMS Osborne* were sitting. Prince Louis had been placed *"below the salt,"* since Russian protocol evidently dictated that he be put in a place that befitted his morganatic status. It was unbelievable since Louis and Sasha were first cousins and, this, understandably, set Victoria's teeth on edge. Atypically, Victoria said nothing about the matter, not wanting to spoil her sister's wedding day. Louis was certainly offended, but it appeared as though he preferred sitting with his navy fellows.[35] Grand Duke Ludwig later said something to Sasha, and Sasha remarked simply that the Prussians had wanted it that way. Obviously, the Tsar of Russia could have arranged the seating in any way he chose.

When the feasting was over, the wedding party accompanied the bride and groom to the Sergueivjia Palace, Serge's home in St. Petersburg. The Emperor and Empress arrived first, and met the couple at their own doorstep with bread and salt. According to Russian tradition, it was Serge's parents who were supposed to perform this ritual. Since they were deceased, it became the responsibility of the Imperial couple to perform this parental task.

Soon afterward, the English and Danish Royal parties boarded the Osborne. The Queen had graciously sent the Royal Yacht to facilitate her family's return to their various homes following the festivities. The yacht was an elegant paddle steamer where all could relax and enjoy their luxury cruise home. They had adequate time to talk about all the events, parties, and ceremonies that had taken place, and also, it is logical to assume that Alix was thinking about her new relationship with her cousin Nicky.

Victoria, ever vigilant of the feelings of her family, was particularly concerned for her father and wrote during the voyage: *"It was difficult for us all, but especially for you to say goodbye to Ella..."*[36] She went on with the cheering news that they would meet again soon in either Seeheim or Jugenheim. Her mind was already involved in making arrangements.

****

That summer, Victoria discovered that she was expecting a child. She spent much of her time walking, driving, and exploring the countryside around Sennicotts. She also made a visit to Romsey, which would be so important to her family later on. The Queen, as was her usual custom, was even more involved since it was Victoria who was in this interesting condition, and kept very close tabs on all that she was doing. *"I hope you walk regularly every day? It is the one thing to be attended to."*[37]

Her marriage to Prince Louis was developing along the lines that could be expected knowing both of their characters. Each was highly competitive, intelligent, and had a strong personality. It was inevitable that they would have their occasional clashes. Victoria, in her tomboyish manner, was extremely careless with her appearance, which grated on the elegant Louis. Louis admired Victoria's mind, which was analytical and questioning, though her constant chatter sometimes annoyed him. She would often say that there were only three people in the world who could tell her to shut up: her grandmother Victoria, her son, Dickie, and, of course, her husband – she hardly seemed offended by this. It was said that Victoria was argumentative to the point of perversity, however, *"she leavened the somewhat doctrinaire formality of Prince Louis."*[38] Nevertheless, to all appearances and observations, including those of his sister, Princess Marie of Erbach-Schönberg, they were a very happy and devoted couple.[39]

Prince Louis wrote to a friend:

Now that I am married, I positively hate going to a ball, as I could not dance with the only woman I could care to. I should so much like you to make my wife's acquaintance. She is really more English than German, and we invariable speak English together, which may seem strange at first sight. ... Now that I have got such a splendid lift through the yacht, I am more keen than ever about serving on, and she is ready to go anywhere with me.[40]

Victoria never forgot her obligations to her siblings and was constantly writing to the young ones left at home, Irène, Alix, and most important, Ernie. As seemed usual in his boyhood, Victoria had to encourage him to work hard and listen to his tutor, Herr Müther. *"I hope I shall hear only praise from Herr Müther & that you have been working hard & getting on nicely like a great big fellow of your age should, if he ever wishes to become a real man & a sensible prince."*[41] Later she would encourage him, in her absence, to take charge and comfort his family if they feel sad, and be a *"help and comfort to Papa like a loving thoughtful boy, as dear Mama would have wished."*[42] However, she never hesitated to correct him in a motherly way. *"I must tell you by the by that when you address your letters to me, you should write Princess Louis Battenberg – like Princess Karl ..."*[43]

That summer was also the beginning of the struggle between Princess Beatrice and Queen Victoria over the matter of the Princess's determination to marry Prince Henry. Almost as soon as the Royal party returned to England, Beatrice wrote to her mother revealing her feelings and explaining the matter. According to Victoria, she received a *"really hard answer."*[44] Victoria went on to tell her father that the Queen was sure that it was just a fancy and that he, the Grand Duke, had told her, the Queen that Liko was not looking in Beatrice's direction at all. However, even the Queen could not be stern with Beatrice for long and told her that she had never thought that she *"who was so plausible & matter of fact, would, on so short an acquaintance, allow [herself] to care so deeply for anyone."*[45]

During the winter of 1884-85, Victoria became more involved with the continuing controversy. Luckily, unlike her father's unfortunate debacle, this one had a happy outcome. The couple wanted to marry, and of course, this was insupportable to the Queen. Beatrice had announced her intentions to her mother shortly after they returned from Victoria's wedding and the two had ceased speaking to one another. Queen Victoria had always expected her youngest daughter, her 'Benjamina,' as she called her, to stay with her, and made no secret that she did not want the girl to marry.

Nevertheless, love would prevail. Beatrice and the Queen, miserably, continued their silence with one another, passing notes in order to communicate. By November 1884, Beatrice had made it sufficiently obvious that she would not back down. Clearly, the Queen objected to Liko only because he was about to take her baby away from her and this she would not have. Liko, not deterred, went to Louis and Victoria at Sennicotts, staying there while continuing his courtship with Beatrice. Initially, and lasting for nearly six months after the wedding, the Queen would not even discuss the issue. However, in November, (by which time Liko was staying at Sennicotts, and with great encouragement from Louis) she was slowly and reluctantly *"getting used to the idea."*[46]

Liko finally got up the required courage to ask for Beatrice's hand on December 23, when they had all been invited to Osborne for Christmas. Once the Queen had settled that the couple would live, always, with her, she was able to accept them and give her consent to the marriage. Some thought that these conditions were too hard on Liko, but he chose them willingly. There was evidently great drama in Berlin, as the couple caused quite a fury with the Hohenzollerns since Liko was not considered to be of proper geblüt (stock). Characteristically, the Queen was much more upset about this slight than about her daughter's impending marriage. She gleefully quoted Lord Granville who said: *"If a Queen of England thinks a person good enough for her daughter what have other people got to say?"*[47] Uncle Bertie of Wales was also happy – his little sister Beatrice, he said, had found her Lohengrin. According to Victoria, the Prince advised Liko that *"as long as he shows tact and discretion in political, social and family matters, everything should go smoothly....[Uncle Bertie]* always *wants to give him good advice if, with a little dig at Grandmama, it will be allowed."*[48] As a side note, poor, unhappy Princess Victoria of Prussia, whose engagement to Alexander of Bulgaria was by this time extremely precarious, cried when she heard that Victoria and Louis were getting married. Beatrice and Liko's engagement just twisted the knife in deeper for the jealous and frustrated young woman.

Weddings in the family, no matter how numerous, always caused great excitement and Victoria herself, even though she was near to her confinement, could not resist making arrangements and giving orders to Ernie. She wrote to him, soon after the engagement was announced that, *"Grandmama is full of plans for the wedding already. She wants it to take place here at Whippingham in July & you are all to come. Aunty wants to have eight of her nieces as bridesmaids. The 3 Wales, our two girls, Aunt Helena's 2 & the eldest little Edinburghs."*[49]

In other letters to Ernie during that time and until the birth of her daughter, Alice, Victoria told him of her arrangements for him. She gave him directions on where he was to stay when he arrived for the wedding, what clothing he was to wear, and more importantly where he was to buy his clothing – London, she advised, since the tailors and material were so superior to those in Darmstadt.

While Victoria was arranging Ernie, her grandmother was doing some arranging of her own. Louis and Victoria, now heavily pregnant, traveled to Windsor from Osborne on February 14, staying near the Tapestry rooms. Queen Victoria, who, as usual, did not trust foreign doctors, insisted that Victoria have her lying-in at Windsor. She was to have the very same rooms her own mother had occupied during her birth. The couple felt extremely grand staying at the castle while the Queen was not in residence; however, being so near her time, it is hard to imagine Victoria enjoying the large spaces between halls and rooms very much.

The Queen arrived some days later, not intending to miss the impending event. But as usual for the time, when births were to occur, there were anxious moments. Irène wrote to the Queen, *"I am so pleased Victoria is keeping well for I cannot help feeling rather anxious."*[50] As the last days of February wore on, Victoria was getting restless, and not feeling herself. After a day of *"not feeling well"* a doctor was sent for, and she went into labor on February 24.

She labored through the night and on the following morning, the Queen described her in her journal as having had a bad night. She had in fact, sat with Victoria, holding her hand, stroking her arms, and wiping her forehead, the entire subsequent day of her labor – not leaving her side – just as she had done for her daughter Alice, when Victoria was born. Louis, too, had remained attentive and patient and also, hardly left Victoria's side. The Queen stayed with her *"on & off, till at length, at 20 mi. to 5 in the afternoon, the child, a little girl, was born. The relief was great, for poor Victoria had had such a long hard time, which always makes one anxious. How strange & indeed affecting, it was, to see her lying in the same room, & in the same bed, in which she herself was born."*[51]

Victoria's first child was called Victoria Alice Elisabeth Julie Marie, after her grandmothers and great-grandmothers. The baby, however, would always be called Alice.

The Queen described the infant as being very small and very dark. She held it for just a few moments in her arms. Victoria had already pulled herself together and Louis was described as *"radiant."*[52]

Naturally, those who had been quite anxious, in this case, Irène, now wrote to her grandmother in great relief, *"We were so pleased to hear of the Birth of Victoria's little girl. Your first great grandchild born in England!"*[53] Alice would be christened in Darmstadt in the spring. Irène was happy because it was an occasion for the whole family to be together once again.

Alice was beautiful, and would go on to be called one of the most beautiful Princesses in Europe. Victoria thanked Ernie for his letters about the baby and penned an amusing description of her new niece:

I hope you will think her pretty when you see her. She has nice big dark grey eyes, which everybody says will turn brown soon & a pair of capital eyebrows, such as I never possessed, so I should say she will be more like L[ouis] than me – but at present she has got a true baby's face, with a nice little nose & a mouth, which she opens like a fish...[A]lso she makes dreadful faces when angry so that sometimes she looks startlingly like Sir William Jenner & at such times she turns as red as an old turkey cock.[54]

Undoubtedly, Victoria felt that the beautiful child did not inherit her looks. She would often say that Alice looked like the Battenbergs.

There is a famous photograph – one from the period in sepia, where people usually look so stiff and glum – showing Queen Victoria, Princess Beatrice, and Victoria, dandling little Alice - fat, round-faced, light-eyed Alice - on her knee. The interesting part of this photograph is something not necessarily seen in the thousands of photographs of Queen Victoria – she's actually smiling. She's not only smiling, but she has her eyes squeezed shut, and she looks like she's in the middle of a giggle. Ella was, in fact, moved to write to Louis that this particular photograph *"of the four generations is charming."*[55] It's not known what caused such merriment, probably Alice did something outrageous; but that side of the Queen was seen so rarely that most people would not have credited its existence.

Alice's outrageous behavior towards her grandmother, however, was legend, and a source of many good stories. There is an incident, often told, that happened when the child was about four or five. She had been dressed to the nines, and presented to her Great-Grandmother. The little girl had been instructed that she was to kiss her Grandmama's hand. However, when the crucial moment arrived, she stoutly refused. The Queen was affronted by this disobedience, and scolded,

"Naughty, Alice."

Whereupon Alice replied, defiantly,

"Naughty, Grandmama."

Naturally, the naughty little girl was quickly spirited out of her Great-Grandmother's presence.

Louis and Victoria had begun their family with the girl who would have such a fascinating and in some ways tragic destiny.

Chapter V

March 1885 – May 1888

In those early years of her marriage, Victoria began what would become a pattern of constant visiting and travel. Much of her time was spent in Darmstadt with her younger siblings, especially while Louis was away on voyages. As events unfolded, however, she began a long series of visits to her married sisters in Russia and Prussia and spent less time in Darmstadt proper. Instead, as her family grew, she preferred to spend Louis' leaves at the Heiligenberg, or visiting Ernie at Wolfsgarten. Later, when Louis had various different jobs that kept him on land, Victoria would spend more time in England. They lived, usually in rented houses, and ultimately at the Admiralty in The Mall, or Kent House, on the Isle of Wight. In the final years, Victoria lived alone at Kensington Palace. However, while Queen Victoria was alive, she frequently visited her in whatever palace she happened to be living at the time.

In the first years of Louis and Victoria's marriage, they were both much occupied with matters pertaining to Louis' younger brothers. On one hand, there were Prince Alexander's very serious difficulties with Bulgaria, along with his ill-fated engagement to Princess Victoria of Prussia. On the other, though far more felicitous, was the wedding of Prince Henry to Princess Beatrice. Victoria continued to be occupied with her Hessian siblings as well as absorbed in her new baby and young husband – when he was present.

Though the Queen, as Victoria's closest confidant, had expressed her happiness at her choice of husband, defending it constantly to the royal snobs of Europe, she seemed determined to make sure that Victoria, herself, understood how lucky she was. Queen Victoria was certainly susceptible to a handsome face, but she did not suffer fools lightly. If Louis had not measured up, she would have said so decidedly to her granddaughter. However, this was not the case – she came to love Louis like a son, and when she died, he was one of the executors of her estate. She wrote to her granddaughter: *"Let me just add what I said before, how I have learnt to esteem your dear Louis – what a motherly feeling I have for him & what an exceptionally tender kind & excellent Husband you have in him! – You can never show him too much devotion & affection."*[1]

In fact, her grandmother often chided Victoria for not showing enough affection. This was highly characteristic of the young woman, as it had been the girl. Victoria did not give public demonstrations of affection, even at family gatherings, and there are several other letters in which the Queen mentioned that Victoria should be more loving and warm. It was simply not in her nature to be so public about private emotions. The things that were deepest in her heart were the things she found most difficult to express. She responded that she would not *"forget what you say about my duty to Louis, & indeed it will be easy to fulfill it, for I love him with all my heart & if I have seemed to think of Papa more than him, it is only because I am so afraid of my happy married life making me neglect poor Papa, who has always been the kindest of fathers to me."*[2]

Soon after the birth of Alice, while Victoria and Louis were still in England, the Hesses suffered a family death. The Grand Duke Ludwig's mother, Elisabeth, the widow of Prince Karl, died at the age of sixty-nine. Her death occurred in March of that year, and Victoria, who had been anxiously awaiting her return home to *"Grandmama ... and to showing her the baby*"[3] was now *"not looking forward at all to home."*[4] The young mother was not yet strong enough to make the trip, but Louis and Liko quickly went back to Hesse in order to attend the funeral. Victoria traveled to Darmstadt with the baby and Queen Victoria at the end of that month.

Alice was christened on April 25, 1885, by the same Pastor Binder, who had christened Victoria twenty-two years before. As an addition to the ceremonies, Ernie was confirmed that very day in the chapel of the Schloss. According to *The Times*[5], the ceremony was short and simple. Ella, keeping her promise to visit Darmstadt, was present for both of these auspicious occasions. She and Serge attended the ceremony with the Queen. The promised visits, however, did not often materialize in the intervening years. Ella and Serge never visited Hesse or England as much as they and most certainly as much as Ella, herself, might have liked. Primarily, it was a question of time and distance. However, it was true that the Queen's dislike of all things Russian may have made Ella, and certainly Serge, feel slightly uncomfortable – though, as Queen Victoria often emphasized, she had nothing against Serge or, later, Nicky, personally.

During that month, however, the romance between Prince Alexander, Louis' younger brother and Princess Victoria of Prussia was the prime topic of conversation. It absorbed not only members of the various families, but political enemies and friends, alike. Chancellor von Bismarck felt strongly that Sandro ought to give up the Princess in order to court Russian favor. This had initially been completely unacceptable to Sandro for several reasons. Primarily, he was lonely in Sofia, and desperately wanted to get married. The Princess was an excellent candidate and was very much in love with him. Second, he was anxious to free Bulgaria from Russian influence, and was in no mood to court any such favor from the cousin who had shown him nothing but contempt.

Ultimately, after all the constant contention, Sandro was becoming tired and completely discouraged. By the end of that April, he had reached the end of his tether. Submitting to both Chancellor von Bismarck and the Tsar of Russia, Sandro ended, as chivalrously as possible, his engagement to Princess Victoria of Prussia. The renunciation, however, didn't satisfy the Tsar, who disliked Sandro immensely. Moreover, Sandro's father, Prince Alexander of Hesse, was becoming more and more distressed since there had been threats on his son's life. Nevertheless, the young man made an attempt to continue his work in Sofia, even with enemies both at home and abroad working against him.

Irène, as was her tendency, was sympathetic and uncritical. She wrote to her grandmother about how people in Darmstadt were working hard for the Bulgarian wounded and how they were terribly anxious about Sandro. *"I do hope that all will now be settled peaceably for poor Sandro... It is quite astonishing how much all the people here are giving in aid of the Bulgarians, & how very kindly they think of poor Sandro."*[6] Interestingly enough, this particular situation got the usually reticent Irène's hackles up, and her initial sympathy turned into militant partisanship. *"I scarcely think that anyone will as yet abuse dear Sandro or any of his family to me, & if they did I do not think that they would care to try the experiment again – for it might turn out more or less disagreeably for them. I may be timid or shy, but if any we love are abused, this disappears in a second & I know how to speak out, even if it costs me ever so great a struggle."*[7] Many times, she dug down deeply for the strength and it did cost her dearly.

Victoria also had compassion for her brother-in-law as events become more difficult. Nevertheless, it must be remembered that it was she who said that if he gave up there it would be a sign of a very weak spirit. Perhaps as time went on, she became less censorious. Victoria, herself, had a great deal of determination and had a difficult time understanding why others, in time of great need, did not have a wellspring of strength, as did she.

Mostly, however, she was devoted to her new daughter. After Alice's christening, the family went straight back to England and to Sennicotts. Victoria's main concern at this time was getting the right rattle with rubber netting so the baby would not hurt herself. In fact, it was such an important assignment that she turned it over to Ernie to look in Darmstadt. If he felt that he could not perform the commission, then he, in turn, was to give it over to Orchie, who was still with the younger members of the family.

In June, the families were again preparing to come together for another royal event, the wedding of Beatrice and Liko. Victoria couldn't resist arranging her family as she had always done. Letters sped back and forth in a flurry and naturally Ernie, as usual, was in the forefront of Victoria's concerns. *"You are all to come over on the Victoria & Albert & Louis & I have planned out the cabins & find there will be plenty of room for everybody. I am afraid poor Aunt Julie will be rather nervous at sea. You are to arrive on the 20th I hear, & the wedding to be on the 23rd."*[8] Ernie kept up his end in corresponding with his sister, whom he loved deeply and to whom he often expressed his feelings. He never seemed to resent Victoria's "bossiness' – perhaps, he truly believed that it was for his good, though, usually, that was something younger brothers rarely believe.

In a letter during this time, Ernie related to Victoria that he had met the Solms-Hohensolms-Lich children on a visit to the small principality. He described the family: *"Lich's girls have grown up & are very amusing & very pretty."*[9] There were two boys in the family that were older than Ernie as well as the amusing girls. One of those girls, Eleonore, would, much later, become Ernie's second wife.

****

On July 23, Beatrice and Liko were married at the beautiful chapel of St. Mildred's, Whippingham, near Osborne House, on the Isle of Wight. Liko, who was fond of uniforms, looked quite splendid and almost Ruritanian. The bride, too, looked lovely, and thin. Beatrice, who had a tendency to plumpness, had lost weight because of all the complications she had suffered with her mother, the Queen, and because of all the insults to Liko in the English and Continental press. Added to her stress was the loud and vocal disapproval from the Prussian side of the family, who, naturally, had difficulty countenancing Battenbergs as relatives by marriage.

The Russians, the Scandinavians, as well as the extended German and British connections of both the bride and groom, had all come to attend the wedding. Conspicuous by their absence were the disapproving Prussians. Though the engagement was technically at an end, poor Princess Victoria of Prussia was to be kept away from Sandro at all costs. The actual truth was, to the relief of many, they had not been invited. The Queen had decided against having them, wishing to avoid problems. Victoria wrote to her father that she felt that *"nobody can take offence at Liko's parents if only the English and our family attend."*[10]

Victoria, Alice, and Louis were firmly ensconced at Kent House, which belonged to Victoria's Aunt Louise and her husband the Marquess of Lorne. Louis met a great deal of the company at Flushing, Holland, with the royal yacht, the *Victoria and Albert*. Victoria worried about her mother-in-law since the crossing lasted sixteen hours and was most unusually difficult. Princess Marie, Louis' sister, wrote a harrowing account of the crossing and how everyone suffered from sea sickness – *"my maid was literally howling with the misery of mal de mer..."*[11] The waves were pummeling the ship, and, most of the passengers were sitting glassy-eyed and apathetic, or were completely prostrate in their beds. At last, when all were, no doubt, convinced they were going to die, they anchored off Cowes and came ashore, thankfully, to their welcome accommodations.

The wedding ceremony was performed by the Archbishop of Canterbury, a little white in the face since he had also suffered that terrible crossing. After the ceremony, the bridal couple traveled back to Osborne, in the *"golden sunshine."*[12] The roads were lined with holiday makers, wishing the pale Princess and her handsome Prince well. Upon their arrival, the wedding breakfast was served in tents at Osborne. There were ten pipers in Highland dress piping their way around the table that held the huge bridal cake, weighing nearly four hundred and fifty pounds. The guests milled around the lawn and paid tribute to the most important attendee, Queen Victoria, and then the bridal couple. Though the Queen was hardly losing a daughter, and most definitely gaining a son, she still managed to look glum as the couple departed for their very short honeymoon. In the evening, there was a large state dinner for the royalty and the diplomatic corps that had attended. The Queen and the Grand Duke Ludwig doubtless consoled each other in their various losses.

In all, as time went on, the wedding, so dreaded by the Queen, actually gave her much happiness in the coming years. She loved having a handsome man in the house and called Liko the sunshine of their home. His sister Princess Marie described him as someone who loved gadgets, and drove the first motor-cars. He loved to shoot, and loved the theater. His own sister did not consider him overly intelligent, certainly not nearly as intelligent as his new wife, but, nevertheless, she was adamant that he was interested in everything. Most importantly, the Princess observed that the couple was very happy together.

****

A little less than a month after the wedding, Victoria, having given up Sennicotts for good, left Osborne and made her way back to Darmstadt. At the end of August, Prince Louis was promoted to Commander, and went on half-pay so that he could spend some time with his new family. They spent a little of that time with the Hesses at Wolfsgarten. Though Victoria was a married woman with a child, the Queen nevertheless continued to give her advice about every aspect of her life. Victoria would always be an avid reader. She was interested in everything and willing to give almost any book a try. In a letter, the Queen admonished Victoria to never neglect church attendance, and, had expressed her feeling that "[o]nly reading is not good,"[13] and young girls ought to have other occupations besides. Therefore, it was quite a concession for her to implore Victoria to read only good and improving books, not "*materialistic & controversial* ones for they are bad for everyone...."[14] The Queen never ceased trying to mold, advise and guide Victoria throughout her young adulthood. It was a project that was to continue for the rest of the older woman's life. One always had the impression that she wasn't quite succeeding as much as she might have liked. All the same, she never gave up.

Ernie was getting older, but Victoria still felt the need to put some jam on any pill she was sending him in the form of managing, admonishment, or (face it) nagging. That fall she wrote him a tremendously amusing account of a visit by her first cousin, Aunt Helena's son, Prince Albert of Schleswig Holstein. *"Abby [as the family called Albert] is great fun & we chaff him dreadfully – he is indefatigable at criket [sic] & rounders, which take place on the old croquet road. It is very hot work & it is a sight to see Irène with dress tucked up puffing & panting up & down between the wickets, these latter being constructed out of a heep [sic] of waterproofs & jackets."*[15] Though it was an attempt to amuse Ernie, Victoria, herself, was no doubt as amused as she wrote. She never lost her sense of fun and tomboyishness, even as a married woman and mother.

That winter, too, Louis and Victoria worked on a project together. It was a pamphlet that they assembled detailing his sister, Princess Marie of Erbach-Schönberg's visit along with her husband, Prince Gustav, to Sandro in Bulgaria in 1885. Marie wrote an absorbing account of her time there, describing the sights and sounds in and around Varna and Sofia. She was fascinated with the people, many dressed in their colorful native costumes, and the quaint villages and towns. She was also most impressed with the welcome that the Prince of Bulgaria's family received from the people of that country, and the joy they seemed to take in their Prince. The account, for the most part, can be read in her memoirs.

Louis and Victoria both supervised the story from the beginning stages to the finished product since Louis knew a great deal about printing and fine arts.[16] Such opportunities for the couple to be at home and work together were quite rare, and therefore to be cherished. They would remain so for the first twenty years of their married life, since Louis was at sea most of the time.

****

During the spring of 1886, events in Bulgaria were coming to a crisis point. Prince Alexander was a national hero, but, as things evolved, he could come to no understanding with his Cousin Alexander III of Russia. Great consternation spread throughout the offices of the Tsar and his ministers in St. Petersburg. They were dismayed at how well-liked Sandro was in Bulgaria, and resolved to do something about it quickly. First, they tried to remove him by circulating vicious rumors, some of the worst being his having venereal disease, or, having embroiled himself into the Turkish taste, which in plain language meant homosexual affairs; this last, really being ludicrous to anyone who knew him. However, these kinds of accusations seemed to have the reverse affect on the people of Bulgaria who were extremely satisfied with their ruler. Having failed in these clumsy attempts, the Tsar began to foment discord among the officers on Sandro's staff and the Prince was struck off the Russian military list.

Since none of these stratagems worked, in August 1886, the Tsar acted in desperation. Louis and Victoria received word that officers of Sandro's general staff, whose dissatisfaction had been exploited, had kidnapped him. It was a completely transparent effort, and all knew that the Tsar was responsible. His plot had gone into full swing, with disgruntled Bulgarian officers snatching both Sandro and, his brother, Franz Joseph, who was with him at the time. The brothers were taken at gunpoint to a steamer and whisked out of the country under the most abominable of circumstances. They were locked in the hold and most certainly beaten.

Victoria described the scene to her Uncle Bertie of Wales in a letter:

Sandro telegraphed yesterday evening from Reni in Bessarabia, saying that he had been set free at last, & that he & *Franz Joseph were coming straight home via Breslau. He says that he was carried down the Danube on his own yacht, guarded by what he calls "Russische Polizeiten" [Russian Policemen] , & as far as we can make out from the laconic words of the telegram, put into a Russian prison at Reni. He says that he & his brother are quite broken & crushed by the way they have treated... The fate of the Emperor Maximilian of Mexico naturally occurred to [my parents-in-law] at first, when S. was supposed to be a prisoner in Bulgaria...*[17]

It would be natural to assume that Victoria was worried not only about her two brothers-in-law, but also, her husband who traveled immediately to join his brothers. She kept her uncle abreast of all that occurred as quickly as it happened. The Bulgarians were outraged by the kidnapping, and demanded the return of their Prince. At the end of the month, looking ill and strained, Sandro returned to Sofia. He was received with great enthusiasm, according to Victoria, *"Louis telegraphed yesterday afternoon from Rustchuk [Bulgaria] that Sandro's reception there had been perfectly wonderful. ... [Louis] will only be able after a day or two to decide his next move; as long as he can be of direct use to his brother he will remain in the neighborhood."*[18]

In the beginning of September 1886, Sandro sent a private telegram in code to his cousin Sasha of Russia, telling him that since he, the Tsar, had given him the crown, he, Sandro, would return it to his hands if that was what Sasha wanted. The Tsar made this telegram public as well as his answer. Prince Louis, in explaining the entire situation to Queen Victoria, wrote that *"[t]he Tsar replied that he could not approve of Prince Alexander's return, 'foreseeing its sinister consequences for the country which has already been so severely tried,' but that the Prince must decide his course himself."*[19] Given such an obvious choice, the Tsar was telling him to go, in so many words, and Sandro abdicated. In the end, he felt that there were just too many members of military and government plotting to get rid of him. Further, Louis told the Queen, *"[o]ne mistake I admit Sandro and I made; we imagined that the son of our good and noble Aunt had still somewhere about him one remaining spark of gentlemanly and generous feeling. That was of course a fatal mistake, but one which all honest and true men should readily forgive..."*[20] Victoria echoed this sentiment nearly exactly in a letter to her father saying, *"[t]he only mistake Sandro made is that he has too high an opinion of his cousin's honor."*[21]

The Queen's response to all of this was quite heated and her language was unguarded:

- *And now what an infamous answer from the Emperor to Sandro's (I think <u>too civil</u>) message! It is very stupid as well as wicked of Russia for she thereby admits almost that she approves of the monstrous plot.*[22]

Sandro and Franz Joseph returned to Hesse where they received, according to Victoria and Irène, a warm reception. *"It was so nice meeting all together at Jugenheim again after these dreadful times. It seemed almost as if the 4 Brothers had never seperated [sic]. Sandro looked well but Franzjos rather dragged & hollow."*[23] Victoria thought both brothers were overtaxed, and in particular, that all that had happened to Sandro showed on his face.

Indeed, Sandro had more stories of treachery to tell his family – the duplicity of his own loyal officers and the ridicule he suffered at the hands of the Russians. Ultimately, even the Prussians got into the act, Victoria wrote to her father, when the legate from Berlin told Sandro, unnecessarily and quite unsolicited, *"that the Kaiser did not wish to see him in*

Berlin, or anywhere else."[24] Not, Victoria hastened to add, that he would have thought of it anyway. It is interesting to note that at the end of this particular letter, she felt it necessary to warn her father to be discreet about what she said. *"Behind the screens certain high gentlemen have behaved nothing less than dishonorably, so do not tell everything I am writing."*[25]

Towards the end of the month, Louis wrote again to the Queen giving her the family's final decisions on what was to be done,

> *Sandro's cause can at this present moment be best served by allowing all this excitement to calm down...His own idea is that he may some day be called upon to play a prominent part in the East once more; but, he has done with the country at present, and wild horses would not drag him back there, if he were to be re-elected now.*[26]

Victoria, perhaps, had a much better understanding of the subject when she wrote: *"Sandro had none of the born politician's subtlety and his talents were decidedly military ones."*[27]

****

Ernie came of age during that tumultuous year. He had spent several years at the University of Leipzig and passed his military exam, becoming a member of the First Guard Regiment at Potsdam. On his birthday, Victoria wrote a very sweet and loving congratulatory letter. It was very important to her that he know that he had grown up in a way that would have pleased his mother.

> *On my last birthday, when she was with us in '78, ... she told me that...I must try & watch over the others & you especially, to whom I was often rough, & that is what I want you to know, now that you too are no more a child; & ask you to believe that I really love you very much, though we don't speak about it & that whatever the future may bring you may be sure this won't change, & that if ever you are worried by anything, or get into any trouble, as young men sometimes, through nothing wrong, will get – you will remember this & know that I will always do my very best to help you, for dear Mama's sake & for your own.*[28]

The relationship between Victoria and Ernie would always be a very special one. Although she often told Ella that she was like Ernie's mother, the reality was that Victoria was in many ways the cornerstone of Ernie's life. When the horrors of war and loss would separate them, their relationship would most easily be mended because of its firm and deep foundation.

****

Victoria would spend Christmas 1886 in Darmstadt. Louis, who was serving on *HMS Cambridge* at Milford Haven, joined the family for Alice's second Christmas. Irène, who had just left England where she had been visiting the Queen, wrote to her grandmother about the general celebrations that took place. *"All here are looking very well, & the dear Baby delightfully fat & pretty with such a merry laugh. At 5 she had been taken down to Uncle Alexander's by Victoria & L[ouis] where they all had their Xmas tree together."*[29]

The romantic and marital tribulations of Irène, in fact, would now come to the forefront of the family. She was over twenty at this point and had someone definite in mind.

However that didn't stop her grandmother from speculating and, of course, worrying about where her future might lay. In early 1886, Irène and the Grand Duke traveled to St. Petersburg to visit Ella. Queen Victoria immediately became wildly suspicious.

> *I must tell you how annoyed & grieved I am at dear Papa & Irene's going to Petersburg – now – after the monstrous way in wh[ich] dear Sandro has been treated & in fact is so still! I think it most unfortunate. And then for poor Irène, it is most awkward for no end of reports have been spread, & I know that Olga Cécile* is bent upon Micha's** marrying her! I shall never forgive it, if she also is to go to that horrid, corrupt Country – & I sh[ou]ld break with Papa if he did it!*[30]

Victoria quickly came to the defense of her father and sister saying that they had planned the trip for some time and that Ella would have been disappointed had the Grand Duke put it off. She explained further that she and Irène had a long talk about the situation, and Irène had not shown the slightest inclination or desire to marry in Russia. In addition, Grand Duke Ludwig was completely adverse to the idea, according to his eldest daughter.

In the beginning of 1887, Irène went against her grandmother and the establishment for the first and last time in her life when she announced her engagement to Aunt Vicky's son, Prince Heinrich (Henry) of Prussia (who, incidentally, was also going against the wishes of his family to marry Irène). Though it was obviously not as repugnant as a Russian engagement, Queen Victoria was against the match since she didn't like Henry for a number of reasons. She considered Henry a heedless, non-intellectual, whose elder brother, Willy wrote his speeches for him. She also felt that he had behaved badly in the Sandro-Moretta romance, and was unkind about Liko's marrying her daughter, Beatrice. Therefore, the Queen intensely disliked the idea that he would be Sandro, Liko, and Louis' brother-in-law.

A more serious issue was the fact that Irène and Henry were first cousins on their mothers' side, as well as being closely related on their fathers' and the Queen was always apprehensive about close cousins marrying. This, especially in view of what could be inherited by children of a closely related couple. A more emotional issue was that the Queen felt that Henry did not treat his mother, Aunt Vicky, with respect. Aunt Vicky, conversely, was extremely pleased with the match since she liked Irène very much. In the end, however, the deepest cut of all was that the Queen learned about the engagement through the newspapers and had not been first informed as she ought to have been.

The Queen reacted angrily in a letter to Victoria from Osborne: *"It is impossible for me to tell you what a shock your letter gave me! Indeed I felt quite ill – for I am so deeply hurt at Irène's conduct <u>towards me</u>... [S]he <u>assured</u> me <u>again</u> & <u>again</u> that she w[ou]ld <u>never</u> <u>do</u> that! How can I trust her again after such conduct?"*[31] The Queen was angry, but being a pragmatist, she was quick to reconcile herself to matters as they lay. She remained hurt over what she considered Irene's dishonesty in the matter, and felt that the girl would have an awkward position the Prussian court. The entire Hessian family, would, she was sure, be treated rudely in Berlin, for all the reasons stated. She was firm that *"Henry must be brought*

(*) *Olga Cécile, formerly Princess Cäcilia Augusta of Baden, now Grand Duchess Olga Feodorovna married to Grand Duke Michael Nicholaevich, youngest brother of Tsar Alexander II.*

(**) *Grand Duchess Olga's son, Grand Duke Michael Mikhailovich, known in the family as 'Micha" or Miche-Miche." Victoria had once had a short, adolescent flirtation with this Grand Duke, who desperately criss-crossed Europe in search for an equal wife. He ended marrying morganatically.*

round to a <u>right</u> view of things...."[32]

The Hessian family closed ranks and came to the rescue, embracing Henry as they had embraced Louis and Serge before him. Ernie, always sensitive to his sisters' feelings, wrote to Victoria that "[d]*arling, Irene is so very happy with Henry and a more dear boy one really could never have seen.*"[33] While Victoria, always the go-between, reassured her grandmother that Henry was "*a very nice fellow – frank, good natured & full of high spirits; he behaved so nicely & naturally on seeing Sandro, that it pleased the latter very much.*"[34]

Irène came timidly to the defense once more as she tried to persuade her grandmother how "*open-hearted and true*"[35] Henry was. Just a few days later she reassured her grandmother that they were indeed very happy and that, "*Harry* [as Henry was called in the family] *is really the good angel here & go between in all difficulties I have already seen & felt, & that I scarcely deserve him too.*"[36] And, just a few days after that, she asked her grandmother to invite Henry to the upcoming Jubilee celebrations. She would, she wrote "*feel that you had quite forgiven me...I hope you are not angry with me for asking this?*"[37] In the end, a more inoffensive marriage could not be found. Irène and Henry got along with everyone so that they were called the "*Very Amiables*"[38] by their relations.

The Queen was no longer angry, and in fact, had moved decisively on. Just a month later, she got back to work. She began plotting once again for matches for her last remaining precious Hessian granddaughter – Alix. She had in mind either of Uncle Bertie's sons, Albert Victor or George, and was adamant that all must be done to prevent, "*<u>further</u> Russians or other people <u>coming</u> to snap her up.*"[39] However practical she was in these matters, she sometimes gave over to feeling sorry for herself, and directing some guilt to Victoria. "*I feel very deeply that my opinion and my advice are never listened to and that it is almost useless to give any.*"[40] She may have been right in this case; however, all marriage arrangements were put aside for a much more important event: the Queen's Golden Jubilee, to take place in June 1887.

****

Fifty years on the throne was a great achievement and the celebration reflected this as well as the fact that the people loved their Queen. They were thrilled to see her show herself on her and the Empire's special day. Queen Victoria had been sure that they had forgotten her and was, perhaps, most surprised and happy about this, even above all the honor of so many crowned heads attending.

The month leading up to this unforgettable day was filled with preparations and a desperate worry. Victoria contracted typhoid and was laid up, seriously ill, for the entire month before the Jubilee. She later speculated that she had caught the disease on a trip to Frankfurt, since, as with diphtheria, it can be caught from contaminated water. She manifested all the symptoms of the disease: being alternately hot or shivering with cold; her skin broke out in a rash; and, her stomach was distended. Naturally, the Queen was tremendously concerned, but no more so than Victoria's husband, who tenderly nursed her. Louis did his best to give progress reports, but he was usually just too busy. Irène wrote more details

In the evening they gave her a very good medicine called Anti febrin, which took the fever down to 38 degrees c... Naturally she felt ever so much better & cheerful. It makes her

perspire. At 2 she had no measure taken... Dear L[ouis] is so touchingly devoted to her & she feels quite unhappy when he is away from her for even so short a time.[41]

Her illness was serious and it was only thanks to the loving care of Louis and her family that she began to improve. All were concerned, including her Uncle Affie of Edinburgh, who wrote to his mother: *"I had only casually heard that Victoria Battenberg was ill but until hearing from you I had no idea of the seriousness of her illness. I hope still she will be strong enough ... to come to England with the other guests."*[42]

There could be little doubt that Victoria would have been utterly distraught had she missed the festivities. However, thanks to her strong constitution, which had previously overcome several other life-threatening diseases, not only did she survive, but would be permitted to attend some of the festivities. Curtailing her activities didn't bother her nearly as much as not being permitted to see Alice. The little girl was just beginning to babble, and though she was unintelligible, Victoria enjoyed her emphatic attempts at conversation in what appeared to be her own private language.

By the beginning of June, Victoria was finding her strength once again, and took up her correspondence. It seemed that the Queen felt it incumbent upon herself to remind her granddaughter, once again, about what a wonderful and devoted husband she had. *"You have been most tenderly lovingly nursed by one of the kindest & best of Husbands whose love & unbounded devotion you can never sufficiently repay."*[43] On June 20, Victoria and her family traveled with the Queen from Windsor to Buckingham Palace, where they lived during the Jubilee celebrations.

The large-scale events took place on June 20-21, 1887, and Victoria was able to attend most of the ceremonies with her family. It was a stellar event and most of the top dignitaries of the world attended, including monarchs from all over Europe and as far away as exotic Persia, Siam, Japan, and Hawaii. Naturally, the Queen's huge family circle was there in force. On the evening of June 20, there was a large family dinner with the royalties in attendance. The Queen listed all the attendees in her journal: *"I went at once to the Picture Gallery, where all the Royalties were assembled ... – an enormous party. Afterwards I received the Queen of Hawaii, and then saw, in quick succession, the Japanese Prince Komatzu and the Siamese Prince, and finally the Persian Prince, who speaks no English."*[44]

The following morning the Thanksgiving Service and Celebration took place at Westminster Abbey. The Queen traveled there in an open landau, so that all might see her. She was surprised and deeply touched by the enthusiasm of her subjects. She had hardly appeared in public since Prince Albert died twenty-six years before. Many of her subjects had never seen her before, and were annoyed about this, so much so that there had even been some strong republican movements afoot. However, that day, as she rode through the streets and listened to the cheers of her subjects, there was no thought of removing the Queen-Empress.

Following the Queen in procession were her three sons, five sons-in-law, and nine grandsons, along with Louis, on horseback. In the carriage with Queen Victoria was her eldest daughter, Aunt Vicky and her daughter-in-law, Aunt Alix of Wales. She was dressed with her usual bonnet, however, in a concession to the grand occasion, it was trimmed with white lace instead of black and with diamonds woven into the material. Her sons and daughters had tried to talk her out of wearing her bonnet, for once, but Queen Victoria was adamant.

After the Queen, the loudest cheers from the crowds came as Uncle Fritz of Prussia rode slowly by. He was extremely impressive and handsome with his gleaming white uniform and imposing bearing. What was unknown to the cheering crowds was that the Crown Prince was ill – growths had been found in his throat. Several operations had been performed and doctors were confident that they had removed the diseased tissue. However, the family was aware that he was in terrible pain, and Uncle Fritz rode stoically, although nobly, through the cheering and admiring crowd.

The procession made its way to the Abbey, where the Archbishop of Canterbury met Queen Victoria. The members of the congregation were in their places as the Queen made her way to the altar, walking slowly to the majestic strains of Handel. She looked impressive in her dress, which was made of black silk so elegant and stiff that the congregation must have heard it rustle as she proceeded up the aisle. The Archbishop was wearing the velvet and gold robes that had been worn by the presiding Archbishop at her coronation, fifty years before. She made her way to the coronation chair, under which rested the famous Stone of Scone - the prize that Edward the First had wrested from the Scots all those hundreds of years ago. Then, the organ played Prince Albert's composition, the Te Deum. No doubt, as the music played, the Queen thought about her darling Albert, and the fact that he was not there (she had written the day before that she was *"all alone"*[45]), and what joy and meaning could she derive from such a moment without him? Then, as the organ and choir swelled, all her daughters, one by one, came up to the chair and curtsied to their mother, and kissed her. When her eldest daughter, Vicky, approached, the Queen embraced her warmly, and for many more seconds than the other Aunts and Uncles. It was an emotional moment. Afterward, the service continued with more tributes, and, as the finale, the congregation, along with three thousand schoolboys, rose as one, and sang God Save the Queen.

Dinner that evening was, as expected, a large gala. However, Victoria was excluded from the festivities and made to go to her room and rest. Clearly, she would have been irked to be left out of festivities, since she loved being with her extended family, however, she was under strict orders from the Queen. After the bulk of the festivities were over, Victoria, Louis and the Queen returned to Windsor where Victoria continued her convalescence.

By July, when Victoria had recovered completely, the family returned to Darmstadt. Louis immersed himself in his career, and was appointed second in command of *HMS Dreadnought*. Though his time with the Victoria and Albert was pleasant, in that it afforded him the opportunity of spending time with his family, he was certainly much happier with a real ship, rather than what he undoubtedly would have termed, a pleasure cruiser. In his capacity as Commander, he stirred up mean-spirited comments of favoritism from his colleagues in the Navy. His close relationship to the Queen would have had to encourage promotions, and as a consequence, would make him a constant target of envy. Moreover, his German accent and phrasing would make him a victim of xenophobia.[46] Louis was not a typical British naval officer and was philosophical about it, but one can imagine that Victoria raged at the injustice of it all.

Nevertheless, Louis certainly had his defenders. In a letter to *The Times* of London, one such gentleman praised his abilities, calling him well-qualified on a theoretical or pragmatic level for any position in the Royal Navy. Indeed, the writer was surprised that he had not received such an appointment sooner.[47]

In October of that year, Victoria set out with little Alice, to join Louis at his new post on the island of Malta. Located at the cross-roads of the Mediterranean, south of Italy, Malta was Britain's stepping-stone to Africa and the Middle East, and was thus, extremely strategic. It was ideally suited for the Royal Navy and her Mediterranean Fleet - a good jumping-off point to all destinations in the Near and Far East. Victoria's Uncle Alfred of

Edinburgh was the Commander-in-Chief of the Fleet and it was at his official residence, San Antonio, where Victoria and Alice initially stayed.

Victoria was fascinated with the island, its history, and scenery. From the Neolithic landscapes and ancient temples, the island was the home of many wayfaring and battling cultures: Phoenician, Carthaginians, Romans, Arabs, and Normans. Having a long history of being the scene of so many battles, and being a bastion of Southern Europe, Malta was covered with defensive forts and battlements. It was also the home of the Order of St. John, more popularly known as the Knights of Malta. These monk-knights would defend Europe against the infidel, and help pilgrims and crusaders on their journeys to the Holy Land. They protected Southern Europe against the Moslem invaders in the fifteenth and sixteenth centuries and built the fortress city of Valetta. Victoria's fertile imagination undoubtedly fed on her eerie, mysterious, and exotic surroundings.

Staying in Malta became a special pleasure for Victoria. She, who had suffered so badly from chilblains as a child, also had circulatory problems which stayed with her for her entire life. The warm and breezy weather was a balm for her condition. More importantly, she had the company of close and congenial family in the Edinburghs. Her Aunt Marie of Edinburgh was far happier in Malta than she had been in England. Perhaps it was not equivalent to her position as the Tsar's only daughter, but she was the First Lady of the island, and need not take a back seat to anyone as she had grudgingly done in England.

Victoria spent hours exploring the island. She loved the unusual landscapes where she cultivated her interests in botany, cartography, and archeology. However, she particularly enjoyed getting to know her Aunt and Uncle as well as her little Edinburgh cousins. Though they were ten years younger and more, they were wild and independent, and full of good cheer, especially the two oldest daughters.

The eldest was Marie, whom the family called "Missy." She would eventually become the Queen of Romania. The second was Victoria Melita, called "Ducky," whose ultimate destiny, after a sad detour, lay in Russia. The third was Sandra, who loved to tag along on her very small pony, and, lastly, the baby, Beatrice, a playmate for Alice, who was called "Baby Bee" even into advanced old age.

Victoria joined her young cousins on wild gallops all over the island. It was very hilly, full of slopes, and strange and fascinating geological formations - but there wasn't a river or a mountain in sight. The girls' mother often scolded them for acting like hooligans. Indeed, Victoria heard echoes of her grandmother in the admonishments – how the Queen had taken her to task about her own wild riding and that it made young Princesses 'fast'. Victoria, nevertheless, felt very free on that small island.

The wild rides would end in an al fresco tea or picnic at various fortresses, naturally presided over by Aunt Marie. Sometimes, there would be favored naval officers in attendance. All the girls had their pets among the officers, and Captains, as did Aunt Marie. Victoria described their activities:

Here we are leading a quiet pleasant life, making driving expeditions of an afternoon or taking long rides of which the 3 girls are passionately fond. They all ride very nicely & don't know what it is to be nervous. Alice & Baby Bee romp & play together & I am sorry to say quarrel besides – they are both rather spoiled so their games often end in pitched battle, in which poor Baby Bee generally comes off worse, as Alice slaps & even bites her, before she has time to realize what is happening...[48]

Victoria enjoyed this sojourn immensely, although she commented about some of the most common residents of the island, namely *"the goats* [who were]... *more numerous and met with in every street."*[49] Nor did Victoria neglect her grandmother. She wrote long descriptions of everything and everyone and the Queen was most appreciative as she vicariously observed her granddaughter's life. *"Your descriptions of your voyage & your life at Malta are very vivid & enable me to follow all in thought."*[50]

Just before Christmas, Uncle Alfred and Louis returned to Malta. Victoria and Louis moved to Number 1, Molino Avento, a small corner house with no separate nursery and a flat next door which was also rented out. The house was modest and their dining room only seated six. When the men were home from voyages, Victoria's life was much different. Instead of the intimate family gatherings, gallops and excursions around the island, there was a vigorous social life with the naval officers and the dignitaries of the island. They dined a great deal at Aunt Marie and Uncle Alfred's either in large parties, or en famille, and were invited to balls and other parties.

On Christmas Day, Victoria and Louis *"went aboard the Dreadnought for service ... and round the mess decks afterwards."*[51] The ship had been specially decorated for the season. Afterwards, everyone gathered at the Edinburgh's residence, San Antonio, for Christmas dinner and the opening of presents. One present, particularly precious to Victoria, was a leather bound book with a lock on it in which she listed the books she had read, a habit she maintained from childhood and throughout her life. It was inscribed *"From L's Mother Xmas 1887 Malta."* She began to use the notebook in January of 1888. This particular volume continued until 1902. Examples of some of the books she read that first month were *Life of George Washington, Principles of Constitutional Law,* as well as several novels.[52]

However far away, though, and whatever the season, Victoria found time for her family and those of her siblings still at home. On Boxing Day, she wrote Ernie a letter lecturing him about his bad spelling, but softened the criticism by telling him that, *"Georgy* is nearly as bad on this point, but in French chiefly...He is much at San Antonio & also comes here sometimes & all are fond of him..."*[53]

Little Alix was about to be confirmed, and already exhibiting religious fervor and an interest in the occult. Irène wrote to her grandmother about the date of Alix's confirmation, but also included the news that *"Papa intends Alix to be confirmed at <u>Whitsuntide</u> as in that way Miss Jackson's leaving would be more agreeable for all and a natural end to her remaining."*[54] After some twenty years, "Madgie" was leaving her charges, and moving back to England.

Meanwhile, Irène, in a similar position as Victoria had been when planning her wedding, was now trying to do so with little help. As with Victoria, there was illness and tragic events that would have to be considered as time went on. However, paramount with Irène, as it had been and would be for all the Hessian children, was the attendance of the Queen. Irène wrote to her grandmother more than six months before the wedding with the hope that she would attend. If the Queen didn't wish to come to Berlin, then Potsdam would be the location of the wedding, and most definitely, nothing would be fixed until she heard from he grandmother. In the end, the Queen attended neither Irène's wedding nor Alix's confirmation.

By November of that year, there was much anxiety over Prince Henry's father,

---

(*) *Then Prince George of Wales. He received the title of Duke of York from Grandmama Victoria. Later, during the reign of his father, King Edward VII, George was Prince of Wales and in 1910 succeeded as King George V.*

Uncle Fritz of Prussia. As the New Year dawned, not only Irène worried about his illness, but her grandmother's family at large, as well. He had endured several operations in which the growths, originally thought to be benign, had been removed from the Crown Prince's throat. However, by the end of 1887, the doctors were finding more that they described as *"alarming,"*[55] and only days later classified as malignant. A tracheotomy was performed at Villa Zirio in San Remo in early February 1888, and Irène, as well as her father, the Grand Duke Ludwig IV, were at Aunt Vicky's side during the operation. Victoria, however, in a letter to Ernie, thought that even needing the operation was a bad sign. To add to Victoria's unease, Louis developed Malta fever, a disease prevalent in the Mediterranean area. Though not known for a high mortality rate, it was nevertheless annoying in its long debilitating fever, and chronic relapses. It was particularly virulent at military garrisons. Thus, the Princess spent anxious moments taking care of Louis and reading aloud to him.

It was not only Uncle Fritz having throat cancer, but his father, the old Emperor, Wilhelm I, was mortally ill after a series of strokes.[56] The old man died in March 9, 1888. This complicated matters and caused an atmosphere of great tension in Berlin. Uncle Fritz was Emperor for a mere three months. Perceiving his grave condition, most people considered him an interim ruler. The situation was completely 'up in the air', all waiting for the ultimate end of the new Emperor and the accession of his callow son, Cousin Willy. To add to the confusion, the Hessian family was now fully engaged in planning Irène's wedding that would take place on May 24th of that year. Victoria wrote, *"The great change the Emperor's death will cause & the anxiety we feel about Uncle Fritz – it fills our thoughts & we are most anxious for news – as we are so out of the way of everything here. I fancy all of this may cause some change in the plans of Irène's wedding."*[57]

The one ray of sunshine as spring came, was that Prince Louis was much better and convalescing from the Malta fever. Queen Victoria was staying in Florence at the time and Victoria wrote to her describing wedding arrangements. *"Irène's wedding is to be at Charlottenburg on May 24 provided this illness does not make advisable to hurry it on, & will naturally be a very quiet one."*[58]

Oddly enough, the issue of Sandro and Moretta would come up officially one last time just before the wedding. Though, Sandro had renounced Moretta several years before, the romantic Princess and her mother, Aunt Vicky, continued to live in hope that perhaps, since the death of his father, Uncle Fritz would now approve of the marriage. These were futile hopes at this time, as Chancellor Prince von Bismarck and Cousin Willy would never let this marriage happen. Indeed, Sandro, denied a commission in the German Army, had met the woman he would marry, and was fixed upon that idea. He, by this point, actively wanted to get out of the uncomfortable situation and had asked Victoria to explain to, a now strange ally, Willy. The explanation would be as follows: the marriage could no longer be possible, and that he, Willy, should write a letter to Sandro, verifying that he *"under no condition agree to the marriage. This letter Sandro could then forward to Aunt Vicky, withdrawing from his engagement."*[59]

Queen Victoria, who had been in favor of the marriage five years before, now had to take the bull by the horns and write to her daughter,

I only hope you will see your way to put an end to a state of things which is quite ruinous... Unfortunately, there is no denying that this unfortunate project, which in itself was so natural, has been the indirect cause of all his [Sandro's] misfortunes. I know your one wish was to help him and therefore I feel if you and Vicky really love him, you ought to set him free...[60]

It would all simply end in misery for both the young people if the two women persisted.

In the end, not only did Sandro give up a throne for private life, but, also gave up, entirely, and it should be said at this point, the idea of marrying Princess Victoria of Prussia. He was given the title of Count von Hartenau by permission of the Grand Duke Ludwig, and joined the Austrian army. He married a beautiful young opera singer, Johanna Loisinger, in February 1889, and had two children. *The Times* seemed to feel that this marriage *"finally seals his renunciation of the Bulgarian crown,"*[61] though it was obvious from September 1886, that Sandro had no intention of returning as Bulgaria's Prince even if Prussia and Russia would have permitted it. Victoria was philosophical about the marriage that naturally some would have called a misalliance. She told her father that her feeling was *"that the poor man has had to go through so much in the past few years, has lost so much and led such a lonely miserable life, this marriage will perhaps make him happier than anything else could. I believe Frl. Loisinger has an unblemished reputation..."*[62] She wrote further: *"Of course this marriage is a grief to us, as he could have done so much better for himself & such marriages are always risky – however I who have seen how lonely & depressed he was feeling all last year, try to hope that a wife may be some comfort to him..."*[63]

Sandro could hardly help but be cognizant of what such a marriage would do to his prestige and reputation. He was extremely anxious, according to Victoria, about what his cousin, the Grand Duke Ludwig, would think. She wrote to her father, "The poor man was terrified how we would react, he was quaking at your reaction, as you have always been so good to him."[64] Queen Victoria was less sanguine about the situation.

> *We were dreadfully startled and upset ... that Sandro had married a Fräulein Loisinger ..., and had taken the name of Count Hartenau! We could not believe it though it was in to-day's papers. But Liko came to say he had had a long letter from Sandro, giving his reasons. Having met with rebuffs and refusals everywhere, having no money, no occupation, he was driven to desperation, and was determined at least to have a quiet happy home; and the lady was charming and good. It is, however, very sad, and Liko feels it dreadfully.*[65]

Sandro seemed, however, to be most concerned about what the Queen would think about his marriage. It appeared that the Queen's favor was more significant to members of her family, than, at least in some instances, their own happiness. Though this was not the case with Sandro, he obviously felt that he owed her an explanation for his actions and, accordingly, wrote a letter of apology:

> *I cannot find words to tell you how profoundly unhappy I was at the thought of having lost your Majesty's favour for ever, and how happy I am now to know that in your magnanimity you have pardoned the brother of your son-in-law.*
>
> *The thought of having ruined Liko's position pursued me constantly, and it was consideration for your daughter that made me give up my name.*[66]

Weakened, perhaps, by a case of small pox in 1887, Sandro died at the early age of thirty-five in 1892. Though the far more malleable Ferdinand of Saxe Coburg and Gotha, who eventually proclaimed himself Tsar of Bulgaria, was already in power at this point, the

Bulgarians clamored to have their Prince back. Victoria wrote: *"The Bulgarian Government speaking for the people, asked that their first prince should be buried at Sofia, to which with his usual political wisdom King Ferdinand cordially agreed."*[67] His body was returned to the people who truly loved him, and Sandro was buried in Sofia, Bulgaria.*

(*) *Sandro and Johanna had two children: Assen and Svetlana. Assen dropped the title of Count von Hartenau and married in 1944, with no issue. Johanna Losinger survived until 1951.*

Chapter VI

May 1888 – December 1893

As outside events complicated the lives of the Hessian extended family, Victoria's life also became more complex. She had noticed earlier that Alice was babbling in a language of her own. While this was precious while she was a toddler, it became a reason for concern as Alice passed her fourth birthday. Victoria mentioned that Alice was slow in learning how to speak several times to her grandmother. She thought, perhaps, that Alice was slightly behind. The little girl pronounced words improperly and didn't look around or speak when she was spoken to. Victoria briefly considered the possibility that her daughter had become ill-mannered. In a letter to the Queen, Victoria remarked how very much Alice had grown but that she was *"decidedly backward of speech, using all sorts of self invented words & pronouncing others very indistinctly so that strangers find it difficult to understand her."*[1]

It was the little child's other grandmother, Princess Julie of Battenberg, who first suspected the cause of the problem. She urged Victoria to take Alice to an ear specialist. The diagnosis was, due to blocked Eustachian tubes, possibly a birth defect, Alice was almost completely deaf. Her parents were also informed that the defect was inoperable. Once Victoria understood the problem, she characteristically swung into action. She immediately engaged an instructor to teach Alice how to lip-read, and she, herself, spent hours working with the child. In a matter of months, Alice learned to lip-read and to speak more clearly. In fact, by the time she was fifteen years old, Alice could lip-read in three languages.

Victoria, however, was determined not to indulge Alice because of her handicap. She wanted Alice to appear as normal as possible and the little girl was instructed by her mother and various governesses never to indicate by a sign or a gesture that she had any kind of disability. Though this initially resulted in dismaying confusion for Alice, especially in crowded rooms, as the years went by, people who didn't know her intimately were unaware of her problem. While this may sound cruel, it was certainly part of the ethos of the time, especially for a royal person. It probably was no more dismaying than the *"cercle."* Royal princesses were instructed in the process of walking around a circle of chairs – completely empty – and conversing and being pleasant as if these chairs were filled with the most interesting people imaginable. It promoted the obvious attributes for a princess, namely to be sociable and agreeable no matter what the circumstances. Alice's ordeals in crowded rooms seemed no worse to her mother, and were also a process of making her more outgoing and amenable. Victoria wanted to make sure that no one felt sorry for Alice or treated her any differently. As a result, Alice did learn and was neither treated specially nor pitied.

Alice, however, was only one of Victoria's concerns as the last decade of the nineteenth century began. Having two siblings at home in Hesse, the matter of engagements and weddings was to absorb Victoria, her grandmother, and, indeed, the entire extended family. Ernie was in his early twenties, and quite immature still, while Alix was just coming of age. Much thought was put into likely candidates for these two, and though Ernie showed little inclination for marriage, the Queen continued to be especially apprehensive about her young granddaughter and the inevitable pitfalls of her marrying a Russian.

****

On May 24, 1888, Irène and Henry were married in the Royal Chapel at Charlottenburg near Berlin. Though extremely disappointed that her grandmother would not attend the ceremony, Irène wrote, with great affection, *"I shall always try to keep your kind advice in remembrance and to be deserving of my name, wh*[ich] *is always my great wish."*[2]

The months before the ceremony had been full of worries. Irène was intimately involved in what would be the last illness of Uncle Fritz, her future father-in-law, the Emperor Friedrich III. Naturally, she confided in the Queen: *"I have never seen a braver woman than dear Aunt Vicky, who is all our admiration."*[3] Besides her feelings for Uncle Fritz, Irène, like Victoria, was deeply concerned about leaving her father. She consoled herself with the idea that the Grand Duke would be happy about her union since he was very fond of Henry, and he would, as he promised, make frequent visits to Berlin.

Just before the wedding, Alix, who was nearly sixteen years old, was confirmed. She was profoundly disappointed that neither Victoria nor Ella could attend the ceremonies in Darmstadt. However, the rest of her close family was there to witness the service. Alix was growing up to be a painfully shy girl, and the performance of reciting the creed proved extremely arduous for her. Though she was afraid of the whole thing, she did a creditable job and, appeared, according to Irène, very self-possessed.

At last on that day in May, Irène's wedding took place. The bride wore a dress of white satin, with a long train, trimmed with her mother's wedding lace, orange blossoms, and sprigs of myrtle. In attendance were both the Prussian and Hessian connections, Uncle Bertie of Wales, representing Queen Victoria, as well as Serge and Ella. At this point, Uncle Fritz was mortally ill and almost completely bedridden. Nevertheless, he stoically rose from his sickbed with assistance of a cane, and attended the wedding. He sat with his mother and wife and *"rose without difficulty at the usual points in the service; he was not disturbed by coughing."*[4] When the ceremony was finished, *"he walked out unaided."*[5] The wedding was to be his last official engagement. As he had been at the Golden Jubilee, he was, again, a tremendously dignified and noble sight in full dress uniform wearing Hessian and Prussian orders. His illness put an unavoidable pall over the wedding festivities, which had an unmistakably funereal feeling to them. It was uncomfortably similar to Princess Alice's wedding, twenty six years before, following so soon as it did, after the death of Prince Albert.

Henry's brother, the future Kaiser wrote:

When...my brother Henry was married to the Princess Irène... the solemnization ... was entirely dominated by the profound sorrow caused in all those present by the terribly emaciated appearance of my father. He insisted ...while the rings were being exchanged, on rising and remaining standing, like a hero of old, supported upon his stick, but directly after had to leave the chapel. Never again have I attended a wedding like this, at which not joy but sorrow filled all the hearts.[6]

The end came for the Emperor several weeks later on June 15, 1888. Queen Victoria, though distraught at the death of her first and very beloved son-in-law, was content that, though she had not attended the wedding, she had been able to say goodbye to her dear Fritz when she visited Berlin that previous April. Irène wrote to Louis about the deathbed scene and how peaceful he had been at the end: *"Dear Uncle had repeatedly asked for Harry* [Henry]

& when we came into the room he recognized us & seemed so pleased, putting his hands on my head as if for a blessing." Aunt Vicky, she said, broke down a great deal, but was progressively doing better as time passed.

Irène and Henry, whose romance was initially caught in the dramatic end of two reigns and the unfortunate bickering that ensued afterward, were, thereafter, a quiet and content couple. Victoria wrote from Wolfsgarten, where she had gone after the wedding, *"Irène is coming on a fortnight's visit to us next week, while Henry is at sea – her new home is very pretty & she seems pleased & contented with her new life."*[8]

Cousin Willy became German Kaiser Wilhelm II and it must be said that his accession was not a cause for unfettered joy in the family. Most had no confidence in his abilities either as a ruler, or his compassion as a son to his newly-widowed mother, Aunt Vicky. Queen Victoria characteristically had a lot to say. She was angered at the way in which Willy and his wife, "Dona," Kaiserin Augusta Victoria, had completely taken over and callously brushed the Dowager Empress aside. Indeed, she had no hesitation in saying so frankly to Victoria: *"It is too dreadful for us all to think of Willy & Bismarck & Dona – being the supreme head of all now! Two so unfit & one so wicked. He spoke so shamefully about dear Auntie V[icky] to Uncle Bertie & A[un]t Alix."*[9]

After waiting to succeed for so many years, a mere few months for her eldest daughter as Empress, was an enormously frustrating outcome. The Queen wrote constant letters to her family complaining about Willy's heartlessness and viciousness towards all his relations, but most especially towards his mother. In addition, she continually worried about the persecution that her own daughter might suffer at the hands of her weak and autocratic grandson. She enlisted any reasonable family member, including Victoria, to help her to make Willy see reason:

I beg you to entreat [Wilhelm] to let bygones be bygones…Tell him that the more respect he shows to her & his father & the more consideration for her wishes, the more he will be liked by his Country & all of us. – The reverse w[ou]ld do him immense harm. You can say this best as he trusts you. I have written very kindly to him & also hinted at it, in thanking him for his birthday letter to me.[10]

Irène, once again, put herself in the role of peace-maker. "[I]f [Aunt Vicky] *would only try & look more kindly on people's motives, she would really be happier. Just the same about Dona, who I know deeply sympathises for poor Aunt Mama & has often told me that she was so terribly unhappy how often she was misunderstood by her whenever she tried to do anything to please her & that she tries her best."*[11] One can imagine what the Queen though of these sentiments. That Dona was well-meaning can only be understood, and even wondered at, in the context of a long history of misunderstandings and inter-familial conflicts.

Victoria was spending most of the fall and winter in Wolfsgarten, though she went back to Malta by November. During that time, Ella and Serge went on a pilgrimage to Jerusalem. Ella was worried about her childlessness and wanted to pray for children in the Holy City. While they were there, they dedicated a Russian Orthodox Church, the Church of St. Mary Magdalen, to Serge's mother, the Empress Marie Alexandrovna. Located at the foot of the Mount of Olives, the church, with its onion domes, stood on the earth where the Orthodox believed the Garden of Gethsemane was located.

Ella wrote fascinating letters to Victoria and the Queen conveying the character of the Holy Land as being both extraordinarily beautiful as well as being dilapidated at the same time. She described their tours of Nazareth, Mount Tabor, and finally Jerusalem. The Ottomans had neglected the land shamelessly, most of it being barren or derelict. There were pockets of Christians, Jews, and Moslems living in the few cities that had continued from ancient times, as well as the Bedouin, who wandered around the whole area along with their livestock, and without thought of boundaries. There was, however, no development – no modern progress of any kind. It was a land that time hadn't just neglected, but completely forgotten.

Jerusalem, however, was radiant. Ella told her grandmother about the colorlessness of the stone, but how it rather grew on one. There was a golden glow to the indigenous stone as the sun touched the walls. She had gone to the dank and dark burial place of Christ at the Church of the Holy Sepulcher which she wrote about rapturously, and had walked the twelve Stations of the Cross. In the end, she exclaimed, prophetically as it turned out, that she was "[d]*eeply affected by all this... 'How I should like to be buried here!'*"[12]

In many ways a strange and cruel man, Serge was, oddly, a very religious one. Certainly, it meant a great deal to him that several years after the dedication of the church and the pilgrimage, Ella decided to convert to Russian Orthodoxy. This conversion would have a great influence on her sisters in years to come.

****

That fall also saw more personal tragedy unfold in Prince Louis' family. His father, Prince Alexander, whose health was undermined by the terrible trials of his son, Sandro, was diagnosed with inoperable cancer of the stomach. In the middle of December, the once dashing darling of the Russian court, died at the age of sixty-five at the Heiligenberg with his family around him. Having worked closely with his sons their entire lives, his death was a terrible blow to Louis and his brothers. For obvious reasons, there was more than likely a mentality among the Battenberg men – 'us against the world' – and Louis' father, Uncle Alexander, was the rock. He had stood by Louis through his difficult days as a cadet and an officer in the Royal Navy, he was at Sandro's side through his disastrous tenure in Bulgaria, and was there to buck up Liko, when he was ridiculed in the British and Prussian press and by the various royalties when he had married Beatrice. Perhaps his younger sons didn't suffer quite the difficulties of the older ones, but the unit was complete and self-contained. Now, its stalwart was gone. *"Poor Louis is terribly unhappy, he always got on so very well with his father..."*[13] Victoria told her grandmother.

As the oldest son, Louis inherited the Heiligenberg, and Victoria, from thence onward, considered it her true home. Since there were a number of business matters that needed attention, instead of returning to Malta, Victoria and Louis wintered in Hesse with her father, the Grand Duke. As the least of his duties, Louis, along with Princess Julie, had to discharge his father's various bequests. One such keepsake was sent to Ella and Serge, who were genuinely touched by *"the souvenirs your Mother is sending us & will treasure them very dearly in remembrance of your beloved Father."*[14]

In January of 1889, Alix and her father traveled to St. Petersburg to stay with Ella and Serge. Alix often expressed how much she loved Russia, so it was matter of great delight to her that her first ball would take place there. Alix's cousins, the children of Alexander III and Marie Feodorovna, made sure that every minute of Alix's day was filled with activity.

She went skating, sledding, dancing and to parties, theater evenings, and cotillions – all accompanied by Cousin Nicky and his sister Xenia. The Tsarevitch was particularly attentive. On January 29, as a culmination of all the fun and festivities, Alix had her 'coming out' ball – an opulent and glittering affair. Orchie, no doubt, shed a tear as she readied her beautiful charge for her first ball. Indeed, Alix was beautiful, dressed in white, and resplendent with diamonds and flowers in her hair. Naturally, when she returned to Darmstadt, besides the inevitable let-down that the end of such wonderful times would always have, there was little doubt that she left her heart with Nicky in Russia.

Although the Queen fretted about this, she and Victoria had several other important events to discuss. In the beginning of that year, Victoria discovered that she was expecting her second child. The pregnancy was more difficult than her first one had been, and she felt listless and lethargic. Naturally, the Queen shot off letter after letter telling Victoria to walk more, exercise more, even to move more, but this time she did not feel like listening. Her vigor seemed drained. To make matters worse, she was suffering from acute hay fever which was always debilitating.

A sad distraction from her unusual languor came on January 30 when the gruesome events at Mayerling took place. Archduke Rudolf, only son and heir of Emperor Franz Joseph, killed himself after shooting his young lover, Baroness Marie Vetsera at the Mayerling Hunting Lodge outside of Vienna. The resulting uproar was a royal scandal of immense proportions. The Queen wrote to Victoria that the death of the two was quite terrible. There was no doubt in the Queen's mind that the Crown Prince had led a debauched life, "*& that this unfortunate girl said to be one of the prettiest & I hear fastest in Vienna Mlle. Marie Vetsera only 19 – was found dead, on his bed, both dead, & shot – & a pistol in his hand. ... The poor, poor Emperor & the Empress are g[rea]tly to be pitied – for it is awful altogether.*"[15]*

Irène was more charitable. Her comment about the tragedy was that it was too sad for words and what a "*terrible blow to his poor Parents, & to Stephanie above all left alone with her little girl.*"[16] Victoria in a more circumspect mood years later, meditated on the Archduchess Stephanie, who was a daughter of her cousin Leopold II of Belgium. As the wife of the unfortunate Rudolf, she was one of the main victims of the calamity. "*I knew Stephanie, his wife, since our visits to Brussels in our childhood. I never considered her clever then, or after I had seen her again many years later did I find cause to reverse my opinion.*"[17]

****

Happier news came that March when Irène, who became pregnant very soon after her wedding, gave birth to her first child at Kiel. Irène presented her husband with a little boy whose names were: Waldemar Ludwig Wilhelm Friedrich Victor, though he was always called Toddy. Henry was tremendously excited about the new baby, writing to Queen Victoria: "*I have been, and am nearly still mad with delight and happiness...*"[18] He also asked the Queen to be godmother to the baby, telling her that the christening would take place in May. Like her mother and her sister, Victoria, Irène, too, breast-fed her babies, to the extreme annoyance of her English grandmother. On a sadder note, the boy very soon began to exhibit signs of hemophilia. This ailment, which eventually took Toddy's life, prompted

---

(*) *In an odd sideline to the tragedy, Sandro, now Count von Hartenau, had actually been invited to Mayerling that weekend by his longtime friend Crown Prince Rudolf, but the Count had to decline as he was traveling elsewhere.*

Irène to want to live a private life away from the Prussian court and its controversies.

Victoria spent the summer of 1889 at the Heiligenberg awaiting the birth of her second child. Her condition was more delicate than usual, and she wrote to her father that she could not travel by coach by the end of June because *"I do not dare to risk the shaking about and the climbing into of the carriages."*[19]* She received numerous letters from Queen Victoria discussing her current pet project of matching Prince Albert Victor of Wales, known as "Eddy" to his family, and Alix. Unfortunately for the Queen, it wasn't going at all as she hoped. Eddy had never been an object of Alix's affection, though she had said that she loved him as a cousin, and would try very hard if Grandmama really wished it. The idea, however, was doomed from the start since Alix's heart was firmly engaged elsewhere. Victoria, having an obvious interest, was the receptacle of all of her grandmother's discourses on the subject.

> *And now let me say a word about Alicky. Is there no hope ab[ou]t E[ddy].? She is not 19 – & she shl[ou]d be made to reflect seriously on the folly of throwing away the chance of a very good...position wh[ich] is second to <u>none</u> in <u>the</u> <u>world</u>! Dear Uncle & Aunt wish it so much & poor E[ddy] is so unhappy at the thought of losing her also! Can you & Ernie not do any good? What fancy has she got in her head?*[20]

Victoria was well aware of what fancies Alix had in her head, but as the summer wore on, she had more immediate concerns. She went into premature labor and on July 13 1889, Princess Louise Alexandra Marie, Victoria and Louis' second daughter, was born. The second name was in memory of Uncle Alexander. *"Unlike Alice, who was a fine sturdy baby, Louise was rather a miserable little object, and the nickname 'Shrimp' which Louis then gave her remained attached to her during her childhood..."*[21], and frequently the way he addressed her in letters. It had been a difficult pregnancy, a difficult labor, and it took Victoria some time to recover. However, once the Queen knew that Victoria was on the mend, she returned to her current favorite subject of Alix and Eddy.

> *We have just a <u>faint</u> <u>lingering</u> hope that Alicky <u>might</u> <u>in</u> <u>time</u> look to see what a pleasant home, and what a useful position she will lose if she ultimately persists in not yielding to Eddy's <u>really</u> earnest <u>wishes</u>. He wrote to me he should not give up the idea (though it is considered for the <u>present</u> <u>at</u> <u>an</u> <u>end</u>) –...*[22]

·Irène made an effort to mitigate the situation for her grandmother. *"Alicky is always so reserved that it is difficult to speak of such things with her, but I really think it only wants time – for she is so young – & then these fancies against E[ddy] may come right."*[23] Alicky, she explained, had just come out, and loved her freedom. Also, it appeared that she was self-conscious about the issue because she was afraid that she might be dragged into marriage against her will. Further, Irène also put forth the interesting idea that Aunt Vicky wanted her daughter, the disappointed fiancée of Sandro, Victoria of Prussia, to marry Eddy, since there was a time that Eddy had been interested in the young princess. Irène, too, has an interesting idea. *"I believe however that ever since a small child Alicky cared for Georgy of Wales most – but do not know now."*[24]

The Queen, however, was not to be placated, and went on to lament that there

---

(*) *In the same letter Victoria mentioned that the Almanach de Gotha for that year made no mention of the death of Prince Alexander of Hesse. More proof of the snobbery against the Battenbergs – she speculated that the Prussian Heraldry Office or Duke Ernest of Coburg, who liked to make trouble for Queen Victoria, were behind this.*

were very few matrimonial possibilities for Alix being the youngest daughter in a small German Grand Duchy. Though a beautiful girl, she would be lucky to find a suitable match when other granddaughters were unable to find any. Eddy, though in line for the throne of England, was highly problematic as well. He has been called slow-witted, and barely seemed able to function in society. He had been put in the navy with his younger brother, where he had an extremely undistinguished career. Now, at the age of twenty-six, he was doing very little more than wearing uniforms and being pleasant. To make matters worse, he was rather odd-looking with an abnormally long neck, and arms that seemed to hang much lower than they ought. His uniforms were made up specially, with high collars to hide the neck and longer cuffs to hide the length of his arms. Uncle Bertie of Wales made fun of him and told all the children in the family to call him *"Collars and Cuffs."**

Queen Victoria was quite aware of Eddy's tragic short-comings and looked about for a gentle princess – good-looking and sweet – who would be able to manage Eddy, and make him see that there were things that he simply must do. He was just returning from a tour of India and the Queen voiced the hope that he would be much *"improved and developed as we must hope he will be – who could he marry? Do tell me."*[25] As Alix seemed to be set against the match, she searched endlessly for other possibilities.

Victoria, acting as an intermediary between her sister and the Queen wrote: *"I think it would perhaps be best not to disturb Ali[x]'s mind about Eddie just at present – but will try & speak with her about him in spring, when I get home. I really know of nobody who would suit him so well as a wife – though there are several young princesses I believe who are about her age & said to be nice..."*[26] Did Victoria know that her sister would not accept Eddy and that she had someone else strongly in mind? Likely she was trying to prepare her grandmother for what she knew was the inevitable outcome.

By the time Louis was appointed to his first command, *HMS Scout,* Victoria was ready to go back to Malta. This time, however, the couple went without the children, who would remain with their *"Grossmama Julie,"* Aunt Julie Battenberg, at the Alexanderpalais. Louis and Victoria settled back in Malta and again, they had the delightful company of the Edinburghs, who would soon leave the island for another command. One of the highlights of the stay that year had been the arrival of Victoria's Hessian family for a visit. Not only had the Grand Duke, Alix, and Ernie come from Darmstadt, but Irène, had arrived with baby Toddy. She had sailed to Malta with Henry, a Captain in the Prussian Navy, who was in command of the ship, Irène, anchored off of Valletta.

As in her last stay, Victoria enjoyed this sojourn in Malta. Though Louis was away a great deal, she had her interests to keep her busy. Louis' absences were never easy for Victoria, but she had the advantage of being able to cope on her own and as an only parent, since she had done so, very frequently, during her own father's constant absences. By spring, however, Victoria was back in Darmstadt, happy to be with Alice and baby Louise. She continued to be the main recipient of the Queen's ruminations about Alix, and the all encompassing matter of her engagement. Alix had gone to visit the Queen that spring, but nothing had come of her meetings with her male Wales cousins. Queen Victoria, tenacious as ever, refused to be put off. Moreover she refused to consider another Russian marriage: *"[T]ell Ella that no marriage for Alicky in Russia w[ou]ld be allowed, then there will be an end of it[.]"*[27]

Most unhappily for the Queen, the Grand Duke was planning to take his family to

---

(*) *This is the orthodox view of Eddy, although it has recently been questioned.*

see Ella at their country home outside of Moscow, Illyinskoje, at the end of that summer of 1890. At this point, the Queen was secure in the fact that Alix and Nicky would not marry because of their religious differences and because Nicky's parents had no interest in the match. She was sure, however, that there were other Russian Princes and Grand Dukes just lying in wait for the opportunity to pluck the Hessian rose. Once again, Victoria tried to sooth her grandmother saying quite truthfully that, *"I do not think you need have any fear of Alix becoming engaged to some Grand Duke..."*[28] Irène echoed the same sentiment when she told her grandmother that "[Alix] *would never wish to marry there."*[29]

Victoria went on the Russia trip with her Darmstadt family and spent until the end of September with Ella and Serge at Illyinskoje. They had an idyllic time, playing lawn tennis and visiting their neighbors, the Youssoupovs and the Galitzines, the great aristocratic families of Russia. In addition to neighbors, there was plenty of company in the house since many officers of Serge's regiment, the Preobrajensky guard, were staying there. Victoria and Ella sat on the beautiful wood veranda at the rear of the house, facing the Moskva River, and had many discussions.

Mostly they concerned an issue that Ella had now decided. She was going to convert to Russian Orthodoxy, and did so, later, in March of 1891. Her reasons, which she confided in Victoria, would soon be known to the rest of the family. First, she wished Alix to see that going from Lutheranism to Orthodoxy wasn't as difficult as she might imagine. Next, she felt that, perhaps, as a consequence, God would then grant her children, but only lastly, that it would make her husband happy. Ella was adamant and made it absolutely clear to her family that she was not coerced by any member of the Imperial Family to convert – that it was completely her own decision.* Victoria, who throughout her life would change her views on religion, spirituality, and even in the way she believed in God, supported Ella in this.

The rest of Ella's family were not nearly so understanding. Her father was *"so depressed about it..."*[30], and Irène, by her own admission, *"cried so much and ... [was] ... so miserable."*[31] Irène was convinced that Ella was entirely too impressionable and that she was fascinated with the mysterious rituals of orthodoxy and that Protestantism was just too cold and matter-of-fact for her. In the end, that she was a Christian was all that really mattered to Irène, though she thought her mother would have been heart-broken over it.

Victoria returned to Malta that fall, and though she was lonely without the Edinburghs, this time both her children accompanied her. Alice who was now five years old was some company as Victoria continued to work with her on her speech and lip-reading. Victoria had, since childhood, often expressed a wish, if she could have had a vocation, that she would have been a teacher. Helping her daughter mastering these basic skills must have been highly satisfying for her.

Victoria, the voracious reader and life-long student, continued her education with courses, one such, being a series of lectures on geology with a Professor Lepsius. Along with tutorials, she longed to expand her mind with books lent to her from such diverse sources as Serge and Ernie. She continued to be very methodical in her book lists, marking down

---

(*) *Though Ella was adamant, The Times of London, nevertheless, printed assertions that she had been coerced... "I repeat most positively my assertion that Princess Elizabeth of Hesse is not changing her religion willingly, but is only yielding to moral coercion of a very brutal kind, and such as ought to be taken into consideration by all those reigning families of Europe who, in giving away their daughters to Russian Grand Dukes, have treated Russia as a civilized State acting as other civilized States do in respecting marriage contracts."* (The Times of London, *March 21, 1891*). *The author's outrage notwithstanding, in view of her outstanding devotion and work within the church, Ella's word may be taken on this issue.*

books she had already read and books she was reading for the first time.

As in her youth, Victoria continued to have a total lack of vanity. She rarely worried about her appearance, and had her hair done in a very stark manner *"brushed and tied tight back..."*[32] Though she had an adolescent flirtation with clothes, that time had most definitely passed. Her sartorial sense, if not completely lacking was somewhat blind. This used to irritate Louis who was absolutely immaculate in dress, however, it just wasn't important enough to Victoria worry about a straight seam or a hanging thread.

Queen Victoria also continued to think about Alix and now that marriage to Eddy was not in the cards, she greatly feared Alix's marrying Nicky. After Christmas, the Queen wrote Victoria a particularly agitated letter about the matter.

> *I know it for certain, that in spite of all your (Papa's Ernie's and your) objections and still more contrary to the positive wish of his Parents* [Tsar Alexander III and Tsarina Marie Feodorovna] *who do not wish him* [Tsarevitch Nicholas] *to marry A[lix] As they feel, as everyone must do, for the youngest Sister to marry the son of the Emperor – would never answer, and lead to no happiness, – well in spite of all this behind all your backs, Ella and Serge do all they can to bring it about, encouraging and even urging the Boy to do it? ...*

> *The state of Russia is so bad, so rotten that any moment something dreadful might happen and though it may not signify to Ella, the wife of the Thronfolger* [heir to the throne] *is in a most difficult and precarious position.*[33]

The Queen said she heard these things from Aunt Alix of Wales, who had in turn heard them from her sister the Tsarina Marie Feodorovna. She continued to be furious about the events that were inevitably leading to a possible engagement between Alix and Nicky, and, most of all blaming Serge and Ella for promoting it. Always hopeful, the Queen refused to see the engagement as an inevitability.

****

The following year, 1891, though absorbed as it was in the beginning by Ella's conversion, was more or less quiet on the Alix-Nicky front. The Queen's fascination with the marriages of her grandchildren was unquenchable, and she tried to assuage her own fears of Russians by suggesting other possible suitors. Now the handsome, and wealthy, Prince Max of Baden came under her antennae for Alix.

> *You know how much dear Papa & I wish dear Alicky sh[ou]ld some day marry Max of Baden, whom I <u>formerly</u> wished for Maud* [of Wales, Uncle Bertie's daughter]... *Then I heard that he did not at all wish to marry an English Pr[ince]ss: If (as I anticipate) nothing comes of this I hope dear Papa will <u>lose no time</u> in inviting him.*[34]

In addition to Alix, the Queen was now scrutinizing brides for Ernie. The Queen initially thought that Princess Maud of Wales might be a possibility for Ernie, but she had some sensible worries as well. Maud was somewhat sickly, and because *"of the symptoms in dear Irène's beautiful boy tho' these I think will get better, it w[ou]ld not be advisable."*[35] Sadly, little Toddy, by all indications, was a hemophiliac. This is probably the first time the dreaded malady was positively mentioned in connection with the second generation, the grandchildren of Queen Victoria, and the first time that it showed up in the families of the Hessian children.

In a completely different matter, the Queen, completely without prompting from Louis or Victoria, also used her influence in getting Prince Louis a promotion. She wrote to the First Lord of the Admiralty, Lord George Hamilton:

> [the Queen] *hopes and expects that Prince Louis of Battenberg ... will get his promotion at the end of the year, for several junior to him have been promoted over his head. There is a belief that the Admiralty are afraid of promoting officers who are Princes on account of the Radical attacks of the low papers and scurrilous ones; but the Queen cannot credit this. She will always maintain that if a Prince is unfit for promotion in the Navy or Army he should not be promoted because he is Prince. But if he is fit, he should be treated as any other officer, who can rise to the highest post in the service. This the Queen will insist on, whoever the Prince may be. But she knows how excellent an officer her grandson-in-law is, and she therefore trusts there will be no further delay in giving him what he deserves.*[36]

The Queen was obviously extremely aware of the charges of nepotism that hounded Louis. In view of the above letter, she would hardly have been surprised at the extreme prejudice from which he would suffer throughout his naval career and, later, the egregious accusations of spying. Nonetheless, the Queen's wishes were swiftly granted and Louis was promoted to Captain in December 1891.

During that winter, Louis also invented a navigating instrument which was subsequently called the Battenberg Course Indicator. Several years later, the Admiralty adopted his invention and it was later used by the Air Force during World War I.*

In the beginning of 1892, Eddy, Alix's erstwhile suitor, and heir presumptive of the British throne, died. The young man, who, like his three sisters, had never been the picture of robust health, succumbed to pneumonia in January. Victoria wrote her condolences to the Queen. "[T]*he only bright spot in this dark time, is the thought that ... all his life was fair & good, an example to his contemporaries & his people.*"[37]

Just a month before Eddy's death in December of 1891, he had finally got himself engaged to Princess Mary of Teck, known as "May" in the family. Alix, who was no doubt relieved that the pressure was off, wrote: "*Yes, darling Grandmama, I was glad to hear of Eddy's engagement ... I did not write to congratulate* [May], *as we never corresponded & it would have been rather difficult, and I am sure if you thought I ought to have done so, you would have told me.*"[38] May would become a lifelong friend of Victoria's, who wrote to her grandmother in order to congratulate her on the engagement, noting that "*it will be a great load off your mind.*"[39] And it was for a short time. However, with his death, the Queen began her accustomed lamentations about death. "*Was there anything so sad, so tragic* [?]"[40] ... "*When you think that his poor young Bride who had come to spend his birthday with him, came to see him die – ...It would sound unnatural and overdrawn if it was put into a Novel.*"[41]

Alix was now, like everyone else, plunged into mourning. The Queen, however,

---

(*) *A few years after its adoption by the Royal Navy, Victoria was visiting Alix in Russia. They were both aboard one of the Tsar's men-of-war, the Captain showed Nicky his Course Indicator and Victoria exclaimed: "'Why, that is Louis's invention.' The Emperor then said to the Captain: 'That is the instrument which my brother-in-law, Prince Louis of Battenberg, invented,' and the Captain replied that it was found to be so good and useful that the Navy Department were going to order it for all ships." (Kerr, 119).*

never one to take defeat, continued to talk about George of Wales for her. After Eddy's death, George began to look a great deal more attractive, though he was, according to his Grandmother the Queen, *"thin, his hair cut quite short and the merriment gone out of him at present."*[42] He was, at least, intelligent and good-looking, but, also, far more important, because he was now the heir presumptive.

That winter, Grand Duke Ludwig had begun slowly to fail. Initially, there were hopes that he might rally and Victoria wrote to her grandmother: *"I'm happy to say that Papa is so much better...Dr. Eigenbrodt wrote to me, that if he takes a little care of himself the whole thing will pass off without leaving any weakness."*[43] There were even discussions about whether the family would go to Eddy's funeral, but the Doctor had decided that the Grand Duke should not travel, Alix wrote her grandmother, since *"the journey might do him harm, as every great excitement and emotion..."*[44]

Henry, very much wanted to represent both the Prussian Family and his wife at Eddy's funeral, but Willy would not permit it. There was no reason given for this, but Irène was extremely upset. Afterward, oddly enough, Willy, according to Irène, regretted his recalcitrance, and, hoped that Uncle Bertie would understand. She begged the Queen *"not to think too harshly of his Brother* [Willy] *for he was really sorry afterwards not to have sent Harry."*[45] It must have been difficult for Irène to be in the middle of the two families, feeling obliged, as was her tendency, to rationalize Willy's ill-treatment of his mother's family, to her grandmother. It was a tribute to her sanguine nature that she was able to do this, but it must have been a thankless task.

The Grand Duke's condition, which was described as an enlarged heart, began to worsen, and all were gravely concerned. Victoria wrote constant letters to the Queen apprising her of the Grand Duke's health. During this difficult time, as was usual, Victoria was the stalwart of her family. She was, according to Irène, *"the one to whom we go for everything & is the one to keep us all up ... – I cannot imagine what it would have been without her."*[46] She was tired and worn, but always, according to her sister, the one who tried to make sure that all should be as their father might wish. Alix, was, of course, devastated that her one remaining parent was mortally ill. She later wrote, *"It is often so hard & difficult to be brave & quiet when ones heart is bleeding, but one must not let the others notice it, but must try to help them & make them happy."*[47] But the sisters and their brother had to brace for the inevitable.

Any hopes for a cure came to naught when, in March of 1892, the Grand Duke died of heart disease and stroke. *"A dreadful day,"* the Queen remarked in her journal, *"one of those one can hardly write about."*[48] Ludwig had been lonely up until the end, not reconciling himself to losing his daughters to marriage or what he considered his one chance of happiness with Alexandrine de Kolemine.

Ernie was now the Grand Duke of Hesse and by Rhine. An attractive young man of twenty-three, he was completely overwhelmed by work for which he was not yet prepared. Alix, the only sister now remaining at home, was broken-hearted and extremely uncertain as to how to proceed. The Queen, completely aware of the situation wrote: *"Poor darling Ernie, how he is to be pitied with his great youth burdened now with responsibilities, and poor sweet Alicky, without a parent, and I the only one left of the grandparents."*[49] Unfortunately, Alix found it difficult to cope with her new position and sometimes seemed snobbish and hostile though the reality was she was only painfully shy and withdrawn. She had little idea how to make herself appealing. Alix, who was only six when her mother died, did not have the instruction necessary to be the "first lady" of the Grand Duchy. Consequently, she was hardly what the Hessians thought of as a *"Landsmütter."*

Victoria and her brother and sisters were truly orphans now, and once again, plunged into mourning. Victoria kept up the morale of her brother and sisters, always trying to *"cheer & help us ... & to help all to feel comfortable..."*[50] According to Irène, it continued to exhaust her. Queen Victoria, who had considered herself their mother for many years, along with their husbands and children, also provided much comfort, and came to visit the bereft family the following month. It was as painful for the Queen as for the family and she confided to her journal,

> *I could not sleep much and felt very nervous in thinking of Darmstadt... How one missed darling L[udwig], who always used to jump into carriage and welcome us with such joy. Dear Ernie, in plain clothes, and the three poor dear girls, Victoria, Irène, and Alicky, in deepest mourning with long veils, were standing on the platform. ... Ernie and Victoria drove with me, the others following, and we went straight to the poor dear Neues Palais, where we are always so at home.*[51]

While she was in Darmstadt she tried to give Ernie an abbreviated course in ruling. Fortunately, Ernie eventually proved a far more successful ruler than his grandmother and family, had, perhaps, thought he would at the time of his succession. He was a man of great sensitivity and artistic temperament and initiated *"an extremely progressive programme of social and health legislation [as well as] an outstanding patron of science and the arts."*[52] In his youth, he was greatly influenced by the artists of the day, particularly enjoying Art Nouveau. He set aside one of the parks, the Mathildenhöhe, in Darmstadt for up-and-coming architects and artists. There, they were given freedom to design their own houses as well as for others living on the estate. It was called the Darmstadt Artist's Colony, and was made possible not only because of his monetary support but *"also his initiative and enthusiasm."*[53]

It was also around this time that Victoria discovered that she was once again pregnant. Luckily, this pregnancy was unlike her previous one in that she felt vigorous and full of energy. This was all just as well, as the Queen continued her matrimonial musings not just for Alix, but was now focused on Ernie as well. She was convinced, quite rightly, that it was important for the Grand Duchy to have a Grand Duchess, and that Ernie needed the help that a good wife could give. In any event, all could see that Alix with her particular personality was of little use, though she certainly tried to *"do all to help [Ernie], as his life will not be so easy for him now, and he is still so young. I only wish I were as clever as Victoria, as then I could be of far more use to him..."*[54] Victoria also tried to help with, perhaps, better results, by taking over the presidency of the group her mother began, the Alice Frauen Verein. But, her peripatetic ways made it crucial to eventually give this office to someone who would be present and could handle it full-time.

As the summer came, there was much thought and discussion between the Queen and her confidantes, particularly with Victoria. The main thought now was that perhaps one of the Edinburgh cousins might do for Ernie. True, they were first cousins, however, the Queen consulted with her physician, Sir William Jenner, who seemed to feel that there would be no problems with such a union. Victoria was relieved at this prognosis, telling the Queen, *"I am very glad Sir W. Jenner does not seem to think it would be unwise of Erny [sic] to marry one of the Edinburgh cousins for the responsibility of giving life to delicate or sickly children is very grave."*[55] Victoria must have felt this very strongly.

The cousin, however, would not be the oldest girl, Missy, who, at the very tender age of sixteen, was betrothed to Ferdinand, heir to the throne of Romania. The Queen was surprised at the announcement, *"We have been much startled lately to hear of Missy's Engagement to Ferdinand of Rumania. He is nice I believe & the Parents are charming – but the Country is very insecure & the immorality of the Society at Bucharest quite awful."*[56] Alix, who, herself, was about twenty, was astonished about her little cousin's engagement. Quite rightly she felt that, *"[s]he is still so very young, almost a Baby..."*[57] After this surprising news, the Queen was more eager than ever to secure one of the Edinburgh cousins for Ernie. Especially, since Marie's engagement was another matrimonial disappointment.*

Victoria gave this scant attention as fall came to the Heiligenberg. She was more interested in appointing Alice's first governess – Miss Robson, who had been the governess of her Cousin Margaret of Connaught. There were also visitors of note. Cousin George of Wales came to visit and remarked upon it in his diary: *"Louis met us at the station & drove us to his pretty place Jugenheim, where we found Victoria & her two dear little girls Alice & Louise. We had tea & they showed me over the house. ... They showed me their collection of Naval medals which was most interesting."*[58] But more exciting for Victoria was that her beloved sister Ella was coming, and expected to be in Darmstadt in the beginning of November, while she was awaiting the birth of her next child.

On November 6, 1892, Victoria gave birth to her first son. Coming just a little more than six months after the death of her father, it was especially emotional for her. The baby was born at the Old Schloss in Darmstadt, and named for his Cousin George of Wales, Aunt Vicky of Prussia as well as Victoria's father and her two brothers-in-law, Serge and Henry. So, he was George Louis Victor Henry Serge, but the family called him "Georgie." Near the end of the month, when Victoria was fit, she wrote, thanking her grandmother for her congratulations on the birth of her thirteenth great-grandchild:

> *The baby seems a strong, healthy child & is a source of the greatest pleasure & interest to his sisters. Louis left us yesterday & hopes to see you soon, when he will be able to tell you all about me & the child. I am so pleased and proud he has got this appointment & trust I shall be able to be a good deal with him in England to have the pleasure of seeing you from time to time.*[59]

Indeed, Louis had been appointed Naval Advisor to War Office, Chief Secretary to joint Naval and Military Committee of Defense. Victoria was no doubt sorry to leave their base in Malta, but the family would return there often. They rented a house in London at 37 Eccleston Square, Pimlico. The house was inexpensive and Victoria thought it very unfashionable, however it had the great advantage of being walking distance from Buckingham Palace and the Queen.

Among other reasons, Louis was appointed to this position because of his great tact. The British had begun to worry about the German threat and the Kaiser's jealousy of the Royal Navy. Louis' superiors were aware that the Kaiser was always indiscreet with him, showing him drawings of battleships and constantly boasting about his Navy and his plans. Louis was invited to inspect ships of the German Manoeuver Squadron of the North Sea and he wrote a report to the admiralty about this and all else he had learned from his incautious cousin.

(*) *Marie's father, the Duke of Edinburgh, had hoped that Marie and Prince George of Wales might marry. His wife, however, would not have any of it. Marie Alexandrovna did not want her daughters future to be England.*

Christmas of that year was spent with the family at Osborne. It was doubtless here that Victoria and her grandmother had further discussions of what began to be a constant theme – a match for Ernie. However, now the field was narrowed to just one – Victoria Melita, little Ducky of Edinburgh.

Chapter VII

December 1893 – June 1896

The Queen relished the idea of Ducky's marrying Ernie for several reasons. She felt that they had a great deal in common: their sense of humor, musical tastes and both were extremely artistic. And, as if to clinch the matter, they shared the same birthday. However, while Ernie was quiet and sensitive, Ducky was a strong, painfully honest, passionate and fearless person. She was a girl of extremely high spirits and, Ernie, with Alix, still in the depths of mourning, was hardly used to such a volatile and large personality. Nevertheless, the Queen was captivated with the idea, and lobbied for it persistently. As in the past, her modus operandi was to enlist other members of the family to facilitate her plans.

> *You will be seeing dear Uncle Arthur & A[un]t Louischen tomorrow & on Saturday I think Uncle Alfred A[un]t Marie & the girls & Alfred will be coming & I am very anxious that shl[ou]d hint to Ernie to be very kind & posé [level headed] & not tease Ducky or make silly jokes, wh[ich] might destroy our hopes & wishes – I know you understand what I mean. He has doubtless shewn you the copy of what I wrote to Uncle A[rthur] last week also of what Sir Wm. Jenner wrote.[1]*

Before he had died, the Grand Duke, had expressed an interest in the match, and Victoria talked to Ernie about it as well. Evidently, Dr. Eigenbrodt, their physician in Darmstadt, was not of the same opinion as Sir William Jenner. He did not like the idea of such closely related people marrying – for that matter, neither did Victoria. She wrote to Ernie in the strongest terms:

> *If [Dr. Eigenbrodt] has other reasons besides the fear of an illness like Uncle Leo's against our family especially intermarrying it would be well to know them – for I think it is one of the duties of a man in your position especially, to try & have healthy descendants & I know besides from experience that to see ones children not quite strong, or with some little ailment like Alice hearing, is a cause of worry & pain to the parents.*

> *...I hope you won't think I am fussing you, but I so fear the newspapers will soon be discussing engagements between you & Ducky & then Grandmama etc. & Uncle Affie will again try to hurry you ... so do please seriously think the question of relationship over once more so that if in the end you do marry Ducky you may not later have to reproach yourself at having done so without careful consideration.[2]*

Once, again, however, the family provided some distraction. Cousin George of Wales had proved to be as unappealing to Alix as Cousin Eddy had been. Fate and propinquity took a hand, and he took for his bride, the fiancée of his elder brother, Princess May of Teck. The wedding was set for the beginning of July and was the subject of intense letter writing. *"The wedding,"* Victoria told Ernie, *"is to take place ... in the Chapel Royal at St. James Palace.*

It will be a quiet one, as poor Aunt Alix could not bear a big one. The Wales girls, Thora*, & Edinburghs, Ena**, Alice Albany*** (& if now on account of her grandfather's death she cannot probably our Alice) will be the bridesmaids."[3] Ernie was to usher Queen Victoria in the procession.

Louis and Victoria were now in another rented house, Undercliff House, Sandgate, Folkestone. During most of that summer, they went up and down from town attending lunches, dinners and eventually the festivities leading up to the royal wedding. Of the luminaries attending the wedding, representing the Tsar, was his son, Nicky. No doubt he was extremely disappointed that Alix had elected not to go to the wedding since she wished to avoid meeting him again. Nevertheless, romance was in the air, since Ducky and Ernie had a chance to meet again.

The most interesting part for Victoria, however, was that her daughter, Alice, though Alice of Albany did, in the end, attend, was also asked to be a bridesmaid. She was developing into a very pretty child and held her own against the equally lovely Connaught sisters. After the wedding, there continued social events in which the family participated. Again there were dinners, lunches, and musical evenings. The highlight of which took place some days afterwards. At Windsor, the remaining guests were treated to a performance of two one-act operas, *L'Amico Fritz* and *Cavalleria Rusticana* conducted by their composer, Pietro Mascagni.

Later that summer, on August 22, Ernest II, Duke of Saxe-Coburg & Gotha died at Reinhardsbrunn at the age of seventy-five. He was the brother of Queen Victoria's beloved Albert, the Prince Consort. Though the Queen thought her brother-in-law and husband extremely dissimilar, his death was the end of yet another of the Queen's generation, and most especially, a precious link to Albert. Victoria was sensitive as to how this death might impact her. *"I am sure that the death of dear Grandpapa's brother will have much grieved you...The change will be a great one to Uncle Affie & Aunt Marie..."*[4] for the Edinburghs were the heirs to the Duchy of Saxe-Coburg & Gotha and would now have to take up residence in Coburg.

Victoria went back to Darmstadt in the fall and spent a great deal of time with Ernie and Alix. Unquestionably, they were discussing the matrimonial prospects that both were entertaining, and in Ernie's case, getting a great deal of prodding from the Queen. *"I have written twice to Ernie ab*[ou]*t The necessity of his showing some attention & interest. Pray tell it him & say he must answer me. – Aunt Marie fears he no longer wishes it, wh*[ich] *I am sure is not the case. Georgie lost Missy by waiting & waiting."*[5]****

Meanwhile, Victoria was concentrating on the Alice Frauen Verein. Since Alix could not manage, it was necessary for Victoria, even when living in England, to try to keep it all under control and to inform Ernie about what the Central Committee intended to do about a myriad of issues. *"I enclose a letter I have just received from Frl. Winter of the hospital; as she explains better than I could, the hopes & wishes the Verein entertains regarding the new street which is to pass through the Mathilden Höhe [sic] – ... If it is possible not to*

(*) *Princess Helena Victoria of Schleswig-Holstein-Sonderburg-Augustenburg, daughter of Prince Christian and Princess Helena, Queen Victoria's daughter.*
(**) *Princess Victoria Eugenie of Battenberg, daughter of Henry of Battenberg and Princess Beatrice, Queen Victoria's youngest daughter.*
(***) *Princess Alice of Albany, daughter of Prince Leopold, Duke of Albany, and Princess Helene of Waldeck and Pyrmont.*
(****) *The reality was that George of Wales, who was indeed interested in Missy of Edinburgh, lost her because her mother did not wish Missy to marry anyone from England.*

*lay the street so very near to the house..."*⁶ Later in the letter, after talking about who was appointed Secretary of the Central Committee, she made a telling remark: *"I am so sorry you have to lead such a lonely monotonous life – but hope it may not be for long – if you get a nice wife, that will make a great difference in many ways."*⁷

As the year got old, Victoria and Louis had more personal worries. Louise, who was now a delicate four-year-old, had a glandular problem in her throat that necessitated an operation. Her physician was Sir Frederick Treves, who would later operate on Uncle Bertie of Wales when he suffered from appendicitis. Louise recovered, however, in November of that year, Sandro of Bulgaria died in Graz. The family had known that he was ill, and the Queen wrote in her journal,

> *No more news of dear Sandro early, but whist we were having luncheon before one, Liko telegraphed that they feared the worst, and that he was starting this afternoon – L[ouis], having hurt his eye, being unable to accompany him. ... [Beatrice] came in saying, 'He is gone.' She is much distressed, and feels so much for the whole family. Dear, noble, charming, splendid Sandro to be snatched away like this at thirty-six, just when there was every reason to expect he would rise very high and play a great part in the future.*⁸

All were shocked and unhappy at this sad turn of events. On November 20, at Windsor, there was a memorial service held for the Prince. Louis and his family received numerous condolences, including one from Ella, who wrote from Russia,

> *We were dreadfully <u>pained</u> receiving Ernie's telegram how deeply you must feel the sudden shock...as you know what real affection we had for dear Sandro. We had a funeral service for him yesterday in our little church. ...Poor boy his was not a happy life I fear & it would give you pleasure to hear with what sympathy all speak of him here – of course there were mistakes on both sides & the choice of the people sent him from here was disastrous like all clever will acknowledge.*9

Irène felt deeply saddened by his death, and related to her grandmother how Willy had seen Sandro in Austria and had acted toward him. This was yet another case of her trying to justify the Kaiser's bad behavior, going on to mention how kind his wife, Dona, had been in telling her the sad news. She continued,

> *Indeed, I also felt poor Sandro's death deeply, he had always been so kind & dear to me – & it was so horribly sudden. [It is a] ...comfort...to know that his now poor, forlorn wife <u>really</u> made him <u>happy</u>...Aunt Vicky does not like to hear that his poor wife made him happy – ...if only young Vicky had never seen him it would have spared him much sorrow.*¹⁰

Victoria, who had expected a great deal from her brother-in-law when he was ruler of Bulgaria, was now much more sympathetic. The Bulgarians wanted their Prince back, and he was buried in Sofia. They also provided pensions for his children. Victoria wrote *"it is sad that poor Sandro now can never know, that his many trials & difficulties during his troubled reign served to so greatly endear him to his people."*¹¹

****

The family spent Christmas with the Queen at Osborne. As the year went out, there were further discourses about Ernie and Ducky and their engagement. As Queen Victoria's arguments became more urgent, those in Darmstadt, at last, took notice. Ernie had visited Ducky in Coburg and it began to look as though he would finally and decisively come to the point. Alix wrote to her grandmother saying that it was wonderful for Ernie to be engaged, but she was surely feeling a little *"de trop."*[12] Victoria, however, never feeling 'de trop', now felt impelled to dole out a little sage matrimonial advice to her brother.

> *I feel almost sure she will ... depend very much on you – for in marriage, if it is to be a really happy one – both people must learn to understand each other – and when the wife is still so young, she will continue to develop very much as the husband influences her – and that will not happen suddenly but by imperceptible degrees as each grows to know the other better and to see and tolerate lovingly the faults that every human being naturally has!*[13]

In the beginning of the New Year, events came to their conclusion. Ernie proposed to Ducky and was accepted, and on January 10, the betrothal was officially announced. A truly luke-warm affair, though, both were certainly devoted friends, who enjoyed each other's company and hoped that their marriage would work. Victoria wasted no time in writing her congratulations and to *"[g]ive my best love to all & tell Uncle Affie I don't forget how in '87, the first winter I was at Malta, he pointed out Duckie [sic] to me one day in the garden of San Antonio & said: that is the future Grand Duchess of Hesse I hope!"*[14]

Perhaps, it was not a good omen that Ernie needed so much prodding and encouragement to propose to Ducky. The match, so energetically promoted by the Queen, would be, as she herself would later say, the last attempt at such a pursuit. Victoria, level-headed and sensible as she was, was happy to see that her brother had found a life companion to assuage his loneliness. Knowing the personalities, tastes, and dispositions of both the young people as she did, she may have had pause – and not just for health reasons.

Nevertheless, for Victoria and her sisters, family gatherings were a cause for rejoicing. They loved seeing family, and were always thrilled when they could get together, dispersed as they were, for talks and advice, as in the old days. Though Aunt Marie of Coburg didn't approve of marriage between first cousins*, this was her first big family gathering as the Duchess of Saxe-Coburg and Gotha, and it would be, as the newspapers called it, another 'Wedding of the Decade.' Despite the Duchess's reservations, the rest of the family was delighted with the match and all the 'Royal Mob' – the Romanovs, the Hohenzollerns, many various Germans, Uncle Bertie of Wales, and of course, Queen Victoria – came together in April of 1894 for the event.

The family was to gather at the Schloss Ehrenburg, the town residence of the Dukes of Saxe-Coburg & Gotha, naturally, in the center of town. Coburg was another one of those beautifully quaint German market towns, surrounded by hills, and a great many castles. There was the fortress - the Coburg Citadel, called the Veste, as well as the Schloss Rosenau, where the Prince Consort spent much of his youth, and the Schloss Callenberg, the hunting lodge of the family. Schloss Ehrenburg was a lovely palace without the wedding-cake look of some of the other castles in Germany. It sat on a square where the children of the town played.

Victoria had spent those few months after the January announcement of Ernie's

---

(*) *Marriage between first cousins was forbidden in the Russian Orthodox Church.*

engagement, at the Eccleston Square house in London. However, before she left to attend the wedding, she and Louis rented a charming house in the country, Elm Grove, at Walton-on-Thames. They would keep this house until the end of summer when they returned to Darmstadt.

As the month of the wedding drew near, there was a great deal of activity. The Queen had already left, spending some time in Florence before coming to Coburg, and Victoria, stopped in Darmstadt on her way to the wedding.

Upon their arrival, Louis and Victoria were lodged at the Villa Coburg in the palace park, and the following day, Queen Victoria arrived. That evening, April 17, there was a torch-light serenade at Schloss Ehrenburg. Afterwards, the family went into a candlelight dinner, in the Thronsaal, and dined to the sublime music of Mendelssohn and Wagner.[15] Ducky and Ernie were married several days later, on April 19, 1894, during a ceremony unique in that it was attended, as *The Times* pointed out, by four generations of the British Royal Family: The Queen, her daughter, Aunt Vicky of Prussia, her daughter, Princess Charlotte of Saxe-Meiningen, and, finally, the Queen's great-granddaughter, Princess Feodora of Saxe-Meiningen. Nevertheless, the great drama was not focused on these eminent attendees or even the matrimonial event, but on a completely different pair of lovers.

Alix and Nicky of Russia became the main interest during the days leading up to the wedding and several days afterward. Nicky had taken this opportunity to strenuously court Alix, and try to persuade her to marry him. The big problem for Alix was that she could not conceive of converting from Lutheranism to Russian Orthodoxy. It was a tremendous mental struggle for her that had not been much eased by Ella doing so several years before. Since a Tsarina of Russia had to be Russian Orthodox, for Alix, the idea of marriage appeared to be impossible.

Strangely, as the young woman's resolve began to weaken, it was the combined arguments of Kaiser Wilhelm II, and Ella, who were able to convince her about conversion to the Russian Orthodox faith, and that this was the right course. More than likely, Ella's own experience and her constant assurances that the faiths had marked similarities with which Alix could live, were more compelling than Wilhelm's bombastic political arguments.

****

There exists a famous set of photographs that were taken during the wedding festivities. It seemed as if there were more Queen Victoria descendants and crowned heads, crowded on steps at the rear of the Edinburgh Palais, in order to mark the occasion, than ever before. The Queen wrote that *"in the garden, the whole of our large family party were photographed by English, as well as German photographers. Many groups were taken, and some of me with Vicky and my three sons and Wil[helm]."*[16] The principal photographer was the Coburg court photographer, Professor Uhlenhut. He took many of the pictures and had about thirty of the guests sitting in all kinds of poses and combination. These photographs were circulated all over Europe, and are in nearly every book about Queen Victoria ever published.

For the most famous sitting, there was the Queen, surrounded by Aunt Vicky, Kaiser Wilhelm, the Edinburghs, the Hesse sisters with their husbands, and as many of the Aunts and Uncles, and Cousins who could attend – and who could fit in the picture.

Standing in the crowd, next to Alix, was her new fiancé, Nicholas of Russia.

All the discussions that had gone back and forth during the previous day, as well as all the advice given from sisters, and most assuredly unwanted guidance from Cousin Willy, had helped Alix make her decision. Most important, in Nicky's case, there were desperate entreaties to capitulate and consent, since he was deeply in love with Alix. Obviously, it was an agonizing time for the young woman. However, after everyone had had their say in the matter, Nicky proposed to her for a second time, and she said 'yes.' As in all the other cases, the Queen was philosophical:

Breakfasted alone with Beatrice. Soon after Ella came in, much agitated, to say that Alicky and Nicky were engaged, and begging they might come in. I was quite thunderstruck, as, though I knew Nicky much wished it, I thought Alicky was not sure of her mind. Saw them both. Alicky had tears in her eyes, but looked very bright and I kissed them both. Nicky said "She is much too good for me." I told him he must make the religious difficulties as easy as he could for her, which he promised to do. People generally seem pleased at the engagement, which as the drawback that Russia is so far away, the position a difficult one, as well as the question of religion. But, as her brother is married now, and they are really attached to one another, it is perhaps better so.[17]

It is also possible that the Queen thought that the engagement might improve relations between England and Russia.

Almost immediately after the wedding, as had been the custom for all her Hessian granddaughters, Alix left for Windsor in order to spend her last single days with her grandmother. Queen Victoria felt deeply obligated to instruct the young woman regarding her immense responsibilities as the Tsarina. There were the issues of leading such a public life, and because she was going to Russia, the very important security matters, as well as long discussions about family, health and court protocol. In addition, Alix was learning Russian and being instructed in Russian Orthodoxy by Father John Yanishev. In her typical manner, she took very strongly to Russian Orthodoxy.

During her stay, Alix intended to go to Harrogate, just west of York, for a cure as she suffered greatly from sciatica, and wanted her legs cured before the wedding. Taking the alias of Baroness Starckenburg, she stayed in at the spa town for nearly a month, hoping that she would benefit from the baths and drinking the waters there. Alix brought her tutors with her so that she was able to continue being instructed in religion and the Russian language. As Alix learned more about her new religion, there is little doubt that it had a great appeal since she had inherited her mother's love of mysticism.

In June, Victoria and Alice joined her for a portion of the visit and the two sisters amused themselves racing around in bath chairs. Alix enjoyed her stay, living, as she noted, for the first time, in a house, and emphatically expressing the desire that all treat her as an ordinary woman. Though the object of unwanted publicity during her visit, she was delighted to be asked to be godmother to her landlady's twins, christened Nicholas and Alexandra.[18]

Victoria could not fail to see how much happier her sister was now that her future was settled and she was going to marry the man she loved. She wrote to her grandmother 1894:

If you could see, as I do, what a great difference Alicky's engagement to the man she has so long been devoted to, has made in her – how much brighter & happier she really is, you would feel that there is one great good in this engagement, which must counterbalance many of those disadvantages you mention – & that is the deep & sincere love that Alix & Nicky will begin their married life with – & you, who better than any one else, know the difficulties and penalties attached to a high position, know too by experience, the great blessing that sincere love between husband & wife is to all...As to living in Russia – it is not as if she were going quite among strangers for Ella is there too...[T]he nihilists there are really not more dangerous than the anarchists we have in the rest of Europe.[19]

As the future wife of the Heir to the Russian Imperial Throne, Alix was inundated with invitations to balls, dinners, and parties, however, the Queen was adamant that this to be a quiet time for the young woman. She was explicit in directions that Alix was to partake in no amusements, but most especially not with the Marlborough House set with Uncle Bertie and Aunt Alix.

Victoria, along with Louis, followed the others back to England at the end of May. They were at their house in Walton-on-the-Thames, and Victoria seemed to be the main recipient of complaints, mostly from Uncle Bertie and Aunt Alix, that Alix was not able to freely visit all family members. Victoria, in turn, tactfully wrote to her grandmother that perhaps this wasn't exactly the right course since Alix had visited their Aunt Helena and Uncle Christian of Schleswig-Holstein. *"I trust you will forgive me for mentioning it,"* she began, *"but I hear Uncle Bertie & Aunt Alix are much grieved, that you did not allow Ali[x] to go to them ... – they are distressed that she may visit other relations & not them."*[20]

Once again, however, the Queen was unwavering. This was to be a time that Alix could convalesce, learn about Russia, its religion and customs, and above all, to attempt, with her grandmother's help, to comprehend the position into which she was being thrust. Alix spent much time reassuring her grandmother that her new role, though

full of trials and difficulties, ...with God's help & that of a loving husband it will be easier than we now picture it to ourselves...I cling to you more than ever now that I am quite an orphan...Please do not think that my marrying will make a difference in my love to you – certainly it will not, and when I am far away, I shall long to think that there is one, the dearest and kindest woman alive who loves me a little bit.[21]

Queen Victoria continued to have her doubts on the wisdom of this marriage and Alix's capabilities in handling her tremendous position. She brooded about it, and was quite angered at those, particularly Ella, whom she thought ought to have discouraged Alix instead of persuading her to say 'yes'. She wrote to Victoria in a most prescient fashion that

[a]ll my fears about her future marriage now show themselves so strongly & my blood runs cold when I think of her so young most likely placed on that very unsafe Throne, her dear life & above all her Husband's constantly threatened...It is a great additional anxiety in my declining years!...[Alix] has no Parents and I am her only Grandparent and feel I have a claim on her! She is like my own Child as you all are my dear Children but she and he* are orphans.[22]

(*) *This was written when it seemed likely that Alexander III was mortally ill.*

After leaving Harrogate, Alix went to stay with Victoria and Louis at Walton-on-Thames in their little house. It was an idyllic life, and near the end of June, Nicholas arrived on the Imperial Yacht, the *Polar Star*, to join the party. The engaged couple were openly affectionate toward one another, and mostly unchaperoned. It would be the last time in their lives together that they could be completely private and themselves. Certainly when they left the house to see the Queen, open demonstrations of such a nature, would never be permitted, since she disliked it so much.

Victoria read one of her beloved Marion Crawford* novels to the couple, during those few peaceful days, all, of course, over much too soon. As Victoria later wrote, "[T] *his private intermezzo came to an end and we four were fetched by a Royal carriage with an outrider to go to Windsor much to the surprise of the Waltonians, who never realized who the important people stopping with us had been.*"23

An unprecedented event for the Empire happened during Alix and Nicky's stay at the little house at Walton. On June 23, George of Wales' wife, Princess May, gave birth at White Lodge, Richmond Park, to her first child – a boy, who would now be in line for the throne of England, and would be known as David. Later, of course, he would be Edward VIII, and briefly King, until his abdication to marry Wallis Simpson. But on that June day, the possibilities of such a debacle would have been so remote as to be considered ridiculous. Certainly not when one of the Queen's granddaughters was about to marry the Tsar of all the Russias and rule over one of the largest empires the world had ever known.

It was a landmark event in English history there were three living heirs to the throne.

****

Victoria, her family, and Alix finally left England at the end of July. It was a little sad for the Queen, who wrote, a trifle wistfully, "[t]*ook leave with the greatest regret of darling Ali*[x], *whom I had watched over since May.*"24 The sisters spent the rest of the summer at the Heiligenberg, enlivened by a visit from Irène and her family. As fall was approaching, the news from Russia was ominous. It appeared that Alexander III, only in his late forties, was seriously ill. He was suffering from kidney disease – nephritis, a malady that could lead to kidney failure at anytime. By October, Nicholas summoned Alix to be with him at his father's deathbed.

This necessitated a 'mad dash' for Victoria, Alix, accompanied by Orchie, to Warsaw, where Ella waited to escort the young princess the rest of the way to Livadia, in the Crimea. Evidently, since Ella was meeting her in Warsaw, Ernie decided it was not necessary for him to accompany the two women. Irène explained to her grandmother that though he would not be going, she was happy that Victoria was attending their sister since she had "*never seen anyone have such a way of cheering & helping on in distress like Victoria.*"25 As the Tsar had become worse, with little hope of recovery, the doctors recommended that he go to a climate that would be more temperate. They had suggested Corfu, but it is probable that he was aware that he had very little time, and had no wish to die anywhere but Russia, and therefore their villa in Livadia was chosen.

The two women arrived at Simferopol, where Nicky and Serge met them. Alix and Nicky were overjoyed to be together again, though the circumstances were dire. Indeed, as the days wore on Alexander III's condition worsened. Some days he would be restless, and the family would be called every couple of hours for last rites. At other times, he would sleep through the night and the family would become optimistic again.

It was a roller coaster existence. However, about ten days after Alix arrived, on November 2, the family was again called to the drawing room where Alexander III was given Holy Communion while sitting in an armchair. This time, according to accounts, he kissed his wife, and after a few light convulsions, he died. Nicky and his family immediately burst into tears. Alix was a witness to Nicholas' nearly paralyzing fear of what was to come, and between sobs, Nicky had said, "*what am I going to do? I am not prepared to be a Tsar.*" His father's lack of foresight in providing the needed training and Nicky's lack of readiness dogged him for the rest of his life. The truth was neither of the young people was ready for the grave responsibilities that lay ahead.

Alix was accepted into the Orthodox faith, and was, for a week, Grand Duchess Alexandra Feodorovna. Initially, Alix had wanted to take Catherine as her Russian name, however, it was preferred that she take the name of Nicky's great-grandmother, the wife of the first Tsar Nicholas. So she, too, became Alexandra. *The Times* of London saw Alix as a strong and intelligent woman, evidenced by the fact that she insisted that certain ceremonies, which she felt might be offensive to her Hessian family and her former religion, were omitted from the process. The newspaper saw this as evidence that Alix had a great deal of influence on her husband, which was predictive of *The Times*, to say the least.[26]

A few weeks after the death of the Emperor, on November 26, Nicky and Alix were married. The event took place in the Chapel of the Winter Palace and although mourning was discarded for this one day, the atmosphere was grave. It was another one of those weddings in the family that had a funereal atmosphere. According to the reports, there were possibly eight thousand people present at the palace. It must have been a great comfort to Alix that some of her family: George of Wales, Uncle Bertie, Uncle Affie, Aunt Marie, and most importantly, Ernie, were in attendance.

Nicky, arriving before Alix was dressed in the uniform of the Hussars of the Lifeguard. Having taken over an hour just to put on her dress, she arrived at the ceremony wearing a tiara and the same wedding crown that Ella wore on her head, and her hair arranged down, in curls, over both her shoulders. She wore a dress of silver brocade tissue edged with fur over stiff petticoats. Her Imperial mantle was cloth-of-gold bordered in ermine. She was adorned with orders and brooches and ropes of pearls, and from every report, looked breathtakingly beautiful. However, the entire outfit was so heavy that Alix moved with great difficulty.

The ceremony took about an hour, and after kneeling for prayers, Alix became the Empress of Russia. The couple changed into traveling clothes, stopping at Nicholas' mother, the now Dowager Empress Marie Feodorovna's palace, the Anichkov Palace. She welcomed them as Serge and Ella had been welcomed nearly ten years before, with salt and bread. The Grand Duchess of Hesse, Ducky, did not come to the wedding since she was fairly far-gone with her first pregnancy. That evening, Ernie, who was also at the palace, ate supper with the newlywed couple.

Immediately following, and with no ceremony whatsoever, they went up to their bedrooms. Though they never had an official honeymoon, it could be said that their entire marriage was a honeymoon. Through all their travails, their one great and enduring love and loyalty was steadfastly to one another. Alix described her wedding and the subsequent days to Victoria:

The ceremony in church reminded me so much of '84*, only both our fathers were missing – that was fearful – no kiss, no blessing from either. But I cannot speak about that day nor of all the sad ceremonies before. One's feelings you can imagine. One day in deepest mourning, lamenting a beloved one, the next in smartest clothes being married. There cannot be a great contrast, but it drew us more together, if possible. Aunt Minny is so sweet and patient in her great grief. She touches one with her gentleness. To-day was again a hard day, the fortieth day at the fortress. We two have just now been for five days at Zarskoe [sic], alone with a lady and gentleman, the rest and quiet did one good. We walked and drove and enjoyed the beautiful country air. Here we get out but little, as Nicky sees people almost all day and then has to read through his papers and to write. Only tea we have together, all the other meals upstairs with the rest. I cannot yet realize that I am married, living here with the others, it seems like being on a visit. ...

It was horrid saying goodbye to dear ones when they left again for home – poor Gretchen!** But one must not think of that. For my Nicky's sake I must be good, so as to cheer him up.

If I could find words to tell you of my happiness – daily it grows more and my love greater. Never can I thank God enough for having given me such a treasure.[27]

In spite of her great personal content, Alix gave birth to four daughters, and lived in constant fear of not producing the necessary male heir. Unlike her sister Ella, who had learned to get along with the Romanovs and was a great favorite, Alix was completely different. Because of her extreme shyness, she made a negative impression on her 'in-laws'. She loved a quiet family life and felt strongly that it was necessary to keep her husband and children away from a majority of the other Romanovs who were in her opinion, completely degenerate, and worse, undutiful. Obviously, this attitude did not endear her to the Imperial Family, who had many other grievances against the Empress as well.

Nevertheless, those early days were blissfully content. Alix kept in constant touch with Victoria, who, unhappily, was unable to attend her sister's wedding. Instead, she joined Louis at Malta. Over that winter, however, she had many letters from Alix, talking about her new life in St. Petersburg. So much was different yet, she never *"thought one could be as happy as I am now, life is so different to what it was in the past – tho' there are many difficulties, & all is not easy where one comes first into a new country & has to speak another language..."*[28] There is a wistfulness about her former life, a sadness that she is not home with her father to celebrate Christmas, but in the end, she was completely happy.

****

Though Victoria and her children continued living in Malta through some of 1895, she nevertheless, appeared to dispense much advice to the Darmstadt newlyweds. Ernie, though interested in his mother's charities, had thought that once he was married, his wife would take up the performance of the duties at the Alice Frauen Verein. However, this was not the case, and Victoria continued to pick up the slack, asking Ernie about the

---

(*) *Serge and Ella's wedding.*
(**) *Alix's Maid of Honor, Baroness Margarethe Olga von Fabrice.*

appointment of the Central Committee and advising him. *"I know you take a real interest in the work dear Mama began & in the hospital built as a memorial to her & that its welfare is safe in the hands of its 'protector'."*[29]

Ducky, however, did fulfill her duties as a wife, when on March 11, 1895, she gave birth to their daughter, Princess Elisabeth of Hesse and by Rhine. The little girl was born in the Neues Palais and from that time until her untimely death at the age of eight from a rare form of ambulatory typhoid, the little girl was a particular favorite of the Hessian people. Queen Victoria was thrilled at this new great-grandchild, but very unhappy with Ducky and Ernie. It seems that over a year in to their marriage, they had still not sent out 'thank you' notes for their wedding presents. Indeed the couple didn't seem to answer correspondence even from their Grandmother. Victoria was entreated to intercede. *"I do wish you c[ou]ld get Ernie to be less neglectful in answering letters and telegrams....[H]e is neglectful even to me I have to send message on message by telegram....Do, I entreat you do what you can to make him more punctual & more attentive."*[30]

The Queen visited Ducky and Ernie in Darmstadt in April and saw the new baby. What she didn't know was that the couple was already having problems. The following month, Victoria visited Jugenheim where Ernie and Ducky brought their new baby Elisabeth with them, which *"for a time eased the situation between [Ernie and Ducky]."*[31]

****

No such problems were associated with Alix and Nicholas, whose marriage continued to and would always be a true meeting of minds and hearts. Queen Victoria wrote: *"How impossible it seems that gentle little simple Ali[x] should be the great Empress of Russia."* However, by the time of the coronation of Nicholas and Alexandra in May of 1896, *"gentle little simple"* Alix had not only been a wife for over a year, but was the mother of a daughter, Olga, who had been born in December 1895. More important, she was now in the throes of planning this momentous occasion.

There were two deaths in the family before the big event. Victoria's mother-in-law, Aunt Julie, Princess of Battenberg, sweet, but always resolute and determined, died in the early fall of 1895 at Heiligenberg. She was a woman who always put her sons and daughter first and was tremendously ambitious for them. The Princess did everything in her limited power to make sure that their unequal birth would not hinder them. Queen Victoria, who loved the Battenberg children, loved and respected their mother as well. Perhaps this was because Princess Julie never put herself forward in a way that would cause anyone else discomfort about her less than royal origins. She was admired for this tact, especially by the Queen. Victoria's daughter Alice was very close to her grandmother, having spent a great deal of time with her, and missed her tremendously. After Princess Julie's death, Victoria and Louis sold their town residence in Darmstadt, the Alexanderpalais. The property, which was later destroyed, eventually housed a Post Office. Alix sent a sympathy letter which summed up the feelings now that both of Louis' parents were gone.

What a homecoming! Words are too poor to express all I feel for you in this great sorrow, & I can only pray for God to give you strength and comfort – What a loss! the dear old house quite broken up now! And that you should have been too far away when that woeful news came! Poor Marie must be quite broken-hearted – it will do her good to see you, I am sure. It is so hard being far away, & knowing you all in such sadness – written words are so cold & cannot convey the sympathy one wishes to show, – so I shall not write any more today.[32]

In late 1895, King Prempeh of Kumasi was engaged in raiding the Gold Coast for slaves. Appealing directly to the war office for permission, Louis' brother, Liko, Prince Henry of Battenberg, left England to join the Ashanti Expedition in West Africa. Though Prince Henry and Princess Beatrice had made an agreement to live with Queen Victoria without an establishment of their own, Henry, particularly, was becoming increasingly restless with this living arrangement. Having obtained the permission, Queen Victoria had no choice but to also permit the relatively young man to accompany the expedition. Undoubtedly, the primary concern for the Queen, besides being left without the man of the house, was the disease and peril in the path of such an undertaking.

On December 27, the Prince joined a column of men marching inland. The Queen's reluctance proved prophetic, since he contracted malaria. His health was, according to the doctors, improving and he was put aboard a ship, the *HMS Blonde* in order to sail for home. However, the improvement was only temporary and he died off the coast of Sierra Leone. Since they did not have burial facilities at sea, they were forced to put the body in a coffin made of biscuit tins and filled with rum. Oddly enough, some people found this morbidly humorous. Others however, reacted much differently. *"What a horrible thing the death of poor Henry Battenberg! He has given his life for a country where he is not loved at all. It is very sad."*[33] Closer to home, the Queen lamented that *"[t]he sunbeam in our Home is gone."*[34]

He was buried on the Isle of Wight. Henry's sad and untimely death left Beatrice alone with three sons and a daughter. One of the sons was a hemophiliac, and only one of the three survived to marry. Their daughter Victoria Eugenie ("Ena") became Queen of Spain when she married Alfonso XIII in 1906. Sadly, she, too, would carry on the hemophilia gene into the next generation.

****

December 14, 1895, the sad, old Queen noted in her journal, *"[t]his terrible anniversary returned for the thirty-fourth time. When I went to my dressing-room found telegrams saying that dear May had been safely delivered of a son at three this morning. Georgie's first feeling was regret that this dear child should be born on such a sad day. I have a feeling it may be a blessing for the dear little boy, and may be looked upon as a gift from God!"*[35] The birth of the boy who would later become George VI, but known in the family as "Bertie" provided, perhaps, some relief. Maybe it would be possible that this significant date could now have a joyous connotation – the birth of the fourth living heir to the British Throne.

The whirl of life continued into the year of the last coronation of Imperial Russia. Henry and Irène bought a picturesque property called Schloss Hemmelmarck in Eckernförde located near Kiel, Holstein, which would become their permanent home. The Empress Friedrich described the house as a nice sized property with a barn and large woods around the place. However, she thought it rough, but noted that Henry and Irène loved it – it gave them *"perfect liberty."*[36] Rumors circulated about Serge and Ella, that their marriage was a sham and that they didn't love each other. Ella, herself, annoyed that such things were said about her personal life, was more concerned about Ernie's failing marriage, and Alix's already apparent failure to connect with the Russian people.

None of this mattered in the face of what would occur in May of 1896 – the coronation of Nicholas and Alexandra. The family gathered that month without, of course, the Queen, who had the excuse of protocol to keep her from going to hated Russia – a country she continued to consider full of peril. Irène, who was in the early stages of her second pregnancy, and feeling ill, was also absent. Uncle Arthur and Aunt Louise of Connaught represented Queen Victoria, along with Uncle Affie and Aunt Marie of Edinburgh, who were the senior members of the British family present. However, as usual, Victoria was the primary reporter of all the events to her grandmother, and all the news of her Russian granddaughters. *"We lunched with Alicky & Nicky yesterday she is looking so well & happy, quite a different person & has developed into a big, handsome woman rosy cheeked & broad shouldered making Ella look small near her ... but there is nothing left of the sad & drooping look, she used to have & otherwise she is quite unchanged."*[37] It is obvious from photographs from that period on that Alix regained her doleful expression once again, but, perhaps, just for this moment in time, it was gone.

The city of Moscow was completely wired with tiny electric lights that would be illuminated the night of the coronation. Wooden bleachers lined the streets, which were festooned with ribbons and every sort of banner. It seemed as though all the residents had planted beautiful flowers and plants to decorate the avenues along which the lengthy processions would wind. Above all, there were thousands of people who had come expressly to attend this lavish and momentous occasion, swelling the city to proportions it could hardly accommodate. However, for that moment in time, the joy of a new Imperial couple ruling Russia was deeply and spiritually felt. The fact that the country itself was plodding, when everyone else was sprinting towards the twentieth century, paled in significance to the astounding and wondrous ceremony that would take place. It was the zenith of the Romanovs, though they were oblivious to it at the time.

The Coronation encompassed several days of festivities, beginning with the entrance of the Imperial Family to Moscow along with hundreds of necessary security men. The day was sunny and the procession of the Imperial family also included the Imperial guards, the Cossacks, Nobility, and the Tsar, himself, along with a grand processional of princes, princesses, and grand dukes, all winding up at the Kremlin. The different guards and regiments rode through the streets to the moderate cheers of the people. Victoria had a feeling of dread on this day, and observed that the Russians seemed to have much less enthusiasm for their rulers, even on this day when their relationship was being renewed. The restraint of the crowd, however, was more than made up for by the grandeur of the parade.

Nicky, usually a shy young man rode through the avenues on a white horse and a plain uniform. His face was serious as he held his right hand in a perpetual salute. His mother, the Dowager Empress rode in a carriage behind him and Alix followed in an incredibly ornate carriage of state which was terribly stuffy. The crowds could see her through the windows and her face was unsmiling and serious. She was, doubtless enervated and uncomfortable, and because of her discomfort, people saw an unhappy face. She was, very possibly, pregnant at the time, and the strain of the ceremonies may have resulted in a miscarriage. She, nevertheless, looked beautiful in a white gown covered with jewels. The procession finally ended at the Kremlin, where a special *Te Deum* was sung.

Five days later, on May 26, the coronation, itself, took place at Uspensky Cathedral. The Imperial Couple slowly and solemnly entered the cathedral which was full to the rafters. Alix looked exquisite in a Russian Court dress of silver brocade and silver tissue. Over her dress, she wore an extremely heavy mantle, the order of St. Catherine on her breast, and around her neck she wore five strands of pearls. Nicholas crowned himself and then Alix, who was now the Empress Alexandra Feodorovna. The crowd was awe-struck as the two sat on thrones thickly decorated with jewels, while all paid reverence to the newly crowned monarchs. The heat was intense and the air filled with holy incense, as the choir swelled with Russian Chant. They sat on the diamond-encrusted thrones and received homage, and then the Imperial Couple eventually rose and went to the top of the Red Staircase to show themselves to the crowds, bowing to them three times. The rest of the participants filed out slowly. The Imperial Coronation was astonishing in its length and pomp. Each event was more exhausting and exhaustive than the preceding one.

Victoria, in describing the events to her grandmother commented that she had never beheld *"sadder eyes"* than Aunt Minnie's who looked young and lovely. It looked to Victoria as though she kept back tears only with a great effort of will. She described the crowning saying that *"Ella & I should have kissed Ali[x]'s hand, but she would not let us."*[38] Most important, *"Ella wore a beautiful creamy velvet costume embroidered with gold branches of wild roses & wore the most beautiful set of emeralds. ... I wore a pale blue dress & blue & silver train, which had belonged to the Grand Duchess Mathilde which Papa gave me for Ella's wedding & which is remarkably handsome."*[39] In all, Victoria thought the whole ceremony from beginning to end was wonderfully well rehearsed and everyone was calm, and unhurried.

That afternoon there was a coronation banquet for nearly two thousand people. Alix, Nicky and Aunt Minnie ate on a raised platform in the Hall of Facets, while people entered humbly to pay their respects to the Imperial Couple. The food was surprisingly good, being simple Russian fare, and the guests ate it with alacrity. That evening, all the small electric lights that had decorated the streets and buildings of Moscow were turned on all at once, resembling nothing so much as the stars in the firmament. The Kremlin, completely outlined in the darkness by the tiny lights, was magnificent.

During the coronation banquet, Victoria was struck by a strange mixture of people standing around one of the smaller reception rooms. She asked and was told that *"these people were all descendants of men who had saved their Sovereign's life, from the old Tsar times downwards. It was an old custom to invite these representatives to the Coronation."*[40] She also noticed *"Prince Ferdinand of Bulgaria* (later King) [who] *was at that moment very much in the black books of the Holy See. He, a Roman Catholic without any warning to the Vatican, had had his son and heir Boris, baptized into the Orthodox Church. On his way to the Coronation banquet as he passed through the room in which the cardinal [papal nuncio] was standing, the latter, to mark his contempt, made the gesture of spitting at him, and Ferdinand, not to be beaten, spat back!"*[41]

The festivities continued on for days, but were afterward tragically marred by a horrendous calamity. It was May 30th, four days after the Coronation and a special feast for the public was set up in a large military parade ground just outside Moscow called Khodynka Field. The field had barracks on one side and the other was a road leading out of the town. There would be free meat and beer, as well as a souvenir mug of the Coronation given to everyone who attended. The people had been gathering from the night before in order to partake of the Imperial largesse. By daybreak, with the workers coming in, the crowd swelled to nearly half a million people. Suddenly, as the crowd heard that the gifts were being distributed they pressed forward. Exacerbated by the rumors circulating that there wasn't enough for everyone, the crowds panicked. Some said that those rumors provoked the crush, and crush it literally was. Over fourteen hundred people were killed, falling into trenches dug on the field used for army exercises, and either trampled or suffocated or both and thousands more seriously wounded.

That night, there was to be a ball at the French Ambassador's. The French had spent exorbitant amounts to make the most lavish of parties, and the ball had been planned for months. The Imperial Couple pleaded with the family and with Nicholas' uncles in particular, to cancel the affair. Alix had been crying since she had word of the tragedy, and her face and eyes were red and swollen. Nicholas' uncles, however, insisted that they attend the ball. After all, they reasoned, the French were allies, and had spent a lot of money on the ball. They would be extremely insulted if the affair was canceled. To their credit, Nicholas and Alix were appalled, but the uncles were adamant, and they were literally forced to go. Needless to say, many, including other members of the family and the court, were outraged that they attended these festivities. The image of Nero fiddling while Rome burned was mentioned, indeed, the city was stunned that they had gone. After making an appearance for three and a half hours, they returned to the palace. The couple were both in complete despair.

The Queen, writing from Balmoral Castle in Scotland, was also completely stunned over the uncles' insistence that Alix and Nicky attend that ball. *"But oh! How awful & dreadful is that fearful catastrophe of that Fête!...Would it not have been better to have stopped the Balls etc. for it looks so unfeeling to go on just the same. It must throw a gloom over everything..."*[42]

She, again, evinced prescience in her assessment of the situation a few days later.

I fear the number of poor victims has increased. The papers speak of a very angry feeling being evinced amongst the people in Moscow. Trust there is [no] *cause for alarm or danger to the Emperor and Empress. Also fear poor Serge as Governor* [of Moscow] *may be blamed.*

There seems to have been lamentable want of proper prudence, i.e. allowing such a number of people to collect in one spot, and to keep order. It is most grievous.[43]

It is, as well, lamentable that the Queen was not alive during the first decades of the twentieth century to advise the Imperial Couple. Though, with the coming years, Nicky and Alix became more obdurate and isolated and it is more than probable they wouldn't have listened even to such sage advice as the old monarch could have provided.

Chapter VIII

June 1896 – January 1901

As the nineteenth century drew to a close, the Royal Families of Europe were at their zenith. Queen Victoria, who rightly called herself the 'Doyenne of Monarchs,' was growing old, but her mind was still razor sharp. Uncle Bertie of Wales, who was certainly aging, continued to do his best to live the life of a young playboy. In the process, he accomplished his goal of annoying, and more important, getting the attention of the Queen. Her grandchildren were marrying at a fast and furious rate, thereby producing even more royal offspring, who in their turn were doing the same. The sun never set on the British Empire and Europe was still composed primarily of monarchies, many of whom were headed by members of the Queen's family.

Those waning years of the century, like most years, were peppered with monumental events for the Hessian sisters and their families. A year after the Imperial Coronation and the Khodynka Field tragedy, Queen Victoria's Diamond Jubilee, the celebration of sixty years as Queen-Empress, took place. Victoria, with several children in tow, continued to visit back and forth, wandering from Moscow and St. Petersburg to visit Alix and Ella, to the Heiligenberg and to Wolfsgarten in Hesse to Ernie, and so to Kiel and Irène, and thence back to Windsor, and the Queen. It was something of a nomadic existence, with a mostly absent husband, but it satisfied Victoria's independent and endlessly curious nature.

Alice was growing up to be quite a young lady, and already showing signs of extraordinary beauty. She coped well with her deafness, and was adept at lip-reading. She was bright, strong, and had the love for exoticism and mysticism that other women of the Hessian family had shown. Louise, though not classically pretty, nevertheless, had the Battenberg bone structure: the long high-bridged nose, the intense eyes, and the molded cheekbones. She might never be beautiful, but she would always be striking, tall, and thin, like her Aunt Alix, with an extremely elegant look. She was as determined as Alice, though a "talker" like her mother. As for Georgie, he was an active five-year-old, always getting into everything and wanting to do anything that older boys and girls could do. He was, naturally, destined for the Royal Navy. Unlike some children, far from resenting this predestination, Georgie embraced it, loving everything naval. Indeed, when he did leave the navy later on, it was with real regret.

****

After the coronation, the Imperial Couple along with Victoria went to Ella's country home, Illyinskoje, for a rest after the exhausting ceremonies. They spent the mid-summer of 1896 boating, riding, swimming and picnicking with their closest neighbors, the fabulously wealthy and aristocratic Youssoupov family, at Archangelskoe. Ducky, and her sister Marie of Romania, stayed with the Youssoupovs, along with Aunt Marie of Coburg. Archangelskoe was built in the 18th century Classical style, and offered the same outdoor pursuits as the much simpler Illyinskoje – riding, boating, and picnics.

That September, Ella and Serge met Victoria, Ducky, and Ernie in Munich, and from there they went to Venice to explore the city together and go antique hunting. Unknown to the others at the time, Ducky had fallen, what appeared to her at the time, as hopelessly in love. It had happened during the coronation, when she and her Cousin Kyrill Vladimirovich, the son of the Grand Duke Vladimir Alexandrovich, Alexander III's younger brother, were thrown together. She and her sister Marie, who was, herself, having a flirtation with Boris Vladimirovich, Kyrill's brother, were reckless in their attentions to their cousins, and people anxiously noticed.

Also during that September, Alix and Nicky visited Queen Victoria at Balmoral. The Queen found her granddaughter distant and aloof. Alix's discomfort with being the Empress was already apparent to the old lady. She had worried so much about Ella's getting too 'grand', but in the end, it appeared to her that Alix was the one becoming more and more remote. Having never been uncomfortable around her grandmother before, the Queen didn't recognize Alix's hauteur as most likely profound shyness, and an inability to cope with her new position. In addition, the Queen found it difficult to deal with Nicholas, who appeared to be weak and wavering. In all, it was not a happy visit, though the Queen enjoyed her great-granddaughter, Olga.

The Imperial couple went back to Europe in October, visiting Ernie and Ducky at Wolfsgarten. Victoria, who was also present, remembered Nicky as envying Ernie for being a constitutional monarch.

> *Under other circumstances, Nicky would have made a remarkably good constitutional Sovereign, for he was in no way narrow minded, nor obsessed by his high position. If one could have boiled down Nicky and William in one pot you would have produced an ideal Emperor of Russia. His father's dominating personality had stunted any gifts for initiative in Nicky.*[1]

In November of that year, Irène had her second child – a boy. Born at Kiel, he was called Sigismund, according to Irène, *"after Harry's little brother that died."*[2] Thereafter, known in the family as "Bobby," he would be the only completely healthy child that Irène bore. After that, Irène often complained about what an awful bother it was to find dresses now that her figure was changing and she couldn't stand anything tight. It is entirely possible that the gaps between Irène's children bespoke of someone who had difficulties conceiving or maintaining pregnancies. Her letters were full of taking time off for rests in various isolated locations, and complaining to her grandmother of various female maladies. That together with the fact that her first son was a hemophiliac seemed as much of a reason to make her withdraw to the background of the Prussian Court, as her more liberal beliefs and Darmstadt upbringing.

The following spring, Victoria joined Queen Victoria at the Excelsior Hotel Regina, in Nice. There was much company there – the Battenbergs, Aunt Helena's daughter, Princess Helena Victoria, and the Grand Duke Peter Nicholaevich, who was there with his wife, the Grand Duchess Militza Nicholaevna, and her unmarried sister, Princess Anna of Montenegro. Louis' brother, Franz Joseph, was still unattached and had spent a good deal of time searching for a suitable bride. Consuelo Vanderbilt Balsan, the former Duchess of Marlborough, had written in her memoirs that Franzjos had an interest in offering for her – and this, indeed, was quite true. This was the period when Consuelo was considered eminently suitable and marriageable, and she and her mother, Alva Vanderbilt were traveling about Europe meeting people. Alva Vanderbilt had brought her to Paris before her subsequent marriage to the Duke, purely and simply, to be auctioned off to the highest bidder – the more important the title the better. Certainly, Franzjos, as a minor royal, interestingly enough, conspiring, still, to get back the crown of Bulgaria, was far more important than a common English Duke. Alva temporarily entertained great hopes.

Consuelo was no more to blame for this mercenary behavior than Franzjos was in looking for a wife with money. Each had something that the other needed. He considered the young heiress, who, in her memoirs, wrote some rather biting sentences about the Prince, who, after all, was not well off, and was looking for an affluent bride. However, Consuelo might have been more understanding about him so much later on in her life. She remarked that he was rather oily, suave with too much dubious Continental charm for her. He may not have been lucky enough to fascinate Consuelo, but he was, at any rate, charming enough to capture the heart of Princess Anna of Montenegro in 1897.

The couple began the process of driving out together in Nice, and dining together with the Queen and the Princess's sister. After several weeks of this, the engagement was announced. Aunt Julie of Battenberg would have been pleased at the idea of another princess for her youngest son. Naturally, the Queen, herself, was also pleased at this engagement because of her attachment to the Battenberg family. She wrote to Aunt Vicky, that she would be

greatly surprised to hear Franzjos was engaged the night before last to the Princess Anna of Montenegro, a charming girl who is quite determined to marry him and is devoted to him. We are all most pleased as it is in every way a good match, being a near connection with Italy and also Russia. The Prince of Montenegro arrived yesterday and I saw him today. He is a great man.[3]

Franzjos, it should be remembered, fought along side his brother, Sandro, during his tenure in Bulgaria. Upon his marriage, he would become a Colonel in the Montenegrin Army. Nevertheless, he was, overall, an intellectual more than a soldier and earned a PhD from the University of Leipzig.

The Queen happily wrote, *"I really think he could not have found a nicer wife anywhere, nor one who could have been fonder of him."*[4] Victoria was also delighted, telling Ernie that she was a charming girl, *"– so natural and merry and warm-hearted. … Of course the finances are the weak point – but she is not spoiled & I think will be practical, which poor F. J. is not particularly…"*[5] The couple were married in May.

It was during this year that Victoria, encouraged by Louis, engaged a lady-in-waiting for herself, who would also see to the education of her children. The young lady was Nona Kerr, the daughter of Admiral Lord Frederick Kerr, and the sister of Mark Kerr, a naval comrade of Louis' who would later, at Victoria's request, be his biographer. Nona was a constant companion for Victoria, who shared in her travels and her life until her marriage nineteen years later. Even after she went to live with her husband, she *"remained… [Victoria's]… closest friend."*[6] She became an integral member of the family and one who, in some ways, served as a buffer between Louis and Victoria.

It is interesting to note, that as she did with Louis, Victoria was unable to express herself well to her very closest friend.

I have never managed to say to you, though I've wanted to all along, that I thank you much for doing a great deal more than just jobs for me all this time & that I should have missed you very much if you had not been there. I don't know why I am afflicted with (I fear) incurable complaint of never being able to speak out decently even when I much want to – but perhaps you know it & so will continue to be patient with me.[7]

Nona wasn't the only one who evidently needed patience with Victoria. Louis, whom she had been married to for more than fifteen years, must have understood her reticence and lived well with it. They were, in many ways, a union of opposites, but there was never a breath of scandal about their marriage. It is apparent from all that has been written, that it was truly a happy one, and even that rarest of pairings – a love match.

Nona was engaged just before another jubilee, the final one for Queen Victoria – her Diamond Jubilee. Once again services of Thanksgiving, processions and dinners were planned. They did not, however, quite compete with the grandeur of the Golden Jubilee. One reason was because of the Queen's age, near blindness, and other infirmities, it was decided that she would not go up the stairs of St. Paul's. However, when the all-important day finally came, she not only rose to the occasion, but she towered above it.

On that sunny day, June 20, at St George's chapel at Windsor, the Queen, as she had during her Golden Jubilee, heard her beloved Prince Albert's *Te Deum*. The following day, she triumphantly entered London from Paddington Station and eventually ended her progress at Buckingham Palace. As on that day ten years ago, she looked regal in her black silk with panels of gray satin. She was veiled in black net, dusted with diamonds, and had not abandoned her bonnet.

That evening, there was a family dinner with various royalties,* special envoys, and dignitaries from all over the world. The most interesting, since most of the exotic monarchs from Persia and the like, didn't come as they had ten years earlier, was President McKinley of America. Everyone was dressed formally, with every possible medal, decoration, and sash that they could possibly dig up for the occasion. Even the Queen, wearing a dress made in India, with the whole front embroidered in gold, was looking quite as grand as she could in her unfashionable silks and satins. She wore the inevitable widow's cap with diamonds, and a diamond necklace. President McKinley, however, stood out. He wore plain black evening dress, and was all the more conspicuous because of the plainness of it.**

The following day, June 22, was the big celebration. It was, Queen Victoria wrote with a large degree of satisfaction, "[a] *never-to-be-forgotten day. No one ever, I believe, has met with such an ovation as was given to me....The crowds were quite indescribable, and their enthusiasm truly marvellous and deeply touching. The cheering was quite deafening, and every face seemed to be filled with real joy. I was much moved and gratified.*"[8]..."*Before leaving I touched an electric button, by which I started a message which was telegraphed throughout the whole Empire. It was the following: 'From my heart I thank my beloved people, May God bless them!'*"[9] The thanksgiving service took place at St. Paul's at eleven in the morning. The Queen's coach stopped in front of the cathedral at the foot of the steps.

Afterward, the coach continued for a long six mile procession through the streets of London, starting in South London, on to Westminster Bridge, and finally to the Houses of Parliament. The Queen rode in the coach with Aunt Alix of Wales, who took the Queen's hands in hers and pressed them to comfort the old lady as she was overcome with emotion. The Queen had tears in her eyes, and was amazed and continually surprised and touched

---

(*) *The Queen had decreed that no other reigning sovereigns should attend since she was just too old.*
(**) *He was assassinated on Septemb 6, 1901, at the Pan-American Exposition in New York City , by an anarchist, Leon Czolgosz.*

at the devotion of her subjects. Victoria drove in the Procession with cousins Margaret of Connaught, and Beatrice of Edinburgh. Louis rode behind the coach, as he had done in the previous jubilee. A movie was photographed of the occasion and beacons were lit that evening. The celebrations went on for days, culminating on July 2. Though, not nearly as elaborate as the previous celebrations had been, it was overwhelmingly emotional for the Queen and her family. It was the capstone of her reign.

****

In the beginning of 1898, Victoria was at Hemmelmarck, once again, visiting her sister. Irène was alone there with the children since her husband Henry had left for China on a two year cruise on the Deutschland; Irène was delighted to welcome her sister. Afterward, Irène, herself, now began the rounds of visits with her two boys. In the late spring she and the boys went to Windsor to visit the Queen. She was pleased to find herself living in the Tapestry rooms where *"Aunt Vicky generally does & where Victoria was born."*[10]

Later that year, Victoria dealt with a small crisis with her younger daughter Louise. She seemed to be a sickly little girl, starting with her glandular problems, and now a new ailment, a possible curvature of the spine, appeared. She was smaller than her sister, continuing to earn the name her father had given her in babyhood – 'shrimp'; however, she weathered this problem as she always would. Victoria had her examined by a Dr. Vulpius at Heidelberg, who confirmed that her back wasn't straight. He was able to suggest a course of exercises that were apparently successful.

Irène was thrilled to be permitted by her brother-in-law, Cousin Willy, to join Henry for part of his cruise. The Kaiser was very controlling and manipulative which was aggravated by the fact that Irène was much insistent for reasons already mentioned that she and her family distance themselves from Berlin. She was adamant in steering her immediate family on a course of self-determination and isolation from what she considered Prussian ways and was surprisingly strong in her objective. It is interesting to note that her sister, Alix, did the same thing in Russia, with tragic consequences. However, Irène's course, because of her lesser position, was successful, and beneficial to her family. Nevertheless, she still needed Wilhelm's permission to go on the cruise, and obtaining it required all of Irène's tact and peace making skills.[11] In this case, she was, again, successful and she delightedly joined Henry in China in the beginning of 1899.

Louis was finally appointed to the equivalent of shore duty, when he assumed his new position as Assistant Director of Naval Intelligence. Their life would now be much more stable, as opposed to the constant wandering and separations. They rented a house in London at 40 Grosvenor Gardens.

Alix and Nicholas visited Wolfsgarten in September of that year, and Victoria and her children joined them. Alix now had three girls, Olga, Tatiana and Marie, and was naturally worried about not having provided a male heir to the throne. This was a constant anxiety and obsession with the young Empress. Her family was sensitive to her health and Irène cautioned Ernie to *"please take care of* [Alix] *& see that she does not stand or walk much ... & if one does not remind her she forgets to sit down..."*[12] In photos beginning at this time, it is possible to see her lips, drawn in a very thin line, and the first signs of premature aging.

There were no Russian Orthodox Churches in Darmstadt, and Nicholas had commissioned the building of a chapel in 1896, as a gift for his wife. The chapel was completed several years later. In the beginning of October, 1899, during their visit, the Imperial couple consecrated the Russian Chapel. It was called, as the church in Jerusalem had been called, the Church of St. Mary Magdalene and was situated near the artist colony with which Ernie was currently involved, the Mathildenhöhe. It was also quite close to the Hesse family mausoleum, the Rosenhöhe.[13]

Victoria and her family were now leading a less itinerate existence in their rented London home. Louis and Victoria visited the Queen at Windsor, and spent the time acquainting the children with the great landmarks of London, the tower of London and so on. It was also at this time that the Boer War began and they often saw the troops leaving Victoria Station for the South African War.

Ernie and Ducky's marriage, based on temperaments that were worlds apart was continuing its slow deterioration. In a last ditch attempt to salvage something from their relationship, they rejoiced in Ducky's second pregnancy. Ernie happily wrote to Victoria,

Ducky expects the baby next June. ... You can well think [of] *our joy and how happy we are together sometimes I can hardly realize it, it seems too good for words. Ducky is very well...*[14]

...words that hardly boded well for the future. However, they do show that despite the fact that Victoria had played mother to Ernie for much of his adolescence, he never resented her advice. Indeed, he confided in her, and trusted her implicitly. Some months later, he wrote: "Don't we two really understand each other the best?"[15]

Ducky, however, was not the only one in the family about to have a child at this time. Victoria and Irène were both carrying their last children. In the beginning of 1900, Irène's youngest son, Heinrich, was born at Kiel and christened in May of that year. Victoria, who was not due until June, moved to Frogmore in April. She was nearing her thirty-seventh birthday and possibly was urged by the Queen to move there because it was far more peaceful and healthful than London. It was also a place where Victoria could walk and exercise in the way that the Queen had always prescribed. The Queen visited back and forth with Victoria during this time, lunching, chatting and stopping by whenever the fancy took her. No doubt afterwards, Victoria was grateful for this last small interlude with her grandmother.

On June 25, the Queen wrote in her journal: "*I heard on waking that dear Victoria had got a little boy, born at 6 this morning, ... it was a great pleasure. ...saw the pretty little Baby & also dear Victoria, just for a moment. She was very well.*" Victoria's second son was christened Louis Francis Victor Albert Nicholas, named presumably for his father, uncles and naturally both the Queen and Prince Albert.

Victoria consulted the other three children about a nickname for their new little brother. Someone suggested "Nicky" but it was thought that that would confuse the little boy with the Tsar, though why is a mystery. Then someone else suggested "Dickie" not knowing that "Dickie-bird" was Victoria's pet nick-name for Louis. After some further discussion, "Dickie" won out, and "Dickie" he was known for his entire life.

He was the last great-grandson with whom Queen Victoria was photographed, as well as her last godson. She observed him to be a strong and vigorous child and noted that during their session, the infant knocked off her spectacles, and got his little hand stuck in her cap-veil, which she thought was quite amusing. It is interesting to note that both of

Victoria's sons escaped hemophilia. Whether this was luck or Victoria simply didn't carry the gene is not known.

Dickie was a sunny child with a great love for small animals, a slightly artistic bent, and a true calling for the Royal Navy. He inherited the Battenberg tendency (undoubtedly because of the persecution that his father and uncles suffered), of needing to prove how royal he was. In addition, he inherited his Uncle Liko's vanity, being much interested in his appearance. Certainly, that was one attribute he didn't inherit from his mother.

To cloud the joy of this event was the news of the death of Prince Alfred, Duke of Edinburgh and Saxe-Coburg & Gotha. Queen Victoria lost her third grown-up child in July of 1900, and the Hessian family lost a beloved Uncle. He, who had encouraged Louis to join the navy, and, along with Aunt Marie been such companions to the Battenbergs while they lived in Malta, had died of cancer.

Also, that August, Victoria received a letter from her grandmother. A small note, it read, simply, *"Darling Victoria, I read your dear letter without the Enclosure & sent £10 for the poor women & if it is safe enough will send more. Ever your devoted Grandmama, V.R.I."*[16] It is not apparent what exactly this little gift of charity was, however, it was the last letter that Victoria received from the Queen and the end of a long and copious correspondence that lasted nearly thirty-three years.

The Queen was began failing physically in earnest now, and as fall of 1900 turned to winter, the signs were beginning to emerge. She was extremely rheumatic, and because she was nearly blind, Beatrice read state documents, letters and all important papers out loud to her as well as writing letters for her. The responsibility was enormous and it has been wondered if the Princess understood the gravity of her position. Certainly, there were those that expressed the opinion that she did not.

If Beatrice wasn't around then several other useful daughters or granddaughters were found to perform the little tasks that the Queen needed. However, as much as people could hardly comprehend it, it now looked as though the end was, at last, drawing near. Irène was, in fact, with her grandmother that last fall at Balmoral, along with Princess May. Victoria observed that though she was in fragile health, on December 14, 1900, she *"still attended the usual service in the Mausoleum ... at which we and most of the family were present."*[17] This was, of course, the anniversary of the Prince Consort's, and Princess Alice's death, and every year since the Prince's death in 1861, a very sad day. By the end of the year, the Queen began to settle the final details of her life, one of which was appointing Louis Battenberg, as a sign of her great regard for him, as an Executor to her private money.

The Queen was slowly weakening as the New Year came, and Louis and Victoria were summoned to Osborne in January of 1901. The old lady had been brought low with several pieces of bad news. The Boer War made her very unhappy, though it never completely doused her spirits. As ever, her fortitude and determination had nothing to do with her health, and she blocked out the probability of anything but a complete victory. A famous quote, spoken when her minister, Mr. Balfour, visited her after a particularly bad patch of the war, illustrates this best. When Balfour attempted to commiserate with her, she replied, *"Please understand that there is no one depressed in this house; we are not interested in the possibilities of defeat; they do not exist."** She was indomitable in a way that can hardly be explained today. Added to the war, which still continued, was the death of her son, Affie, and the serious illness, cancer of the spine, of her eldest daughter, Vicky. Dying did not

---

(*) *During the so-called 'Black Week', December 1899.*

bother her, though she lay there languishing for about a week. Queen Victoria died on January 22, 1901 at Osborne House.

As in every other death in her life, the Queen was much preoccupied with her own and her only concern was that her ladies made sure to carry out her instructions for burial to the letter. She had given very clear and concise directions about how she wished to be dressed: in a white silk dressing gown, with the order of the Garter resting from her shoulder to waist and her wedding veil over her face. In addition, she was extremely specific about the things that she wanted placed in her coffin.

Her retainers and Dr. Reid, without any of the family present, were instructed to put into her coffin all sorts of mementos and keepsakes. Among them were some of her favorite jewels, a photograph of John Brown, some shawls, Prince Albert's dressing gown embroidered by his beloved second daughter, Princess Alice, and various other photographs. In the end, Queen Victoria rested with well-beloved things about her. The Victorian preoccupation with death and mourning served her well. Her death, for so many in her family and in the empire itself, was an explosive and seminal event; so completely shattering that afterwards so many said that their lives were changed beyond recognition.

Victoria and, her brother, and sisters, lost the woman who, for nearly twenty-three years, had been like a mother, and, certainly in Victoria's case, one of her closest confidants. For the Hessians it was such a drastic change, that it was hard to even place it in a context in which it was possible to understand or even cope. When their mother died, it was bad enough, but there were many around to help with recovery – Papa, all the Aunts and Uncles, the Cousins, and above all, the Queen, Grandmama. However, now that person who represented an entire generation, indeed an entire world was gone, and the grief was nearly unbearable. Victoria wrote:

> *Grandmama's death was a great personal loss to me. On account of our having lost our mother when we were so young, Grandmama had taken a special interest in her beloved daughter's children. Her affection for us was very warm and sincere and she proved it on every occasion. As the one of us, who was the most in England, I was the one who was in closest touch with her. After my marriage she became very fond of Louis and relied on his judgment, tact and discretion, so that she discussed not only many private, but also public matter with him – and she nominated him as one of the Executors of her Will.*

> *My understanding of Grandmama grew with the years. In childhood, I had known her as a middle aged woman, and as I was approaching middle age, she had become a very old lady...In my early youth, Grandmama was a very formidable person in my mind, some one whom my mother regarded with respect and awe. ...She herself, tho' very gracious to her grandchildren, expected perfect manners and immediate obedience from them and would look and speak severely to any offender. ... My mother's death broke through many of these outward barriers and the constant signs of affectionate pity and interest, gave to our intercourse a more natural ease.*[18]

Victoria went on to describe her grandmother as flexible, and hardly someone that would be thought of as Victorian. She never wore the famous widow's cap in the privacy of her rooms and smelled faintly of orange blossoms. Though she met many distinguished people at her table, she was, nevertheless, a shy person. She had, according to her granddaughter, a tendency to listen to men more than to women and was always susceptible to a handsome face. She had been, through her entire life, extremely proud of being a soldier's daughter and the Admiralty deeply offended her when they refused to give the Prince Consort an honorary rank.

To understand her best, was to understand her womanly nature, and that the *"secret of Lord Beaconsfield's charm for her [was] he never overlooked the woman in the Sovereign"*[19] And, this was the key to one of strongest parts of the Queen's character. Her likes and dislikes were strengthened by personal contacts. She loved Louis, who after his marriage to Victoria had spent much time around the Queen. Because of their long association and the Queen's regard for the Battenbergs, she trusted him, as mentioned, as one of the Executors of her estate as well as being her naval aide-de-camp. Incidentally, Louis would go on to fill that role with Bertie, now Edward VII and later George, who became George V.

Several days after Queen Victoria's death, the Battenbergs went to London, and Uncle Bertie, now King, had his first council. He was proclaimed King by the Privy Council and the Cabinet. There, he made what was thought to be a startling announcement – he proclaimed himself Edward VII; startling, because the Queen had very much wished him to reign as King Albert. He explained that it was because the Prince Consort, as Albert the Good, ought to stand alone in people's hearts, and that he, Edward, would be different. Naturally, many believed something quite to the contrary. Much, there is little doubt, was owed to the resentment he had felt for this man who was constantly brought up to him as a paragon of perfection. This was coupled with the manner in which his mother treated him, especially with regard to his future position. She never let him look at a state paper. Possibly not being King Albert the First was the middle-aged King's first declaration of independence.

Alix, who was pregnant with her fourth child and unable to attend, and Ella were absent from this last and very important ritual in the life of Queen Victoria, but Victoria, Irène and Ernie attended. Like so many, Alix eloquently expressed her regrets, and a disbelief that the world had changed so dramatically,

How I envy you being able to see beloved Grandmama being taken to her last rest. I cannot believe she is really gone, that we shall never see her any more. It seems impossible. Since one can remember, she was in our life, and a dearer kinder being never was. The whole world sorrows over her. England without the Queen seems impossible. How thankful, that she was spared all physical suffering.[20]

Aunt Vicky of Prussia was on her own death bed by this time and expressed her thoughts eloquently, *"the best of mothers and the greatest of Queens, our centre and help and support – all seems a blank, a terrible awful dream. Realise it one cannot."*

The new King returned to Osborne, before the body was borne away, to oversee the arrangements for Queen's military funeral. She preferred this to a royal funeral, because the less flamboyant dignity of the military was much more to her taste, as well as the fact, already mentioned, of her pride in being a soldier's daughter. In addition, it has to be remembered that England was at war at the time. As with all such occasions, London swelled to many thousands more than its usual population.

Victoria and Louis, during this time were housed at the Admiralty, and helped receive the family that came for the Queen's funeral. No doubt that the entire week took on an air of unreality. Even Cousin Willy, who had held his dying grandmother on his good arm for two hours before she slipped away, had managed to stay quiet, extremely sorrowful throughout the entire process, and above all, respectful. He had been awarded the Order of the Garter by his Uncles Bertie and Arthur, right after the Queen's death. In addition, Bertie's son George, now the heir apparent to the throne, was quite ill with German measles and naturally very upset at not being able to participate in his grandmother's funeral.

The coffin was brought from Osborne on February 1 and made its sad and slow procession through London on the following day. There were many people - family members and other royalties, following the coffin through the streets, a spectacle, according to the *New York Times* (and strangely echoing the Queen's words) *"never to be forgotten."* It made its way, in virtual silence, through a grieving capital, swathed in black. The procession, two hours long, eventually ended at Paddington Station from where the coffin would be taken to Windsor. Then, the sad, flag-draped coffin would take a much smaller journey to Frogmore where she would be laid, at last, next to her husband in eternal rest.[21]

It was when the funeral train arrived at Windsor that an unexpected event occurred. Prince Louis was there to put it to rights, though it made his fellow military services extremely jealous. When the coffin bearing the Queen arrived at the station, there was a gun carriage with two pairs of horses waiting to carry her up to the mausoleum. Because the horses had been waiting for several hours, they were evidently no longer inclined to move. The horses *"had grown cold from long waiting in the biting wind, [and] became restive..."*[22] When the coffin was placed on the caisson, the forward horses balked while one of the back horses reared up and collapsed in a heap, hopelessly entangling all the horses in the harnesses and lines.

Everyone stood aghast having no idea what to do about the situation. They were standing about somewhat dumbly, until it occurred to Louis what must be done. He suggested that the traces be cut, and a whole group of his sailors pull the entire carriage up to Windsor. After that and some other alternate plans were discussed, it was decided to convey this singular honor upon Louis' men.

They looked, smart and according to reports were *"clean-shaven...men [who] evoked the admiration of all by the speed with which they removed the refractory horses, improvised ropes out of traces, and started the gun carriage with it precious burden toward the chapel."*[23] It was obvious that they were thrilled and honored to do this last task for the Queen, but the other services, the cavalry and artillery were much put out. It made for an impressively moving procession to the chapel, and Prince Louis received a private message of thanks from the new King.

The Queen lay in the Albert Memorial Chapel until February 4, and then she was taken to the Mausoleum where she would be placed next to her dear husband. The place she had longed to be, so she averred, since his death in 1861.

For the Hessian sisters, the rest of the family and the world, nothing would ever be quite the same.

Part III

January 1901 – September 1921

At right: Prince Ludwig of Hesse and by Rhine was the candidate best suited to gain the hand of Princess Alice of Great Britain and Ireland. Her father, the Prince Consort, gave his blessing to the union and that settled matters. Ludwig and Alice were married at Osborne House, Isle of Wight, on July 1, 1862.

Below left: Princess Elisabeth and Princess Victoria, the two eldest children of Ludwig and Alice of Hesse and by Rhine.

Below right: And baby makes three. From left: Princess Alice, Princess Victoria, Prince Ludwig holding Princess Irène. On the foreground is Princess Elisabeth.

Princess Victoria of Hesse and by Rhine.

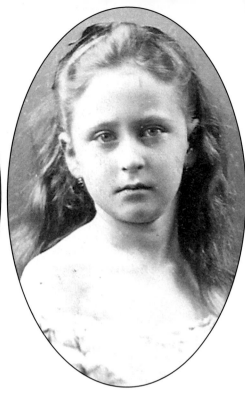

Princess Elisabeth of Hesse and by Rhine.

Princess Irène of Hesse and by Rhine.

Princess Alix of Hesse and by Rhine.

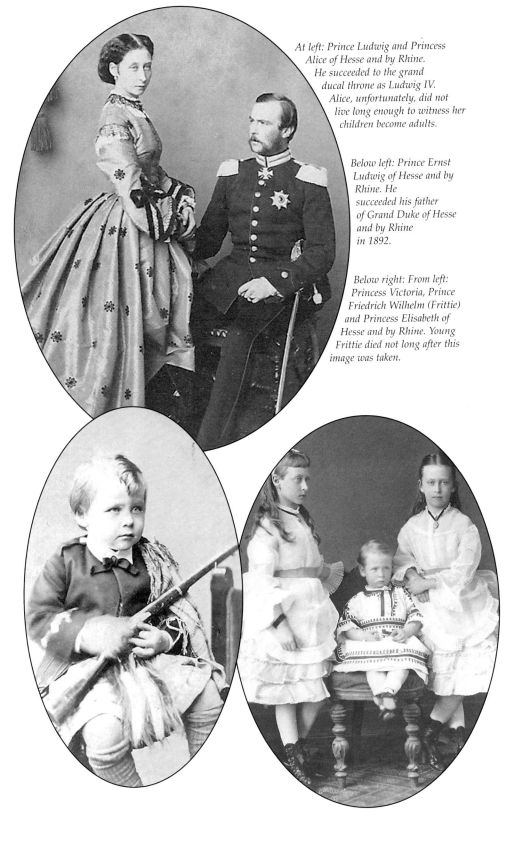

At left: Prince Ludwig and Princess Alice of Hesse and by Rhine. He succeeded to the grand ducal throne as Ludwig IV. Alice, unfortunately, did not live long enough to witness her children become adults.

Below left: Prince Ernst Ludwig of Hesse and by Rhine. He succeeded his father of Grand Duke of Hesse and by Rhine in 1892.

Below right: From left: Princess Victoria, Prince Friedrich Wilhelm (Frittie) and Princess Elisabeth of Hesse and by Rhine. Young Frittie died not long after this image was taken.

The three eldest Hessian sisters: Princess Victoria, Princess Elisabeth and Princess Irène. From Darmstadt, they were destined to spend their lives in London, Moscow and Berlin.

At center, Grand Duchess Alice holding Princess Marie. Around their mother and sister, clockwise from top: Princess Victoria, Hereditary Grand Duke Ernst Ludwig, Princess Irène, Princess Alix and Princess Elisabeth.

The Hessian children enjoyed an idylic life surrounded by loving parents and grandparents, dedicated nanies and tutors. All that happiness turned to be ephemeral when tragedy struck in 1878. In this photo from the early 1870s are Princess Irène and her brother Prince Ernst Ludwig with one of their pet birds.

Victoria and Alice, the two eldest daughters of Queen Victoria, were extremely talented. In spite of Hesse and Prussia being on opposite sides during the war of 1866, relations between Darmstadt and Berlin were quickly restored after the arrival of peace. Both living in Germany, Victoria and Alice, along with their children, visited each other with frequency.

Grand Duchess Alice of Hesse and by Rhine.
(1843-1878)

At right: Grand Duchess Alice wearing the famed Hessian diamond tiara, one of the most precious pieces of jewelry owned by the grand ducal family.

Below, left: Grand Duchess Alice and her only surviving son, Ernst Ludwig, an artistic and sensitive child who was deeply touched by the loss of his mother.

At right: Just before tragedy struck and desolated the Hessian family, Princess Marie and Princess Alix pose for a lovely photograph. Within a short time, Marie fell to the same illness that ultimately took the life of their mother.

Grand Duke Ludwig IV of Hesse and by Rhine.
(1837-1892)

The Hessian siblings photographed in the early 1880s. From left: Princess Elisabeth, Hereditary Grand Duke Ernst Ludwig, Princess Victoria, Princess Alix and Princess Irène.

From left: Princess Victoria, Queen Victoria, Princess Alix and Princess Elisabeth. After Alice's death, the Queen remained very close to her Hessian grandchildren.

At right, from left: Princess Alix of Hesse and by Rhine, Princess Louis of Battenberg, Grand Duchess Elisabeth Feodorovna of Russia and Princess Irène of Prussia.

Above, left: The two youngest daughters of Grand Duchess Alice: Princess Alix and Princess Irène in the mid-1880s.

Above, right: Prince Henry of Prussia and his fiancée Princess Irène of Hesse and by Rhine. Behind them are two of her siblings: Alix and Ernst Ludwig of Hesse and by Rhine, c. 1888.

At right: And the marriages begin: Grand Duke Serge Alexandrovich and Grand Duchess Elisabeth Feodorovna of Russia, Princes Louis and Princess Victoria of Battenberg, and Grand Duke Ludwig IV of Hesse and by Rhine.

The Hessian siblings mourn the loss of their father. Seated, from left: Princess Irène of Prussia, Princess Alix of Hesse and by Rhine and Grand Duchess Elisabeth Feodorovna of Russia. Behind them: Grand Duke Ernst Ludwig of Hesse and by Rhine and Princess Victoria of Battenberg.

At left: A photo of Princess Victoria of Hesse and by Rhine on her wedding day.

Below, right: Prince Louis and Princess Victoria of Battenberg while living in Malta, where he was stationed for some time.

Bottom, right: Prince Louis and Princess Victoria with three of their children: Louise, Georgie and Dickie.

Bottom, left: A young Princess Victoria.

The Four Graces and their brother remained very close in spite of many challenges confronting them. In 1903, the siblings reunited in Darmstadt for the wedding of Princess Alice of Battenberg and Prince Andrew of Greece. This was the last time Grand Duke Ernst Ludwig played host to his brothers-in-law. Within two years, Serge Alexandrvich was dead. From left: Grand Duke Ernst Ludwig of Hesse and by Rhine, Empress Alexandra Feodorovna and Tsar Nicholas II of Russia, Princess Irène and Prince Henry of Prussia, Grand Duchess Elisabeth Feodorovna and Grand Duke Serge Alexandrovich of Russia, Princess Victoria and Prince Louis of Battenberg.

Standing in back, from left: Prince George, Princess Victoria and Prince Louis Jr. of Battenberg. Seated, in same order; Princess Margarita of Greece, Princess Louise of Battenberg, Prince Louis of Battenberg holding Princess Theodora of Greece, and Princess Alice of Greece.

At right: Princess Victoria of Battenberg attending a charity event with Queen Amelie of Portugal and Princess Alice of Teck, who in 1917 also lost her husband's title and became Countess of Athlone.

Below: Victoria during a visit to Russia just before the outbreak of War.

One of the last images taken of the Four Graces and their brother. From left: Princess Irène of Prussia, Grand Duke Ernst Ludwig of Hesse and by Rhine, Grand Duchess Elisabeth Feodorovna of Russia, Princess Victoria of Battenberg and Empress Alexandra Feodorovna of Russia.

At right: In 1917, Prince Louis of Battenberg relinquished his German titles and became Marquess of Milford Haven. This image dates from 1921 and is among the last known photos of him. With Louis and Victoria are their son Georgie with his wife Nada and their children, Tatiana and David.

Below: Victoria, Dowager Marchioness of Milford Haven, visiting her daughter Louise in Sweden.

In 1928, Andrew and Alice of Greece celebrated their silver wedding anniversary while living in exile in France. Standing in back: Princess Cecile and Princess Sophie. At front: Princess Margarita, Prince Philip, Princess Alice, Prince Andrew and Princess Theodora.

At right: In the 1920s, the remaining unmarried children of the Dowager Marchioness of Milford Haven found spouses: Lady Louise Mountbatten married Crown Prince Gustav Adolf of Sweden in 1923; Lord Louis Mountbatten had married Edwina Ashley the year before. In this image, Victoria Milford Haven is photographed with her four children and their spouses. Back row, from left: Crown Prince Gustav Adolf of Sweden, Lord Louis Mountbatten, the Marquess of Milford Haven, Prince Andrew of Greece. At front, same order: Crown Princess Louise of Sweden, Lady Edwina Mountbatten, Victoria, the Marchioness of Milford Haven and Princess Alice of Greece.

Below: After the end of the Second World War, travel around Europe resumed. In this image we see the Dowager Marchioness of Milford Haven surrounded by family members. From left: Crown Prince Gustav Adolf of Sweden, Lady Patricia and her mother Lady Edwina Mountbatten, Victoria, Crown Princess Louise of Sweden, Lady Pamela and Lord Louis Mountbatten, soon to become Earl Mountbatten of Burma.

A gathering of the "Royal Mob" in Coburg, April 1894. From left: Duke Alfred of Saxe-Coburg & Gotha (Uncle Alfred), the Prince of Wales (Uncle Bertie) and the Duke of Connaught (Uncle Arthur).

In 1884, Princess Elisabeth of Hesse and by Rhine married her Russian cousin Grand Duke Serge Alexandrovich.

Grand Duchess Elisabeth Feodorovna in a stylish and form-fitting fashionable dress.

Grand Duchess Elisabeth Feodorova in full Russian court dress and spectacular jewelry.

Serge and his brother Paul were particularly close. In this early 1890s photo they pose with Elisabeth.

At left: Paul Alexandrovich became a widower in 1891. To help him cope with life, Serge and Elisabeth became surrogate parents to his two children, Marie and Dmitri. In this image we see: Paul standing in back; while Serge, Elisabeth, Marie of Greece and Marie Pavlovna Jr. seat in front.

Below: Grand Duchess Elisabeth Feodorovna in court dress.

Above: Paul Alexandrovich and Elisabeth Feodorovna dressed for the famed 1903 Imperial Court Ball.

At right: Grand Duke Serge Alexandrovich in full military uniform.

Above: Princess Victoria of Battenberg visiting Russia. In this image, from about 1908, Victoria poses with her sister Elisabeth and other family members. From left: Grand Duchess Elisabeth Feodorovna, Princess Victoria of Battenberg, Grand Duchess Marie Pavlovna Jr., Prince William of Sweden and Grand Duke Dmitri Pavlovich.

At right: Grand Duchess Elisabeth Feodorovna with her nephews Hereditary Grand Duke Georg Donatus and Prince Ludwig of Hesse and by Rhine. The image was taken at Hemmelmark, Henry and Irène of Prussia's estate in Schleswig-Holstein.

At right: Prince Henry of Prussia.

Below: Princess Iréne of Hesse and by Rhine.

Prince Henry of Prussia and Princess Irène of Hesse and by Rhine were one of two sets of Queen Victoria's grandchildren to marry each other. The other couple was formed by Ernst Ludwig, Irène's brother, and their cousin Princess Victoria Melita of Edinburgh and Saxe-Coburg & Gotha. This rare image was taken during Henry and Irène's wedding ceremony at Schloß Charlottenburg, Berlin, on May 24, 1888.

At right: Prince Waldemar of Prussia.

Below: Prince Sigismund of Prussia.

A photograph taken to commemorate the silver wedding of Prince Henry and Princess Irène of Prussia, 1913.

The Henrys of Prussia and their family. From left: Prince Sigismund, Princess Irène, Prince Henry holding his grandson Prince Alfred, Princess Charlotte-Agnes and her daughter Princess Barbara, Princess Calixta and Prince Waldemar.

At right: Princess Irène of Prussia.

Below: Prince Henry of Prussia at seat. He was an avid sailor.

Princess Irène and Prince Henry of Prussia.

Prince Waldemar of Prussia in later life.

Prince Sigismund of Prussia, who lived in Costa Rica.

Prince Alfred of Prussia in Costa Rica.

At right: Princess Alix of Hesse and by Rhine.

Below: Tsar Nicholas II of Russia.

Tsar Nicholas II and Empress Alexandra Feodorovna at tea with their children: Grand Duchesses Olga, Tatiana, Marie, Anastasia and Tsarevich Alexei.

Prince Edward of Wales, Tsar Nicholas II, Tsarevich Alexei and the Prince of Wales (George V).

Empress Alexandra Feodorovna dressed for the part she was simply unable and unprepared to play.

Empress Alexandra Feodorovna surrounded by her daughters: Olga, Anastasia, Tatiana and Marie.

Tsar Nicholas II smoking by the seashore. Photo taken by Grand Duchess Helen Vladimirovna.

A family gathering at Tsarskoe Selo's Vladimir Villa, from left: Grand Duchess Tatiana Nicholaevna, Duchess Antoinette of Mecklenburg-Schwerin, Grand Duchess Victoria Feodorovna, Grand Duchess Olga Nicholaevna, Grand Duchess Marie Pavlovna, Grand Duke Kyrill Vladimirovich, Empress Alexandra Feodorovna, Princess Elisabeth of Greece, Tsar Nicholas II, Princess Olga of Greece, Grand Duchess Helen Vladimirovna, Grand Duchess Anastasia Nicholaevna, Princess Marina of Greece, Grand Duke Boris Vladimirovich, Grand Duchess Marie Nicholaevna and Grand Duke Andrei Vladimirovich.

Tsar Nicholas II and Tsarevich Alexei Nicholaevich during WWI.

The long and difficult exile began in Tobolsk, Siberia. With Nicholas II is his daughter Olga.

Three cousins: Prince Alfred of Edinburgh, Hereditary Grand Duke Ernst Ludwig of Hesse and by Rhine and Prince George of Wales (George V).

Grand Duke Ernst Ludwig of Hesse and by Rhine.

Wedding of Ernst Ludwig and Victoria Melita, May 1894.

Crown Princess Marie of Romania and her sister Victoria Melita of Hesse and by Rhine in fancy dress.

Hereditary Grand Duchess Cecile of Hesse and by Rhine.

Stunned by the tragic deaths of five members of his family, Prince Ludwig of Hesse and by Rhine married the Hon. Margaret Geddes quietly before presiding over the grand ducal funeral in Darmstadt.

Victoria, Dowager Marchioness of Milford Haven.

Grand Duke Ernst Luwig of Hesse and by Rhine.

Princess Irène of Prussia.

This image was taken at the Rosenhöhe in Darmstadt during the funeral of the Hessian grand ducal family. Prince Ludwig of Hesse served the unenviable post of chief mourner, his new wife by his side. Behind them are, among countless others: Hereditary Prince Gottfried of Hohenlohe-Langenburg (in uniform and white sash) with his wife Margarita; Prince Christopher of Greece, Princess Sophie of Hesse, Prince Andrew of Greece, Margrave Berhold and Margravine Theodora of Baden, Lord Louise Mountbatten, Prince Philip of Greece and the Dowager Marchioness of Milford Haven. Princess Alice was unable to attend her daughter's funeral.

The Neues Palais, Darmstadt.

Schloß Wolfsgarten, Hesse.

*The
Alexander
Palace,
Tsarskoe Selo,
Russia.*

Schloß Hemmelmarck, Schleswig-Holstein.

The Napolnaya School, Alapaievsk, Russia.

Chapter IX

January 1901 – February 1905

A fter the Queen's death, it was all too apparent that the deep core of the family would not hold together. Small tears began to develop in the carefully and intricately woven fabric of her extended relations. Such was inevitable, however, since the hub was gone. The Queen's eldest daughter, the Empress Friedrich, Aunt Vicky, lay at Friedrichshof dying, while Ernie and Ducky's marriage approached a crisis. There were some sad deaths of children which brought down the spirits of the family, as well as events in Russia which were coming to a violent head. The impact of all of these things would spill over cruelly into the sisters' lives.

Queen Victoria's legacy was being tampered with in more material ways as well. Her daughter Beatrice had taken upon herself the task of copying out all of the Queen's diaries and burn the originals. It is not known, particularly, what kind of editing she did, but perhaps the only tangible benefit was that Beatrice's handwriting was much easier to read than the old Queen's. The task took her thirty-nine years, and historians lament the losses, and question again and again, her fitness for the task.

On February 14, 1901, for the first time in long memory, Parliament opened without Queen Victoria. Prince Louis, who was, after all, one of Uncle Bertie's favorite cousins, was appointed the new King's Naval Aide-de-Camp. Once all the formalities were over in England, Victoria began her wanderings once again. She went to visit her dying Aunt at the beautiful Friedrichshof. She helped where she was able, sitting with the Empress, reading to her, and helping Aunt Vicky's daughters take care of her. The Dowager Empress was in tremendous pain with spinal cancer and suffered greatly with her last illness.

After that difficult visit, Victoria went to visit Ella at Illyinskoje. On August 6, 1901, while she was in Russia, Aunt Vicky died. The Imperial Family went into mourning and there were services commemorating the Dowager German Empress at Peterhof. The sisters all felt the loss of a beloved aunt; one of the care-givers who, in those early days, had helped the family through the grievous loss of their own mother. Aunt Vicky had, as they remembered, sounded like their mother. Others understood their grief and empathized. The Infanta Eulalia of Spain, who had written to Irène to condole with her on the death of her "Aunty-Mama," received this heartfelt reply:

> *We thank you both from our hearts for your kind sympathy at the death of* [Henry's] *dear mother....Henry's one comfort too was his having been able to say goodbye to her before he left with his vessel - both had the feeling that they would no more meet on this earth, so ill she was already.*[1]

Meanwhile, as autumn began, Ducky and Ernie's marriage broke down irretrievably. It was true that they had not been happy together almost from the beginning, however, the family had always hoped that they'd find some common ground. There was plenty of blame to go around, but the truth was that they were mismatched from the start. Ernie had no idea how to cope with Ducky's strong and passionate nature – his was a more placid and introverted one. This along with Ducky's falling madly in love with her cousin Grand Duke Kyrill Vladimirovich sounded the death knell of their grandmother's last royal match.

Ducky left Darmstadt in October 1901 and went back to Coburg to live with her mother, Aunt Marie. When she left Ernie, she also left her little daughter of six, Elisabeth. She was roundly criticized for this, but there was little doubt that Ducky loved her daughter passionately – the only way she knew how to love. She also knew that as a Princess of Hesse, the little girl had to remain in Darmstadt, at least until further agreements could be reached. Nevertheless, there were many that felt that she was an unfit mother.

Alix emphatically took sides with Ernie against this cousin of whom she'd never been overly fond, and certainly never understood. She made it clear that she would never be welcome at the Russian Imperial Court. However, Alix, herself, as her grandmother had feared, did not do well in court circles. Perhaps one of the prime reasons for this was that she was completely outshone by her mother-in-law, the Dowager Empress Marie Feodorovna. Another would be that Alix could not, and, indeed, would not make any attempt to ingratiate herself with the leaders of the court and society, or even with the other members of Nicky's family. She never hid her views regarding that society, which she found degenerate and unwholesome. That naturally was questionable, but because of her attitude, she made few friends among them. Sadly, later, when, she desperately needed the support of her peers, the support was not there. Perhaps, had the family been more united, things might have been different.

Alix was never comfortable as a public figure. She was shy and extremely uneasy in crowds. In addition, she was completely guarded, and never understood how to show her deep affection for the Russian people. She rarely smiled or seemed friendly. To the people who saw her, this translated as being cold, distant, and unfeeling though she was hardly this to the people she loved. With her husband and children, she was capable of a great warmth and compassion that very few others were privileged to see.

Unlike her younger sister, Victoria took a much more sensible view about Ernie's predicament, and was not so set against Ducky, out of respect, perhaps, to Uncle Affie. However she was extremely aware of how much Ducky had hurt her brother. Ernie certainly hadn't been much in love, despite his comments to the contrary, but his pride, and by extension Hessian pride, was hurt. Victoria was the right sister to console him. As always, her advice was sensible and unclouded with useless emotion and Ernie was grateful for her calm. He wrote a heartfelt letter full of love for his eldest sister,

I had felt very near on the verge of madness & those words of love comforted me & consoled me... Every word you say is true & now that I am calmer I see the absolute impossibility of going on leading a life which was killing her & driving me nearly mad... If I had not loved her so, I would have given it up long ago...Don't worry yourself darling you have been a sister to me like there are few... But in one way I led a nearly still more solitary life than she, I was allone [sic] she had her family & I was only with one of you when she wanted it. One inexplicable feeling has come over me, I feel that I am given back to you my sisters. Why I have it, don't aske [sic] me...Henry is such a help...God bless you for all your love my own darling, darling Victoria.[2]

Because of Victoria's pragmatism and sense of fairness, she also became Ducky's confidant. During one of their discussions, Victoria confessed that she knew well that it was better for them to part, and indeed it was. Ducky accused Ernie of homosexuality, an accusation that continues to this day. However, there are only the letters she wrote and her discussions with her niece that bear this out. She was, possibly, trying to convince others that she had been right to leave. In those letters, she wrote that he had stable boys and nearly any other young boy upon whom he could get his hands, in his bed. However, no external evidence of this exists. No one else, throughout the years, in letters or diaries, when it no longer would have mattered, has stepped forward to confirm the scurrilous rumors.

Eventually, Ducky and Kyrill were married in October 1905. This occurred after the birth, at last, of the heir to the Russian throne, Alexis Nicholaevich, the previous year. Kyrill had been waiting to see how Alix's latest pregnancy would turn out. There were those who said that had it been another girl, perhaps Kyrill, the heir presumptive and an opportunist (and perhaps the 'marble man', as his new sister-in-law, Marie of Romania would call him), would not have so quickly married Ducky. At any rate, the couple were exiled by Nicky from Russia since Ducky was a divorcee, as well as Kyrill's first cousin. However, the fact that Ducky had been married to the Tsarina's own brother was probably the deciding factor. Kyrill was struck off the Imperial rolls, stripped of his titles and decorations as well as his allowances. The couple went into exile in Paris. Victoria wrote:

> *I was really less surprised and startled by her decision than he. Tho' both had done their best to make a success of their marriage, it had been a failure. Their characters and temperaments were quite unsuited to each other and I had noticed how they were gradually drifting apart. As I had known Ducky well from a child, since the time that she lived with her parents at San Antonio, she had often spoken freely to me on the subject of her married life. She had confidence that I hope was not misplaced, in my fairness of judgment, and in spite of my being devoted to my brother. I can only say that I thought then, and still think, that it was best for both that they should part from each other.*[3]

Alix, who was furious about the entire affair, and was extremely slow in forgiving Ducky or receiving the couple, wrote: *"Divorce is a terrible thing, but now I can only thank God that it happened as it did, otherwise my brother's spirit would have been utterly broken."*[4]

As usual, the most afflicted party was the couple's little girl, the Princess Elisabeth of Hesse and by Rhine. In December of 1901, when the divorce became final, one of the agreements put in place by the couple was that Elisabeth would live with each parent half of the year. So, the child began the sad limbo typical of children of divorce, shuttled from parent to parent. When she went to her mother in Coburg, Ernie wrote to Victoria, that *"it was terrible to see her misery at leaving, for she has such a pronounced feeling for her home. I did everything I could to make it easy for her but alas that child feels herself such a Hessian..."*[5]

Happily for Ernie and other members of the family, they had great events to distract them. Most important, of course, was Uncle Bertie's coronation, set to take place in June of 1902. Indeed, Ernie would also travel, at the end of the year to be present at the Coronation Durbar in India. In that early summer, however, royalties gathered, and for the Hessians, there was a reunion of sorts, at least with Irène, Ernie, and Victoria. Victoria's daughter Alice, fresh from her finishing school in Darmstadt also attended with her parents. She was becoming more lovely every day with her blonde hair and blue eyes. During this visit, she met Prince Andrew of Greece and Denmark, and was strongly drawn to him. However, Victoria and Louis felt just as strongly that Alice was too young, and wanted to do nothing about the young couple's attachment until both were much older.

Unfortunately for all that gathered for the great day, it, in fact, had to be canceled.

The King had become very ill and went through an emergency appendectomy on June 24. Convinced he was going to die on the operating table, instead, the King came through the operation extremely well, sitting up and smoking a cigar in the bed the following day. However, there had to be a period of recuperation and many of the royalties, deprived of their show, drifted back home.

Victoria went back to the Heiligenberg during the month of July, and as a matter of fact, celebrated the fifth year of Nona Kerr's, her stalwart lady-in-waiting, service. With a self-deprecating sense of humor, Victoria wrote that Nona deserved a statue struck in her honor *"in the stable grounds,"*[5] for sticking it out with her, Louis and the children. To Victoria's credit, she was well capable of self-analysis and knew how difficult she could be at times. Though she rarely voiced it, she wrote it often to her friend – her deep appreciation of Nona's devotion and care to her and her children.

Victoria also became deeply aware that her daughter was impatient to begin her life, and wanted very much to become engaged to Andrew. The young people had seen more and more of each other that summer, at Darmstadt, where she and Louise continued their studies and he was a dashing member of the Hessian 23rd Dragoon Guards. Their attraction grew quickly to love, and they sought Victoria and Louis' permission to become engaged. Though it was against Victoria's wishes, she acquiesced, and wrote to Nona: *"Little doubt about Andrea becoming my son-in-law."*[7]

The following month, those who could, hurriedly returned to London, where Edward VII was at last crowned on August 9, 1902. Victoria and her family were there as well as Henry and Irène, all staying at Buckingham Palace. The new King liked Henry and made him a Vice-Admiral of the British Fleet and also conferred upon him the Royal Victorian Chain.[8] Alice's new fiancé, Prince Andrew, also returned to attend the festivities. Their engagement would not be official until May of the following year, but, more or less, from the coronation onward, they were unofficially engaged. The official engagement was announced by Cousin George, now the Prince of Wales, when Prince Andrew was twenty-one. Though Alice was now seventeen, both Louis and Victoria continued to feel that Alice was far too young and the Greek monarchy too insecure. Nevertheless, they allowed Alice to have her way.

About the insecurity of Andrew's family's throne in Greece, they were undoubtedly right as events would later prove. Greece had only become a monarchy in the last seventy years, and King George, who had been Prince William of Denmark, and Aunt Alix's brother, had only gone to Greece in 1863. The Greeks seemed a bellicose people with expansionist ideas. Undoubtedly, sensible Victoria wasn't excited about the prospect of her daughter in a volatile Balkan state, even if she would be nowhere near the throne. As the decades rolled along, Alice and Andrew were in and out of exile, as was the entire Greek Royal Family.

Putting her doubts aside, Victoria began planning what would, again, be called a 'Wedding of the Decade' by the newspapers. This would be one of the last gatherings of the 'Royal Mob' before the Great War. Victoria, as was natural for her, spent her time writing letters and making arrangements. Though there would be many members of the family attending Alice's wedding, Darmstadt would be able to handle the situation. Being a minor Grand Duchy, Darmstadt could, nevertheless, easily provide the entire family with lodgings at the Old and New Schlosses. In addition to that, if the wedding would take place in September or October Alix and Nicky would also be able to attend, and there really would be a full complement of Hessians.

Ernie continued to write to Victoria about the fact that he believed her to be his greatest friend in matters of his little girl Elisabeth and that

> *my child has been worrying me very much and especially because I can't do anything in the matter and you are the only one who can say anything to her. I fear it will be of no use but anyhow I thank you once more with all my heart.*[9]

It appeared that Victoria was the only one in the family who could discuss issues of visits and such with Ducky. Once again, Victoria was the 'go-between' in difficult family issues.

> *She, of course, was traveling back and forth from England, where Louis was now the Director of Naval Intelligence, and constantly visiting with her sisters. Ella came in October of 1902, and all were gathered at Darmstadt for a mini-reunion. Victoria moved on to Irène's later in the year, and spent Christmas at Kiel. She wrote of an amusing incident, which characterized Henry's love for gadgets, and his great love for motor cars. He always had the most up-to-date ones; however, there were some drawbacks since, you had to replenish the boiler, stopping at some farmhouse on the way to get water in a bucket. Then, in accordance with the force of the draught created by the car, flames and steam would envelop the passengers in the back seat, and the temperature would become uncomfortably high. Coming back from Hemmelmarck I was frozen up to the waist by the icy wind we faced, while the lower part of my body was being roasted like St. Laurence on the gridiron!*[10]

In the spring of that year, an event occurred that would change Ella's life. Earlier, in September of 1891, her husband's brother and one of his closest companions, Grand Duke Paul Alexandrovich, lost his wife, the Grand Duchess Alexandra, who had formerly been Princess Alexandra of Greece and Denmark, only five days after giving birth to their son, Dmitri. Paul was inconsolable, and had to be physically restrained by Serge and his other brother, Alexander III, from throwing himself on his poor wife's coffin. In the intervening years, Paul immersed himself in his military career and left his two children, Marie and Dmitri in the care of Serge and Ella. They were the children's unofficial guardians, but because Paul made a morganatic marriage in 1903, the two little ones were officially put in Ella and Serge's care.

So, nearly twenty years into their marriage, they became the parents of their brother's children. Young Marie's memoirs certainly gave the feeling that she and her brother felt abandoned by their father. She was also bitter that Ella did not seem to reciprocate the worshipful feelings she had for the Aunt with whom she lived. As a matter of fact, she portrayed the Grand Duchess as cold and unfeeling towards her. Knowing the Grand Duke's outwardly cold disposition, perhaps a clue to understanding Ella's treatment of Marie was a result of her own jealousy of Serge's tenderness towards the two motherless children. There is also some evidence that Serge was jealous of the love that Marie and Dmitri had for their father, Paul. According to Marie, *"in spite of the great sorrow that my uncle felt at his brother's misalliance, he could not conceal the joy he felt at the fact that from now on he would be able to keep us entirely to himself."*[11] Sadly, it wasn't quite the happy ending that many would have hoped. Dmitri, it appeared, was easier for Ella. So in their household, there was a convolution of conflicting emotions, leading to misunderstandings and jealousies.

Those troubles were all put aside when in October 1903, the 'Royal Mob' gathered once again for the occasion of Princess Alice's wedding to Prince Andrew. It would be the last time there would be a strong Romanov presence at a family event – and Nicky and Alix were there, as well, as Ella, Serge, Irène, and Henry. Queen Alexandra of England, as well as Andrew's parents the King and Queen of Greece also attended, though Uncle Bertie did not. However, Prince George and Princess May came along with the Queen. More poignantly, it was probably one of the last carefree times in which the various Royal families would meet before the Great War. Luckily, Darmstadt was a convenient and central meeting place for the Royal contingent, scattered, as they were, throughout Europe.

Doubtless, it was times such as these, when the family gathered, that Victoria missed her grandmother the most. For all the Queen's calling her extended family the 'Royal Mob,' and complaining that these occasions were tedious and tiring, she certainly, enjoyed them, at least in secret.

Ernie was slowly recovering from his problems, but, naturally, for the first time, there was not a strong Edinburgh presence at a big family event. It was just as well since Alix's hostility towards Ducky and by extension, the rest of that family was palpable – and Alix was now by no means just a difficult and shy younger sister.

Louise, who was fourteen, and one of her sister's bridesmaids, looked slim, elegant, and quite grown-up in her long dress. Louise would perhaps never come close to her sister's beauty, but she had a tremendously attractive way about her, and was extremely intelligent. She began to lose some of her reticence and Victoria began to think of her as excellent company, which, indeed, she had become. Her father had hoped this would happen, writing to Louise that

In years to come I will probably be much at sea, and there must always be these long & bitter separations, which one feels more & more, the older one gets. It will always be a comfort to me to know that Mama has a helpful companion in you especially since Alice found her happiness, & thus left us so early![12]

On October 6, the civil wedding was celebrated after which there was luncheon at the Old Schloss. Princess Marie of Erbach-Schönberg, Louis' sister, described the day:

The procession of their Greek Majesties with a military escort, three four-horsed carriages à la Daumont, with outriders, and many pair-horsed carriages, was splendid...In the evening there was a gala performance in the theatre, and on the evening of the 6th October a dinner with the suites in the Kaisersaal of the castle. Then there was a reception by Louis and Victoria in the ballroom of the Old Palace, with music and a supper, the same ballroom where I and all of us had come out at our first balls. There were about three hundred people present... Alice looked charming and radiant, and no less handsome and radiant was her father, my dear brother Louis, who wore the uniform of the Hessian artillery.[13]

The following day the religious rites were celebrated. First, Alice married Andrew in a Protestant ceremony at the Schlosskirche at 3 p.m. and then in the new Russian chapel on the Mathildenhöhe, for the Orthodox Service. Princess Marie continued:

The wedding day broke hot and sunny. At half-past three the Protestant marriage was solemnized in the castle...The bridal couple...stood on a carpet of rose-coloured silk a symbol of the path of life. The four crown-bearers, Princes George and Christopher of Greece, Prince Albert of Holstein, and Victor [Marie's son] stood behind them...They had been brought from Petersburg, and were the wedding-crowns of Catherine II...We then gathered again in the

Old Palace, where a family dinner took place at once.[14]

The royal festivities culminated with the wedding banquet, which was a rather raucous affair. From all accounts, their subjects would be amazed at how silly many of the family members could be at these parties. Much of it had to do with being together with so many members of the family, which was, to say the least, a rare occasion, and being able to behave naturally, and not be constantly on ones' dignity. No less a factor, undoubtedly, was a great sufficiency of champagne and other imbibable potables.

When Alice and Andrew left in their new motorcar, a gift from Nicky and Alix, some members of the family, to the dismay of the ever-present detectives, began chasing the car. There were cheering crowds determined to get a look at the newlyweds, as well as others just out to get a glimpse of the entire royal splendor that had converged on their little town. Nicky, evidently feeling very free and secure in Darmstadt, was the ringleader of the gang chasing the car. They caught up to the car and flung another slipper at Alice along with more rice. Alice laughingly flung the slipper back at Nicky, whom it was reported, she called a silly ass. He, it was further reported, was doubled over in the middle of the street, convulsed with laughter. The young couple spent a week in Jugenheim, and then returned to the Old Palace until about the end of the year.

Victoria, now a mother-in-law at the tender age of forty, was wistful. She wrote to Nona: *"It is ridiculous how old I begin to feel, not physically, but mentally."*[15] She wintered in London at her house at 70 Cadogan Square. But just as all was calm for a few months, tragedy struck once again. On November 16, 1903, little Elisabeth of Hesse died, at the age of eight, at one of the Tsar's hunting lodges at Skierniewice, Poland.

The little girl had been visiting her cousins, the Imperial Family, at the Emperor's shooting lodge at Spala near Skierniewice where they customarily spent their autumn. There, she sickened with a rare form of ambulatory typhoid and very quickly died. She had been Ernie's mainstay during the difficult years after his divorce. One need only look at pictures of this little Princess to be struck by her beauty – she would have been another of the great Hessian beauties. Naturally, both her parents loved Elisabeth and were shattered by her death. As mentioned, the divorce agreement provided that she stay alternately with them during the year, and Victoria wrote that *"her nurse, Wilson, told me the child was very unhappy at the separation of her parents as she loved them both. Happy as she was with her mother, she always longed for Hesse which she considered her real home."*[16] As much as Elisabeth loved Hesse, Hesse evidently loved her. The entire Duchy was grief-stricken since this little girl was so obviously a very great favorite. The city decked itself out in white and Elisabeth was buried in a white coffin with great pomp and ceremony.

Victoria comforted Ernie as best she could, rushing back to Darmstadt to help him with the funeral arrangements – though, who truly feels comforted at the death of a child? Little Elisabeth was, at that lonely time, an important part of his life and the Neues Palais was particularly desolate with no sisters, no little daughter, and only Ernie glumly clattering around. Naturally, because of this, all of his sisters worried for him.

Victoria, as his confidant, was especially concerned, though she was optimistic about his recuperative powers. She wrote to Nona: *"He will continue missing his dear little child terribly but there is no reason to fear he will brood & mope over his loss..."*[17] However, there was some reason for concern. Ernie was alone in Darmstadt on that dreaded date, December 14, the date of their mother and grandfather's death. Victoria wrote a long letter of sympathy to Ernie that shows the depth of their relationship. She wrote that he had *so lately learnt to understand how greatly dear Mama suffered at the loss of her little ones, by the bitter loss that has come into your life…Always I have remembered those last words I ever heard her speak, when I saw her at the doors of Papa's room, on her return from seeing Aunt Marie at the station. 'Ich bin so müde' she said; & I felt it even at the moment, that she was not only tired in her body, but weary in her heart of all the anxiety & grief she had gone through – She was but as old as you are now, & she has been at rest since then. But the work she did in that short life of hers has lasted & born fruit – & if one day the same can be said of us, then shall we not have been unworthy of her.[18]*

The family continued to be doleful, and extremely anxious about Ernie. This would be a pattern for the sisters – they would surround Ernie and try to spare him from any great sorrow, as though they all knew that he couldn't bear such adversity. At the end of the year, Irène, closest in proximity to her brother, was eager to discover his plans for Christmas. The thought of him being alone with his grief at the Schloss was more than she could bear. However, in the end, Alice and Andrew, who were living in the Schloss while Andrew continued his military service, spent the time with their Uncle as well as Franzjos and Anna Battenberg. But Irène had the last word with a wish for the New Year that *"time help to soften the great pain you suffer from, & bear so bravely…Oh! Ernie dear, it makes ones heart ache to think how you must suffer."*[19]

Neither was Irène spared as the New Year of 1904 rang in. In February, Irène's youngest child had an accident. Ernie wrote to Victoria to apprise her of the situation:

I got a telegram from Henry today, saying that their baby had fallen from a chair two days ago & suffers from headaches & sickness, they hear it may be a hemorrhage to the brain & return to Kiel today. Perhaps it is not quite so bad as they think poor things.[20]

At that point, Victoria was in England attending the marriage of her cousin Alice of Albany, daughter of Uncle Leopold, to Alexander of Teck, the brother of Princess May of Wales. The young couple was married at St. George's Chapel at Windsor.

The condition of little Heinrich, who was suffering from fevers and headaches, was grave. There was no hope for the child, Ernie subsequently wrote to Victoria, but Irène was brave and only broke down occasionally. A few weeks later, at the end of February, Irène lost her youngest little boy to hemophilia. He died at Kiel and was just four years old. That left her with just two boys: her eldest, Toddy, who also had the dreaded disease, but seemed to manage and even grow up; and, little Bobby – Sigismund, who was completely free from the disease. Victoria, as contemplative and practical as she was, must have marveled endlessly at the miracle that prevented her boys from suffering from the disease. Naturally she rushed to attend the funeral.

Irène never failed to appreciate the attentions of her family. She wrote to Ernie only a few weeks later about how wonderful he had been in those sad days that little Heinrich died. She was already trying to 'buck up' and do the normal everyday things in life to get back on track. *"Once more from the depth of my heart – God bless for your love and help & all you did & suffered for us in those terrible days & Kisses over & over again fr. Yr. Sorrowing old Irène…"*[21]

The Infanta Eulalia, whose son was also ill at this time, wrote to Irène and Irène, unfailingly considerate, thanked her.

Let me thank you for your loving sympathy in our great grief in which Henry also begs to be allowed to join his thanks. Indeed it has been a terrible shock to us, and the daily life seems so hard without that sunny bright angel near us – he was so full of life and the three children were all so different in their way – but he is saved further pain and sorrow for him it is better, but for us.... But I ought not to speak so of my grief when you are in such anxiety about your youngest darling [the Infante Luis Fernando]...

Henry remembers so often your great kindness to him at Madrid, and your pretty house you showed him then.[22]

****

Happily, in Ernie's case, there was some balm for the great sorrow and loss of both these small children, when the young man, in time, found another princess to marry. Ernie would probably never rid himself of his great fears of abandonment, and his childhood wish not to die alone. Because of these issues, which were obvious to his sisters, undoubtedly their prayers were literally answered when Eleonore of Solms-Hohensolms-Lich consented to be his wife. She was a sweet, simple girl, and therefore, nothing like the far more flamboyant and complex Ducky. Her family had been friends of the Hesse and by Rhine family, and she, in fact, had spent time in Darmstadt the previous winter of 1904, when her mother, Princess Agnes, was ill, and was receiving medical treatment. They became friends, and there was little doubt that she was far more suited to Ernie, who had no idea how to cope with complicated women – not that he'd ever been much inclined to try.

In February 1905, Louis and Victoria went to Darmstadt to be present at their wedding which took place in the Court Chapel of the Old Schloss. Their marriage was smooth and serene, and Ernie finally got what he really wanted – two beautiful boys, Georg (George) Donatus, "Don," and, Ludwig whom the family called "Lu." Victoria wrote that

Ernie's second marriage was a great success. She understood him perfectly, thanks to her unselfish but very intelligent nature and they were deeply devoted to each other. There are few people whom I have learned so to respect, love and admire, as my sister-in-law Onor [as Eleonore was called].[23]

****

Prince Louis continued to rise in the navy and in July of 1904 was promoted to Rear-Admiral. This was achieved, in spite of and not because of his position as Prince Battenberg and the husband of one of Queen Victoria's granddaughters. There were objections in the Admiralty from the likes of Lords Beresford and Lambton, who for various reasons, possibly xenophobia, nepotism, or jealousy, did not like the Prince. Nevertheless, he did advance. That summer, Victoria and her children who were still at home, spent their time at yet another rented house. Chief among their visitors that year were Irène and Henry. Later that summer, Louis went to Peterhof to represent Uncle Bertie at the christening of Alexis Nicholaevich, the new little son of Alix and Nicky.

By autumn, Victoria and her family were back at Cadogan Square, and looking forward to spending a quiet Christmas at Osborne Cottage with Aunt Beatrice, while the Connaughts spent it close by with Aunt Louise, at Kent House. As though to put a period on the idyllic year, Victoria recorded that *"I picked primroses in the Osborne grounds on the last day of that year."*[24]

****

In February of 1904, Russia declared war on Japan and new troubles began. Ella, however, was in her element organizing hospitals and caring for the wounded and sick. But even these humanitarian projects did little to add luster to Serge's reputation. There was always another way to see such altruism. *"During the war with Japan* [the Grand Duchess] *collected funds to equip a hospital train, but this humane project never materialized, because someone embezzled the large sums subscribed in response to Ella's appeal, and it was said in some quarters that Serge himself was implicated in the fraud."*[25]

Russia could not conceive of Japan having the power to defeat her and was shocked when news of Japanese victories began to arrive. As the year wore on, the war incited more domestic unrest. Reforms were proposed that were completely at odds with Serge's policies since he had taken the office of governor. He was implacable about such changes and chose to resign as Governor General after thirteen years in office, rather than acquiesce. It was later given out to the press that the Grand Duke's resignation was for reasons of health.[26] After his resignation, and because he was worried about his family's security, he moved them into the safety of the Kremlin. Serge officially gave up his post on January 1, 1905.

Whatever reluctant measures the Tsar put forward were not enough to quell the continuing turmoil. The beginning of 1905 marked a watershed in Russian history. On January 22, workers under the leadership of a priest organized a strike, and from all accounts, went on a peaceful march, to the Winter Palace. They were interested in presenting a list of grievances to their Tsar, and call for a constituent assembly. They quietly walked through the streets to do so.

When they reached the huge snowy square of the palace, Serge's Preobrajensky Guard was set up and waiting in front of the ornately columned building – a long line of mounted soldiers with swords drawn. They were stationed there to meet the crowd, having been told there might be trouble. Though the crowd had remained peaceable during their walk to the palace, the Guard's orders were, nevertheless, to disperse them by any necessary means. Nicky, in any case, was not there but at Tsarskoye Selo. What happened next was sheer panic and the guard began firing on the amassed demonstrators, killing many. What resulted was a tragic melee, where scores of people were killed and wounded. It was another stupidly handled fiasco and became the infamous events known as "Bloody Sunday." After this horrific incident, the Tsar was no longer seen by the peasants and workers as their "Little Father" but as "Nicholas the Bloody."

As January led into February, one contemporary historian said that Serge had the look of someone with the foreknowledge of what was to come. *"He wore a haggard, haunted, frightened look which seemed to betray a premonition of the tragic fate in store for him."*[27] With the lack of wisdom in which so many of these incidents of discontent were handled, it is hardly surprising that the human face of repression, the Grand Duke Serge Alexandrovich, would become a primary target of assassination.

As in his father's case, there was more than one attempt made on Serge's life. On

February 13, 1905, however, the attempt was successful. At three o'clock in the afternoon, when his carriage was inside the Kremlin walls, a bomb was thrown and Serge was blown to bits. Ella had heard the explosion from her rooms and rushed out to see what had happened. She numbly began to gather the parts of the body strewed everywhere saying: *"Hurry, hurry, Serge hates blood and mess."*[28] Though little remained, at her direction, the pieces of her husband were placed on a stretcher, covered by a cloak, and taken to the Nicholas Palace. Ella wrote telegrams informing the family, though Alix and Nicky were advised not to attend the funeral, and did not.

Victoria rushed from London to be at her side. Louis, however, was unable to go since he was obliged to leave for his new commission on the *HMS Drake*, and his new appointment as Rear-Admiral. The Prince could hardly have been comfortable letting Victoria, Louise, and Nona go to Russia after such an anti-monarchical incident, and the assassination of a close family member. Nevertheless, Victoria was determined to be with Ella and she left for Moscow on February 18. They were eventually joined by Ernie and Onor. Henry and Irène joined as well, though they were unable to go all the way to Moscow but only traveled with Victoria for several days through Germany. Wilhelm *"met me at the Berlin station and gave me supper. He was very kind and thoughtful and much worried about Ella, for whom during his student days he had felt a strong devotion."*[29] Marie of Erbach-Schönberg also joined the supper group at Berlin. She described the meeting:

> *The train came in soon, and we all went to the railway-carriage. Victoria had Baron Riedesel with her. She had left London the evening before. It was a painful meeting. At table Victoria sat between the Kaiser and me; we talked about many things, not only about the unfortunate Sergius. When it was time for her to leave we went with Victoria to the carriage in which she would have to continue her journey for another forty-eight hours.*[30]

On February 19, Ella went to Taganka Prison to speak with the man who had murdered her husband, Kaliaev. Naively, she asked him why he committed such an act and tried to reconcile him with God. He answered her that the things he had done were perfectly consistent with his principles and that he had no regrets. He did tell her, however, that he had actually restrained himself from throwing a bomb when she and Marie and Dmitri were in the carriage. Ella left him a holy picture which he evidently kept. She had not wanted this visit to be generally known, but it soon became well publicized.

When Victoria reached Moscow the following day, along with Aunt Marie of Coburg, and her youngest daughter Beatrice, she found Ella very brave, calm, and collected. She was, however, pale and trance-like and Victoria noted that her sister could neither eat nor sleep. Ella moved her bed into her niece's, the Grand Duchess Marie Pavlovna, room, taking comfort, for once, in the children that Serge had so loved. Thirty-seven years later, Victoria wrote in her memoirs that,

> contrary to the general belief [,] she and Serge had led a happy married life, tho' it was he who was completely the head and master of the house. Ella was very willing that he should be it and he was full of affectionate attentions to her. As to bringing up Paul's children, she left it entirely to him, who was a devoted uncle to them. Both Ella and Serge were very fond of children and it was sad that they never had had any of their own.[31]

One would hardly think that Victoria need cover-up for her sister so many years after the events, and with so many of the players dead.

Ella arranged the funeral which, as stated, Alix and Nicky did not attend, since it was deemed too dangerous for the pair to be seen publicly after such a violent act against the throne and the family. After much ceremony, and sincere mourning from some segments of the population, Serge was put to rest in a crypt of the Chudov Monastery in the Kremlin.

After all the rituals attached to the death of her husband were completed, Ella began to think about her future. She knew that she loved Moscow and wished to remain there. While Victoria was with her, she and Ella discussed her plans for the future and what Ella would do as a widow. Victoria wrote to Nona about some of what they discussed, although she was somewhat surprised at some of the plans Ella proposed for her future. What surprised her more, though, was Ella's devotion to her niece and nephew. She was sure that with Ella's

unselfish character, high sense of duty, healthy nerves & energetic mind, I have no doubt of her being able to shape her future life wisely & well by herself, & her great sorrow she has born [sic] bravely from the first. For the next years certainly, I think she will retain the charge of Marie & Dimitri, & as they cling to her in a touching fashion, she will have them to love & care for –[32]

Ella's other decisions, however, were, perhaps, a little more unexpected to the rest of her family – though not so much to Victoria. She stopped eating meat, had her bedroom stripped of its luxuries, divided all of her jewelry in three groups – some went to the crown, some to the family and the remainder was sold. This began her withdrawal from the world, and the beginning of her decision to found a convent order and become a nun herself.

Ella began to study the ways and means in which she could begin a monastic order. Her interest was creating something unique in the Russian Orthodox monastic system – she wanted to start a nursing order that would be involved with the physical nursing of patients and building hospitals. Her requests to begin such an order were initially rejected by the establishment. It was hard for some to believe that the Metropolitans would ever let her, a convert to Russian Orthodoxy, do this – especially the way in which she proposed. It all reeked too much of Protestantism for them. Ella had her own ideas of the way a nunnery should be organized. She wanted her sisters to be able to go out in the world, and have holidays with their families. It was, possibly, because she never wanted them to forget that they were human beings, so that they could better take care of other human beings.

The initial refusal by the church hierarchy was not at all surprising. However, Ella was not discouraged about this. She continued sending them proposals, and having discussions about such a nursing order. It seemed that Ella not only had a true calling but a great deal of determination. In the end, it was by the sheer force of this determination that got Ella what she wanted – the Convent of SS Martha and Mary.

Chapter X

March 1905 – May 1913

A month later, Victoria left her grieving sister and traveled back to the Heiligenberg. As difficult as it may have been for her to go, she left a woman who had already set out on the purpose that would drive the rest of her life – the commencement of which would gradually take form in the next five years. On a broader level, the political events of 1905, the war and the Revolution, absorbed the entire family from a personal as well as a public point of view, and the violence of the twentieth century was just beginning.

Victoria's son, Georgie, graduated from Cheam, and became a Naval Cadet at Royal Naval College at Osborne. Uncle Bertie had, it seemed, no use for his old childhood home and gave it, except for the Family Pavilion, to the Royal Navy. Though the Queen's grandchildren, who had spent such happy moments there, no doubt had difficulty imagining how he could so easily give away Queen Victoria's precious house, perhaps the King's childhood memories gave him little pleasure. Or perhaps, it was too middle class and plain for him.

In April of that year, Victoria traveled to Athens for the birth of Alice's first child. She arrived at the seaport city of Patras on April 7, and attended the First International Archeological Congress at the Parthenon. As an aficionado of archeology, one can only imagine her delight. Prince Andrew, knowing how to please his mother-in-law, took her on sight seeing excursions in his car. Together they drove to the bridges of Pentelikon, famous for its marble quarries, just northeast of Athens and then further to Elensis.[1]

On April 18, Princess Margarita of Greece and Denmark was born in Athens at 12 a.m., and at the tender age of forty-two, Victoria was a grandmother. The little girl and her next sister, Theodora, called "Dolla," who would come one year later, were destined to be very good friends with Victoria's son, Dickie. There are many family pictures of Dickie playing with the two little girls, no doubt delighted that there were now children in the family over whom he was senior.

Louis arrived in Greece on the *HMS Drake* and joined the family. The christening took place in May with Victoria and King George I of the Hellenes acting as godparents. Afterward, Victoria returned to her children, who were staying with their Uncle Ernie and Aunt Onor in Hesse, and went to the Heiligenberg, where they spent the rest of the summer. Louise was confirmed that June, however, Louis, back on the Drake, was unable to attend. Louise, in an introspective mood, wrote to her father and reassured him on a point that was extremely close to his heart. *"I will always try and be a helpful companion, now that I am getting older to dear Mama."*[2] Louise always kept her promise to her father, and did so until her late marriage.

After the traumatic events of early 1905, Victoria recalled that summer months were hot, lazy days, but above all peaceful. The family brought a new gramophone and made their own records. Her recollections are rambling about this period of her life. There were interesting new-fangled inventions to talk about from the installation of telephones to the cinema, and what she thought of both. She loved telephones and made a point to answer them before servants or anyone else in the house for the obvious reason that she adored talking. That was, however, the reason she was not quite as enchanted with the wireless radio – she couldn't talk back to it. In addition, she did not like the cinema since the flickering of the film was, in her opinion, difficult on the eyes.

Victoria recalled one of the first films made of her family, in 1896. Alix and Nicky and other family members were visiting their grandmother at Balmoral in Scotland. The instruction the cameraman gave must have been something to the effect of 'walk around, but for heaven sakes, try to stay within the range of the camera', and the film, today, is rather hilarious because that is exactly what the family members did. They walked in and out of the frame milling around in a rather aimless and silly manner. It is fascinating, however, to see these figures as living and animated people. In all, the cinema did not have a great attraction for Victoria, though Dickie wanted her to be more 'film minded'. Dickie loved it, as he would later prove on his honeymoon. He and his new wife Edwina made a stop in Hollywood and acted with their friend Charlie Chaplin in a small, privately shot film.[3]

Victoria's sister-in-law Onor had a miscarriage in September 1905, and the following month, a charming memorial to the little Princess Elisabeth of Hesse was unveiled in a park in Darmstadt. Victoria was able to hand over the reins of the Alice Frauen Verein, which had not interested Ducky, on to her new sister-in-law. She wrote to Onor:

> On Thursday the General Meeting of the...Institute is taking place...I am sending you the invitation...Ernie has never come and Papa only did it in remembrance of my mother. Of course you would give the institute great pleasure if you appear...do what you think fit.[4]

Onor happily embraced the leadership of the Frauen Verein and through the years became a greatly beloved Grand Duchess, extremely involved with the people, the institutions founded by Alice, and the duchy itself, a true '*landsmütter*'.

In the fall, Louis, in his capacity as Rear Admiral, Commander of the Second Cruiser Squadron and the *HMS Drake* was off to North America and the United States for a good-will tour. In November, the squadron was shown gracious hospitality when it arrived in Baltimore Harbor. The Americans treated all the British Officers with friendliness and consideration, though that consideration might have sprung from the fact that the British did not look upon the Americans as foreigners. It might have been more accurate to say that they were looked upon as eccentric cousins. *The Times*, of course, could not resist saying that an "*exhibition of naval smartness will be fully appreciated by the people of the United States.*"[5]

Louis had the good fortune to be received by the President, the energetic and often exhausting Theodore Roosevelt. Having been Secretary of the Navy before he became Vice-President under McKinley, he was also extremely knowledgeable about naval matters. Both Prince Louis and the President were admirers of Admiral Alfred Thayer Mahan who wrote *The Importance of Sea Power in History*, a primer of naval imperialism, and consequently, there was much for the two to discuss. They talked about their concern about the Kaiser and his build-up of what was becoming a monumental German navy. Cousin Willy, too, kept a copy of Admiral Mahan's vital book on his night table, and took its lessons eagerly to heart. Louis evidently left the official White House dinner hungry. He and the President were so deeply in conversation that he had waved away dishes and touched little on his plate.

After leaving Washington, Prince Louis and his party went to New York. There, they attended a reception with the current Secretary of the Navy, Charles J. Bonaparte.* They spent nearly eleven days in the city. One evening, there was a banquet at a Chinese Restaurant with singing waiters, one of whom was the future great popular composer, Irving Berlin. Many years later, during World War Two, Berlin, who remembered serving Chinese food to the Prince, told the story to Victoria, who in turn, told it to Dickie.[6]

We had another U.S.A. officer, who was taking the well known song writer Irving Berlin from Bristol to London, the latter being our chief guest. I sat near him & he told me that the first time his name ever appeared in a paper, was on the occasion of Papa's visit with the cruiser squadron to New York in 1905. Berlin was then a waiter in China Town & one of the numerous extra hands (& singing waiter), employed at a dinner for our fleet. He seems to have been given the job to attend upon the drinks & serve Papa & one of the newspapers mentioned him by name. He still treasures the cutting from it.[7]

The Prince left America with a great love of that country, which he passed on to his children.

Oddly enough, the German community of New York took Louis' visit as an opportunity to stage a protest. They felt that his being there was *"part of a cunningly contrived plan to create an impression abroad that a secret alliance exists between England and the United States, and that this alliance is specially directed towards intimidating Germany."*[8] This is especially ironic in view of the treachery of which Louis was accused later on at the beginning of the Great War.

That following spring, members of the family spent a jolly holiday in Venice, where they met a ship of Louis'. Ernie and Onor were keen to go to antique shops and Princess Marie of Erbach-Schönberg was particularly excited that she would finally be able to visit one of Louis' commands. Marie remarked, movingly, in her memoirs that they all particularly remembered Sandro who loved the city as much as they did. Her poignant comment was *"the city of crumbling dreams, it suited us all, but me particularly, who am always listening to the slowly dying tones that sound from the dream-like past..."*[9] And, indeed, the end of the dream-like past was coming.

The spring of 1906 was punctuated by another Royal Wedding. Henry of Battenberg and Princess Beatrice's only daughter, Ena, the sisters' tall, blonde, beautiful cousin, was to be married to Alfonso XIII of Spain. Alfonso was a small, dark, odd little fellow, who stood up rather poorly to the Junoesque Ena; moreover, she was not his first choice. Alfonso had already made the rounds with her other cousins, first setting his sights on Princess Margaret, whom the family called Daisy, of Connaught. Then, when Crown Prince Gustav Adolf of Sweden won her, he cheerfully shifted the photographs in his wallet and his attentions to her sister, Patricia, called Patsy.

Despite the fact that Ena was the granddaughter of a morganatic marriage, something that mattered to the Spaniards, and a Protestant (which mattered even more), Alfonso chose to overlook these obstacles. He settled upon Ena, a very popular Princess in

---

(*) *Secretary of the Navy Charles J. Bonaparte was an American-born descendant of the French Imperial Family. His father, Jerome Bonaparte, was a son of Jérôme Bonaparte, former King of Westphalia and youngest brother of Emperor Napoléon I, and of his first wife Elizabeth Patterson. The couple's marriage was not accepted by the Emperor, who asked the Pope for an annulment. When the Vatican denied the request, Napoléon took the unprecedented act of declaring the marriage annulled. Jérôme became King of Westphalia in 1807, ruling for six years. He was married off to Princess Catherine of Württemberg, daughter of King Friedrich I and his first wife Augusta of Brunswick-Wolfenbüttel. The descendants of Jérôme's second marriage form today's French Imperial Family.*

England, who happily accepted him.* She was known as Queen Victoria Eugenie when she married Alfonso in a solemn ceremony in Madrid in May 1906. It was one of those events that attracted many of the various royal families. As was often true, this wedding took place under threats of violence. The church was crowded with family and press, and after their vows were made, the couple rode in a procession to the royal palace. En route, a deranged young assassin threw a bouquet of flowers at the couple. It concealed a bomb.

Pandemonium ensued as the horse guards scrambled around the crowds looking for the murderer. The blast killed twenty-four people and injured dozens. Shaken, the newlyweds could only try to calmly change carriages and proceed to the palace. Like Khodynka Field for Nicholas and Alexandra, this boded ill for the two. Unlike Nicholas and Alexandra, they lacked a solid relationship to see them through the hardships ahead.

****

For the next several years, Victoria spent her summers with Ella in Russia. She traveled with her constant companions, Nona Kerr, Dickie, and Louise, when the latter wasn't having her lessons at Fraulein Textor's Pension for English girls. By 1906, the Russo-Japanese War was lost and naturally the Russian people were unhappy about this, and so many other things. Unfortunately, changes in the government were about as quick as a man running through quicksand. Ella, who was still reeling from the violent death of her husband, was nursing wounded soldiers at Illyinskoje. The unrest and disturbances were a major problem that continued with threats and assassinations endemic. If fear of assassination had been part of the Romanov's lives before, it was even a more insidious problem now. It was so much so, in fact, that when Victoria visited Russia in July, the Governor General who received her at the railroad station, actually did so at risk of his life.

The two sisters spent most of their time out of Moscow at Illyinskoje. Here Ella, according to her wards, Marie and Dmitri, continued to "spoil" her patients.[10] Indeed, they were quite vocal in their complaints since Victoria heard about them during her visit and remarked upon them to Onor. Ella, however, was not well, at this time, possibly because of the violent events she had experienced. She had faced the days following the death of Serge with great stoicism, and it is quite possible that her ill-health was a reaction to the enormous stress.

Victoria, in a letter to her sister-in-law Onor, took it upon herself to reassure her and Ernie, as well as Irène about Ella's mental and physical health. After thanking Onor for looking after her children who had not traveled with her this time, she went on to say that Ella looked pale and thin but no longer had that 'staring' look, and can *"laugh quite naturally about something funny."*[11] She argued further that Ella had simply transferred her attention from Serge and his well-being to the soldiers' and therefore, she saw nothing harmful or unhealthy in her sister's preoccupation.

In later letters, Onor invited Ella to come to Darmstadt for a stay, but Ella, according to Victoria, was afraid to leave Alix in case any possible misfortune might occur. Victoria lamented: *"If only the bloody shadows of revolution would not spoil and darken everything. Not every hour and every second, no one could stand that, but it lurks in the background and the life for thinking people here has become very serious."*[12]

(*) *Because having a Protestant queen was anathema to Spaniards, Ena converted to Roman Catholicism.*

Ella, however, had made her decision to embark upon an entirely different life. Her bedrooms and sitting rooms no longer displayed the sumptuous furnishing and precious objects that Serge had so adored. She began to institute what she hoped would become a plain life devoted to self-perfection, and dedicated to service. She became a vegetarian, spent most of her days either in prayer or helping the sick and the poor, and had begun to sell much of her worldly goods to raise funds for her order and convent.

Laudatory as these effort were, and even with Serge gone, they did not make Ella immune to gossip and innuendo. Because of the great interest in the various Royal Families, newspapers often took pieces of gossip wherever they could find them and printed them true or false – a practice that continues to this day with politicians and celebrities, though to a far more irresponsible degree. Nona Kerr sent Victoria a newspaper article about Ella and Ernie.

The gossip about Ella, which you sent me a cutting of, has appeared with yet more untrue details in some papers I hear, which say that she was secretly married last year already to a Count Strogonoff I believe – & that I went to Illyinskoje for the christening of their child.[13]

All silly trash she continued, along with the rumors in English papers saying that Ernie was getting a second divorce.

The following year, Victoria and Nona were off to Russia again. During this visit, Victoria, Ella, and Nona went on visits to hospitals and convents. Ella was completing her plans for starting the nursing order and as a part of that, they went to visit the houses in Moscow that Ella bought for the Convent of SS Martha and Mary.

It wasn't, however, Victoria's usual summer visit. This year, it was in celebration of the engagement of Ella's niece, Marie Pavlovna Junior and Prince William of Sweden, Duke of Södermanland. In her memoirs Marie complained that she had given her consent to the luke-warm union while she was ill. Marie's father, the Grand Duke Paul was incensed that he had never had the opportunity to confer with Marie on this matter, and completely disapproved of the marriage as did the court. Indeed, many thought that the precipitous nature of this engagement, since Marie was only seventeen at the time, was in preparation for Ella's new life and the founding of the convent that she envisioned. It was felt that she simply wanted to get rid of her niece and put her in a situation of which she could hardly complain. This judgment may have been too harsh, but the truth was that the marriage, which was performed in May of 1908, was extremely unsuccessful and the couple divorced in 1913.

****

By 1908, Prince Louis was appointed a Vice-Admiral, and later that year Commander-in-Chief of the Atlantic Fleet. Those days continued to be idyllic and sweet for Victoria and her family. She traveled constantly; Georgie Battenberg flourished brilliantly in the Royal Navy, and Alice continued to present her mother and father with grandchildren. Victoria was most probably only slightly reconciled to the fact of being a grandmother, but was of a pragmatic and philosophical breed. By 1914, Alice and Andrew had two more daughters making a total of four. For a long period, as with her Aunt Alix before her, Alice had no son.

That January, Ella, who continued to work on her plans for the convent was diagnosed with a non-malignant tumor. She was successfully operated upon and slowly recovered. Irène traveled to Russia to be at her side. Prince Louis' only sister, Princess Marie suffered the tragic loss of her husband that month. The Prince of Erbach-Schönberg died in Darmstadt and Louis, who was in Malta, left immediately to be at his sister's side.

The Battenbergs had taken up residence in London at the beautiful Admiralty House where, Louis, in his capacity as the Commander-in-Chief of the Atlantic Fleet, was now housed. Louis, who was a progressive man, continued to move up in the navy. He wanted more than anything to institute needed reforms which, as he often said, would bring the navy into the twentieth century. Consequently, he made enemies among the conservatives and those who harbored jealousy. Some of those jealousies were cloaked in the form of xenophobia. Even Louis' friends, including the First Sea Lord, Admiral Fisher, to whom Louis was extremely loyal, were concerned. The Admiral worried each time Victoria and Louis went to Germany and even Greece for family events. Many in the Admiralty and in the press made much of the couples' constant junkets to the continent. Even when they went to Prince Erbach-Schönberg's funeral, there were insulting remarks and 'talk' – it didn't look well.

Though some were horrified that a German Prince held such a dominant spot in the Royal Navy, he was strongly supported by Winston Churchill, the head of the Admiralty. Indeed, when Churchill came into that office, there was great consternation in the camp of Louis' enemies. Winston was a great admirer of Admiral Fisher, and, therefore, extremely well disposed towards Louis. Victoria and Louis dined a great deal with Churchill and his wife, Clementine. Victoria, who so loved books herself, remarked upon *"his ingenious arrangement for lodging his large number of books. On deep shelves the books stood in two lines, the rear-most sufficiently raised for one to be able to read their titles over the backs of the front row."*[14]

Some in the Admiralty thought it was an advantage that Louis had such close contacts with the various Royal Houses, and in particular, the Prussian one. However, not everyone saw this as an advantage. There were constant snide comments issued forth about the possibility at some point of having a German in the office of First Sea Lord. The newspapers, always eager for slander, published these innuendos. Louis never answered these calumnies. He simply continued his work, hoping that it would in the end, speak for itself.

However, more important to the Royal Navy and the government, was the fact that Cousin Willy lost no opportunity to engage Prince Louis in discussion about all aspects of his navy. Most of the time, his pride, and conceit usually overpowered his discretion. Hard as it is to believe, it seemed that the Emperor was not worried about to whom else Prince Louis might relate their discussions. Indeed, he was heard to remark, in a patronizing fashion, that Louis, with his *"intelligent comprehension of the state of affairs..."*[15] could be most useful to Germany. The reality was that Louis was most useful to the British Admiralty, instead, and made detailed reports to his superiors about all his talks with his Imperial cousin.

Prince Henry was also involved in the talks and discussions about the strengths and intentions of the German Navy before the war. David Duff relates a talk between the Prince and Frederick Ponsonby, Assistant Private Secretary to the King, which took place several years later in 1910. Ponsonby told Henry that it was thought that the German Navy was building its strength for an invasion, and Henry responded that the Germans thought the same thing about the British Navy. This 'tit for tat' was later thought to be Henry simply trying to smooth over the aggressiveness of his brother. Unfortunately for Irène and Henry, this was not the only discussion that was misunderstood.

At this time Victoria and Louis, who were always looking for ways to increase their comparatively meager income, met an American Colonel Thompson, who helped with their American investments. Victoria related a story that said a great deal about the Colonel.

He said, 'The Navy is the very worst preparation a man can have for business. The whole outlook of the naval officer being so different.' To explain this, he told me, that when in his youth he had gone into business after leaving the Navy, he had had an interview with a very able man with whom he had dealings. The man listened silently to Thompson's explanation of the situation and, at the end he said; 'Young man, you will get on all right, as you know when it is advisable to tell the truth.' Poor Thompson had never thought of doing anything else! He was very rich at one time, having been nicknamed 'The Copper King.'[16]

Along with her worries about Louis and the Admiralty, Victoria and her family were completely aware and beginning to despair of Alix's situation in Russia. It seemed that most of the letters and discussions between the siblings from this time on were about 'handling' Alix. They spoke of trying to talk to Nicky when Alix was not in the room, or about Ella trying to talk sense into Alix without risking a curt dismissal, possibly never being able to enter her presence again. That March, Ernie and Onor planned to go to Russia to see Alix and Nicky. Victoria told Onor:

It is also good for Nicky and his people if Ernie can talk freely about things with him. I have discovered that he is very fond of Ernie, and it does him good to speak with him, which he cannot do with others. But one has to force out Nicky as well – due to circumstances both of them have shut themselves off so much and therefore the push for freer speech will have to come from Ernie. Every time I managed to touch on political matters with Nicky, in Alix's absence, I found him willing to let me talk and also to answer, although I did not do it much and very rarely, as I do not feel competent to do so.[17]

Victoria and Ella fretted a great deal about the situation developing in the Russian Court and the insularity and self-deception in which Alix was engaged. Her sisters, along with so many others, were well aware of the hatred that the Tsarina had engendered and how far her conception of her role in Russia was from the actual truth. However, they were also beginning to discover that Alix would stubbornly refuse to speak about anything to do with Russia and its governance, and woe betide any sister who tried to reason or address any of the issues with her.

There was times when both Victoria and Ella tried, but their attempts ultimately came to naught. Victoria had to content herself with her continued close relationship to Ella and to walk on eggshells when it came to Alix. She delighted in spending time at Illyinskoje and in some odd way felt safe there from the troubles that were brewing. Victoria enjoyed the more relaxed atmosphere, since there was no need for the tight security that Nicky, in light of Serge's assassination, had insisted upon. However, as time went on, that proved not to be the case. The sisters were not permitted to leave the grounds because threats continued against the lives of the Imperial Family. Illyinskoje was never the same and Ella would leave the house to Dmitri when she moved into her convent.

During those summer days at Illyinskoje, there were still moments of happiness. There were teas on the back verandas with many young cousins about, including, Alix's four girls. The eldest was Olga, just short of thirteen, and turning into quite a handful for her mother. Alix was aghast at the independent spirit of this oldest child who actually had the temerity to talk back to her. Tatiana, eleven at the time, and was, of the four, the most typical Hessian princess. She was tall, slim, beautiful, had a mind of her own, and a decided air of authority. She was the leader of the children in her family. Then there was nine year old Marie, who had apple cheeks, enormous blue eyes, and masses of brown wavy hair. The youngest sister, Anastasia, was about seven that summer, and a very devil of mischief. She wasn't as pretty as her sisters, but there was something taking, even memorable, about her. Perhaps, it was that her unique personality made her stand out from the rest, or perhaps that was just hindsight because of what came later. Anastasia was definitely herself, a merciless tease, and prankster, who was sometimes even a bit cruel. Alix, however, was always quick to make sure she understood her actions and she inevitably apologized to the person who was the butt of one of her jokes.

Ella, by virtue of Imperial Order, was finally given permission by the Synod to build her convent, and would, in April of 1910, take the veil. She had chosen some land on the banks of her beloved Moskva River, and continued the construction of the Convent of SS Martha and Mary, the cornerstone of which had actually been laid several years before, in that summer of 1908. The construction would eventually encompass a convent house, a beautiful onion-domed Church of St. Mary Magdalen, as well as a hospital, an old age home, a home for consumptive women, and lushly planted gardens. There were also plans for an orphanage. This endeavor utterly absorbed her, and she never again accepted any social engagements. Instead, she would visit her sisters, and be present only on so-called family occasions, the same thing that she had decided for all the nuns of the convent. However, unlike most convents in Russia, these women would not be completely cloistered. They would be allowed holidays to visit their relatives on a regular basis.

Ella and Victoria spent many happy hours conferring about all aspects of the convent and what it would and would not comprise. They discussed the way in which the nuns should set up their days, when they should be required to say prayers, and when not – what their mode of dress should be, and even what they should eat. Again, because this was the first of such liberal institutions in Russia, they would often have to improvise answers as the problems and issues would arise.

By following summer 1909, Victoria and Nona visited Ella at her house and hospital. She was already living there. It

> *consisted of a group of buildings, one of which was the hospital. Then there were the buildings which contained the Dispensary and the rooms in which lighter cases were treated. In another small building near the entrance gates, Ella lived, as did Mme. Gordeef a friend, who had entered the sisterhood at the same time as Ella and superintended the domestic affairs of the foundation...The gardens of the different buildings, which had been private houses before were all thrown together, so that the "Obitel" had very nice grounds. A little removed from the main group of buildings stood one which now houses the orphan girls, that were under the care of the chaplain, who had before been military chaplain to one of Ella's regiments and who had moved with his family and the little girls into the "Obitel" chaplain's house.[18]*

Together, the sisters visited various charitable institutions. Ella often had to hold hands of the dying, in one case *the husband, who was very devoted to his wife, was a communist, and he and Ella each held the hand of the dying woman. The husband afterwards said to one of the nurses 'that if all the members of the Imperial family were like this one, the first one he had ever met, his opinion of them would be different.'*[19]

Victoria returned to the Heiligenberg near the end of August and had an interesting reunion – a visit from Sandro's young son.

Assen, Louis' nephew, the son of Sandro and Countess Hartenau, who was stopping at Schoenberg [sic] *came over for a few nights – a nice youth, but hampered in his movements by a paralysis of his right arm and leg, which he had from birth. I only met him again years afterwards when he was a grey haired man, and had come to London with an Austrian Mission, having been employed in the Financial Department of the recently defunct Austrian state.*[20]

Little else was said about Sandro's children by his opera singer wife.

Victoria and Louis, now in command of the *HMS Prince of Wales*, celebrated their Silver Anniversary very quietly and with no fanfare at the seaside town of Margate *"in a very empty hotel."*[21] They had just had the good news of their eldest son, Georgie, who passed fourth in his class from Dartmouth. In June, Georgie started his cadet training on the *HMS Cornwall*. During his tenure on the ship, he often made requests to visit relations at the ports at which they called, so much so that the commander began to be suspicious of his having so many relatives in so many different places.

The next few years, the last before the war, unfolded gently with very few ripples. The sisters visited back and forth, their children played together, the controversies between Alix, and her extended family and, indeed, her country continued, and the others sought in some way, any way, to mitigate these controversies. It was a losing battle, but it was fought earnestly. The end of that pre-war world, however, was coming. Many marked it in different events, but certainly one of the most significant was the death of King Edward VII in May 6, 1910 after a short reign of nine years.

Louis and Victoria as well as the rest of the family truly mourned this man who had played such an important part in their lives.

His loss cast a sad gloom over all those who had known and loved him. Louis, personally felt it very much, for ever since he had been a cadet in the Ariadne *in 1869, Uncle Bertie had been the kindest of friends to him.*[22]

It was Uncle Bertie who befriended Louis during his young and difficult years in the navy; it was Uncle Bertie who insisted on Louis' staying with him whenever Louis was on shore leave, so that Louis actually had his own bedroom at Marlborough House; and, it was Uncle Bertie who insisted that Louis be his Naval Aide-de-Camp as he had been for Queen Victoria, and as he would now be, for Bertie's son, Cousin George. Victoria wrote in a heartfelt letter to the now Queen Mary, that *"Uncle Bertie was always so kind & good to us, his sister's children ... that we mourn his loss as a personal one to ourselves."*[23]

The King's funeral was a grand affair, attended by many royal families. There was the so called 'March of Kings', in which nine sovereigns took part in the funeral procession. The monarchs followed the coffin, as it wound slowly through London. Among those included in the procession were: Alfonso XIII of Spain, Willy, Manoel of Portugal, and Mr. Theodore Roosevelt, now the former President. On May 17, the actual funeral service took place at Windsor. Louis, on foot, personally escorted the gun carriage carrying the King's body

That fall, there was one of the last meetings of the family of sisters and brother, with all their available children and spouses in Hesse. Alix continued to be sickly and suffering from sciatica and possible heart problems, ailments that she had persistently suffered from since before her marriage. The symptoms were exacerbated now by anxiety over her hemophiliac son and the worsening political situation in Russia. Because of this, she wished to take the waters at Bad Nauheim. Naturally, with so many members of the family coming at once, it was necessary to organize and Victoria, with her usual efficiency, was up to the task. Letters flew between her and Ernie, trying to set up accommodations and amusements for the Imperial visitors.

There must be somebody to help in occupying Nicky although he is so touchingly kind never expecting anything. Irene's idea of the hotel is quite out of the question. Firstly the season is not over, so they would be mobbed the moment anyone of them put their nose out of the house. Then as to guarding the house & all the surrounding streets, that also is not favorable. The quiet which Alix wants she would never get. In Friedberg that is all possible.[24]

However, Ernie was not only concerned with domestic matters but, more urgently with security matters since the Imperial Family could never be without their massive protection apparatus. The towns that they might visit were swept not only by the Okhrana agents, but the local constabularies were on full alert.[25]

The Imperial Family arrived in August, and spent until nearly the end of October at the Schloss in Friedberg while Alix went to the spa in Bad Nauheim. During the visit, Henry and Irène arrived with their children as well as Victoria, Louis along with Louise, Georgie and Dickie, Alice and Andrew and their children. All the cousins played together, with a firm eye kept on all of them by their respective nannies. There were luncheons and dinners, some informal and some alas, formal, when the Kaiser showed up for several days and required everyone to dress in their uniforms. However, besides this inconvenience, it was a private and relaxing visit.

When Alix had had enough of the waters, they returned to Wolfsgarten and spent some quiet days there. There are some last group pictures of the sisters at their beloved childhood home and Ella now in her nun's habit. She looked, her cousin, Princess Marie of Erbach-Schönberg remarked, like Elisabeth in Tannhäuser.

Ella had become the Abbess of her convent in April of that year after the long hard battle to get the permissions she needed. If not exactly a complete hindrance, Alix found it difficult to understand Ella's desire to embrace the religious life, and doubted her sincerity. Victoria wrote to Onor that

there is something extraordinary about a person who has high ideals and tries to live in accordance with them – something shaming and refreshing for us ordinary people – this is what I find at Ella's home, and I am very sorry that Alix is so full of doubt, mistrust and envy about Ella and her undertakings; she doesn't really know Ella's art of living and I fear sometimes does not want to know. Ella and I are totally different in character and opinions, and still I feel I understand her.[26]

Eventually, Alix would try to understand something of Ella's desires and was a help to get the last authorizations to open her convent.

Victoria, being the daughter of her mother, was caught up in good works. Besides building a club house for youth at Jugenheim, she was also busy while she was in residence in London. She, Nona and Louise did a great deal of charity work at the East End providing entertainment and games, for poor boys. They participated in the Sailor's Orphan Girls School and the Friends of the Poor as well as handing out prizes and purses for The National Federation of Christian Workers among Poor Children.

In March 1911, the family lived in Admiralty House at Sheerness. More important to Victoria's immediate family, however, was the birth of Alice's third child — another daughter. Princess Cecile was born June 22 at Tatoi. Louis was away at sea a great deal, but not for as long periods as before. During this time, Victoria entertained a bit, giving a series of dinners and *"even a garden party."*[27] In June, the family attended the first courts and then, on the twenty-third of that month, the coronation of King George V and Queen Mary. Victoria stayed with her Aunt Louise Lorne at Kensington Palace. Though it was not the custom for the dowager Queen to attend the Coronation Ceremonies, and Aunt Alix, quite rightly, stayed away, there was quite another reason that her entourage encouraged her to stay home. She was evidently lamenting, to the embarrassment of all that George not Eddy was to be crowned. Aunt Alix in her grief and delusion ignored the sad fact of his demise. However, England was certainly eager enough to forget a prince that may have been ill-qualified to serve as its ruler. Only his mother, to the discomposure of her court, remembered poor Eddy.

More interesting, was that May and George were the first Imperial Couple to go that winter to India for the Coronation Durbar at Delhi, at the end of the Coronation year. The Durbar was a time when delegations of Indian Princes and Rajas would pay homage to the representatives of the Queen-Empress or the King-Emperor. However, this would be a far more festive event since the Imperial Couple would actually attend. And because of their unprecedented attendance (and more important because such jewels could not be taken out of Britain), it was also paramount that a new crown be made – named appropriately enough, The Crown of India. Victoria's son Georgie accompanied George and May to the Durbar and attended as their guest. One can only imagine the envy Victoria had for her son for such an interesting and exotic assignment.

However, the summer at Sheerness was glorious. Louis was busy training aeroplane pilots for the navy – his idea – and, at the time, an entirely new concept. Victoria, in fact, became the first princess to fly. *"The planes were not made to carry passengers and for our short flight – for Louis would not allow me to be taken on a long one – we perched securely attached, on a little stool hung on to the flyers back."*[28] Dickie and Louise went up with Victoria for the short flight.

The summer may have been brilliant, but the winter was horrid. Besides suffering from circulatory problems from the cold and damp, Victoria was obliged, nevertheless to keep the windows open. As it happened, there were gunnery defenses near by who were constantly firing so therefore it would not do to have the windows closed lest they shatter. So, besides being extremely cold, it was tremendously noisy as well. Suffice to say that Sheerness, with the noise, the cold, and the lingering smell of glue, was not one of Victoria's favorite residences.

That year she also said goodbye to her youngest child as Dickie went to boarding school, Locker's Park, Hemel Hemsted. While there, the boy received constant encouragement by letter from his mother.

> *She was particularly close to her youngest child and Dickie had always been sure of her interest and her backing...Victoria knew that her boy was impulsive, enthusiastic and trusting, anxious to please easily hurt...She taught him to be proud of his family's standards and not to flinch...Dickie had grown up thoughtful, loyal and sweet-tempered.*[29]

In October of 1911, the Naval War Staff was created. Prince Louis, because of his intelligence trips to Germany, knew better than anyone the necessity of trying to prepare the Royal Navy for war. In December, along with being King George's Aide-de-Camp, Louis was now appointed Second Sea Lord. Churchill had wanted him as First Sea Lord, however, there was some difficulty. People asked the crucial question: Should a German be in such a position of importance? Nevertheless, he was now one of the top men in the navy – a man well thought of and extremely capable. Victoria constantly received laudatory notes and letters from the men under his command saying what an able and fair leader he was, how intelligent, organized, as well as completely dedicated to his men.

At this point, difficulties with Germany took a temporary backseat to the problems brewing in the Balkans. Greece continued to have troubles and conflicts that were rapidly becoming chronic. Between 1912 and 1913, she fought a series of wars called the First and Second Balkan wars, mainly, it seemed, for territorial acquisition. Macedonia, which had previously belonged to the Turks, was now coveted by many countries, including Bulgaria, as well as Serbia and Greece. The first battles in 1912 were between Turkey, whose Ottoman Empire was dying, yet still limping painfully along, and the aforementioned countries. The following year, Greece and Serbia fought Bulgaria. The outcome after both wars was the Treaty of Bucharest. Greece was greatly expanded, adding the southern part of Macedonia, some of the Aegean Islands, and Crete.

Naturally, during this troublesome period, Victoria worried constantly about Alice and the girls. Prince Andrew joined Crown Prince Constantine as a Major at the front in Turkey. At her own request, Nona went to Greece in order to help Alice. There, true to family inclinations, Alice was working and organizing hospital facilities. Nona wrote that the atmosphere in Athens was one of high exhilaration – typical of wartime exuberance. However, such high spirits could easily be quenched and the Greeks would no doubt rid themselves of their current rulers if all did not go well. The Royal Family was simply not well enough entrenched, and the Greeks certainly not all that attached. And, as if to illustrate the point, in March 1913, King George I of the Hellenes, the brother of both Queen Alexandra of Britain and the Dowager Empress Marie Feodorovna of Russia, was assassinated in Salonika. Prince Andrew's brother Constantine now became King of Greece.

In summer of 1912, Victoria headed off for her penultimate trip to Russia. She stayed with Ella at her convent and tried out her Russian. However, her conversation, she wrote, was severely limited and she was *"at a complete loss"*[30] if Ella was not present. This trip, more than any others, was quite a strain since Alix was becoming more and more mystical, introspective, neurotic and, worst of all dependent on Rasputin. To the Empress, Rasputin was the only person who could ease her son's sufferings during his horrific bleeding episodes. Rasputin became more and more powerful as the years passed, and more and more corrupt. The Romanovs, outside of Alix's immediate family circle, hated the so-called holy man and worked desperately to persuade Nicholas to send him back to his village, which he did . . . once. Nicholas, however, could not resist his wife's entreaties or his young son's suffering and brought the starets back. In addition, Alix would never believe any account of the monk's excesses. She thought that malignant undercurrents were there to destroy her delicate son and the rest of her immediate family.

The other Romanov family members were not the only group who noticed the malevolent influence. Scurrilous cartoons about the Empress, the Grand Duchesses and their 'sexual escapades' with Rasputin appeared in newspapers. It was apparent that whatever small bit of popularity the Imperial Family may have had, was dwindling fast. Victoria tried hard to soothe some of the controversy between Alix and Ella as well as the ill-feelings of the other Romanovs. Alix, however, would hear nothing against Rasputin. In fact, when Ella was sent by the family to talk to Alix she was curtly told to leave. The sisters, for the first time in their lives, became estranged, though not for long.

Alexei had a serious hemophilia episode at the Imperial Family's hunting lodge in Spala, Poland in fall 1912. Though the doctors gave up hope, Rasputin was enlisted by the Empress, who miraculously seemed to alleviate Alexei's sufferings. Alix firmly believed that Rasputin cured him. She was used to seeing strong women rely on 'peasants', such as her grandmother did with John Brown and later the Munshi. She believed implicitly in their sincerity and their lack of guile and couldn't be talked out of her association. Since she was stronger but no cleverer than Nicky, she dictated and he listened, an obvious recipe for disaster. Interestingly enough, during the Spala episode, Irène was with Alix. No doubt Alix found her the only sympathetic sister, since she, herself, had hemophiliac sons.

*****

In the winter of 1912, Louis was appointed First Sea Lord and the Head of Royal Navy. Victoria was happy at Admiralty House and wrote to Ernie that,

> our...house is most comfortable, it has a very big dining room & study on the ground floor & above them a large drawing-room & sitting room, half-way, off the marble staircase, is a sort of gallery-room which makes another, though not very private sitting-room. On the two floors above these are the bed-rooms, amongst them two for guests, which I hope you & Onor will once inhabit.[31]

The appointment did not go without controversy because of Louis' origins. It was also possible that the man he replaced, Admiral Sir Francis Bridgeman, was bitter, though the reason publicly given for his resignation was illness.

That Christmas, Henry and Irène visited Sandringham as guests of George and May. Victoria, Louis and their family, excepting Alice, were also there. Undoubtedly, Victoria enjoyed spending the holiday season with this particular sister. Compared to Alix and even Ella, she was calm, restful, and peaceful, living up to her name, and at the moment, there was no controversy around her. Sandringham was a large edifice, constantly expanded and rebuilt to accommodate the family. In its latest incarnation, it was more gingerbread Victorian house than anything else and very homey. It had originally been bought for Uncle Bertie and Aunt Alix when they first married, and served as their private country residence. It was far cozier than Balmoral, and certainly much warmer.

The family had their usual festivities before Christmas. Tree trimming and carol singing and all joined in with the Christmas charades and games. Inevitably, there was a lot of talk about hostilities between the allies and the so-called Triple Alliance of Germany, Austria-Hungary and Italy. With war a very grave and real possibility, none of the royal family with their German ancestry, wanted to fight Germany. However, they all knew that none of them would hesitate if they were called upon to do so.

While Henry was at Sandringham, he took the opportunity to talk to George and Louis about the state of affairs between their two countries. Henry, to all intents and purposes, appeared, as usual, to be coached by Willy about what precisely he must say to his cousins. He asked them, *"If Germany and Austria attacked France and Russia would England come to the aid of the latter?"* It was an informal question asking whether England would act if her allies were attacked. Georgie replied, *"Undoubtedly yes – under certain circumstances."* Henry seemed happy with this answer and later took it back to his brother, who undoubtedly interpreted it as a stance of neutrality, as though there could be no such circumstances in which the British would intervene during such an attack.[32]

Oddly enough, Henry had this same conversation at Buckingham Palace with George a second time. In the fateful summer of 1914, he was once again, sent back on the same mission. This was only days before the hostilities of the Great War began. Possibly, the Kaiser wanted some kind of confirmation of the previous talk and what he considered a policy of neutrality. When asked the same question, the King said that he did not know what *"we shall do, we have no quarrel with anyone and hope we shall remain neutral."*[33] But if Germany declared war on Russia, and France joined Russia, then the King indicated that England would most certainly be dragged in. At the close of the talks, George said that he and the government would do all they could to prevent a European war.[34] However, we now know, due to the revelation of private conversations King George V had with Sir Edward Grey , his Foreign Secretary, that the monarch asked for war. When Grey told the King that the cabinet had not found a justifiable reason to go to war, King George V replied, *"You have got to find a rerason, Grey."*[35] George V was afraid that Germany's defeat of France would lead to the German' complete domination of European politics.

Henry returned to Kiel on July 28, several days later and repeated the discussion to his brother. From these declarations, the Kaiser was sure that England would remain neutral and had telegraphed the American President, Woodrow Wilson, saying he had been so assured. The brothers seemed happy and satisfied with the news that George and his government would not act. Naturally this was not at all what the King meant, nor what happened. It is strange that Henry would have made such a misinterpretation of statements. Later on, when he was implicated in all sorts of nefarious deeds, including being responsible for starting the war (which, of course, was utterly ridiculous), these conversations were brought to light and discussed, ad infinitum. One can only conclude that it was absurd that Willy had not sought clarification himself, and Henry admitted after the war that he'd misconstrued George's statements, that he had interpreted an *"anxious hope as definite assurance."* He had transmitted to Willy his version of the comments, which seemed an assertion of neutrality, rather than just the hope of it. Despite the trust that the brothers had for one another, it can only be interpreted as poor judgment to accept such important declarations without further clarification.

****

In May, 1913, another Royal Wedding would take place in the family. The engagement of

Princess Viktoria-Luise of Prussia*, the Kaiser's only daughter, to Prince Ernest August of Hanover was reported in *The Times*.[36] The date was set to coincide with Queen Victoria's birthday, and coincidentally, Irène and Henry's Silver Anniversary, May 24. Unlike that sad time in 1888 when Henry's father was about to breathe his last, this was a happy occasion and a love-match between the young couple. However, the wedding would be the last gathering of the 'Royal Mob' before the Great War engulfed them all.

The family gathered at the lovely Neues Palais at Potsdam, near Berlin, for the nuptials. There was a feigned amount of camaraderie between the Emperors Nicholas and Wilhelm and George, for by now, it seemed the battle-lines had been drawn and it was only a matter of time. Indeed, it was the last time all the German Royalties met with their English and Russian cousins and counterparts. Willy was in his element, hosting his family and feeling important. Alix did not attend, pleading illness, but Nicky attended with several of his daughters. So, the sisters were not together at this last time with the extended family. This occasion was between Henry's ill-fated talks with George, and all steered clear of any controversial subjects.

As in a dream before the war swept away so many of the Emperors, Kings, and Princes, they all assembled interacting, dancing, talking, whispering, and watching each other. On the evening of the ceremony, the bride and groom participated in the traditional torch dance. With pages lining the room with torches, the bride danced with her father, her father-in-law, then with the other Emperors present that evening. The conversations between the cousins, Emperors for only a heartbeat more, can only be imagined.

There was George waltzing around the room with the bride, while May was talking to her Aunt Augusta of Mecklenburg-Strelitz, a lady in her early nineties. Aunt Augusta was a Cambridge, and sister to the Queen's mother. She, like so many members of the royal family, was very unhappy when the war started. It was, of course, so incredibly difficult to have allegiances that were contrary to one's inclination.

Also attending were Willy's six sons – all bon vivants, and not averse to getting drunk on any occasion. All six would survive the war, though later on, one of the sons, Joachim, in despair over the defeat of Germany, would commit suicide. He could not bear to live through the end of the Second Reich, and his mother pined away and died probably as a direct result of his suicide. Willy was obviously incapable of teaching them anything about having a backbone - he would have had to have had one himself.

Crown Princess Marie of Romania, was also there. There had been a matchmaking exercise between Alix's daughter, Olga, and Marie's son, Carol. However neither of the young people, having any inclination toward each other, was persuaded in that direction.

There were Princess Beatrice's sons, Alexander, Leopold, and Maurice – all three looking young and handsome, and none, at that point, married. Leopold and Maurice died young, and would never marry. Eventually, however, Alexander did marry and produce one daughter who had, to say the least, a rather checkered career.

Then, there was the bride, the new Duchess of Brunswick-Lüneburg, radiantly happy. Willy had not liked young Ernest August, nor the Hanover royal family, since they had refused to bow to the suzerainty of the Hohenzollerns. She was, perhaps, the only one to enjoy that evening with unbridled joy, for the dream would soon be over for all of them.

(*) *HRH Princess Viktoria-Luise of Prussia (1892-1980) and HRH Prince Ernest August of Hanover, Prince of Great Britain and Ireland, later Duke of Brünswick-Lüneburg (1887-1953). The groom was a first cousin of both King George V and Tsar Nicholas II. Viktoria-Luise and Ernest August's children included Queen Frederika of Greece.*

Chapter XI

June 1913 – July 1918

The years of the first decade of the twentieth century, which some historians have called the pleasantest years on our planet[1], were in reality the beginning of some of the most catastrophic and violent times that mankind has ever known. Victoria later wrote: *"The feeling of increasing political tension was very disquieting to us, especially as Louis took a rather pessimistic view of the situation in Europe."*[2] His pessimism was sadly rewarded. The peace of Europe was shattered forever by the coming juggernaut, and as if fate was mocking them, the sisters and their families had one last halcyon time together. The Imperial Family came to Hesse in 1913 and spent a great deal of the summer at Wolfsgarten. This was the final gathering.

Victoria was recovering from an appendectomy and Ella came to care for her and to keep her company. Once the family joined them, they spent their time playing tennis, riding, and having picnics and parties. This was also when Victoria's Dickie, who was somewhat younger than his Romanov cousin, told his mother seriously, that he meant to marry Marie Nicholaevna when he grew up. It was no joke to him. He had very strong feelings for her that lasted his entire life. He had a particularly lovely drawing of her that he always kept near him.

But fall inevitably came and Victoria went back to London and the house in the Mall. Irène and Alice, with her two oldest girls, came for a visit and Victoria related an amusing anecdote in her memoirs. She introduced her two granddaughters to her own Uncle Arthur of Connaught, as the girls' great-great uncle, *"Whereupon Uncle Arthur, in a horrified voice exclaimed 'My dear, you are making an ancestor of me!'"*[3]

Victoria also discovered that her Aunt Louise was making a gift to her and Louis of Kent House on the Isle of Wight. It would serve as their family home. She was pleased with the gift and wrote to Nona:

We think that Kent House (a free gift as it would be) will suit us & our children.... The Prince & I have lived in it in old times & though the garden was much smaller then, found one was neither overlooked or disturbed by ones neighbours & that we were very comfortable, both summer & winter, in the house.[4]

The house was a lovely gated Tudor-style building made of stone, with a bay of mullion windows overlooking the water and a garden with a wood.

The year 1914 started quietly. Irène and Henry took a seven week tour of South America. There was the usual sadness over a death in the family – Victoria and Louis' benefactress, Aunt Louise, lost her husband, the Duke of Argyll, who died in May of inflammation of the lungs. Nevertheless, the round of traveling and visits continued. Victoria spent June and July with Alice in Corfu and attended the birth of her fourth granddaughter, who was born at Mon Repos.

This island is wonderfully picturesque & green, very different from Malta. Mon

Repos is a charming property fronting the sea all along one side & full of fine trees, olives, palms, oaks, magnolias, cypresses & lots of oleander bushes all in full bloom now. Though the sun is very hot, yet there is still a breeze every afternoon & evening from the sea, which makes the heat bearable...Alice is fit & well, but rather worried at the delay in the arrival of the baby... I often bathe with the children & we gather flowers & arrange them in the vases daily, quite a proper grandmotherly occupation.[5]

Though the birth was late, the little girl was healthy and sturdy. Victoria wrote a long detailed letter to Ernie about the baby granddaughter and about her plans for the summer. Alice, she wrote, had her baby, named Sophie *"(needless to say not in honour of Sophie*, but because Andrea & Alice like it & because it is a name known in all countries)."*[6] She mentioned her plans to leave for Russia on July 15, and she also began to make arrangements for the fall. *"Would it suit you & Onor if we came to you early in September? Alix cannot have us for long as she is going to the Crimea in that month."*[7]

Prince Louis, too, free for the moment, spent the beginning of the summer in Darmstadt. He wrote to his sister, Princess Marie of Erbach-Schönberg: *"Oh! I shall come now every year to you, to rest. That is at last possible, now that I don't go to sea anymore, but live in London."*[8] Yet, this would be the last time he visited Darmstadt. Prince Louis was back at his post by July and the Royal Navy was in a fevered pitch, ready for a full test mobilization. Prince Louis had wanted to do this test for many years and King George V inspected the fleet and all went remarkably well. However, as events began to unfold, Louis had the incredibly difficult decision of whether to stand down after the tests were completed, or remain mobilized. It was an issue of whether the navy appeared weak or seemed as though it was saber rattling. As it was, he showed excellent judgment by leaving the fleet standing in readiness.

At the end of June, with the calamitous assassination of the Archduke Franz Ferdinand of Austria and his unfortunate wife, Sophie, Duchess of Hohenberg, there was a marked exacerbation of the effects of anti-German feeling on Victoria and Louis. In an atmosphere where people were kicking dachshunds on the street and sauerkraut was called 'Liberty Cabbage,' resentment against the Royal Family and anyone with a German surname was intense. Though, he was hard at work for the war effort, the existing prejudices against Louis remained. The Prince would be accused personally of everything from sinking British ships to spying for Germany. And, many continued to complain about Louis and Victoria's close personal ties to various German Royal Families, though Louis had been a conduit for passing intelligence he had gained from these ties for years.

The summer of 1914 was Victoria's last trip to Russia. Victoria, Louise, and Nona stayed at Ella's convent. Afterward, they planned to tour Russia together during which each one would visit the places that she found most interesting. They took their trip on a yacht. Traveling down the *"immense breath of the Volga was most imposing, but the shores were not very picturesque and, owing to the great width of the river, often far off, while the banks of the Kama offered much variety."*[9] There was much to do and see, ranging from lunching with various Governors, going sightseeing and for Ella, the church services. Victoria noticed the Tartars in their oriental costumes. Many of them seemed to have eye diseases. Ella was most anxious to visit the monasteries and convents, while Victoria, Louise, and Nona were

---

(*) *Queen Sophie, a Hohenzollern by birth, came from a family that traditionally did not look upon kindly upon scions of morganatic marriages. Alice, being a Battenberg, was not well-received by some of her haughtier in-laws. Queen Sophie and Grand Duchess Elena Vladimirovna, their sister-in-law, were cold and distant to Princess Alice.*

engaged with the archeological and natural sites. Victoria particularly enjoyed her visit to the Kungur Ice Caves near Perm. According to a tourist pamphlet, Victoria and Louise, like typical travelers, left their names in the caves along with the date.

As they visited towns, many would put on their finest clothes to meet Ella. While Ella visited Alapaievsk, Victoria and Louise continued from Perm and toured the Urals by special train. Victoria enjoyed her visits to caves and platinum mines, and the little towns that they happened upon such as Kishtyn. *"Tho' not the rose, I was near enough to it, being the Empress' sister and we were officially received there during two or three days."*[10] During their travels, they visited Ekaterinburg, and remarked that it was not a particularly welcoming place. They saw the Ipatiev House, which would later be renamed by the Bolsheviks 'The House of Special Purpose,' which lay in a big square. Oddly enough, they also toured the various mines outside the town, and without knowing it, they may have seen the spot where, later, the bodies of the Imperial Family were said to have been found.

It was in the beginning of August that Victoria received a frantic telegram from Louis urging her to return to England as soon as possible since it appeared that war was imminent. Unfortunately, both Louise and Nona became ill and the party had to travel back to St. Petersburg in slow stages. It did not help matters that the troops were beginning the process of mobilization. On August 4, the day Germany violated Belgium's neutrality, they finally reached St. Petersburg and Alix opened the Winter Palace, since *"we felt we could not put up at Peterhof as Alix had intended, the patients having to be kept in bed and there was a risk of spreading the infection."*[11] Back in England, Louis must have felt somewhat lucky. Since he refused to demobilize the navy, they were ready for whatever would come next.

Victoria described their hurried departure from Russia:

Alix, with the two eldest girls came to see Ella and me on the following forenoon and I spent the next day with her and her family at Peterhof....[Alix] came to see us before we left and, with loving forethought, equipped us with thick coats and other serviceable clothing for the sea journey; we only having the lightest of summer clothing with us, also giving us smaller and lighter travelling trunks.

We left St. Petersburg on the afternoon of August 7th. I little dreamt that it was the last time I should ever see my sisters again. We were escorted on the journey home by Mr. Wilton who belonged to the British Embassy. His brother was the Newspaper correspondent who was present at the investigation of the Ekaterinburg murders by the Russian Authorities and who wrote an account of it.

We were taken by special train to the Russian Frontier at Torneo at the head of the Gulf of Bothnia. Lying at the wayside station, I caught sight of another saloon carriage on the line opposite to us in which I recognised Aunt Minnie, her daughter Olga and party sitting at tea. We dashed across to speak to her and get the latest news. Aunt Minnie had come from England and Olga from France and they had been sent out through Berlin and Sweden and were now nearing home.

There is no communication by rail between the Russian frontier and Haparanda, only a high wooden bridge connecting the Russian frontier station and the Swedish town. We walked across to Haparanda and there, with infinite difficulty succeeded in getting a cart to take our luggage to the train and in obtaining a cab for ourselves...[12]

Victoria left her jewelry with Alix for safe keeping and never saw it again.

They eventually got a train to Stockholm.

We spent twelve hours with Gustaf and Daisy at Drottningholm and also visited Charles [Haakon] and Maud at their small summer place on our way through Norway. We boarded the last steamer leaving Bergen. They had managed to secure cabins for us from Oslo. The ship was crowded with the last tourists and anglers coming from distant parts of Norway and people slept on the floor of the dining saloon. We crossed the North Sea going as high up as Petershead and coasting down from Newcastle. We had good weather and an undisturbed voyage, but we found all the warm clothes Alix had provided us with most useful in the fresh sea air. We arrived in London on the 17th of August, ten days after we left St. Petersburg. We found Louis absorbed in his work which went on at night as well as by day. As to Dickie, whose leave from college had begun several days before, he had been quite solitary at the Mall House till we arrive and tried to find occupation in the care of some white mice he had bought for that purpose.[13]

As intuitive as Victoria was, perhaps she had an idea that her world, the beautiful summer worlds of Illyinskoje and Wolfsgarten, the sound of children laughing and playing, a large international extended family melding her past and present, her domestic paradise, the scenes of her love and youth – the Heiligenberg – were all lost to her – for always. The bereavement was, perhaps, akin to the loss, once again, of her Grandmama, for this was the world that she had made.

Victoria saw neither Ella nor Alix again.

****

There was now much to do since war was declared. Alix wrote to Victoria that she was glad that *"for dear Ella's sake that we have been here to cheer her up...She has any amount to do, is energetic, here, there, and everywhere...."*[14] Victoria and Irène had had the foresight to exchange ladies maids, Victoria sent Irène her German one, while Irène sent her English maid back to England. Aside from Henry's position as Grand Admiral of the Prussian Navy* Irène and Henry's sons were both involved in the German war effort. Toddy, impeded by his hemophilia, drove an ambulance and Bobby was in the navy. The couple had been in England that summer of 1914, and had hurriedly to leave in July when their cousin George told them that things were looking very bad indeed.

In mid-October, Louis was admitted into the Privy Council. However, by then, the worst case was already in the works. On October 28, in the face of xenophobic pressure, Louis reluctantly resigned as First Sea Lord. This was hardly a shock to Victoria who saw, with every passing day which way the wind blew, and that his resignation might ultimately be the only outcome. So much had happened before that. Now, there was only this last indignity to be revealed.

Louis, who had been the object of prejudice for most of his career, was now the object of narrow-minded bias from the tabloid press, the clubs, and the public. Louis had

---

(*) *...and ironically, a Vice-Admiral of the Royal Navy, as well as holder of the Order of the Garter, awarded to him by his late uncle, King Edward VII. Henry of Prussia also happened to be a brother of Queen Sophie of Greece, she who was so unwelcoming to Alice of Battenberg, Irène of Prussia's niece.*

been a member of the Royal Navy for over forty-six years and yet, at least partly because of his family connections in Germany, he was accused of being a German spy and the tabloids clamored for his resignation. Digs from writers who hid behind such pseudonyms as John Bull, and Bottomly, were becoming a constant in Louis and Victoria's lives. Anonymous letter writers were more specific in their charges of spying. There were accusations of sending secret signals to German ships, and other allegations of allegiance to the *"germhuns"*– as the press called them. He was being blamed for every ship sunk since hostilities began and every man drowned.

In his letter of resignation, he wrote: *"I have lately been driven to the painful conclusion that at this juncture, my birth and parentage have the effect of impairing in some respects my usefulness on the Board of the Admiralty...."* Besides the upper class diehards who didn't like the influx of German royalty and the German family name, there were members of the press as well as some retired officers who wanted him gone. Others actually felt that it was because of Victoria that he had to resign. Some feared that though she was tremendously patriotic, she was also tactless and talked too much on continental visits – being what her Grandmother had called a 'gasbag'. However, like Louis, she was able to gather much information about the German Navy from Henry and Irène and would then tell anyone who cared to listen all about it. Whatever the reasons, not only Louis and Victoria, but their children were affected deeply by this unfortunate situation. There is a story that when young Dickie heard of his father's resignation, he was a cadet at Osborne. It was said that he stood at attention in front of the Union flag with tears streaming down his face. Whether true or not, Lord Mountbatten certainly spent a great deal of time proving his Royal lineage and working out elaborate family trees. Ironically enough, the first Royal casualty, a Battenberg, happened on that very same day when Aunt Beatrice's son, Prince Maurice of Battenberg was reported killed at Mons.

Curiously, on the night before Louis handed in his resignation, he arranged to see his daughter by Lillie Langtry, Jeanne Marie, for the very first time. She had only learned, perhaps, in the last ten years that Prince Louis was her father since her mother, Lillie, had always posed as her Aunt. Margot Asquith, the wife of the Prime Minister, had taken the liberty of informing Jeanne Marie, at a dinner party, that she was the daughter of Prince Louis. She was so angry that her mother had kept this from her that they never truly made up. She married a very rich young man in society, an Ian Malcolm, who was incidentally a good friend of Winston Churchill.

Though the young woman was furious with her mother, she was evidently not angry with Louis, and came quite willingly that evening before the resignation. Louis' intent was to spare her the humiliation of finding out when the papers announced it. Perhaps, Louis was satisfied that he was at last able to do something honorable for her after conveniently sweeping the problem under the rug so many years.

It goes without saying that Victoria was deeply unhappy over the need for Louis to resign. She wrote to Nona,

What we hoped might not happen, has had to be & when you get this letter Louis will be a simple Admiral on half pay.

It is the penalty of serving a Democracy, the "man in the street" is mighty, & when the fools hour (you remember the article in The Times I cut out and kept) strikes, the wise man who loves his service & the country must for their sake yield to the 'man-in-the-street' & the

ignorance of the 'People.'[15]

Churchill, who had an excellent working relationship with Louis, would have stood by him, but Louis refused to have any such contention at this time of national emergency. There were others, who by way of letters to the editor of *The Times* of London made their views known. From one letter he was called: *"a naval officer of very great ability, who has devoted the whole of his life to the service of England."*[16] In another, the entire Battenberg Family was defended:

> *What proofs are the Battenberg family to afford to satisfy the country of their loyalty? The brother of Prince Louis died in the wars of West Africa, and now his nephew, Prince Maurice, has been killed in fighting the battles of Great Britain.*[17]

In the end, Victoria tried to think of it as a war sacrifice though it was painful for her to remain in London. Therefore, they decided to sit out the war in the house that Princess Louise had given them, Kent House, on the Isle of Wight.

They spent their time in retirement, reading, writing, and gardening. In addition, because of the relative inactivity enforced on the couple because of Louis' resignation, Louis began his memoirs, which would cover his life up until his marriage. Victoria had much more time to brood about her family, her brother and sister in Germany and her two sisters in Russia. She wrote poignantly to Alix that:

> *To-day is our Ernie's birthday, the first time in his life that three sisters can give him no news. How lonely he must be away from his dear ones, in a foreign country and hating the war. . . One's heart bleeds, thinking of all the misery everywhere and what will be afterwards!*[18]

More importantly, however, was the fact that Louise went, in March 1915, to Nevers in France. She joined the Voluntary Aid Detachments (VAD), and was, perhaps, the first and only British Princess to nurse in France during the war. Nona Kerr, too, worked at a military hospital in Rouen. She wrote a sympathetic letter to Louis, illustrating that she had become nearly as close to him as she was to Victoria. He answered, feelingly, writing:

> *When the blow fell I missed you so much. Your presence would have been an additional comfort (for people have been extraordinarily kind) but you form such a real part of our small inner circle, that in any event, happily or the reverse, we miss you. Your dear letter gave me great pleasure. I kept on putting off writing to you for literally all my time while at home was taken up in replying to letters from every where and everyone.*[19]

Though Nona was so obviously an integral part of their household, she now had other concerns. Besides her nursing in France, she had become engaged and married Lt-Col Richard Crichton in February of 1915, an officer, for those romantically inclined, that Nona had nursed.

Victoria took this in stride, hoping that if Crichton didn't mind, she would like Nona to continue on as her companion. Evidently he did not and later offered Louis and Victoria a house on their property, Fishponds, which they gladly accepted. Nona would never attend her again as constantly as she had done prior to the war. That, however, did not stop their constant correspondence when they were apart. That year, Victoria wrote an interesting assessment of her Aunts.

> *Aunt Helena is sometimes a misfortune, as in the case of the nurses pay. She has the reputation of being practical etc with some people & talks quite well, but she is not clever nor judicious & so prejudiced that a person she does not like can do no right...& she is led & run by quite unsuitable persons.*

> *Aunt Beatrice is not clever either, but shows this defect more, & is much more normal & simple, also she is discreet. Her weak point is her want of imagination & being able to feel things in anticipation as it were. Because of my mother, I am fond of all my aunts, but I don't think I respect them & Aunt B. is the one I feel nearest to.*[20]

It was interesting that she did not appear to respect her remaining Aunts, and it was too bad that she did not elaborate further on the reasons behind her rather harsh assessments.

During the war, different branches of the family were able to remain in contact through neutral Sweden. Crown Princess Margaret, Victoria's cousin, Daisy of Connaught, would actually take letters from German or other relatives from the Central Powers, copy them out in her own writing, and then send them along to families who were members of the Allies and vice versa. This letter to Ernie illustrates the process:

> *I enclose a letter for Onor which Victoria asked me to forward & add these few lines to say that if you or Onor want to write to her please send the letters to me & I will make sure of their getting there in much less time than the three months Victoria wrote the last one from Darmstadt had taken. I am too glad if able to be of any use to any of the relations.*[21]

Victoria wrote to Nona about a particular letter from Ernie, which had been sent through Daisy to Alix. According to its contents, Ernie hated the war and never participated in active combat; instead he worked in an ambulance brigade and helped with rehabilitation of wounded men. He wrote, *"You can't think what I go through when I am out there sometimes walking quite alone in the fields & no one to speak to & my heart goes out to my dear ones & I break my head how one could bring peace to the world & I find no answer."*[22] Irène was well, but Victoria felt strongly that it was depressing to get news of her German family in this way, *"... knowing nothing will ever be the same again, except our personal affection for our relations. You know how wholly English we are & yet understand these other feelings & so I have told you what news we got."*[23] As well as Irène, Ernie and his family, there was also the plight of Franzjos and his wife Anna, who were not well off financially, to consider. Luckily, they were in neutral Switzerland.

In September of that year, Victoria was permitted a twenty-four hour pass, and went to Nevers to visit Louise. She spent her time helping around the hospital where she could, helping men to the latrines, and changing bandages. Louise stayed and nursed in various hospitals until 1919 and at no time was treated specially in any way. She cleaned and bandaged wounds, changed bedpans and watched men die. In this way, she continued a tradition, started by her grandmother Alice, of selfless devotion to duty.

Meanwhile, Victoria's son Georgie was serving on the *HMS New Zealand* and already making a name for himself. He was said to be the cleverest and laziest cadet that his master at the Royal Naval College had ever met. He had amazing amount of mechanical ability and creativity. He was able to air condition his cabin and give himself hot and cold running water before these things were commonplace aboard ship. He was able to rig a device to begin his morning tea when his alarm clock went off.[24] He and Dickie were certainly a source of anxiety to Victoria, but she was philosophical, telling Nona that if it is their time to go, they would go.

However, her greatest concerns were for Alix, even though Russia was an ally. Like her grandmother, she had little reason to believe that the Russian people would keep faith with their Tsar and Tsarina and this opinion was reinforced by the build-up of events over the years. Ella, who tried to influence her sister to moderation, was almost persona non grata with Alix. The distance between the sisters was seen as *"unbridgeable,"*[25] however, when the war came and each did their own war work, some of the tension was obviated.

In spite of all that happened to the family during the war, the tensions, the divisions, the conflicts, there were also the happy events, though they could no longer freely share them with one another. Georgie Battenberg had found himself a bride. She was the Countess Nadejda de Torby, the daughter of the Grand Duke Michael Mikhailovich, a cousin of Nicky's and called by his family 'Miche-Miche.' This was the young man who, for a short time, had been a suitor of Victoria's.

Besides being Victoria's suitor, Miche-Miche cut a slightly comical figure within the Romanovs. He contracted a morganatic union with Countess Sophie of Merenberg, the daughter of Prince Nikolaus of Nassau and Natalya Alexandrovna, the daughter of Alexander Pushkin, the great Russian poet. Even with such illustrious antecedents, Miche-Miche's wife was not accepted. With their marriage spurned at the Imperial court, Miche-Miche lived the remainder of his life in exile. From that moment on, he made it his project to pester Nicky into making his wife an Imperial Highness, which Nicky refused to do. A rather amusing incident happened in the beginning of 1908, and was related by Victoria's son Dickie. Miche-Miche, it appeared,

staggered his family by bursting into authorship in 1908 and writing a novel called "Never Say Die." The hero of the book is Prince Franz. The hero falls in love with Princess Margaret, but his mother, the Princess Donnerwetter, who is an imperious and jealous woman, would not hear of the marriage, although the young couple are in every way suited to one another.

I was told that Princess Margaret was supposed to be my mother with whom he had been very much in love, but in fact she would not accept him....

He finally falls in love with an English girl, Ursula, and contracts a morganatic marriage with her, thus paralleling his own life, as the Grand Duke morganatically married Sophie Nicholaevna, Countess de Merenberg, ...On marriage Sophie was created Countess de Torby and her daughters, Nada and Zia, became Countesses de Torby.

An heirloom left to David, the 3rd Marquess of Milford Haven*, was a gold Fabergé cigarette case given by his grandfather (Micha) to his grandmother (Victoria) although they never subsequently married....Nada Milford Haven told me that his brothers clubbed together

---

(*) *Lord David Mountbatten, 3rd Marquess of Milford Haven (1919-1970), Georgie's son. David Mountbatten was very close to his cousin Prince Philip of Greece and Denmark, later to become Prince Philip, Duke of Edinburgh. Their close relationship lasted until David divorced his first wife and married secondly. Divorce not being particularly welcome at Court in Buckingham Palace, David was no longer seen among the royal entourage.*

and bought up the whole edition before it could be put on sale to the public, but too late to avoid the review copies being sent to the Press.[26]

Miche-Miche, from all accounts, was trying to placate Nicky with the marriage between Georgie and Nada. Since he was aware of what great esteem Louis was held by the Tsar, he was certain that his own fortunes might improve by uniting his family to the Battenbergs. He wrote several letters to Nicky in which he took the opportunity, after describing Nada and Georgie's marriage ceremony, to ask for money. In fact, during the engagement period, both Louis and Victoria told Miche-Miche that Georgie had no money. However, Miche-Miche said not to worry about money, since he had enough – or to be more precise, would be able to acquire enough for the couple. He was sure that in that attaching himself with the Battenbergs, the Tsar would be more forthcoming. In the end, he was the sort of relative that, when mentioned, could always illicit an exasperated response from family members.

Nada, as she was called by the family, was a very high profile society figure, a beautiful 'deb' who was often photographed and mentioned in the society pages. She was an active and independent girl who loved lawn tennis, could ride, shoot and loved to dance. She was something of a flamboyant creature, but very sophisticated, which appealed to Georgie. She was dark, petite, and pretty, and in the insecure world in which Georgie now lived, she seemed like something left of the world before.

Georgie has just written a very happy & loving letter. He has seen his beloved Nada & they understand each other & want us to approve of a private engagement to be made public when the war is over. He says: '...that we love each other & appreciate each other for what we are.'[27]

Victoria discussed the matter very thoroughly in a letter to her cousin, the King. Georgie, she wrote,

saw a good deal of her last autumn when she was with her mother at North Berwick & when he last had leave he told us of his affection for her & of his hopes...

Unfortunately we hardly know Nada, but have always heard her well spoken of... Micha & his wife like Georgie [,] & have been most kind about the engagement which is not much of a "partie" as worldly wealth goes, for their daughter...

The one drawback to a marriage between them, which from all other points of view seems a suitable & promising one, is the fact that it will be the wife & not the husband who will have to provide for the greater share of their expenses...[28]

She ended the letter in asking, appropriately for George's consent, which he gladly gave.

Though Alix was far away, she sent a telegram of congratulations. *"Is it possible that Georgie is getting engaged? Seems quite improbable. He is all of 23 and has been at sea all the time."*[29] Louis also got into the act, writing to his daughter Louise,

Nada is the most attractive little thing & won our hearts completely. At any rate one feels that our dear Georgie will be really happy. Micha is an asp, but we need not mind him. His wife (whom we know called "Sophy") is a thoroughly nice, good woman, without a trace of

snobbishness or vulgarity – which seems strange when one remembers that terrible vulgarian, her mother. Nada has some delightful typical Russian ways about her....They are Orthodox... and speak good Russian...At. Alix has written so nicely about it all, also At. Ella...[30]

Georgie's engagement was not the only family event that spring. Dickie was now ending his school life, passing all his exams, and would be entering Dartmouth Naval College. Victoria, who had taught him as a young child, was very close to this youngest child. She wrote him a truly touching and loving benediction,

> *May God help & strengthen you my very dear boy, & never forget that we love you very dearly & have been young ourselves once & shall be able to understand the difficulties outside & in yourself which you may meet in your new life & if we can help by word or deed will always do so.*[31]

Georgie and Nada had initially decided not to get married until after the war, however, a little over six months later, in November 1916, the couple married. The marriage seemed rather quick to Victoria and Louis. Like many men in wartime, Georgie was perhaps just trying to put his life in order.

In a salute to the past, Louis gave his sons a present that Dickie describes in a letter:

> *Papa has given me a lovely shirt stud, with a pearl in the centre & emeralds & diamonds round it, he gave one to Georgie yesterday for his birthday, like it and has kept the third himself so we all 3 got one. They were given by great-grandmama* [Queen Victoria] *to Papa's father when he came over to attend Mama's christening.*[32]

Louise, who was still nursing in France, was able to attend the wedding as a bridesmaid, which took place at Chapel Royal and Russian Embassy Chapel, Welbeck Street. King George V and Queen Mary attended as did Queen Alexandra. There were also some Russian cousins of the bride in attendance. Possibly not the wedding of the decade, it was, nevertheless, called the 'Wedding of the Year.'

George and Nada would prove to be an unconventional couple, since Nada, was, in fact, a known lesbian, or at least bi-sexual. There would be trouble and scandal about this later on, but Victoria was very fond of her daughter-in-law, admired her strength, and always stood by her. They had two children, David and Tatiana, and settled down well enough together. They both shared a love for erotic art and literature and amassed large collections.

In the fall of 1916, Ella went once more to St. Petersburg to persuade Nicky to rid himself of Rasputin. She also saw very clearly that there was a great hatred building up against the Empress, who was seen not only to be pro-German, but also to be passing secrets to her supposed confederates in Germany. Things came to such a pass that even Nicky tried to get Alix to be more discrete, but Alix would not listen.[33] She felt that the peasants were behind her, and also that she must keep Rasputin close to her as he was the only one who could comfort and help Alexis. The extended Imperial Family, who was virtually shut out of Alix and Nicky's lives now, began to think that Alix was going insane. Added to this were the spurious pro-German accusations that were hurtled against Ella, who took shelter in her convent in Moscow.

Meanwhile, Rasputin was murdered in St. Petersburg in December of that year.

In a letter dated December 27, 1916, written by I. Hanbury Williams from the General Headquarters of the Russian Army to Lord Stamfordham, there is much speculation and worry about Alix.

The agitation against the great lady is according to all accounts getting worse every day – and even the cabmen talk about her. The mistake they make is, in thinking that she herself is pro G[erman] – that is not so – but the mix up of influences through her special lady in waiting, who in turn is under the influence of that blackguard Rasputin – is what causes the trouble and her idea that she is playing us in with the G[ermans]s.[34]

Victoria fully realized the hopelessness of the present regime and her sister's lack of comprehension of the situation. *"I do hope that this time the news of Rasputin's death is true – though poor Alix will probably fall ill at it. What harm he has done her! I fear that among the masses in Russia she is hated, chiefly due to that vile creature & a set of people who have always tried to injure her."*[35] She made an interesting comment as speculation increased about who the perpetrators of the crime were. It would later be established that Grand Duke Dmitri Pavlovich, Ella's ward, and Prince Felix Youssoupov were responsible for the murder. However, Victoria pooh-poohed Youssoupov's involvement saying that *"[i]f either Youssoupovs had a direct share in the killing of that brute, I feel sure it was the father, Felix is not made of stern or violent enough stuff."*[36] For Victoria, this was a rare mistake of intuition.

Greece, or at least its new king, Constantine, was very insistent on remaining neutral in the war. England and the Allies thought they ought to declare one way or another, though their Prime Minister Venizelos was puzzled by this insistence. The Greeks wanted to fight, and the Allies had promised them lands in Asia Minor in return for their support. Venizelos went so far as to set up a rival government to King Constantine's. During this altercation, the beloved summer home of the Royal Family, Tatoi, was burned down by arsonists. Alice and the family had all pitched in to fight the flames, but it was no use – Tatoi was lost.

By 1917, it was recognized by Venizelos that the King was not heeding the will of the people and therefore he must go. Constantine, along with his eldest son George, who was thought also to be pro-German, went into exile. Their second son, Alexander became the next King of Greece, though virtually under house arrest. Alice was doing what she could, trying to protect her children, and waiting for the pieces to fall where they might. Soon enough, they had to follow Sophie and Constantine into exile in Switzerland. There, Alice and Andrew waited out the war.

****

As internal events heated up in Russia, it was thought by some in the government that it would be a good idea if someone who knew Nicky well, would talk to him, and try to make him understand the seriousness of the situation. To this end, it was suggested that Louis be sent to Russia because of his unique relationship with the Tsar. People thought that he might be able to talk some 'sense' into his brother-in-law. David Lloyd George, however, objected on the grounds of Louis' German birth and Lord Milner was sent instead and the mission failed completely.

The year 1917 started badly enough with anarchy in St. Petersburg and with crowds shouting, *"Down with the German woman."* It all went from bad to worse. On March 15, Nicky abdicated in favor of his younger brother Grand Duke Michael, known as "Misha" to the family. King George wrote in his journal of that day: *"I fear Alicky is the cause of it all & Nicky has been weak....Heard from Buchanan that the Duma had forced Nicky to sign his abdication & Misha had been appointed Regent, & after he has been 23 years Emperor, I am in despair."*[37]

Interestingly enough, Victoria was not unhappy at news of the abdication. She felt that it was clear that they had never been happy in their high position.

> *I am very grateful that Nicky has abdicated for himself & the boy, for no one can tell how far the revolution may go & whether the socialists & anarchists may not get the upper hand before long & then had Alix still been Empress they might have fallen on her – this danger I hope is now averted. I hope the rumour that they will be sent to the Crimea is true & that later on they can leave Russia.*[38]

Victoria and Irène never worried about Ella during this crisis because she was so well beloved and considered good and deeply religious by the people of Moscow. Indeed, Ella went so far as to give the new provisional government recognition. Victoria told Nona, *"You will have seen in the papers that Ella has acknowledged the new government & asked to be allowed to continue at the head of her sisterhood...."*[39] No, they didn't worry about Ella, but they would worry endlessly about Alix and her family. They were right to do so. Louis complained to his daughter, Louise that there was *"No news from Russia of our dear ones. It is terrible & really all A[un]t Alix' fault."*[40]

In June of 1917, George V, feeling apprehensive about his own German antecedents, renounced all his German names. The Royal Family was no longer of Saxe-Coburg and Gotha, but now, Windsor. The Tecks, of whom May, Queen Mary, was the most illustrious member, now became the Cambridges and Athlones. And, the Battenbergs, were no longer princes or even Serene Highnesses, but now became British peers with the name Mountbatten, and the title Milford Haven.

Oddly enough, with all of Victoria's egalitarian notions, her socialist and progressive ideas, she was extremely conflicted by this turn of events. Possibly it was because of Louis. They had received their title less than sixty years before, and now, it was being swept away. On one hand, she had never been a snob about titles and so-called bloodlines, but on the other, she muttered about how they were in the same class of people as bankers and industrialists. Possibly, she didn't feel herself in the same category because she hadn't accomplished what they had, or, perhaps, she was not the socialist she imagined herself to be. She told Nona that she didn't think that the peers would like having the Battenbergs among them, but that may have been a cover-up. According to Brian Connell, *"[Victoria] never forgot that she was a granddaughter of Queen Victoria, and retained to the last a somewhat archaic insistence on the personal prerogatives of royalty."*[41] That is a possible explanation, but it was, nevertheless, just one more nail in Queen Victoria's coffin, one more deed that changed their world beyond recognition.

Louis became the Marquess of Milford Haven, and Victoria became the Marchioness. Milford Haven was quite an important town and harbor on the Welsh coast, chosen, possibly because of its naval associations. Georgie was the Earl of Medina, a river on the Isle of Wight, near Kent House, and Viscount Alderney after a Channel Island. Louise was plain Lady Louise Mountbatten, as was Dickie, Lord Louis Mountbatten.*

Victoria also gave up her Hessian titles, though Ernie would not have dreamed of requiring her to do so. It wasn't necessary but she though it best to divest herself of any German names. Though, Louis thought this was very noble of her, undoubtedly, Victoria didn't feel the least noble. For the first time, she truly felt alienated from her sisters – as though she didn't belong to anyone anywhere.

For the rest of the family, she wrote to Nona, *"this would be a good occasion to settle & clarify the whole of the positions of [Cousin George's] relatives.*

The decision come to is that the Tecks & we are to translate our family names into English...Dolly, Algy, Louis & Drino are to be made Peers, if Lloyd George does not oppose too much, & he will only be told about it to-day.... [Princess Helena]... her elderly spinster daughters will be Princesses of nothing like the Fifes...L. had thought of something connected with a naval port, which idea George liked & there was a question of Sheerness...It was suggested that I should continue to be Princess Victoria something or other of Nothing, but what is good enough for my husband is good enough for me – & in saying this please don't think I am insulting the British peerage, which is most honourable, it is just a touch of a princely tar-brush that I suffered from in writing like this..."[42]

Louis told Louise, *"Personally, I have always wanted a change of name. I am through with my career & it seems late in life to have such an upheaval."*[43]

Life, however, went on at Kent House, and Christmas that year, was the first that Louis and Victoria had ever spent alone – a unique experience. However, they were delighted with the news of their newest granddaughter. In mid December, Georgie's Nada had given birth to a girl, Lady Tatiana Elizabeth Mountbatten, in Edinburgh, Scotland. Connected to Tatiana's birth is an ironic story. When she was born, according to Mark Kerr, there were rumors that the Grand Duchess Tatiana Nicholaevna had escaped Russia. *"One day Prince Louis received a telegram from his eldest son in Scotland, which read: 'Tatiana has arrived,' on which he said to his wife: 'Then it is true that she has escaped!' but the reality suddenly occurred to the Princess who replied that it evidently was a new Tatiana who had come upon the scene in the fore, for them of a grand-daughter"*[44] Of course, this can only serve to illustrate the uncertainty of the fate of the Imperial Family, and the lack of news.

In the beginning of 1918, another tie with the old days was severed, when Miss Margaret Hardcastle Jackson, Ernie and their sisters, died. Miss Jackson had given them the discipline and the conscience as well as the tools to follow their mother's philanthropic footsteps. When their mother died, she fulfilled the needed feminine presence and gave structure to their young lives.

Alix was certainly trying to emulate the example of her mother and sisters, and even her niece, Alice. She and her eldest daughters, Olga and Tatiana were nursing the soldiers and had set up a hospital in the Alexander Palace. Ella, too, had opened her doors to the wounded. But the revolution changed all that, at least for Alix and her daughters. As

---

(*) * *"The King approves of: Marquess of Milford Haven, Earl of Medina, Viscount Alderney...the titles of the four peerages should be published by you as soon as possible...for the last time, Louis Battenberg. P.S. Princess Louis & I think it desirable that the following note should be appended to the notification of my new titles: Her Grand Ducal Highness Princess Louis of Battenberg, Grand Daughter of Queen Victoria and Daughter of the late Princess Alice, is, with the King's consent, abandoning her rank and title due to her being a Princess of Hesse, and wishes to be known as Marchioness of Milford Haven." Prince Louis to Lord Stanfordham June 20, 1917. RA PS/GV/O 1153/III/61*

1917 wore on, the revolution in Russia became more vicious. Russia seemed completely immobilized in the past, something like a wolf in a trap, so that in the process of getting out of that trap, and incidentally chewing off its leg, no one could be surprised at the ferocity and the utter brutality that would follow from 1917 onwards.

As the year wore on, the Imperial Family was put under house arrest along with those among their household who wished to remain. The Kaiser, Cousin Willy, of course, made a lot of noise about saving the Hessian princesses, especially the love of his youth; however, this could hardly have been seen as helpful. Cousin George of England had offered asylum to the Imperial Family – offered, and then, later, withdrew that offer. King George thought it was bad policy to offer asylum to an autocrat, even if he was an ally, and his first cousin.

Naturally, Lenin, who had the Kaiser's aid in getting back into Russia after years of exile, had no truck with the Allies. In fact, in November of 1917, he signed the Treaty of Brest-Litovsk with the Kaiser to end hostilities and with a stroke of the pen, Russia was out of the war. It had gone from monarchy, to democracy, to socialist paradise, in the space of one year, and no one had any idea what had happened to Alix and her family or Ella, and, more frustra-tingly, no way of finding out. As 1917 turned into 1918, Victoria tried to exert some influence, but her efforts were met with resounding silence.

Back in England, rumor and speculation were rampant. No one knew what had happened to the various members of the Imperial Family and Victoria worried tremendously. She had the idea of writing to Lenin's wife, an appeal from one woman to another, to enquire about the whereabouts of her family. She wrote to Mr. Whittmore of *The Times,*

> *Thank you so much for your letter & the trouble you have taken to talk with your minister at Stockholm about my idea of writing to Lenin's wife. ... I have meanwhile had a telegrame from the King of Spain confirming what the papers mention about the steps he has taken to have the Empress & her daughters sent to him for the duration of the war & he promises to let me know any news he gets about them. He thinks it is true that the Cesarevitch is dead – my poor sister!*[45]

So by that summer, she began to lose hope of seeing her brother-in-law or her nephew again.

However there was a new and desperate proposal on the horizon. King Alfonso XIII of Spain had offered to give asylum to the Imperial Family. Victoria had specifically asked her nephew-in-law to interest himself in the fate of Alix and Nicky and he had responded positively. She related his ideas to her Cousin George:

> *[Alfonso] confirms what the papers say as to the steps he had already taken. He also says he thinks poor little Alexei is dead too. He says: 'My proposition is to let Alix & daughters go to neutral country on my word of honour that they would remain here till the end of the war. Hope all the different sovereigns will aid me.'*

> *I am sure you are willing & ready to do so, but I fear your ministers may not realize how important, for the safety of these poor things it is that there may be as little delay as possible in backing up Alfonso's request. I have just spoken to an American gentleman, recently returned from Russia, who saw Ella this spring just before she was removed from Moscow &*

he agrees with me in thinking she would not want to leave a country where she has created a work & interest for herself in her sisterhood, which she will hope to take up again as soon as possible – after all she has dedicated her life to this & has no family dependent on her. But for poor Alix & her girls it is different & he thinks it of the utmost importance that any steps to get them out of the country should be taken quickly before the Bolshevist rulers powers dwindle so much that their fanatical followers, & Alix's guard will be made up of such, are left without orders from their so called government to do what they like with their prisoners.

Will you, dear George, please therefore do your best that your government may be quick in its support of Alfonso.[46]

Such orders were given out by the government – *"King of Spain having offered the Empress her children and the Dowager Empress his hospitality is believed to have asked the Germans to help them to leave Russia. If you have a chance of helping and saving them Mr. Balfour desires that you should do so."*[47] But by this time, it was a moot point.

Finally, in September, the news of the assassination of Alix, Nicky and their five children, along with members of their household, was given to King George. As Princess Marie Louise of Schleswig-Holstein (or more properly at this point, she would say 'of nowhere'), daughter of Aunt Helena, recounted events, the king told her that *"Nicky, Alix, and their five children have all been murdered by the Bolsheviks at Ekaterinburg. I have ordered that this awful news should not be released to the Press until I have had time to let Victoria know."*[48]

Princess Marie Louise went from Windsor to the Isle of Wight with a letter from George to Victoria explaining what had happened. Marie Louise wrote that *"I have often had to face difficult situations..., but never anything so terrible as to inform someone that their much-loved sister, brother-in-law, and their five children had all been murdered. I took the letter."*[49] When she reached their home, Louis met her and said that it would be better if he gave the letter to Victoria.

After receiving the news, Victoria came to Marie Louise's room to thank her for bringing the letter. They didn't talk about it much as there wasn't much to say about a tragedy of such extraordinary magnitude. Marie Louise felt that she couldn't even condole with Victoria in the usual way, it seemed out of place. Victoria told her, *"Let us go into the garden as there is any amount of work to be done and one gardener cannot do it all by himself."*[50]

The following day, Victoria wrote several letters. The first was to Nona, as she informed her of the awful news:

Loui[s]e arrived yesterday & brought me a kind letter from George Rex with bad news from Russia....Almost I should be grateful if I could believe it & know that they all met their end quickly & suddenly at the same time & that poor Alicky & the girls were spared the misery I have feared for them. I am so afraid that the fact of their murder is true, but that it did not happen together with Nicky's at Ekaterinburg, for the papers not long ago had an account... [T]hose poor girls. I could have wished might have been spared, they were so young they could have recovered from all the horrors & perhaps found some happiness in life still – but again evil things might have been done to them...It is quite nice having Loui[s]e here now, she is tactful & it helps me to pull myself together...[51]

And to her cousin George, she wrote:

> *For my poor Alicky, as you say, one must be grateful that her sufferings are over, life would always have been a misery to her after Nicky & her boy were gone & though those dear girls were young enough to have recovered from the horrors they went through & happier days might have come to them, yet also there was the chance, that haunted me, of great wrong being done them.*
>
> *If I could only believe, as I do now, that all have reached the end of their sufferings, if I could only also feel sure that it was together with Nicky – it is that about which I am still in doubt because the papers not long ago brought the news, I do not know from what source, that a sort of funeral service was held for Nicky after the Czecho-Slovak forces had taken Ekaterinenburg & I don't understand why his family was not mentioned if they died there, when he did. I shall be so grateful to hear from you any further news you may get, I can't help being haunted by the thought that their end took place at a later date & elsewhere. But however that may be God's peace is with them now & it is easier to bear the sense of their loss to me, than the thought of what they have gone through & what might have still been in store for them.*[52]

Marie Louise stayed for three weeks. They gardened, picked blackberries and hunted for mushrooms, but never talked about the contents of the letter. Marie Louise realized that Victoria was working hard all day everyday in order to lessen her pain. Together they knitted items of clothing for the troops overseas, but never ever talked of the news again. Victoria wrote her a letter afterwards saying that not talking about the tragedy helped her get a grip on events far better than discussing in detail all that had happened.

Victoria wrote about Alix: *"Though her loss is pain and grief to me, yet I am grateful that I can think of her as being at peace now. She, her dear husband and children removed from even further suffering."*[53] She would also never allow herself to hope that the stories of their demise were untrue, possibly because she continued to be haunted by the 'evil' things that might have happened to her nieces. Even in the face of such rumors of the horrors, escapes, and some survivors, Victoria was realistic. She wrote to her cousin George:

> *I thank you so much for your kind note enclosing a copy of the information supplied by the Consul at Ekaterinenburg about the fate of Alix & her children.*
>
> *I see that he says: 'they are stated to have been burnt alive'...& further on 'there is still the possibility of their having been taken north by the Bolshevicks' – the latter surmise I think is so unlikely that I can base no hopes on it – the horrid tale of their end however, based only on hearsay, I trust & am inclined to believe is an exaggeration. I should fancy the more probable course of events, when I compare the two sets of news you sent me, is that they were killed almost at the same time as Nicky & then their bodies, his too possibly, removed to another house which was set fire to, to remove all traces of the slaughter. I can but pray that I am right in this guess & that they were spared the other horror.*[54]

But nevertheless, in the face of all this terror, pragmatic Victoria held out hope that Ella, the Mother Superior of the Convent of SS Mary and Martha, might just have been spared.

Chapter XII

August 1918 – September 1921

In April 1918, Ella was handed a note by a group of soldiers informing her that Nicky needed her urgently. She and her companion, Sister Barbara, were given just minutes to get ready and were taken away from the convent by the Bolsheviks. The truth was that Lenin was jealous, and hated her popularity – a Romanov's popularity – in Moscow and wanted to be rid of her by any means possible. The nuns were first taken to Ekaterinburg, and thence to Alapaievsk along with several other members of the Imperial Family: Grand Duke Serge Mikhailovich, three sons of Grand Duke Constantine, and young Prince Paley, the son of Grand Duke Paul Alexandrovich and his second wife, Princess Paley.

At Alapaievsk, they were incarcerated for several months in an empty school house. Besides trying to make their own daily lives as bearable as possible with a normal routine, Ella and Barbara spent much of their time looking after the men. They were able to smuggle out some letters so that others knew these bare facts, but their existence was extremely precarious.

Victoria said much of this in a letter to her cousin, George V:

You may like to know what little information I have had in the course of this summer about Ella. From an American gentleman who saw Ella twice at Easter time in Moscow & brought me a few cautious lines from her, I received the information that she declined to receive the German representative Mirbach – shortly afterwards she was given two hours notice of her intended removal & was taken away...A letter was received from her by the Sisterhood announ-cing her arrival at Alapaëvsk [sic] (this was I think in May). She had passed 3 hours at Ekaterinenburg on her way there but had seen no one. Alapaëvsk is north east of that town, in the Urals. Her guards had treated her considerately on the journey.

The last news I received about her was through Alice in a letter written at the end of July. She informed me that Aunt Olga of Greece had heard from her sister-in-law Elisabeth Mavrikevna (widow of her brother Constantine [and mother of three of the Princes held by the Bolsheviks]) who had been forced to lodge herself with her youngest children & 4 little grandchildren in obscure lodgings in Petrograd, where she would have starved but for the kindness of the King of Sweden, who sent her provisions through his minister. The husband of Hélène of Servia, John, & his brother Igor Constantinovitch....are her elder sons....

From the latter, Elisabeth had received a long letter in the summer telling her that they, Hélène (who must have been taken there by the Bolsheviks), Micha's brother Sergeï & Paul's son by his second wife, were all prisoners together with Ella...in the school house at Alapaëvsk, lodged in adjoining rooms along one corridor as well as their guards. They were allowed to walk in the little town & to the outskirts of a wood.

Since then Elisabeth had heard that her sons & Sergeï had been removed. From earlier rumours & now from the Consul's report we know that these have escaped.

I hope that Ella may still be at Alapaëvsk, where there are evidently people who were still kindly inclined towards the prisoners – but Elisabeth did not know whether Ella & Helène of Servia were there still or not.

Should any news of her reach you, I am sure you will let me know & I thank you once more for your affectionate & sincere sympathy with me in my distress & sorrow.[1]

The letter contained the facts as far as Victoria knew them. However, the Princes and Grand Duke she wrote about did not, in fact, escape. They all shared the same tragic fate. On the night of July 17/18 a truck took them to a spot near Sinyachikha. They were pushed alive into a disused mineshaft by the soldiers who threw in two hand grenades after them. The peasants said that they heard the survivors of the fall singing hymns in English such as *"Hail gentle light..."* Ella, who was probably one of those survivors, comforted and bandaged the wounds of the others in that dark pit. The peasants were evidently too frightened to rescue them, and it was only some ten weeks later, after all were dead of wounds, exposure, and starvation, that a monk by the name of Father Seraphim removed the bodies. He was a great admirer of Ella's and took charge of the coffins of the dead.

Some months later the sad truth was confirmed to Victoria by Lord Robert Cecil. She wrote a letter to Nona that showed her deep understanding of her two sisters.

If ever anyone has met death without fear she would have and her deep and pure faith will have upheld and supported comforted her in all she has gone though so that the misery poor Alicky will have suffered will not have touched Ella's soul and maybe had she lived, years of solitary suffering would have been her lot, for I have recently heard that all her work in Moscow has been destroyed.[2]

Though she had no choice but to accept the ends of her sisters and families as related to her by various relatives and government functionaries, it did not follow that she was reconciled or thought that all had been done to save them. She knew perfectly well that this was not so, and was bitterly angry about it. She directed this anger towards politicians who would not save her relations, and relatives who would or could not. Her comments about the naïve Woodrow Wilson and David Lloyd George show that she did not mince words. They, she said, *"coquette with the Bolsheviks & think to reform them by moral suasion! The fools!!"[3]* In addition, she blamed George V, fairly or not, for abandoning his cousins.

There was much brouhaha about Cousin Willy wanting to save his Hessian cousins, and that Lenin, when the Kaiser's government had provided him with the wherewithal to travel into Russian, had promised him that they, the two German Princesses, would go free. But no one who knew them thought seriously that either Ella or Alix and her family would accept such help. There was one relative, her nephew-in-law, Alfonso XIII, who had offered to provide sanctuary for Ella, Alix and her family, though he was tragically unsuccessful. Victoria wrote him a letter of thanks.

Now that alas there is nothing to hope for for my dear Sister Alix & her children on this earth & that it is almost a positive certainty that death has release them from further suffering..., I feel I must send you a few lines to thank you with all my heart for all you tried to do to save them from their enemies.

She lauded him for his efforts in trying to provide help to the Romanovs and criticized an unnamed closer cousin, in the strongest of terms saying that

> [t]*he sovereign who had the most direct influence on the revolutionary government in Russia, the one who had known my sister as a child, who had the same blood as hers flowing in his veins, who formerly never failed to claim her as of his nationality deserted her, I fear I must believe, in her distress, whilst you to whom she & hers were comparative strangers thought of & strove to help them – I shall never forget the gratitude I owe you for this.*[4]

The war was over and an armistice was signed in November 1918. With a stroke of the pen, it seemed, much of the Royal World ended until it was barely recognizable. Hindsight provides much wisdom, but it must have been unnerving and ironic that Queen Victoria had never wanted Ella and Alix to go to Russia. She knew that disaster would come to them there, and with all the signs that had taken place during her lifetime, the brutality of their eventual fates would not have surprised her. Her relations must have been glad she did not live to see how her world and many members of her family vanished so quickly, and without, in many cases, even a whimper.

Cousin Willy was no longer Kaiser of the Second Reich and went quietly and almost cheerfully into exile in Holland. The Grand-nephew of the late Emperor Franz Joseph of Austria, who, himself had died in 1916, reigned in Austria-Hungary for two years as Emperor Charles and was now also an exile first in Switzerland and then in Madeira. As for all the Princes, Grand Dukes, Dukes, Counts and Electors in Germany – they were all, including Ernie, removed from power.

Interestingly enough, Ernie was allowed to stay at Wolfsgarten and keep the Neues Palais. He abdicated like the rest and no longer had any real power, but he was popular with the people. This may be partly due to what had happened during those days of revolutionary activity in Germany. According to some of his 'closest friends',

> *Hours before the storm broke he was fully aware of the state of things but refused to make use of his cars, which were waiting to take him to some hiding-place in the country. The sound of the mob in the streets of Darmstadt had reached the Palace for some time, but the Grand Duke and his wife stayed to meet them and waited in their Throne Room. Eventually the mob, who had broken into the palace, burst down the doors of the Throne Room and streamed in, shouting, "Down with the Grand Duke!" "Kill the Grand Duke!" As they approached the Grand Duke, those in the front felt ashamed and there was something like a silence in the Throne Room, broke by the Grand Duke, who said in a loud voice: "I can see no Hessian uniforms among you, but you will form a deputation and tell me what you want; in the meantime, as no one has ever been to the palace without being entertained, my wife will make you tea.*[5]

When the deputation was formed, it was, in fact, formed to protect Ernie and his family. He kept his land and his title, though it carried nothing with it, and he and Onor and the children continued, for the most part, just as they always had – Ernie now working with the convalescents, and Onor continuing her role as the benevolent mother figure to the Hessians.

In early November, Irène and Henry along with Toddy, their eldest son, fled from Kiel in their car. They were fleeing the soldiers of the German Revolution and the car was fired upon. According to *The Times* of London Irène was wounded in the arm and a bullet actually went through Henry's coat.[6] After this rather hair-raising escape, the couple eventually returned to their residence in Hemmelmarck almost as though nothing had happened and all was seemingly peaceful once again, though deprived of their titles. Later on, there was the controversy about Henry's misinterpretation of George V's words in 1912 and 1914, but outside of that, their lives went on much as before. At war's end, there was a slight bitterness in the relationship between the two sisters, but it healed as well as could be expected, though, since neither traveled as they had before, they saw each other very infrequently.

The Dowager Empress, Marie Feodorovna, Nicky's mother, along with her daughters, Xenia and Olga, and their husbands, were eventually permitted to leave Russia. The Empress and Xenia were spirited away in the *HMS Marlborough*, while Olga and her husband had a much longer journey due to her pregnancy at the time. Though Kyrill Vladimirovich, Ducky's husband, marched, at least in the beginning of the Revolution, under the red flag, the couple, too, was able to escape. His temporary allegiance to that flag may explain why he wasn't arrested right away, but finally, he was forced to leave by the skin of his teeth. He and Ducky escaped through Finland, and eventually made their way to France. Kyrill announced that he was the Curator of the Romanov throne, and because of that announcement, the Dowager Empress refused to speak to him thereafter.

Marie Feodorovna refused to believe that Nicky and Alix and the children were dead, and consequently never felt that Kyrill had the right to hold court. According to Prince Louis, she was firmly convinced that *"all her dear ones are safe in the hands of that powerful & loyal body, the Old Believers somewhere far North & East."*[7] Indeed, she was so determined to believe this, that she was quite happy. Victoria told Nona that the Empress *"looks wonderfully well & is most plucky & full of confidence that Nicky & family are alive."*[8]

Cousin Marie of Romania continued to be Queen of Romania, but only because Romania had fought on the side of the Allies. Tsar Ferdinand, who had become the monarch of Bulgaria after Sandro Battenberg, abdicated in favor of his son Boris and very quietly left the country. Of the others who retained their thrones, there was Alfonso XIII of Spain, though not for long, and there were the Belgians, the Italians, and the Scandinavians.

Though many lost their throne and their life, Prince Louis was only slightly luckier. He lost his position in the Royal Navy and much of whatever fortune he had possessed. Louis was no longer able to draw on monies he had invested in a platinum mine in Russia and various properties in Germany. This major part of his fortune was for all intents and purposes gone – and the couple almost seemed to be back where they started from, living on navy half-pay, any small inheritances, and some of Victoria's properties that remained intact. In addition, Victoria lost most of her jewels, which she had left in Russia at the beginning of the war. There was a movement to reward people who had helped in the allied victory, and Louis' invention, the Course Indicator, was thought to be a tremendous help. Louis, however, would not accept monetary compensation for this.[9]

Added to all these financial losses, they were compelled to sell the Heiligenberg, and with the devastating financial conditions in Germany, received £30,000, under half of what the estate was actually worth – and that sum became virtually worthless because of the devaluation of the mark. From a pragmatic point of view, their son, Georgie would not have the beautiful home outside Jugenheim to inherit, but from a sentimental point of view, Victoria missed the Heiligenberg, the scene of so many of her youthful larks and later, marital happiness.

Their lives, which Victoria had thought sacrificed by Louis' resignation, were certainly changed. However, during their years at Kent House, they did their war work by sheltering some of the wounded and sick men that came to the Isle of Wight. Several of these men convalesced for long periods at the cottage. It was good for Louis, for he was able to advise the men as he had advised his junior officers. They looked up to him and he began to feel useful again and kept up with several of them for some years afterwards.

The remaining members of the Hessian Family, Ernie, Victoria, and Irène, continued to struggle with the rumors and misinformation that began to seep through to Germany and England about the fate of the Imperial Family and Ella. There were more differing accounts of the events than there were stars in the sky, and people came forward with new and miraculous escapes, or an even grislier version of their sad ends – all incredulous inventions. Later, of course, between Irène, Victoria, the Dowager Empress, and her daughters, now living in exile in Denmark, they would have to contend with all the imposters parading themselves before the world. They claimed to be the Grand Duchess Anastasia, or Marie, or Olga, or Tatiana, and even, Alexis, who couldn't have possibly survived such an ordeal – it was cruel. Irène and Ernie, in particular, would have to deal with the infamous Anna Anderson case. Victoria, no doubt, counted herself lucky that she was not closely involved with this, and would only confirm Ernie and Irène's conclusions when asked.

Victoria's Dickie finished the war as a Sub-Lieutenant, and went off with some of his fellow officers to do courses in Cambridge and catch up on lost time. Georgie and Nada had become parents once again, when their son, David, was born in May in Edinburgh. Victoria was delighted to have a grandson at last. Though Louis was officially put on the retirement list in the beginning of 1919, he was assisting King George V as a Naval Aide-de-camp. In addition, there was news of Irène. Her middle son, Bobby, her only completely well child, was to be married to Princess Charlotte Agnes of Saxe-Altenburg and just a month afterward, Toddy was married to Princess Calixta of Lippe.

Louise, however, was still in France. She continued her nursing, remaining there until 1919. She had always led an independent sort of life, especially during the war, and Victoria and Louis had always felt that she should be permitted to choose her own mate. Certainly, after all she had seen during her nursing, she couldn't have felt like a 'dewy-eyed' Princess. Indeed, she had spurned the proposals of Manoel II of Portugal, and, it was said, Prince Christopher of Greece.

Before the war broke out there was talk of a match with Prince Friedrich of Solms-Baruth in 1913. Onor and Victoria discussed it in letters, but in the end, Louise said no, and Victoria explained, that it was because of lack of attraction, and also because the Solms-Baruth family were *"a totally Prussian family with all their distinct traditions and prejudices, loyalty to the King of Prussia, a member of his nobility, duty bound to the court."*[10] It was obvious at that late hour that such a match would be very awkward for the Battenbergs, father and sons, who served in the English Navy, as well as the thoroughly English Louise.

In any event, she seemed content traveling with her mother visiting relatives in Europe and Russia, and of course, during the war, nursing in France. Early in the war years, she had been engaged to a man, who was never identified, and who was killed. Afterward, she met a fellow nurse, a man that the family called "Shakespeare," identified as the painter, Alexander Stuart-Hill. Louise was very much in love, and they were engaged until Louis put a halt to the attachment. Louise's suitor was not objected to on the basis of being a commoner, or that he was poor, but because he was a homosexual. Louise, in her innocence, had been completely unaware of this.[11]

In the summer of 1919, Victoria did a very scaled-down version of what had once been such grand touring to visit family. In Switzerland, she was able to see Franzjos and Anna, about whom she had worried so much during the war. She also saw Ernie and his family at Thurn for the first time in six years. She approached the meeting with some trepidation, but wrote later that

> *though I knew our love for each other was unchanged yet I own that I rather dreaded our first meeting, for a separation of six years – & such years as we have gone through not only must make us see many from a different point of view, but must also produce unknown effects on our respective characters. Thank God, that in all essentials I have found you the same & I hope that you have found the like in me. I feel too that though I have shrunk from saddening our few days together by speaking too much about our anxieties & griefs for those dear Others in Russia, that you & I share them & our love for them fully. I dare not give myself up to hope....*[12]

With Victoria and Ernie, there can be little doubt that their feelings for each other had not changed. Though Victoria had always said that Ernie was Ella's *"child,"*[13] the closeness with this eldest sister, who had mothered him so completely, was unique. She would never direct her anger at the brother whom she had always protected and shielded from the realities of the world. Any of those heightened anger or bitterness that she cherished, which was very little, she seemed to aim at Irène, her last sister, and that did not last very long. And, in turn, Irène didn't hesitate when she wrote to Victoria, to place the blame where she thought it lay:

> *All the sorrow that fell upon our dear ones originated through the net that was systematically begin drawn round us & Austria for years – as we now know! Europe & the World has to thank the so called Entente for the war & all its consequences. In the End Truth! Will triumph!*[14]

One can only imagine the response Victoria, with all her outspokenness, had to these statements.

That she believed there was no hope for her sisters in Russia safeguarded her from disappointment, and she tried to impart that to Ernie. However, in her compassion, she would not stop him from hoping altogether. She wrote to Onor, that *"if he [Ernie], like poor Aunt Minnie, still has hope, then please do not rob him of this... – time will make this hope disappear in a more gentle way."*[15] Certainly, he knew as little as she did about the circumstances of their deaths, and heard the same odd survival stories. The news that Ernie received from Russia was *"just as sparse & unreliable as all that one has received."*[16] Victoria, herself, had a unique philosophy, even as her grief threatened to overwhelm her. She knew that even as the worst happened that one could still be philosophical and find happiness in life.[17] She tried to share this viewpoint with Ernie.

> *There is one great lesson the passed [sic] years have taught mankind, for the worse sometimes but surely also for the good too & that is not to overvalue this life on earth or to fear death as was the tendency before that – one learns to be really grateful for the small memories & to discover the value & comforts of small daily pleasures. My thoughts are much & often with you & yours, poor Irene & our dear Ones lost to us I fear, but at peace...How little value*

one individual really is to mankind on the whole, it is after all for the sake of our own self respect & good conscience that one must work & live if we satisfy the thousands of our higher nature, we can never be quite unhappy or quite lose courage.[18]

This does not mean that Victoria was always stoic about the tragedies in her life. Despite the stories about working in the garden, Victoria had many tears for her lost sisters. Grand Duke Dmitri Pavlovich*, came to London in the beginning of 1919. He felt obliged to visit Victoria and he recounted his feelings about their encounter in his diary:

Around 11:30 I set off for Kensington Palace to visit old Aunt Victoria Battenberg (now Lady the Marchioness Milford Haven). I have to admit that I was in an awful funk about that interview, because I didn't know how she would feel about me and my activities in the year before the revolution*, which were, of course, against her poor, ill-fated sister Alix. But Victoria was always very observant, and so she has a perfectly correct view of the general state of things. Nonetheless, our conversation was very difficult to bear. She cried the whole time, and managed to draw various pictures for herself of the last moments of her sisters' lives. There's no doubt in her mind that Alix and Aunt Ella have been killed.[19]

Such an emotional scene may seem unlike Victoria, but perhaps it was just too overwhelming to see this young man again. A youth so closely associated with both her sisters and all the lost Romanov relations, and whom she had not seen since before the war.

And as for the relationships between the cousins who had been Queen Victoria's grandchildren? George V's biographer has an answer for that question:

A few weeks after the Armistice, [George V's] son Prince Albert [later George VI]... met the Kaiser's sister, Princess Victoria ["Moretta"]. He wrote to his father: "She asked after you and the family, and hoped that we should be friends again. I told her politely I did not think it was possible for a great many years!!!" The King replied "Your answer to Cousin Vicky (who of course I have known all my life) was quite correct. The sooner she knows the real feeling of bitterness which exists here against her country the better." ... Not until 1935 could [George V] write to ... [Ernie]...: 'That horrible and unnecessary war has made no difference to my feelings for you.[20]

At least the rounds of visiting and travel could continue if in a much limited fashion. At the end of that year, Louis, Victoria and Louise spent Christmas with Alice in Corfu. Afterward they traveled on to Rome. Victoria wanted Louise to *"go away from all old associations to help her restart an after warlife & put the past more into the background."*[21] She noted, too, that "[Louis] *is beginning to show his age rather, he stoops a bit when he walks & does not care*

(*) *Dmitri Pavlovich (1891-1942) was the only son of Grand Duke Paul Alexandrovich and of his first wife, the former Princess Alexandra of Greece, eldest daughter of King George I and Queen Olga. Tsar Nicholas II exiled Dmitri Pavlovich to the Far East as a consequence of the young man's role in Rasputin's murder. This, ironically, saved Dimitri Pavlovich, for when the revolution came, he was able to escape Russia and eventually make his way to Europe. In exile, Dmitri Pavlovich, whose father was executed by the Bolsheviks in 1919, led a rudderless existence. Perennially short of funds and lacking the preparation to build any sort of career, his daily existence centered around a busy social schedule and an endless row of parties. While living in Paris, he had a a relationship with Coco Chanel, before settling his sights on an American heir, Audrey Emery, whom he married morganatically in 1926. They had a one son, Paul, before divorcing in 1937.*

about walking fast – well he is going to be 66, so it is not surprising."[22] For economic reasons and with real regret, they decided to give up Kent House. Instead, they repaired to a little house on Nona and Richard Crichton's estate called Fishponds at Netley Castle. Victoria was determined to make the most out of this time near her best friend and her husband.

In June 1920, there was a slight tempest about the publication of letters between Nicky and Alix in England, America, and Australia. However, Princess Victoria brought forth a suit to stop publication of letters. They were actually published by Messrs. Duckworth & Co. in 1923, and called *The Letters of the Tsaritza to the Tsar 1914-16*. Victoria, however, was sensible enough to know that it was only a matter of time before such exploitive materials became the norm in the publishing world, and that it would be impossible to sue everyone.

In early 1920, Victoria received a phone call from her Aunt Beatrice. The Princess had read in a *London Illustrated News* paper that several coffins were resting in a small chapel in Beijing. The bodies, Princess Beatrice explained, were those of Ella and Sister Barbara, and others who had been murdered with her and they were in Beijing under the care of one Father Seraphim. The article explained how the both the coffins were taken by wagon overland to China by the Father. He stopped in Beijing because he could literally go no further.

Victoria and Louis made inquiries first of all, to find out whether this story was true. Ella was able to inspire true faith and loyalty, and Father Seraphim was evidently inculcated with the necessary zeal to take Ella wherever she wished to be. Moreover, they would find out that he was determined that she be buried in the proper Christian manner. They were informed that many of the faithful, and most particularly the peasants looked upon Ella as a saint, and therefore, there was nothing they wouldn't do to insure that Ella's final wish, if she could not be buried alongside her husband, to be buried in Jerusalem, was carried out.

Victoria slowly learned the details of the events of June and July 1918 and what happened to Ella and the other members of the family who were with her. In a report dated April 24, 1920, Father Seraphim related the story as best as his knowledge. He had been hidden when the assassins brought the party to the mineshaft at Alapaievsk. The group had been taken to Sinyachikha, and was made to walk to the mouth of the shaft. Ella evidently had begun to sing a hymn. The Bolshevik commander pronounced their sentence of death and selected Ella first – she kneeled at the edge of the shaft and said, *'Father, forgive them for they know not what they do'*, and was struck unconscious by a rifle butt and thrown many feet down to the bottom of the shaft. The rest were dealt with in the same way, except Grand Duke Serge Mikhailovich, who protested the outrage and was shot before being flung down.

The priest could not come out, much as he wanted to, and the soldiers also tossed down hand grenades so that though they were mostly alive when they were thrown down, they were mortally wounded by the grenades. When the soldiers left, those hidden could hear them continuing to sing hymns down in the shaft. As the early morning dawned, the hymns began slowly to die out. A peasant who also witnessed the murders stated in Father Seraphim's report that *"en-route to their martyrdom, the Grand Dukes and the other martyrs started religious chants."*[23] In relating the story to Ernie, Victoria added,

I have heard that it was told by one of those who was present at her death that she prayed 'Lord forgive them for they know not what they do' – & I believe it, for how should one not knowing her have thought of putting these words in her mouth. The autopsy on the bodies proved that life was extinct before they were thrown into the pit, so thank God the tales of further suffering are not true.[24]

It is here where we have to conclude that Victoria was once again trying to spare Ernie great sorrow as she had done ever since he was a child, for it is probably not true that they were dead before they were thrown into the pit, though, we will really never know.

Later, when the White Russians were able to take over Alapaievsk, Seraphim was able to go down into the shaft with the help of the soldiers and see the state of the bodies. Ella, it seemed, had been trying to care for the others who had survived the fall. She had torn her nun's veil and bandaged their wounds. When she finally succumbed, her hand, he said, had stiffened into the sign of the cross.

At first, Seraphim took them to his church in Alapaievsk. The bodies were identified, washed, dressed in night-clothes, put in coffins and a funeral mass was said. The Father knew that the Grand Duchess could not stay there long. As the political situation was so unstable, there was no way of knowing if and when the Bolsheviks would return so it was imperative for Seraphim to remove the coffins as soon as possible. This he was finally able to accomplish though it took a great deal of time – nearly a year.

He trekked eastward, with the coffins on wagons, and was actually able to get them on the Trans-Siberian Railway. Besides all the difficulties, the coffins were rescued only in the nick of time from Russian insurgents, by Chinese and Japanese Troops. Later, after many ordeals, he was able to put the coffins on the Chinese Eastern Railway, and eventually they arrived at the Russian Mission in Beijing. It was here that the *Illustrated News* ran the story and Princess Beatrice, useful as ever, had shown it to Victoria.

With the help of Lord Curzon, as well as the British Representative in Beijing, the representative of the Imperial Russian Legation in Paris and Beijing and the Foreign Office, Victoria began her mission to take Ella and her companion to Jerusalem. Having learned that the coffins reposed at an Orthodox chapel in the outskirts of Beijing, together with some of the other Imperial family members killed at Alapaievsk, she began writing letters and telegrams to make arrangements. In correspondence with the representative of the Russian Legation in Paris, M. de Giers, Victoria learned the details of what had happened to Ella and her companions at Alapaievsk, and was able to read Father Seraphim's account. Through the good offices of this same gentleman, she was able to arrange the logistics of the transfer of the coffins from Beijing to Jerusalem; she deposited the necessary funds, and the preparations were made. There was some obligatory haste since Victoria felt that the bodies rested in an environment hostile to Christians. Although she had been advised to leave the bodies in China, after much thought, she decided that taking the coffins to Jerusalem was most fitting. She did not arrive at this decision cavalierly... it was painful for her to remove the remains, but in the end she was convinced it was the only way.

She wrote to M. de Giers,

I am persuaded that, sooner or later, the day will come that the body of my sister will reenter Russia and will find definite repose in Moscow, the city that she loved so much... but until that day comes, I so much want to know, that she is in a safe place. Or, there is only one place which it appears to me which surely the Grand Duchess, herself would have chosen, were Russia not possible, it is Jerusalem.... This city is sacred to all Christians, it is venerated by Moslems and Jews. No revolutionary group would dare to touch its churches and convents. My sister and the Grand Duke Sergei Alexandrovitch have made a pilgrimage; there, in the church, founded by the Empress Marie Alexandrovna, to the consecration of which they took part, where they prayed together, I would like to have transported, the body of my dear sister and that of Varvara [Sister Barbara] Jakovleva, who was faithful to her even in death and whose body has followed these long months on the sad pilgrimage of her dear mistress and abbess.[25]

They were able to coordinate arrangements with Father Seraphim. He and two assistants would leave China on January 15, taking the coffins to Port Said where Louis, Victoria, Louise, and their party would meet them. From there, they would board a train and travel together to Jerusalem.

She was able to relate her plans to Onor,

I could not rest thinking about the remains of our dear Ella and loyal Vari [Sister Barbara] lying in a little unprotected chapel near Peking, in the midst of a European-hating population at this time – and so I have decided to remove them from there and to have them brought to Jerusalem. I think Ella would agree with the thought that her body should find its last resting place in this holy city, and hopefully in the church which was built in memory of Serge's mother, and where she and Serge were present at the consecration.[26]

It was Victoria's intention to go to Rome at the end of the year, and, there, wait for word that the bodies were on their journey. However, before she left, certain events occurred. In October of that year, Aunt Marie of Coburg died. Irène was able to write her details of the Duchess' last moments.

Aunt Marie of Coburg's death [October 24, 1920] will have grieved you, bringing back so many memories, just also of Malta. Quite peacefully she slumbered & neither Ducky nor Baby Bee realized when all was really over – she had had a derangement of her stomach wh[ich] weakened her constitution already underfed & by sorrow & all she has gone through she was a shadow of her former self, and had no strength to resist anything. She is at peace too now – & for her it is also happier so, poor thing.[27]

It was said that Marie could not get over the fact that she was no longer the Duchess of Coburg and became nearly apoplectic when a letter with the envelop addressed to Frau Coburg was delivered to her. However, such stories are usually just that – stories.

Ella's birthday was on November 1, and Irène wrote to Victoria to commiserate on this occasion.

On this day our thoughts will specially be occupied with her & all she was to us – I am sure her memory will ever remain with all those that knew and loved her, & how very many there were – & in Russia surely, through all she achieved with her sisterhood will gradually dawn more and more on all those who were helped by her....[28]

And at the end of the year, she wrote,

God bless you dear for the thought of bringing beloved Ella's remains to Jerusalem & little devoted Vari's – How I wish I could have joined you – alas! That is impossible. Perhaps some day – when it lies in God's will – I may so see her dear grave – & yet for me she is always near me more so than living – & yet it is so hard, so hard to believe she is gone for ever.[29]

It appeared that the two sisters were falling back into their habits of correspondence. There are a few letters from Irène to Victoria from this period, however Irène's pre-war correspondence is lost. In her hasty escape from Kiel in 1918, she burned it all.

The coffins arrived in Port Said on January 25, 1921, where Victoria, Louis, Louise, and the Stroukoffs, (who had been Ella's lady-in-waiting and Private Secretary from the old days) met them. Egypt in January was perhaps, for a Westerner, one of the few bearable months. Usually, the weather was so hot and humid that the natives, themselves, had a problem bearing it. Their first stop had been Alexandria. The British had been in Alexandria since approximately 1880, and the city had been their chief port in the Middle East during the War. From there, they caught a train to Port Said. Upon reaching the port, they learned that the coffins had arrived just hours previously. Victoria described the scene at length for Ernie,

There is a little Greek Church here & the coffins were taken there for the night, so we went to the church; they had just been placed in a small side chapel draped in black & Father Seraphim, the monk who has never left them since Alapaevsk was there, a Greek priest & a couple of Russian people. It was very quiet & private & calm in the little chapel, only one candle burning at the head of each coffin. It seemed so strange to be walking by moonlight in this out of the way town through empty streets to go & meet all that remains of our dear Ella, who had so often come to meet me after a long journey – but it was very peaceful in the chapel. It was too late at night to have a service, one would just say a prayer quietly & it was good to have the faithful Kitty with us, who in 1888 had been with Ella on the journey to Jerusalem & through Egypt. The outer coffins are of Chinese teakwood with brass bindings & a big brass orthodox cross on them, & on the top & head of Ella's, there is a nice photograph of her in her sister's dress fastened on flat in a plain teak frame with a brass crown above it – Vari's [Barbara] is without a picture but otherwise the same, only smaller, for you remember she was a tiny person.

The Monk told us that when the coffins had to be hidden for some months before they were able to leave Siberia, they were in a nunnery, where they were opened, as this was necessary & our Ella's body was not decayed only dried up – The nuns cleansed it & exchanged the grave cloth for a nun's dress & so now it is clothed as she would have like, for she had always intended to withdraw quite from the world, when her Home was well established & end her days as a nun.

This morning the coffins had to leave again by good's train in a special van which is ferried across the canal, we leave this afternoon for El Hautara where we cross & shall find the van attached to the train which starts from there to-night for Jerusalem, where we are due at 2 p.m. to-morrow. The Monk & his 2 novices travel in the van. We are to be met on arrival by hearses & the clergy & after short prayers must pass through the town to the Russian Church of Mary Magdalene which is near the Garden of Gethsamane about 4 kilometers from the station. The Patriarch & church authorities propose that the coffins should stand in the church a few days & that I should decide on the spot where they had better rest afterwards, when there will be a big mass on their removal from the body of the church. I hope to find that they have a vault where they can rest, until they can go to Moscow....

I am so thankful that there was nothing painful or unsuitable at our meeting with the

coffins, all was so simple & peaceful, as she would have liked it.[30]

Their train was fitted with luggage compartments that would fit the coffins and all of Father Seraphim's effects, and those of his two assistants. This was all arranged by General Allenby, a soldier famous for liberating Palestine from the Turks, and who was at this point, British High Commissioner of Egypt. They reached Jerusalem the following day and were met by representatives of the Colonial Government and the High Commissioner, Sir Herbert Samuel, as well as the Russian Orthodox clergymen. The coffins were loaded onto trucks decorated with green ribbons, and two priests in black and silver funeral vestments sat with Ella's coffin. They followed in cars provided by the High Commissioner, and eventually reached the city itself.

As the car made its way down the rocky road that led to the Mount of Olives, many of the faithful began following the cars and trucks. They were determined to participate in the funeral of the beautiful Grand Duchess and her assistant. They drove to the Church of St. Mary Magdalen, the church that Serge and Ella had dedicated in 1888. Built as it was, outside the Damascus Gate, and in the spot that General Charles Gordon had fixed as the site of the crucifixion, it had five onion domes, gleaming white in the winter sun. If one hadn't known better, it might almost have been Moscow. As the cars came to the entrance, there was a bit of a struggle. So many had come for the funeral services being held that day as well as the two days following that there was quite a crush.

Louis took charge and helped direct the unloading of the coffins. Victoria held on to the brass handle of one of them as they climbed the stairs, to the entrance of the church. She wrote of walking over a poor woman who had fallen on her face during the utter crush of the mourners.[31] Luckily, the group was able to get up to the church and into their seats for the service. It was long and drawn out with a congregation that flowed out the door and onto the terrace.

Victoria and her group sat through similar services for the next several days. Though the mandatory government was anxious to extend its hospitality to these most distinguished visitors, they refused all invitations. No doubt, it seemed like a bad idea to have cocktails and tea dances while they were attending the funeral services of a loved one. The greatly devoted Father Seraphim had elected to stay in Jerusalem at the church with Ella and Sister Barbara, living there and praying by the coffins.

The spot was beautiful, Victoria wrote to Nona.

The church lies beautifully on the steep slope of the Mount of Olives in its own grounds surrounded by cypress & fir trees, well back & above the high road, with a lovely view on the town, away from its traffic and turmoil, a really peaceful spot from which you have a lovely view on to the town.[32]

And, to say that they found a peaceful spot in Jerusalem is to say something.

They left Jerusalem in the beginning of February and returned to Rome. From Rome, there was a great deal of letter writing back and forth between Victoria, Irène, and Ernie, discussing what had happened in Jerusalem and their feelings about it. Irène was very moved by the scene at Port Said when Victoria and Louis met the coffins and thought the descriptions of the coffins resting in the little Greek Orthodox Church on a candle lit night, beautiful. As was her inclination, she felt it necessary to close with a conciliatory remark,

Henry beggs [sic] *me quite especially to tell you how deeply he feels for you, & that I am to tell you & dear Ludwig – that for him you both remain in his heart what you were for him before – politics are one thing but old well proved friendship another & he feels as ever that for him he is "his old mate," & sends you both his fond love.*[33]

In a letter dated the following day, Irène asked the key question,

Has...Father Seraphim been able to tell you anything of how beloved Ella's end was? Or how it all happened? However painful his knowledge may have been one longs to know & how one would like to thank him for his faithful care of her last remains...[34]

Though it seems that Victoria knew the details and the truth of what had occurred, it also seems that she chose not to tell Ernie that the victims were alive down in the mineshaft. *"Our Ella's body,"* she told him,

was found quite at the bottom of the mine shaft into which the party from Alapaevsk were thrown. Her skull was fractured & the doctors who examined the body said she cannot have suffered & that most likely the rush of air of the fall sufficed to stop the heart working, as when people have fallen a great distance this has often been the case. I have so long hesitated to touch on these details, they hurt one to know, yet I feel you must hear them sooner or later my poor boy, for they are coming out in publications.[35]

Though it must be supposed that she did not spare Irène, she continued to spare Ernie. That he might not have found out the harsher truth in those self-same publications, for some reason did not occur to her. In the same letter, she explained to Ernie, in the kindest terms possible, the horrors that happened to Alix, Nicky and their family; the end was swift and they would not have been fearful since the soldiers had lied to them, telling them they were to be photographed, which was why they were to wait in the cellar. They were not long kept in suspense. But, she lamented, *"Oh my dear Ernie I fear we shall not have the comfort of being able to do anything for the remains of our other dear ones shot at Ekaterinburg & whose bodies were burnt afterwards."*[36] It was only by a stroke of luck and the faithfulness of a loving monk, that they had the opportunity for Ella. Victoria was deeply cognizant of that bit of fortune.

Victoria, however, moved on with her life and as she got older seemed even more philosophical and pragmatic than she had been as a young girl looking after her growing family. After the unhappiness of the last few years, events at home provided some distractions. The Royal Navy was wearing a bit on Georgie's family life and Victoria had advice for him.

You poor boy. I do so understand how you miss them & Nada & how at times you feel that life is too short to compensate for all this separation. Many a time have Papa & I felt like that in the old times, yet one must try & bear it; ... When you are miserable at the thought of your days spent apart from those you love, just face the fact that you are doing so for others, because of your service & put as much thought & heart into your work as ever you can;....[37]

On June 10, 1921, Alice finally had her longed for boy, Philip, born in the family villa at Mon Repos, Corfu. From the beginning, Victoria took a particular interest in this child, remarking that the precious Philip was the image of Andrew.[38] After so many girls, she along with the entire family was thrilled with this latest addition. Indeed, for a while, after the war, things in Alice's family seemed to go well. The girls were overjoyed to be in Greece again and Andrew was back with his family. Even with these positive developments, things in Greece were politically as precarious as ever. There was constant fighting with Turkey detailed in the newspapers.

In May, 1921, Louis was elected President of the Royal Navy Club. There were many expressions of sorrow over his unfair treatment at the beginning of the war and unlike the usual outcome of such stories, there would be a satisfactory conclusion to his naval woes. In addition, Louis was invited to be the Chair of the Royal Navy Club dinner given in London in July 1921. The dinners were gala affairs given every year to honor the victory of the English Navy over the Spanish Armada and the guest of honor that year would be the current First Sea Lord, Arthur Lee.

After his rejection from the Royal Navy, Louis was extremely satisfied to be chairing this event. When the invitations went out, it was thought that fifty or sixty fellow navy men would be attending. However, when the evening came, on July 21, instead of that small number, eight hundred men, in tribute to their beloved Admiral, attended. Victoria and Louis were amazed and gratified as the men streamed into the room. Apparently, when they heard that Louis was the chair for the evening, they came from everywhere to pay him honor and acknowledgment.

It was a festive celebration full of uniforms and glitter and attended by a tremendous amount of retired admirals, officers, as well as many who were still serving. After dinner, Admiral Lee rose, lifted his glass, and offered a toast to the chair:

To Lord Milford Haven – one of the most able men in the Royal Navy. A man, who, without rancor and acrimony, accepted the low blow that fate had in store for him at the beginning of the Great War – we must all now thank you for what you have done for the navy and the nation - how you prepared her for the war, and the desperate hours that ensued. It is with great pleasure that we wish you and your family well. It is incredible to me the number of men who have come to honor you, Admiral. It is a tribute to the beauty of your character and great accomplishments of your career. No one deserves three cheers more than you do, sir...

And, when he finished these words, there were loud 'hip, hip, hoorays', and a five minute ovation. The men would not stop cheering their admiral – and it was as though he had not been gone from them for the last seven years. Louis was pleased, nearly overcome, as he got up to acknowledge the toast – but the men continued cheering. They would not let him speak and he was momentarily overwhelmed. As modestly as Louis took this heartwarming tribute, there's no doubt that Victoria was thinking along the lines that it was only what he deserved, and the ovation should last an hour.

It was, however, an excellent vindication, and it did not end there. Admiral Lee was greatly impressed by what had occurred the evening of the dinner. Afterwards, he wrote several letters urging Buckingham Palace to give Louis an accolade that would indeed be the supreme vindication.

I am anxious to submit for His Majesty's consideration a proposal which I hope may go some way towards compensating Admiral the Marques of Milford Haven for the unmerited misfortune which fell upon him in October 1914, when circumstances over which he had no control led to his enforced resignation of the post of First Sea Lord.

I need not recall the details of the unhappy controversies of that moment, embittered as they were by the unchivalrous and vindictive conduct of "spy-hunters" who should have known better, but it would be difficult to exaggerate the personal and professional tragedy which befel [sic] one of the most distinguished and universally esteemed Officers in His Majesty's Service, who had just given a signal proof of his capacity and loyalty to his adopted country at the outbreak of war....[39]

Louis was promoted to Admiral of the Fleet on the retired list and given the Grand Cross of Military Division and the Order of the Bath. He was only the second man in British naval history to be so honored. They seemed to want to make amends to their very excellent officer and, from all reports, George V was thrilled to be able to do this for his cousin, whom he, like so many others, had thought so wronged in October of 1914.

The culmination of that unforgettable summer was an invitation, extended by his son, Dickie and his commanding officers for a celebratory cruise on board the battle cruiser the *HMS Repulse*. The thought of being on board one of the cruisers once again boosted Louis' morale considerably. He was sixty-seven years old now, and had, as Victoria had noted, slowed down. The great anticipation of that cruise, sailing across the bounding main as it were, seemed to take thirty years off of his face, and put a little spring back into his step.

They cruised along the northern waters of Scotland, which even during the summer must have been icy cold. Dickie, however, wrote to Victoria that he and Louis were having a fine time with excellent weather. Papa, he told her, was supremely happy and in his element. It was almost a fairy tale ending for his life, getting the honors he deserved, the exoneration that was long time in coming, having one more halcyon cruise, and then dying, very quietly, on September 11, 1921.

Part IV

September 1921 – December 1953

Chapter XIII

September 1921 – April 1929

After Prince Louis' summer cruise, Louise and Victoria, who were on their way to Paris, met him in London for the day. They were anxious to hear about his adventures with Dickie and had some minor concerns about his health. He was staying in the Naval and Military Club in Piccadilly, and the two women took a hotel room nearby. They met for tea and saw that Louis' face was extremely flushed. Louis had caught a chill with a fever during the cruise and was bed-ridden for a few days, but Dickie had written that much to Victoria. Victoria, however, was alarmed and sent Louis straight to bed after their tea. Perhaps she ought to have known by his prompt acquiescence that something was amiss. The doctor was called for straight away, but could find nothing seriously wrong with him.

Victoria and Louise extended their stay in London and kept the Prince in bed the following day, September 11. The doctor came once again and gave Victoria a prescription to fill. When they returned, the housekeeper, weeping told them:

"Oh dear, the Admiral is dead, ma'am."

In answering a letter of sympathy from her cousin George, Victoria wrote what happened:

We had some nice hours together last Saturday & even on Sunday forenoon, for though he had had a rather troubled night with acute rheumatic pains in the shoulders & remained in bed, yet felt much better & the pain was but slight in morning. Then while Louise & I went out to get some lunch, he must have composed himself for a snooze, as I had suggested his doing, & passed away quickly & peacefully in his sleep, for his eyes were closed & nothing disarranged in his bed. When we returned at 1,40 p.m. the housekeeper told us she had found him so about a quarter of an hour before, when she brought in his medicine, at 1,10 when she took him some soup he was still awake & asked if the medicine had come. I am so grateful he was spared any suffering. I thank you so very much that you allowed his body to rest in your chapel, such a calm & peaceful place – it has been a great comfort to me.[1]

She went on to tell her cousin how devoted Louis was to him since they had been shipmates together in the old days and how grateful she was that the King promoted him to Admiral of the Fleet which *"made him very proud & happy & he had what he called 'a very good time' the last 10 days of his life, on board the Repulse – to be once more afloat in a man-of-war, with the old service life going on around him gave him real joy."*[2] She wrote further to Queen Mary that Louis had a very real affection for her and her children *"& was always in the full sense of the words 'at all your service.'"*[3]

It was hard for Victoria to realize that he was gone, but hearing from her cousin did her good as the many other tributes that poured in. She requested that Admiral Mark Kerr,

Nona's brother and a colleague very devoted to Louis and later his biographer, to come to take charge of all the details of the funeral. He would also act as one of the executors of Louis' will. Georgie and Dickie were there, though Alice was unable to reach England until after the funeral. Louis lay at the Private Chapel at Buckingham Palace for several days, and then on the September 19, a procession was arranged. It was all quite impressive starting along The Mall, proceeding through Admiralty Arch, and thence to Westminster Abbey for the service with seven admirals and a Major-General of the Marines as pall-bearers. In attendance were the Duke of Connaught, the Marquess of Carisbrooke, Aunt Beatrice's son, and the royal family sent representatives since their obligations took them elsewhere.

The coffin was taken to Portsmouth and thence to St. Mildred's Chapel, Whippingham on the Isle of Wight, where Princess Beatrice, in her capacity as Governor of the island, Princess Marie Louise and the Marchioness of Carisbrooke, met the party. The funeral took place there, and then, along with Admiral Kerr, Victoria traveled back to Fishponds at Netley, for Alice had finally arrived.

The accolades from friends, colleagues, and common sailors continued and Victoria was gratified and overwhelmed by the letters she received.

I don't think I ever realized till now (nor could he with his utter want of conceit either) how many people really loved and admired Louis. In all my sorrow it was a proud moment for me as a naval man's wife, when as the coffin was taken on board the destroyer the flag of an Admiral of the Fleet was run up for him, & though it hurt I liked to hear them pipe him once more over the side.... I am beginning to feel clearly all I have lost – but as one gets beyond the eager craving for happiness of youth, one can face sorrow more courageously I think & one learns to try & think of others more than oneself – & then there is none of that pain that the thought of my poor sisters last months on earth & of their death will always give me.[4]

One friend that stepped up for Victoria was Queen Mary. The two ladies, who had always respected each other and been friendly, continued that friendship throughout the rest of their lives. Just days after Louis' death, Cousin May's consideration for Victoria was expressed in a monetary gift, which she accepted with warmth and gratitude.

I would like to tell you that ever since I knew you better as a girl when I stopped at White Lodge with your parents & later when we took a walk together soon after your marriage, I have felt more warmly towards you than just as one does to a relation because of the relationship....

Your gift is doubly welcome, for I had set a sum aside to pay for the decoration of a small chapel or rather shrine, under the terrace of the church in Jerusalem where Ella's body rests – so that pilgrims, whom one can't allow to enter the actual chamber where the coffin is, can yet pray near it. This money I shall have to use now & I have been a little worried when & how I should be able to replace it.[5]

Cousin George was also concerned about Victoria's solvency after Louis death and asked questions about her income and where she would live. It was during this time that the King offered Victoria a residence at Frogmore Cottage. She thanked him for his offer, but decided that she would stay at Fishponds for now as the rent was paid up to January, 1922. After that, she told him, she would certainly reconsider his offer.[6] Some days after that, she sent George V a cigarette case that Nicky had given Louis in remembrance of them both. She hoped that he wouldn't think her ungrateful for not accepting the cottage, and asked his advice on her affairs when she has organized them.

She also discussed with her cousin the friendship between her boy, Dickie and his son, the Prince of Wales, whom the family called "David." Dickie, she told him, was loyally devoted to the Prince, but Victoria, forever clear-eyed, had no allusions about her own child. *"Mistakes I fear he is bound to make still, for he is very young, eager and impulsive, but I hope David, as the elder will guide him and the boy is honest and not stupid."*[7]*

As well, a letter of heartfelt love arrived some days after the funeral, which he naturally could not attend, from Ernie:

I had not the courage to write before. My one longing is to be with you & not to be able to come is so very hard. Oh darling it is you I am longing to help for I loved him also and my love to him might have comforted you a little. It is not the words, it is the heart that suffers with one from which one finds strength. I don't know what to write, my heart is too full. Let the heart speak to you, the heart of the brother who loves you so dearly. May my body be not near you, my soul is with you and suffers with you not trying to comfort for that is impossible, only trying to help you to carry this new and greatest sorrow. He is happy, it is only those that have to go on living who's [sic] burden is so terribly hard to bear.

Tell the boys how I feel with them and long to help them. And oh my little Louise my arms are round her and my heart bleeds with her. As to poor solitary Alice she will have a terrible time. All you darlings may God comfort – I can't...[8]**

In the end, Victoria was beautifully philosophical. She wrote to Ernie on the occasion of his birthday:

I shall think so much of you on you birthday & my most loving good wishes are with you. As the years go by & sorrows, trials & worries seem to be more one's lot, it is a comfort & joy to be able to look back to one's young days when there was so much hope & real happiness in one's life & then there always remains with us still to keep our hearts warm the love of each other one knows is able to withstand all the changes that the years have brought. And even for those that we loved & are no longer with us. I think one is grateful to be able to look back on happy times they shared with us, so that one does not grudge them their peace or wish them back into a world that might have more sorrows in store for them. One can always bear one's own pain, it is to see those we love suffer that hurts most.

Do not think of me as too unhappy, there is an emptiness in my life & an ache in my

---

(*) *Interestingly enough, David told Dickie, who broke down and wept when he heard of his father's death, "I envy you a father whom you could love." "If my father died," he said, "we should have felt nothing but relief." (Kenneth Rose, King George V, p.303).*

(**) *Ernie's mention of Alice brings us to the difficult and strange road that she traveled during the 1920s and most of the 1930s. Greece had, not surprisingly, proved extremely fickle, once again. They welcomed King Constantine back after his second son, Alexandr, died of blood poisoning from a monket bite, but it seemed as though he, like his dead son, was virtually under house arrest. King Constantine left Greece forever in September 1922. He died in exile in Sicily a few months later. The monarchy was abolished the following year, forcing the Greek royal family into exile yet another time.*

heart that I must just bear, but I don't sit & mope for that is not my nature – you too have had much sorrow in your life & have a heavy load to bear, but I am sure you are brave & patient about it & for the sake of the children one still can take pleasure in the things that make them happy.[9]

Later, she wrote succinctly: *"Luckily for me, I am not given to worrying over past or coming events & take the present as they come."*[10] That philosophy would serve her well in the days and years to come.

****

The following year was more felicitous for the remaining two sisters and their families. Irène's healthy son, Bobby, decided to start life over in the New World, and moved to Guatemala to start a coffee plantation. Things didn't go quite as well as he planned and he ultimately moved from there to Costa Rica, where he remained for the rest of his life. Irène eventually visited him there, but she could stand *"neither the food nor the climate...."*[11]

Dickie, who had been falling in and out of love since the end of the war, was definitely in love now. He met the Honorable Edwina Ashley, daughter of Sir Wilfred Ashley, and granddaughter of Sir Ernest Cassel. Edwina was a great beauty and one of the most sought after girls of her set. She was one of the 'bright young things' of post-war society as well as one of the wealthiest girls in England. In addition, she was very strong and determined, as well as independent, having been motherless from an early age. Victoria would always have great affection for her, and would give her a ruby from Cartier for her engagement ring. As with Nada, Edwina also adored her mother-in-law and called her Aunt Victoria.

Victoria wrote to Nona that Dickie's letters were full of his love for Edwina. By the end of January, there was an engagement. Dickie had known Edwina long enough to have spoken to Louis about her, which pleased Victoria. *"Louis told him if he knew his own mind he would be pleased at this marriage, & I know he liked Edwina."*[12] In addition, though there is no indication that Dickie married Edwina for her wealth, the Mountbattens had never been wealthy so that marrying her made sense. She, in the future, would help with Alice's care, and Victoria figured that if anything happened to her, that *"Dickie may be able to help Louise when I am gone if necessary...."*[13]

Victoria wrote to her cousin George in order to ask for his consent for the marriage. She told him that Louis had thought her nice and everything that the family had heard about Edwina was positive. Edwina's grandfather, with whom she had been close, died shortly after Prince Louis and Victoria thought the couple might have been drawn together by their mutual sorrow. She didn't hide her pleasure in Edwina's financial status as it relieved her of a great deal of anxiety.[14] However, she wanted to make sure that Edwina's father knew exactly where Dickie stood and asked Georgie to speak to him. *"Be quite frank about Dickie's financial position, present & future with Colonel Ashley if you get a chance of doing so – he need not fancy Dickie is an absolute pauper, even though he will never be really rich himself."*[15]

Victoria spent much of the spring visiting Alice and her family in Greece. She remained for some time in Mon Repos, and thought it a rather out of the way place, but was impressed with the way that Alice had brought up her girls, telling Georgie that they were *"nice and natural."*[16]

Victoria spent her first birthday without Louis with Alice and received an extremely loving letter from Ernie saying that, *"I can't let this day pass without sending a few lines to tell you how I continually think of you and feel with you. You don't know how often we speak of you darling. This day will be hard for you...."*[17]

Victoria, who was not the type to let herself be at a 'loose end', did what women in her family usually did. She made it her business to help others whether they were family or the public. Since the war, she did a great deal of charitable work on behalf of Russian refugees and the Russian Red Cross, and that work along with her work in the East End, sustained her
during these difficult periods.

Another unhappy event took place at Kensington Palace. It was the death of Aunt Beatrice's son, Lord Leopold Mountbatten at the age of thirty-two. Victoria, who was still with Alice, could not be with her Aunt on that sad day, but Georgie and Nada represented her at the funeral.

As with her brother Ernie, she also managed her sons... but as with her brother, her sons always found her advice sensible and not irritating. In her letter to Georgie after Leopold's funeral she wrote:

> *If they* [the King and Queen] *are giving a garden party next month you & Nada should go, unless there is a Court you can attend – & don't forget this time to get a proper pass from the Lord Chamberlain's office for your car & to drive in where the rest of the family do & if it is a garden party arrange with Thora*, who always is well informed to join up with her so as to be at the right spot when the K. & Q. come.*[18]

She added that Georgie should tell his little girl, Tatiana, that baby Philip *"can stand up alone now & sits with bare legs on the hard road & crawls on it without minding the stones. He is in fact just as advanced & sturdy for his age as all the others were & has ... tow-coloured hair."*[19]

Victoria returned in the beginning of the summer for Dickie's wedding which took place in July. She also made the important decision that she would indeed accept rooms from the King and live at Kensington Palace, telling Nona that *"now I am in good training & prepared to make a new start without [Louis] ...."*[20] She and Queen Mary met at the Palace to decide what should be done with the rooms, and if they could be adapted for Victoria's use. The rooms were located in the western part of palace, identified by their lofty arched windows. In actuality, they had been the Chapel Royal, but the rooms were decommissioned in 1901. *"After Queen Victoria's death the chapel was closed and a false ceiling was inserted to allow the first-floor apartments to be enlarged."*[21] Cousin May certainly thought these rooms would do, telling Victoria that living there *"would certainly enable you to put up members of your family."* In addition, she would get the apartments on both sides as soon as they became available.[22]** The King was delighted with the arrangements for his cousin writing, *"I am glad to think that you are going to join what Arthur calls the 'Aunt Heap.'"*[23]

More important, for the moment, than remodeling, was the wedding of Dickie and Edwina, which took place at St. Margaret's, Westminster on July 18, 1922. It was reminiscent of the royal weddings of old in which there was a strong royal presence. David, Cousin George's son and the Prince of Wales, acted as Dickie's best man, and Alice's four girls, the 'Greek Princesses', as they were called in the newspapers, were among the maids of honor.

(*) *Princess Helena Victoria, the eldest daughter of Princess Helena, Queen Victoria's third daughter.*

(**) *It was from Victoria's rooms that Philip went to Westminster Abbey to marry Princess Elizabeth in November 1947.*

The King and Queen attended as well as Aunt Minnie and Aunt Alix, possibly the two most senior surviving royal dowagers. They were venerable now, and neither had many years left. Also attending were the Duke of York, Princess Victoria of Wales, Princess Helena and her daughters, the Duke of Connaught, in fact, all of the Royal family, except Aunt Beatrice, who was still in mourning for her son.

The German contingent, of course, was conspicuous by its pointed absence. Willy and his family were certainly not there, and in addition, Victoria's brother and sister stayed at home. However, Dickie and Edwina paid Ernie a visit the following month to the beloved Wolfsgarten. Ernie reported back about Edwina: *"She is quite charming & won all our hearts being so natural, clever & kindhearted. I wish you could have seen them here."*[24] But, Edwina was a true favorite of Victoria's. Her biographer sums up their relationship saying, *"Aunt Victoria had understood her intelligent, restless daughter-in-law; she had influenced her too. From the time of her marriage, Edwina had followed her mother-in-law's example and kept a daily diary."*[25]*

That fall, Alice's troubles, once again came to the forefront. In September 1922, King Constantine abdicated once again, in response to the military disaster and horrible slaughter of Greek civilians at Smyrna. In October, Andrew was first questioned and then arrested for that same debacle. He was interned in Athens, while Alice lived at Mon Repos under police sur-veillance. By the end of November, six ministers were executed for their part in the campaign and Andrew was reconciled to the fact that he would be next.

However, his relatives strenuously intervened including, Victoria and her son, Georgie. King George V seemed to understand the urgency of making every attempt to get Andrew, Alice and their family out of Greece. Perhaps it was done out of guilt - because he had failed to save Nicky and Alicky. But for whatever reasons, their efforts were successful. In the beginning of December, it was decided that Andrew would be exiled from Greece and suffer army degradation. Andrew was given virtually no time to get out of the country. He was escorted by an Englishman, an emissary from King George, who quickly boarded a Royal Naval vessel, the *HMS Calypso*, and made for Corfu to gather up Alice, the four girls and little Philip. They went into exile once again, though even this time, it wasn't for good.[26]

Victoria wrote, in gratitude to Lord Stamfordham: *"I am indeed rejoiced at the news you send me. In conformity with the King's wish expressed by you, I have telegraphed to my daughter at Brindisi saying: I suggest, by desire, that you break journey arriving here a fortnight hence...."*[27] She was naturally thrilled that they had escaped. Once they reached Paris, there was more controversy about the family coming to London – there seemed some distaste in the Foreign Office of exiled Royalties being hangers-on in London. Victoria wrote once again to Lord Stamfordham wondering what the delay was, and saying that Andrew and his family had more pride than to live off of Prince Christopher in Paris. However, in the end they stayed in France.[28] Alice and her family settled in St. Cloud, in a house lent to them by Princess George of Greece, Marie Bonaparte. Alice decided to open a boutique called Hellas. She sold Greek souvenirs and embroidery, giving the proceeds to charity.

That, however, was just the beginning for Alice. Her journey, through the twenties and thirties, was a sad one fraught with physical and mental illness, and possible religious hysteria. It was a road that denied her the pleasure of closely watching her young son grow up, and being present at the weddings of her daughters, who went on to marry German Princes. As time went on, Alice did, indeed, go into a sanatorium in Switzerland; she was,

---

(*) When Victoria died, Edwina put the diary aside, never writing in it again.

in fact, in and out of it through most of those two decades. Andrew appeared to abdicate much of the responsibility for his children, thinking, possibly, that they would be better off with their aunts, uncles, and grandmother.

The girls and Philip, in particular, spent a lot of time with Victoria, and their uncles Georgie and Dickie. They were also quite close to Nada's sister Anastasia, or Zia, and her husband Sir Harold Wernher. In the end, it was these three men who exerted a great deal of influence over Philip, though, he talked often about how much his father meant to him. Victoria gave her moral support when she could, and tried to make the right decisions about Alice's health. However, it wasn't always in her power to help monetarily because of the losses she sustained during the war. There would be, thankfully, others to pick up the slack, including Edwina, who was always generous when it came to her new husband's family.

Meanwhile, the remodeling continued on Victoria's apartments at Kensington Palace. Queen Mary watched their progress closely and reported to her diary that they would be *"nice when finished..."*[29] which they finally were in the winter of 1922. Victoria moved in that month and immediately after had family members staying with her. Her granddaughters Margarita and Theodora ("Dolla"), Alice's two eldest daughters, who would prove to be frequent visitors, were there for Christmas and Victoria reported to Ernie about how comfortable the apartment was and how much she loved the arrangement of the rooms. There was much correspondence between the two this year and the following mostly worrying about the state of things in Germany – the inflation, the civil war and what Ernie's place might be in a new republic. However, Victoria's letter to Ernie, written a day after Christmas was concentrated on family news. She told him how much she liked Nada's family and especially her sister Zia Wernher, who had invited them over for Christmas and made sure that they all felt like part of the family. There was also Romanov news of Nicky's exiled sister Xenia and her family, who,

> *also lives in London & has all 6 boys over here. The eldest*, who is rather unattractive married some years ago, I don't remember who she was, she works in a millinery shop, they have 2 children, the third boy** married a nice little Vorontzoff. Xenia is a dear & reminds me often of Nicky – her rotten husband lives in Paris – there also lives Paul's Marie & Dimitri.*[30]

And lastly, told him that his cousins, *"George and May always ask me about you, their feelings have not changed about you."*[31]

There would be many changes to report in the New Year. Victoria's sister-in-law, Princess Marie of Erbach-Schönberg, died at Schönberg. She was seventy-one years old, and that left Franzjos as the only remaining Battenberg, and the only one of Louis' siblings still alive. Closer to her home, another of Victoria and Irène's aunts, Princess Helena, died in June after a very short illness and the funeral took place on June 15 at St. George's chapel. That only left Aunts Louise and Beatrice of Queen Victoria's daughters. One of the good things about Kensington Palace was that both the aunts lived there, and Victoria no doubt kept an eye on them, stopping by their doors and visited frequently – which assuaged her loneliness.

Also attending the funeral was Gustav Adolf, the Crown Prince of Sweden. He had

---

(*) *Prince Andrei Alexandrovich of Russia (1897-1981).*
(**) *Prince Nikita Alexandrovich of Russia (1900-1974) married Countess Maria Ilarionovna Vorontzov-Dashkov.*

been visiting England and his Connaught relatives. Gustav Adolf was extremely interested in history and archeology, and was deeply involved in excavations in Greece. He was, in fact, no *"mere dilettante figure-head, but himself worked as hard and as long as any other member...."*[32] of the expedition. Louise, who had had her marital tribulations in the past, had been happy in her apparent spinsterhood. She had also famously declared that she would never marry a king or a widower. At the end of June, she became engaged to Crown Prince Gustav Adolf of Sweden, who would eventually become King of Sweden. He was the widower of Louise's cousin, Prince Margaret of Connaught, whose untimely death in 1920 left five children.

Louise had been at a loose end at the end of the war, poignantly telling her niece, Dolla, that *"all the young men she and her contemporaries had danced with in the palaces of Europe, with whom they had gone on picnics and with whom they had fallen in love, were now dead."*[33] She was described in *The Times* as

> *not at all well known to the general public, and she has not shown any marked taste for social life in London, but is understood to prefer country pursuits. She is said by those who know her to be a lady of much originality and independence of mind, as well as charm of manner.*[34]

Since she was no longer interested in the society that those bygone days might have afforded her, she appeared now to be more content to be involved with social work. She was also used to the idea that she would stay in London and be a companion to her mother, whose company she genuinely enjoyed.

However, the couple had met that spring at a party in London, and met frequently at Georgie and Nada's home. They were seen together at Ascot that year which was highly remarked upon. Beside the fact that pairings of royal persons were always highly remarked upon, Louise's being spotted with anyone, at that point, was also big news.

Louise showed a great deal of reluctance at first. She didn't like the idea of uprooting herself and leaving her family and England, but the match-making plots around her thickened. It seemed that Alice's daughters, Margarita and Dolla, who had a close relationship with their aunt, were staying at Kensington Palace again that summer, and enjoying dances and social events (as they frequently did in those years). They happily aided and abetted Gustav Adolf, contriving to leave the couple alone together. Louise had discouraged his advances, being perfectly happy to remain as she was. However, the more she would plead for the girls not to leave them alone, the more they did so. Eventually, she succumbed to Gustav Adolf's proposal and accepted him. Their official engagement was announced in *The Times* on July 1, 1923.

Victoria, would miss her traveling companion, but understood that Louise could not be with her forever and had to make her own life. She was thrilled that Louise had found someone and wrote to George for permission, saying:

> *To me it is a real joy, for I know he is a thoroughly nice man, who has been desperately lonely since dear Daisy died & I think Louise should be happy as his wife. They have both known sorrow & disappointment & have been able to speak freely & fully together before deciding on this serious step.*[35]

Ernie, too, was happy for his niece, writing:

It is the happiest news I have had since years. God bless the dear child and that it is a real love affair makes me still more happy because one can see so much more peacefully into the future. How I can understand your feelings you dear good old Victoria & I only wish I could fly over to you & have a long & comforting chat together.[36]

The Swedish Government, however, had needed some reassurances that Lady Louise Mountbatten was indeed a member of the Royal Family. Since she was no longer a princess, it was feared that she might actually be a commoner. Naturally, Louise didn't care about such designations any more than did her mother. However, Gustav Adolf would not have been permitted to marry Louise were she a commoner. The Prime Minister of Sweden, therefore, wrote to the British government asking for confirmation that Louise was a member of the royal family. They assured him that she was, indeed, on the list of Royal Precedence and sent them the printed lists, which seemed to satisfy the Swedes.

During the summer, Victoria was in Romrod in Hesse, visiting Ernie and his family. She attended Ernie's sons, Don and Lu's, confirmations along with Irène and Henry. In view of Irène's remark about the Entente being the cause of the world's woes, it's not surprising that Victoria told her son, Dickie that *"only Uncle Ernie & I can freely discuss things, as you know he has more sense & balance than average people."*[37] It seems that their visits became more awkward since the war, and their close sisterly camaraderie would never again exist. It, too, was a casualty of war.

In any case, neither her Aunt Irène nor Uncle Ernie were present at Louise's wedding to Gustav Adolf in November of that year. The event took place at the Chapel Royal, by permission of the King and Queen. Louise, feeling embarrassed and even annoyed in her situation, seemed to feel that she was too old and too thin to be a bride.[38] In any event, she told her niece, Dolla, she would not wear white. Nevertheless, she wore a dress of Indian silver gauze, the sort of material used for saris, which was given to her by Uncle Ernie. Georgie gave the bride away, and all of Alice's daughters and Lady Tatiana Mountbatten were bridesmaids – David, the little Earl of Medina, wearing a white 'man-'o-war' suit, was the only page. The Royal attendance for the wedding, however, was exceptional. Present were not only the King and Queen of England, but the Dowager Queen Alexandra, the King of Sweden, as well as Queen Olga of Greece. However, as with Dickie's wedding, there was no German presence.

When Louise and Gustav Adolf left for Sweden the following month, there was an entire family group as well as the Swedish legation to see them off. There is a sweet anecdote of Gustav Adolf and Louise's departure from St. Pancras station. Her niece, Margarita, took hold of her hand through the open train window, as the train was pulling out of the station. She held on to it for several moments, running along side of the train as it left the station.[39]

Louise's marriage was an unqualified success. She and Gustav Adolf had many interests in common, such as gardening and archeology, and she approached her position in her new country in an extremely intelligent manner. She never proposed to replace the mother that his children lost, though Gustav Adolf's only daughter, Ingrid, felt that her father had remarried too soon. She was known to them as Aunt Louise. Her only sorrow was that after one still-born child, born in May 1925, she had no more children. However, with her astuteness and good humor, she made a beloved Queen of Sweden.*

Victoria, naturally, would be very lonely for her boon companion, but, as was

_____
(*) *and stepgrandmother to the current King of Sweden.*

her wont, carried on. There was an extremely pleasant distraction just a few months later. On Valentine's Day, 1924, Edwina gave birth to their first child, a little girl, called Patricia Edwina Victoria, whose god-mother was Princess Patricia Connaught, Victoria's first cousin. She would become Dickie's adored eldest daughter and throughout his life, they shared a unique and close relationship. She was born while her father was away at sea, but he came home on leave in time for the christening.

Victoria and her new granddaughter also had a wonderful relationship. In discussing her grandmother, Patricia Mountbatten later said that she was wonderful with children and with a penknife could construct a whole miniature tea set from acorns. She played patience and did crosswords, and inculcated her love of reading to her grandchildren. She was always happy to read aloud to them when they were small, and encouraged them to read themselves when they were older. However, the most striking thing that Patricia remembered was that her grandmother was *"a walking encyclopaedia and could answer absolutely any question you asked on any subject. She was also highly intelligent and extremely knowledgeable; I once heard her correcting a Dutch Admiral during the war as to how many cruisers remained in his fleet!"*[40]

However, there were tiresome things such as gall bladder operations that Victoria also had to endure right after Patricia's birth. She spent her birthday in bed, recovering from the operation, and had a note of sympathy as well as birthday wishes from Ernie.

I write to you for your birthday with a heart full of gratitude all the way of recovery. It must have terrible those pains before and after the operation.

I wish I could slip across to be able to help you to get over the times of recovery which will be long and tiresome.[41]

Luckily, she made enough of a recovery to attend Patricia's christening in April of that year.

Contrasting with the birth of Dickie's first child was the sad death of the last Battenberg Prince, Franzjos. He died in that summer in Schaffhausen, Switzerland, where he and Anna had spent the war. Victoria had been visiting Louise and wrote to Dickie from Louise's country home, Sofiero. As ever, Victoria was pragmatic and discussed with her son the need for an allowance for Franzjos' wife Princess Anna, asking him to discuss it with Edwina, whose generosity would extend to her Aunt by marriage. She was more nostalgic with Georgie commenting that this death was *"the last of Papa's brothers, whom I have known all my life & I am greatly grieved..."*[42] Gone now, were the four handsome Battenberg brothers and their sister, Marie – the children of the dashing Alexander of Hesse and his morganatic wife, the Countess Julie von Hauke. Gone was the stunning brood who had so captivated Queen Victoria and enraged at one time or another, the Russian and German Emperors and the great Chancellor Bismarck – all of whom were gone as well.

After interceding with Edwina for an allowance for Anna, a fairly simple task for Victoria, she decided to take upon herself a more daunting challenge. In January of 1925, she wrote the following letter to King George V.

Though not really any business of mine, yet in memory of dear Nicky I must write to you about his poor sister Xenia's distressing financial position. I know how fond you are of her and how generously you have already helped her, yet I appeal to you now for further assistance & an immediate one by way of a loan, repayable on the sum she must sooner or later receive from the man whom the courts last year condemned to refund her for the jewels he tried to swindle her out of.[43]

She went on to explain Xenia's position as told to her by Peter Bark, the former Russian Finance Minster, and said that the Grand Duchess was as ignorant as a baby about money. Xenia had a kind heart and a set of 'useless' sons, *"the eldest of whom I consider to be if not half then at least three-quarter-witted with an adventurous unscrupulous wife. I won't speak of what I think of Sandro, her husband, whom she too has to support."*[44]

Victoria obviously didn't mince words when she was passionate about something and told her cousin that Xenia had the unfortunate responsibility to support at least twenty people and then put forth, in the letter, some sensible ways that the King could help his cousin. The King responded positively to this letter and was determined to act promptly to help Xenia. Far from thinking that Victoria was a busybody, he thanked her for her intercession. *"As for her husband & her eldest son, they are wretched creatures who ought to be supporting her instead of living on her."*[45]

Baroness Sophie von Buxhoevenden, another Russian exile who had made it to England after the tragedies, often stayed with Victoria, and she remarked to Nona that "Isa," as Alix had called her, was wonderful company. These visits, as reflected in Victoria's guest book, were usually about a month and a half long and happened mostly on a yearly basis. Patricia Mountbatten later remarked that she was a charming woman who told great stories. When Victoria set out to write her memoirs in 1942, Isa gave them shape and structure and helped her to write them.

There have been accusations that the Baroness betrayed the Romanovs, taking money and telling the Bolsheviks where the family had jewelry hidden, backed up convincingly by the archives in Ekaterinburg. It was also said that Xenia refused to receive her because of this.[46] However, it is safe to say that if this were generally known or believed at the time, Isa would not have been welcome at Hemmelmarck as she was, nor at Kensington Palace. In fact, she became something of an unofficial lady-in-waiting to Victoria, and it hardly seems possible with Victoria's good judgment and acuity, that Buxhoevenden would have been received if such things were true. A friend of Victoria's, the Countess Merika Kleinmichel, said about the Baroness that *"she was extremely loyal."*[47] The reality was that no one had a bad word to say about the Baroness, including the Grand Duchess Xenia, and that she was neither a bad nor deceitful woman.

Victoria continued that which had sustained her during her married life to a husband that was often absent – the rounds of visits she made. Now it was to Louise in Sweden, then it might be to Ernie at Wolfsgarten, and other times to Irène at Hemmelmarck. That summer in particular, Victoria noticed that Irène, understandably, was still extremely upset about Alix. Nevertheless, Victoria enjoyed the visit, despite Irène's political remarks, and the presence of Henry, she noted, with all his faults. Germany, however, was cheerless, and as the 1920's wore on there was more misery and discontent evident. Inflation, humiliation, political ineptness, and penury were the ingredients of a recipe for coming disaster.

An icon from the past was gone in the autumn of that year of 1925. In November, Aunt Alix, Queen Alexandra, died. It was another connection to that old world, and another reminder that it was lost forever. Victoria, doubtless, recalled that Uncle Bertie and Aunt Alix had been so kind to Louis when he was a young man in the navy. She wrote to George expressing her sympathy and heard from Ernie, who commented about Aunt Alix's death, how sudden it was, as well as how much he loved her. However, Ernie and Onor were vastly cheered by the presence of Alice's daughters, Margarita and Dolla, who were visiting them at Wolfsgarten that year.

> *Alice's girls [he wrote] are a great source of joy to us. I have scarcely found such cheery kind-hearted and clever little companions as them. We are all under their charms. Such humor and so absolutely unspoiled. Alice can be indeed very proud of them and their delightful common sense which is so refreshing.*[48]

This seemed to be the consensus about Alice's daughters, who were constantly praised for being natural and wholesome.

With regard to Alice and her family, there were certain touchy issues that came up, at the end of that year, and into 1926. As with Xenia, Victoria had no hesitation in involving herself fully, writing to the British government and any other powers she thought might be helpful. Those sensitive issues were some questions about how the Greek government would deal with Prince Andrew's house, Mon Repos, and the contents thereof. Victoria wrote to Lord Hardinge, the Permanent Under-Secretary of State at the Foreign Office, to inquire about the property and initially received assurances that the house would not be tampered with. However, during the summer, there were serious worries that the house would be confiscated by the state. Victoria did her best to legally maintain the property with her son, Dickie, the official leaseholder, and wrote the following to Sir Austen Chamberlain,

> *We therefore think it necessary that a copy of the document proving that since the month of May of this year, my son Lord Louis Mountbatten, Lieut.R.N, has become lease-holder of said property should be deposited in safe custody at Athens.*
>
> *The need of producing the lease for the conviction of the Greek Government arising possibly at any moment.*
>
> *By desire of my afore mentioned son and son-in-law [Prince Andrew] I address myself to you and shall be deeply grateful if you would send this document, which I enclose herewith to the British legation at Athens, with instructions for its safe keeping there.*
>
> *My son being an English naval officer, I trust you will find yourself able to comply with my request, especially as he is recognised by The King as a member of the Royal Family.*[49]

However, even with her best efforts, Sir Austen wrote her back denying the request of intervention from the Foreign Office and explaining that since 1924, the Greek Dynasty was considered to be officially at an end and that the properties belonging to it now belonged to the state. The law stated that Mon Repos belonged to the Municipality of Corfu. He went on to enumerate the legalities of the issue and said finally, that it was undesirable for the British Legation to interfere.

> *In all these circumstances I very much regret that I am unable to comply with your request that a copy of this lease, which I return herein, should be sent to the Legation; but I am causing enquiries to be made at Athens as to whether there is not some British bank or alternatively a British legal agent or adviser with whom the lease could be deposited, and to whom instructions could be given to produce it to the Greek government and otherwise act*

in the interest of Prince Andrew of Greece and Lord Louis Mountbatten, should the occasion arise.

Austen Chamberlain.[50]

At the end of that month, Victoria was notified that a chartered accountant was willing to accept the custody of the lease. But, the struggle continued with letters and telegrams, the Greeks insisted that the Mountbattens hand the villa over to them. The Mountbattens never complied, but in 1931 it was taken possession by the Greek authorities, and the State claimed it. However, in 1934, Prince Andrew was legally able to win the estate back from the Greek government. Nevertheless, he sold it that year.

More significantly, the late 20's began the march of the impostors who claimed to be members of the Imperial Family who had survived the terrible slaughter at Ekaterinburg. They usually claimed to be one of the Grand Duchess, though there was no dearth of Alexeis about. Irène, Ernie and Aunt Minnie, the Dowager Empress Marie Feodorovna, now living in exile in Denmark, would have to contend with the claimants, including, the most famous one of all, Anna Anderson, who claimed to be the Grand Duchess Anastasia. Irène saw Miss Anderson, and at some point, briefly acknowledged her, though she quickly took it all back. Oddly, at the end of her life, Irène evidently thought she was mistaken for repudiating the false Anastasia. However, today it seems to have been proven that she was not a member of the Imperial Family. Victoria never saw any of these claimants and left it to the judgment of Ernie and Irène. It was her intention to simply 'go along' with whatever her two siblings thought in the matter.

Victoria's relationship with Ernie continued to be extremely devoted. He always showed a constant affection to the older sister that had been in many ways, like a mother and in some instances, even like a father for him. With all that happened between their two countries, Ernie marveled at the connection they had. He wrote: *"I wonder if there are many other brothers and sisters like us two. What have we not gone through and nothing has ever changed our love to each other."*[51]

Another tremendously meaningful relationship was that with her grandson, Prince Philip. Through time, it continued to grow. He was sent to school at Cheam and Victoria's Kensington Palace apartments became a stopping off place for him for school holidays. In addition, Victoria managed him the way she managed her brother and her sons, giving him instructions on what to wear, where to stay and sending him money for various travels and events. In the meantime, Victoria divided her time between her apartments in Kensington Palace and Edwina's home, Broadlands, which the Dowager Marchioness grew to love.

Meanwhile, Henry and Irène continued their quiet existence. In the 1920's there was barely a ripple in their lives, which had always been tranquil except for some of Irène's health troubles and Henry's lack of perception in dealing with his cousin, George V. A few incidents were reported in *The Times* of London, such as in 1922, Henry wished to fly the Hohenzollern flag on his yacht the *Ayesha*. A group of "Red" demonstrators protested this outrage and the Prince was persuaded to take the flag down. Nothing further came of the protest. In 1927, Henry celebrated the fiftieth year of his entry into the Imperial Navy with a quiet luncheon with some former Admirals. However at the beginning of 1929, Henry became ill and died several months later on April 21. There were newspaper articles asserting that Henry actually had throat cancer like his father, but, according to his son, Toddy, the cause was angina. *The Times* obituary printed an homage to the man they called Germany's Prince Charming and praised for what seemed like an assertion of his Englishness during the war and after the German republican revolution. They wrote:

> *When the dynasty fell he said that he could not, in honour, forswear his house and family; but he promised to give no trouble and kept his word. Republican Germany was well-advised to leave him in peace, and to show that it had no quarrel with a man whose character had been formed from the best qualities of the fallen Hohenzollerns.*[52]

His grandmother might have said that it was her influence and Irène's that led to so positive a tribute.

Chapter XIV

April 1929 – November 1937

The world continued to change as the decade of the thirties began. Both remaining sisters were now widows, and the constant visits that had been so much a part of their lives were sharply tapering off. Victoria, who had once visited the colossal Imperial palaces and the vast expanse of Russia and her natural wonders, had now to content herself with the relative simplicity of Irène or Ernie's various homes in Germany or to those of Louise in Stockholm. Expense, which had not seriously impeded any of them in the past, was now an issue always to be considered.

Henry was laid to rest in the family vault on their Hemmelmarck estate with over four thousand people present according to *The Times*. Some of the attendees included Prince Eitel Friedrich*, representing the Kaiser and several other sons and grandsons of Cousin Willy. Ernie and Onor were there to comfort Irène, but Victoria was not. Victoria had frequently visited Irène at Hemmelmarck in the decade of the twenties, and would continue to do so – later that summer, as well as continuing to stay with Ernie at Wolfsgarten. However, it is possible she felt that she did not want to be seen in such a public fashion, at what became quite a large event in Germany. Maybe the lessons of 1914 were crowding in on her at this volatile time. Indeed, there was virtually no British presence at this grandchild of Queen Victoria's funeral.

Victoria's brood of grandchildren was rounded off with the birth of a little girl, born one day before her Great-Uncle Henry's death, April 20, 1929. Pamela Carmen** Louise Mountbatten, Dickie and Edwina's daughter, was born at the Ritz Hotel in Barcelona, on April 19, and the middle name of Carmen was, among other things, a tribute to her Spanish birth. The Prince of Wales and the King of Spain were present at her christening two months later with, among others, Alfonso and Victoria serving as Godparents.

Later that year, Princess Moretta of Prussia, the highly romantic girl who had so desperately wanted to be the wife of Prince Sandro Battenberg, died. Because she had wanted so dreadfully to marry this handsome prince with whom she fancied herself in love, she became the center of a controversy that involved the Tsar, the Kaiser, the Crown Prince (Willy, at the time) and his Chancellor Bismarck. This alone was her claim to fame until several years before her death, when, still romantic as ever, she fancied herself, once again, in love. The object of her affections was a twenty-seven year old expatriate Russian waiter and the son of a professor of anatomy,[1] Alexander Zoubkoff. She, herself, was sixty-three. They married and the younger man proceeded to spend all of her money and leave her when the funds were depleted. On November 18, 1929, the Princess died and Irène and Prince Adalbert*** represented the former Kaiser at the funeral. Willy had not talked to his hapless sister from the time she started on this last romance – she was, by then, estranged from most of her family.

(*) *HRH Prince Wilhelm Eitel-Friedrich (1883-1942), the Kaiser's second son.*
(**) *...and for her Godmother, the Duchess of Peñaranda de Duero, Carmen Saavedra y Collado, wife of Hernando FitzJames Stuart, XVII Duke of Peñaranda de Duero.*
(***) *HRH Prince Adalbert of Prussia (1884-1948), the Kaiser's third son.*

However, as would be the trend in the twenties and thirties, Victoria's focus would be most particularly on her Greek grandchildren whose parents were separated, and whose mother, Alice, continued to be in difficulties, both in physical and mental health. The five children would find a modicum of stability visiting aunts and uncles, and in the beginning of the decade the four girls all married, while Philip went to school in England.

Oddly enough, it would be the youngest, Sophie, known as "Tiny" in the family, who would steal the march up the aisle on her sisters. Sophie's engagement to Prince Christopher of Hesse* was announced in the summer and their marriage would be celebrated in December of 1930 at Friedrichshof, the old home of Victoria's Aunt Vicky. The Schloss was now in possession of Vicky's youngest daughter Margarete, the Landgravine of Hesse-Kassel. "Cri," as Prince Christopher was called, was killed during the Second World War. It was said that he was an ardent Nazi. However, there was another school of thought that claimed that he had actually been murdered because he had renounced Nazism. His renouncement, if it happened, was after many long years of devoted party service.

Cecile, too, became engaged. She had become interested in her cousin, Ernie's eldest son, George Donatus, known as "Don" in the family. They were in the process of getting to know one another before the beginning of the year. Victoria wrote to her brother, *"I wonder how Cecile strikes you, now you know her better, I personally think well of her character, though of course she has her faults, a good many due to her youth merely."*[2] One wonders if this question was an anxious inquiry on behalf of a love-struck granddaughter, or just the usual discussions and gentle gossip that went on in the family. However, just several weeks later, the engagement of Don and Cecile was announced and Victoria, thrilled with the couple, wrote the following to her granddaughter.

I must send you a few lines through Uncle Ernie, to tell you how pleased I am at your and Don's engagement. That one of my granddaughters should find a home in what was my first one is a joy to me and though I know Don less well than I should have done, had the years of the war not kept us apart, yet what I do personally know of him has given me the best impression as to his character and gifts and I hope you two will be very happy as husband and wife – Uncle Ernie has praised you warmly to me and feels not only that you are suited to Don, but that you are dear [to] his own self too.[3]

They would marry in February of 1931 with Victoria, Irène, Prince Andrew, and Prince Philip in attendance. *The Times* remarked upon the great interest by the inhabitants of Darmstadt and personal popularity the family continued to enjoy.[4]

Alice's other daughters were married into various German Royal Families at about the same time. Soon after Sophie and Cecile's marriages, their elder siblings, too, found partners. Margarita married Gottfried, Hereditary Prince of Hohenlohe-Langenburg**, in April 1931, and Dolla married Berthold, Margrave of Baden***, in August of 1931. All the weddings took place without their mother in attendance. It was certainly, in large measure, Victoria's strength, and determination that kept her grandchildren from going adrift, during

---

(*) *HRH Prince Christoph of Hesse (1901-1943).*
(**) *HSH Gottfried, 8th Fürst of Hohenlohe-Langenburg (1897-1960), only surviving son of the former Princess Alexandra of Edinburgh, a granddaughter of Queen Victoria, and therefore a first cousin of Victoria and her sibilings.*
(***) *HRH Prince Berthold (1906-1963), Margrave of Baden, only son of Princess Marie Louise of Hanover, eldest sister of the Duke of Brünswick and Lüneburg, the same one whose 1913 wedding to Princess Viktoria Luise of Prussia was attended by Louis and Victoria, Henry and Irène, Tsar Nicholas II and King George V and Queen Mary.*

these times of transition. It was also thanks to her daughter-in-law, Edwina, who quietly provided the needed funds. Clearly, this relieved a great part of the burden for Victoria, and evidently, Alice felt that she was being well cared for, as Victoria told Ernie:

> *She says I must not worry, that she is 'so well looked after from every point of view' and that my advice is 'always a wonderful inspiration'. This is a real comfort to me – I should like to be able to put into words all that you and Onor's help & sympathy & understanding have been to me, but it is more than I can express and I can only thank you for it with all my heart.*

And, then added a little family news, *"the Aunts* are well and so are Georgie and May, with whom I had tea yesterday and who all asked after you and when you would at last be coming here."*[5] A very different attitude than they had towards Willy's immediate family.

Promptly thereafter, Don and Cecile presented her with a little boy, and Victoria was made a great-grandmother at the age of sixty-eight.

> *To you and Don I send my best love and good wishes. Now I hope you are well enough to enjoy your baby and that the remembrance of the hours of pain is fading before the lovely feeling of getting well. I am very proud of being Great Grandmother and you must give your boy a special kiss for me. I wonder if Don is as nervous as Papa was in handling all of you – he was quite afraid of holding Margarita for some time....Now you will understand more and more what it is being [a mother] and that love for one's child calls out ones love light through the generations. That is why you are so dear to me and your child too.*[6]

And several weeks later, apropos of tightened purse strings:

> *I am so delighted to hear you and your boy are so well and I thank you and Don very much for asking me to be godmother to my Great-Grandson. I would have loved to be present at his christening, but in these days one's purse tyrannically prevents one's doing many things one would like.*[7]

Nevertheless, Victoria went to Darmstadt and stayed with Ernie at least once a year. As the decade began, she, like many with royal ties in Germany, watched the rise of Nazism, initially with optimism. It was hoped that the Nazi's would restore the Hohenzollerns to the German throne. In addition, the exiled Romanovs also had hopes that the Communist-hating Nazis would rid Russia of Stalin. However, these budding expectations were quickly replaced with dread and revulsion, as Hitler's plans were revealed. And, for those slow to be convinced, when the war came, the various German Princes were eventually thrown out of the German army and even, in some cases, interned in concentration camps.

The entire country was blanketed with red banners with the black swastikas. Early on, even with Hitler's Jewish policies, Victoria looked at the situation pragmatically, writing:

> *I suppose people are furious at the German persecution of the Jews. I think it grossly unjust & most risky, but Anti-Semitism has always been strong in Germany, where the people are wanting in the business & political instincts, which save England & America from the*

(*) Princess Louise (Duchess of Argyll) and Princess Beatrice (widow of Prince Henry of Battenberg).

dread & dislike of Jewish power & push. Hitler has the true German mentality & it is his enthusiasm for a more idealistic outlook on life, which wins him the immense support he gets from the mass of people, who were sick of the low ideals, money-grubbing & place hunting of the Socialists & are utterly averse to communism, except for the factory workers in the big towns. As the Germans do not mind being ordered about, & had their fill of it during the Socialist regime too, they don't seem to object to dictatorship. It remains to be seen however if Hitler is a big enough brain to become the German Mussolini.[8]

Here one can see the typical gentlemanly stereotyping to which even Victoria was prey. However, she was also hard on the Germans, and seemed to understand their character well. Patricia Mountbatten said later that her grandmother *"would have very quickly changed her mind as soon as it became apparent what their policies were – which she absolutely abhorred of course..."*[9] and which she most certainly did. Her grandson, Prince Philip echoed these sentiments when he wrote,

> *I think most people at the time hoped that Hitler would give Germany some effective leadership after the fiasco of the Weimar Republic. I suspect that it was the existence and the behaviour of the uniformed SA and SS which quickly disenchanted any objective observer.*[10]

The Times, however, remarked that by March of 1933, the Nazis were in control in Hesse, completely displacing the Weimar-coalition based government with a virtual dictatorship.

Meanwhile, another cousin, Queen Sophie of Greece, died in January of 1932 at the age of sixty-two. Her funeral took place at Schloss Kronberg. The remains were taken to Florence and then later would be buried along with other royal remains at Tatoi in Greece.

That year, Victoria's son Georgie did something that was no doubt extremely difficult for him to do – he left the navy. There was every indication that he would have gone as far as Prince Louis. He had attained the rank of commander at the time of leaving, but he had a family to support with Nada, of course, having lost all her money at the fall of Imperial Russia. In addition, he missed his family a great deal. He took a job as the Director of Sperry Gyroscope Company and this was no honorary appointment with an illustrious name to put on their stationery masthead. The company really wanted Georgie's expertise, his mathematical brain, and inventiveness. He was happy in the years that he worked there and if he regretted the navy, the family never heard about it.

Georgie spent a lot of time with his nephew, Philip. Philip and Georgie's son, David Milford Haven, were, in fact, very good friends. Georgie's wife Nada and Edwina, were also very good friends and companions, and traveled together to a great many exotic destinations. As Patricia Mountbatten explains, *"Aunt Nada was unconventional and Bohemian in style and she and my mother did some quite adventurous journeys together such as flying across deserts in tiny planes."*[11]

Victoria did her part in continuing to organize young Philip's life writing letters to him and to others arranging for clothing and travel. At one point, she wrote to Nona regarding collecting Philip from Lynden Manor in Bray, the home of Georgie and Nada, to return him to school for his term. Later that year, it was to Cecile that she wrote, having been charged to make his arrangements for Christmas. *"I don't know the date in Jan[uary] when his school begins again, but he will know. He should be back in time to have two full days here, so that the new clothes he may need for the term can be got in London for him."*[12] In addition to clothes, Victoria was constantly telling Philip to whom he should write, giving him addresses where to write to those people and often telling him exactly what to write. In short, she was trying to fulfill the role of a mother as she had done for her own brother and sisters.

That summer, Irène briefly made a splash in *The Times* when she was involved in a car accident returning from a visit to the former Kaiser at Doorn, back to her home in Hemmelmarck. She was not hurt, but her car overturned.[13] Meanwhile, Alice would go to Meran in the South Tyrol for the winter liking it well enough. She was feeling better that year, and improved in her health, but not in her mental state. She later went to a sanatorium in Martinbruhn, and enjoyed that change as well. Victoria, herself, took a break from the care of her grandchildren and the wandering Alice, traveling to Dickie, who was now stationed in Malta, for Christmas. It would be like old times, when Louis and Victoria had been sta-tioned there.

In the beginning of 1933, Victoria gave herself a new project. She decided to ask Admiral Mark Kerr, Louis' very close friend and colleague and Nona's brother, to write a biography of the Prince. Though she spent the beginning of that year on a whirlwind of visits to Alice, who was now taking the waters at Kreuznach, to Irène and Ernie in Darmstadt, then off to Louise in Stockholm, the idea of a book about Louis was completely absorbing and something that she felt he naturally deserved. Later on, when she returned home to Kensington Palace that summer, she started going through Louis' letters and notes in earnest, seeing what could be used for publication. She commented to Dickie:

I have been looking through Papa's letters to me (rather a saddening job) to see if I could find anything which might be of use to Mark Kerr's book – there is hardly anything as your father was very outspoken in them about people & I don't want to be controversial. You are so like him in many ways, my very dear boy & that is a great joy to me.[14]

Today, controversy is so much a matter of course, it is difficult not to wonder what Victoria elected to withhold from the book.

The following year, when the book was published, Victoria was mildly critical of the work. She said that there was too much about royalties in it, and that it was certainly not literature, but otherwise felt it was a decent portrait of Louis.[15] *The Times* review was very subdued when they wrote that *"Admiral Mark Kerr, who served under him in every rank in the Navy, has written an appreciative and affectionate memoir of his old chief."*[16]

Cecile had another son in April of 1933. She named him Alexander, which pleased Victoria immensely. She wrote *"I am so glad the boy will be Alexander, which name has so many connections for us."*[17] The associations, of course, would be thick on the ground – her father-in-law, her brother-in-law, the ill-fated Sandro, and even her nephew Drino, Beatrice's son.

That summer, Victoria sent Philip off with his father, Prince Andrew, for a visit to Wolfsgarten and thence to Salem. Philip's sister, Dolla, now the Margravine of Baden, lived there. Meanwhile, Victoria was free to do some of her beloved reading. Some of her choices that year were Princess Paley's (Grand Duke Paul Alexandrovich's second wife) *Memories of Russia*, *Left Behind* by Baroness Buxhoeveden and *Always a Grand Duke* by Grand Duke Alexander Mikhailovich of Russia, who was married to Xenia of Russia. One can only imagine what Victoria thought about the libelous remarks the Grand Duke made about her brother-in-law Serge.[18]

Though her daughter-in-law Edwina freed Victoria of worrying about the monetary burdens of taking care of Alice and assorted other little things, the Princess still worried about her family and the handling of money. Perhaps, this came from the fact that, comparatively, Victoria had not grown up in the fabulous wealth that some of her relatives had enjoyed, nor had she lived her married life in that manner. However, it also could be seen to come from the privations, relative or otherwise, that many of her relations had suffered after the Great War.

In Ernie's son, Don's case, she would have no compunction in advising him to learn an occupation, so that he could run his estates and understand about his private finances. As was her wont, she didn't hesitate to give both her nephew and her granddaughter the benefit of her thoughts and counsel.

I hope Don will be able this winter to start studying the management etc. of affairs – and if he does not object to my advice, I think it would be well if he insisted on seeing the details of the work which Scharmann can show him – for I am sometimes afraid that Hardenberg... may not look out for your future...Uncle Ernie does not understand private finances, having always had other people to look after them – but is so devoted to Don and Don is so good and tactful a son that I am sure they can talk over affairs freely together.[19]

Count Hardenberg was, in fact, Ernie's chamberlain, and had the running of his household. Besides being interested in their day to day finances, Victoria had something else in mind as well – the former Tsar's fortune. She wrote to Dickie:

The proper German law authorities have now declared that the fortune (shrunk to a 10th & less) of poor Alix & Nicky's children shall fall to the heirs according to German law. Their surviving paternal & maternal nearest relations. In this case: Aunts Xenia & Olga of Russia & the widow of Uncle Nicky's brother, Countess (not Princess) Brassow [sic] & myself Aunt Irène & Uncle Ernie.[20]

Victoria made a claim for her part of the money and was determined to keep the sum in Germany. Her interested was altruistic; she wanted to help Baroness Buxhoeveden and her family as well as Pierre Gilliard, the former tutor to the Imperial children.

That summer, Irène visited her son, Sigismund in Costa Rica. His attempt to start a coffee plantation in Guatemala failed and he moved on to Costa Rica where he stayed. Her grandson, Prince Alfred of Prussia remembers her as a very stern woman who did not like the fact that Bobby was living abroad. After the death of Prince Henry, she wanted him to return to Germany. In fact, the purpose of this trip was to attempt to convince her son to come home. However, Bobby and his family were happy where they were, so Irène was disappointed.[21]* When she returned from Central America, Irène went first to Wolfsgarten to see her brother and sister. Victoria told Georgie that

Poor Aunt Irène arrived a week ago thin & run down & had to go to bed, where she still is, having caught a chill on her way here, which gave her bronchitis....Luckily it went no further & she is recovering steadily. She is bound to be very shaky, when she gets up. She did not stand either the food nor the climate at Costa Rica.[22]

(*) Prince Alfred, who died in June 2013, and his sister Barbara came to study in Europe. After the war, Alfred returned to Costa Rica, while Barbara stayed with their grandmother, who in turn made the young princess her heir. Alfred's return to Costa Rica was through Sweden, a voyage facilitated by his cousin Crown Princess Louise of Sweden.

Towards the end of the summer, a family event, like the ones of old, took place. Princess Marina of Greece, the daughter of Prince Nicholas of Greece and his wife, Grand Duchess Elena Vladimirovna of Russia, became engaged to young Prince George, Cousin George's son, who would later be the Duke of Kent. It would be a modified gathering of the 'Royal Mob', the Greeks and even the Germans were invited. Louise would also be coming, and Victoria was in her element getting people organized and properly attired for the event. She wrote letters to Cecile, who was becoming something of a confidant, telling her what Don should wear for the different events of the Kent wedding. She ended this letter with a refreshing bit of humor: *"Please don't be so 'respectful' when you end your letters to me, it sounds as if I were indeed an ancestress."*[23] – echoing the Duke of Connaught when Victoria had introduced her eldest granddaughters to him some years earlier.

However, as in all events, there was some controversy. She told Cecile that *"I hear Kyril* is coming with his wife and daughter – such a bore for all. He has declined meeting any of Aunt Xenia's sons, so for peace's sake they are not invited, but Aunt Xenia will go for the service at Buck*[ingham] *Pal*[ace] *only."*[24] She was upset about the Grand Duke's appearance at the event because she felt that Kyril was *"the only one of the Russian family whose conduct at the outbreak of the revolution was utterly despicable."*[25] Nevertheless, she was happy that Prince Philip would be invited to the wedding, apparently at the suggestion of Princess Marina.

The following year marked another landmark occasion in the life of Victoria and her remaining cousins, and that exclusive circle – the number of grandchildren of Queen Victoria – was growing smaller. Though Victoria would choose to remain in Malta and not take part in the celebrations, it was King George V's Silver Jubilee on May 6, 1935. Victoria told May,

> It seems to me that the position of the King is so strong now, that if ever, which I pray may not occur, there were a conflict between him and his government, his people would back him up through all, & prefer that the King should rule them, rather than any party dictator, to which other countries have succumbed.[26]

There was a service of Thanksgiving at St. Paul's, on a lovely warm day. George V seemed like the right sort of monarch for the times – unpretentious, ordinary, trustworthy, and above all liked. Victoria's remarks have a ring of prophecy about them when we see what happened just a little over a year later.

Though not present at this event, Victoria would be present at Louise's step-daughter's wedding. Princess Ingrid would marry Frederick of Denmark in Stockholm that same month. While she was there, Victoria had an opportunity to visit Grand Duchess Olga Alexandrovna, Nicky's other surviving sister. She commented to Dickie that *"[Olga] lives in a comfortable house on a farm bought with the proceeds of her inheritance from Aunt Minnie's jewelry etc. & her husband Col. Something-or-other** runs it."* Olga, her husband and sons, lived in Denmark, though Olga enjoyed her visits to Louise and Gustav Adolf in Sweden, and regularly visited there once a year. However, in 1948, feeling imperiled from Soviet troops amassing on the border, she and her family left Denmark for Canada.[27] She would live there until her death in November, 1960.

(*) Grand Duke Kyril Vladimirovich (1876-1938), second husband of Ducky, claimant of the Russian throne.
(**) Colonel Nicholas Koulikovsky (1881-1959) was never truly accepted by his Romanov in-laws.

Victoria continued to comment on her visits to Hesse and Ernie. She was optimistic about her findings. *"Compared with last summer things seem quiet & normal here & the Party seems to be gradually subordinated by & absorbed into the service of the State."*[28] Further, she thought that

> *the mass of the people still have complete confidence in Hitler & his leadership & are working hard & cheerfully – the young Nazi's are less to the fore & when they have done a years real military service will have much of the swagger & conceit taken out of them.*[29]

It is gratuitous to point out how wrong Victoria was, however, it is instructive to see that someone with normally excellent political instincts could hardly have comprehended what was to come. Certainly had that not been the case, Dickie would hardly have permitted his daughters Patricia and Pamela to spend time at the end of that year with their Uncle Ernie in Darmstadt.

Meanwhile, Victoria's life in some respects resumed the pace of old. She read her colorful Cousin Missy's, Queen Marie of Roumania, memoirs, the three volume tome, The Story of My Life. The memoirs were beautifully written and richly illustrated with photographs, and were full of the theatricality of which Missy was most certainly fond. No one could accuse Queen Marie of not believing her own publicity, since she was one of the first self-promoting royals. She even inspired Elinor Glyn, the overwrought romance writer of such classics as His Hour, a romance of the Russian court, to write Three Weeks. This was the writer's most famous opus, also made into a silent film, about a mad and passionate affair between a Balkan Queen and a young man on a continental tour. This Queen, whom the young man worshipfully called 'Queen', used to loll about seductively on tiger skins. This was all very obviously patterned on Marie's exotic behavior. Victoria's interest in Missy's book, far better written than La Glyn's volume, would have been, of course, her thoughts and feelings about the old days, and especially the family and the large number of grandchildren of which she was part. Ultimately, the fascination would have been with all she said but even more, what was not said.

That summer, Victoria visited one of her old 'haunts', the Isle of Wight and spent time with her Aunt Beatrice. She told Cecile that she

> *came here for a week's visit to Aunt Beatrice on Friday – though the trippers swarm around us, there is a sheltered place in the garden, where we sit in the morning, which they can't overlook and in the afternoons we drive to some quiet spot in Osborne grounds, near the sea and take our tea with us and where I can stroll about.*[30]

This was probably one of the last times that they could find anyplace on the grounds of Osborne that was free of tourists.

There were some tragic royal deaths in 1935 and 1936 – some important to the political scheme of things and others more personal in nature, though no less tragic. The young Queen Astrid of the Belgians was killed in a motoring accident in Switzerland that summer, leaving a widower, King Leopold III, and three small children, two of whom, Baudouin and Albert, would later become kings of Belgium. Closer to home, Cousin George's beloved sister, Princess Victoria, died at the end of the year. However, perhaps the most momentous death occurred just in the beginning of 1936, when Cousin George, himself, died. His son, David, came to the throne as Edward VIII. Victoria attended his funeral along with Gustav Adolf and Louise. Then, quickly on the heels of the old King's demise, Victoria Melita, Ernie's first wife, the passionate Ducky, died in March 1936. Victoria was hardly one to dwell on the past, however, it must have occurred to her that her generation was quickly fading.

There were always, however, distractions from the gloom. Ernie was sending his son, Ludwig, known as "Lu" in the family, to England as a cultural attaché of the Third Reich. Victoria anticipated getting to know this nephew with pleasure and wrote about it to Cecile. However, she began to notice that something was amiss with the letters that she received back from her granddaughter. She remarked, wryly, that

> *there is a very zealous customs official at Darmstadt apparently, for all letters nearly, from the New Palace, etc. arrive having been "gesetglich [lawful]" opened – poor man he must have a super – suspicious complex evidently.*[31]

Opening mail was hardly the worst part of the brutal regime tightening its tentacles around the old Grand Duchy.

That summer, Irène celebrated a milestone at Hemmelmarck – her seventieth birthday. Not only were Victoria and Ernie there with her, but also her two grand-nieces, Cecile and Sophie. This would have been one of the last peaceful visits that the family would have together. In August, the infamous Olympic Games took place in Berlin, which Victoria's son Georgie attended, and apparently enjoyed.

******

Philip was growing up in the mid-thirties. Victoria thought him very much like Prince Andrew, with his father's height. His idea for joining the Royal Navy must have started at this time as he had written a letter to his grandmother about it. Victoria told him that

> *Papa has just spent 3 days as my guest here* [Kensington Palace] *& left yesterday again for Paris. I showed him your letter & quite agree to the plan of your getting a naval training later on – it will be useful to you in many ways.*[32]

Philip had initially expressed some preference for the Royal Air Force, but eventually went with the family tradition of sailors. While Philip was making this decision, King George of the Hellenes was invited, by a nationwide plebiscite in 1935, back to that country. No doubt there were those who wondered why the young prince didn't join the Greek Navy. However, the family must have learned their lessons about Greece, a country that continually threw them out, and it was thought that Philip, since, he most certainly was not an heir to the throne, must join a more stable navy – the Royal Navy.

Philip was now going to school at Gordonstoun, in Moray, Scotland, though he spent a great deal of time with his grandmother, stopping there for holidays and for some tenderm loving care when it was needed. Victoria wrote to Dickie that Philip had come to her ill with what she described as an *"inflamed state of the kidneys"* and had to be put to bed with a severe and restricted diet. She ended her letter with the observation that *"children & grandchildren, though a pleasure, are decidedly a worry at times."*[33]

She continued her great care of him in the face of the reburial of King Constantine and Queen Sophie in Tatoi in November of that year. She organized his clothes, remarking that *"I am glad to hear that there is a good tailor at Elgin, so that you can get the necessary clothes made there."*[34] In the same letter she discussed Philip's wardrobe for funerals and what other clothes he would have needed on the continent. Knowing something of the character of impatient young men, whether they were her brother Ernie, her son Dickie, or her grandson, she told him what he should wear, whether he liked it or not. She also informed him when the exact dates of the funerals would take place, telling him *"Dolla has just telegraphed that the funerals at Athens are to take place on Nov. 17, but that she will wire me the exact date of departure. You had better inform Herr Hahn* of this now."*[35] In a later correspondence, she worked out the entire route of his trip to Greece.

While Philip was gone, the Abdication Crisis was taking place in England. Edward VIII abdicated on December 11, 1936. Cousin George had died in the beginning of the year, and by its end, his son could no longer continue without Mrs. Wallis Warfield Simpson, his inamorata, as Victoria called her. Wallis was friendly with both of Victoria's daughters-in-law, Nada and Edwina, and they had traveled together. However, Victoria felt that she exerted a negative influence on David – a double divorcee with two husbands still living. Victoria had never been a religious woman in the style of Ella or even Alice, but this would have been a little much, even for her. His mother, Cousin May, would have absolutely nothing to do with the woman that he loved. It couldn't have been difficult to surmise that a woman, who cheerfully accepted the brother of her dead fiancé because she felt it was her duty to do so, would never accept Mrs. Simpson.

Some thought that this spelled the end of the monarchy in England. However, the young King's abdication seemed to be met with nothing more than slight disquiet or possibly, feeble interest. Taking his place, was George's second son, now George VI, whom the family called "Bertie," his charming wife, Elizabeth Bowes-Lyons, and their two pretty young daughters, Elizabeth, called "Lillibet," and little Margaret. This family stepped easily, without much comment, into the shoes of Bertie's father. It was, in fact, so smooth and quiet, that after a while, few people remembered the months that David had spent on the throne. Dickie, of course, remembered since he was a great friend of David's and David had been in his wedding party. Most agreed, in the end, the whole sorry business turned out in the best possible way.

Victoria had a word to say to Ernie about it all:

Poor David in his infatuation is to be deeply pitied for he has made a sacrifice of his duty & his position for a person I feel is unworthy of it. I can only see tragedy ahead for him. Bertie & Elizabeth will not have David's popularity – much of which he has lost by his selfish action, but I think the people respect them & will be loyal to them, when they find them doing their duty as George & May did. There is still much old fashioned moral sense in the masses.[36]

And, what Victoria did not add and could not know at that moment was that in doing their duty in the worst of times, Bertie and Elizabeth far eclipsed David or even his parents, George and May, in popularity.

The Coronation of King George VI and Queen Elizabeth took place in May of 1937. Victoria was pleased that Queen Mary, now the Queen Mother, had thought to invite Cecile and Don to the event.

(*) *Headmaster of Gordonstoun.*

I am so pleased that you and Don have been invited for the coronation and shall be delighted to put you up....Cousin May says that the stand at the Abbey reserved for the family – both her's and Elizabeth's, will be very full – so she hopes you will have no lady in waiting with you and suggests either no train or a very small one, which you can drag behind you as you walk up the Abbey....I am not going to be present for the coronation festivities except perhaps the naval review.[37]

Before the festivities, Victoria made a trip to Alice. She told Dickie that Alice was *"well & cheerful."*[38] Then she moved on to Darmstadt to see Ernie and Onor. Ernie has had influenza and colitis, but, according to Victoria was now on the mend, though he was a bit thin and shaky. Irène was there also for a visit.

She arrived back in England on May 2 when Don and Cecile were expected on May 4. They all lunched with Queen Mary at Marlborough House on the seventh, just a few days before the Coronation. The festivities were overshadowed for Victoria by the knowledge that Ernie continued to be ill and was not really getting much better. By June she was writing to Cecile:

I enjoyed having you and Don with me for the coronation and only regret I could not keep you longer. Aunt Onor has written to me, that at last a specialist doctor has been called into consultation and that she and Uncle Ernie are going to his clinique at Berlin to-morrow so that the latter can be thoroughly overhauled. I can't help feeling a bit anxious about the result, as he really seems far from well.[39]

Meanwhile, Ernie's younger son, Lu, continued in his post as an honorable cultural attaché for the German Embassy. A year before, he had met a Scottish girl, the Honorable Margaret Geddes, when they were both studying painting and literature in Southern Germany. She was the daughter of Sir Auckland Geddes, who was, among other things, British Ambassador to the United States. Though there were some objections to the young lady, the couple announced their engagement during the summer of 1937. It was never elucidated in any of the letters that flew back and forth, what precisely these objections were. Possibly the political climate was part of the reason. However, Irène wrote to Ernie that,

it has not been easy for you to consent to his wishes I can well imagine, but all you & Onor told me about her & Lu ought to promise a real happiness, even if many a hard time may be in store for each of them in their particular way. May [Peg] become the sunshine of your family.[40]

More important, Ernie continued to be ill. Victoria, who had gone to be with him at Wolfsgarten, told Nona that he was, in fact, feeling completely miserable.

My poor brother is undergoing an X-ray treatment for his lungs, which has made him feel very wretched & he is quite an invalide still, though the photographs show that its effects are good & healing is in progress, but it will take long before he recovers. There is still hope that by the time of Lu's wedding he may be fit enough to come over for it.[41]

There was some temporary improvement and, in fact, the siblings had a last visit, since Irène was there, and Dickie and Edwina came for a short visit in August. However, by the end of

September, Victoria was increasingly concerned, and on October 9, 1937, Ernie was dead.

His wife Onor, as well as his sisters, Victoria and Irène spent a good deal of their time shielding him from the harsh realities of life. He, wrapped in cotton wool, continued the Hessian tradition of cultural and artistic activities, and Onor continued with the nursing and social work that Grand Duchess Alice had started. Ernie, himself, was an avid artist and decorator, enjoying the Art Nouveau school as well as the Surrealist one – some of the drawings he did, even the doodles in the guest book at Wolfsgarten were reminiscent of Salvador Dali. His death, in view of later events, was perhaps, for the best. He was lauded by *The Times* as being a patron of the arts. *"Thanks to his encouragement, many eminent artists settled in Darmstadt in pre-War days, and he was patron of the Great Century Exhibition of German Art held at Darmstadt in 1914."*[42]

His funeral took place on October 12. It was the first time that Alice was seen in public with her family for a very long time. Evidently, Louise had not seen her for five years, and Georgie for seven. However, Victoria took the opportunity to look back. She responded to a letter of sympathy from Cousin May stating that she feared Ernie was one of the last of

> *our old line, who will ever rule in Hesse again & my only pride is that the last reigning Grand Duke was till the very end of his life a model of a broad minded, warm-hearted & conscientious 'father of the people'. I shall stay another week here to help poor Onor a little – their son's marriage will take place quietly on Nov. 20.*
>
> *With love also from Irène....*[43]

Oddly enough, the death of Ernie had rather an astonishing outcome. In thanking Philip for his letter of condolences, Victoria told her grandson that his mother had actually recovered her health and seemed *"quite her old self again, like before she fell ill, and it is a great joy."*[44]

Peg and Lu's wedding, which had been scheduled for October, was postponed to November of that year. Victoria wrote a timely reminder to her grandson: *"Aunt Onor with Cecile & family arrives tomorrow afternoon....You are expected to attend Lu's wedding on Saturday afternoon."*[45] Indeed, the entire Hessian family, the Dowager Grand Duchess, Onor, Don, Cecile, their two boys and various retainers were to fly to England from Hesse in order to attend the festivities.

In line with the terrible calamities that had befallen Victoria and her siblings, fate had one more truly horrifying event in store for her and Irène. On November 16, en-route to Croydon in England, the entire wedding party from Hesse was killed when their plane crashed in Steene, Belgium. Besides the tragic deaths, Cecile's unborn child was also killed. Among the wreckage, the Hessian pearls and the veil of Honiton lace which Princess Alice wore in her wedding were destroyed. Ernie's childhood wish of everyone joining hands and going to heaven together was gruesomely fulfilled. It was perhaps a blessing that he had died just a month before.

Naturally, the family in England was in extreme shock and Victoria, pragmatic as ever, was the one to pull everyone together. She suggested and Sir Auckland, along with the remaining wedding party agreed, that the wedding should take place quietly and right away. Lu would need his wife beside him immediately in order to withstand the ordeal to come. Therefore, Prince Ludwig, now the only remaining member of the Hesse and by Rhine family outside of little Johanna, Cecile and Don's daughter, whom they had left behind in Darmstadt, married Margaret Geddes the following day.

On November 17, 1937, just as his grandmother Alice's wedding to the Grand Duke of Hesse had been over seventy years before, yet another funereal wedding took place. The bride wore black and they spent their honeymoon going to the scene of the tragic accident and taking the coffins back to Hesse for burial. Just two days later, the family assembled to take the coffin to the Rosenhöhe, the family mausoleum. The coffins were placed side by side, the mother, son, daughter-in-law, and two children – Dickie's Edwina wrote in her diary, *"Too ghastly...one by one and quite endless...."*[46] Victoria remarked to May that she was *"thankful that poor Lou [sic] is married, anyhow his wife will be a comfort and help to him in his terrible bereavement...."*[47]

The newlyweds adopted Don and Cecile's daughter, Johanna, but, unhappily, the little girl died of meningitis two years later. Again, instead of perhaps plunging Alice deeper into depression, the death of her daughter and cousin seemed to speed up her recovery, possibly due to the shock of this unbearable family catastrophe. Peg and Lu were stalwarts of the Hesse and by Rhine Family, then and during the war that was coming. During and afterwards, they housed royal refugees at Wolfsgarten. Unfortunately, they were never able to have children and the line effectively died with them.

There was, however, more tragedy to come.

Chapter XV

November 1937 – May 1945

In November 1937, Victoria's son, Georgie, fell and broke his leg while dining at Brook House, the London home of Dickie and Edwina. Naturally, at the time, no one thought much of it. It was mentioned in letters, and Alice wrote to Dickie about it saying that she had been over to Sweden and now was staying with her daughter, Sophie. She was more interested in the political situation in Germany, but was sorry to hear about Georgie's accident. Of more moment to the family was Louise, who had a tendency to be sickly and was having a tonsil operation at the end of the year. Irène visited Victoria in England at the end of 1937, and Victoria continued, as best as she could, to 'mother' Philip.

In the beginning of 1938, the union of Prince Paul of Greece, and Frederika, the daughter of Viktoria-Luise, Willy's daughter, and her husband, Ernest August of Hanover took place. For Victoria, however, major worry had set in regarding Georgie's broken leg – it wasn't healing properly. She wrote to Dickie that the news wasn't good. *"After a good start, the bones are not knitting together as they should & he has frequent pain & is getting thin & pale."*[1] By the end of the month, things had taken a serious turn. In another long letter to Dickie, Victoria detailed Georgie's condition. He had cancer of the bones and had gone for treatment, but, unfortunately, there was little hope of it working. In short, Victoria told Dickie stoically that she didn't know how long he would live and that he was being given heroin for the pain.

As the months wore on, there was no improvement in Georgie's condition. Victoria wrote to Philip: *"Poor Uncle Georgie is making no progress, & all the discomfort & pain of these many weeks in which he has been lying, almost immovable, in bed are running him down, but he keeps up his courage & is most patient."*[2] Life, however, went on during this difficult time. Victoria made arrangements for Philip's school holidays. As ever, she was precise in her instructions. She thought it best that he go to his sister, Dolla at Schloss Salem, and then afterward, *"if it is possible for you to go to Athens still – you could get there by the Orient Express, I think, quite quickly....The car will meet you at the station here on arrival, when I hear definitively from you when that will be."*[3]

April of that year saw Victoria celebrating her 75th birthday, though with Georgie's condition deteriorating by the day, the celebration was quiet and subdued. It would be the last time she received a birthday card from all four of her children. Three days later, George Mountbatten, Second Marquess of Milford Haven, died at the age of forty-six.

Georgie was well liked by everyone who knew him. Queen Elizabeth II, who was seated next to him at a wedding when only a child wrote, *"He was one of the most intelligent and brilliant of people. He spoke to children just as if they were grown up."*[4] In this, he was very much like his mother, of whom this was often said. His brother Dickie said, *"He was the sort of person who, instead of reading detective stories, would sit down and read problems of higher calculus, and solve them in his head."*[5] Patricia Mountbatten seconds this opinion of her Uncle Georgie. Not only was he a charming and good looking person, but he *"had a brilliant mind and had no trouble quickly solving problems which took my father much longer to do through hard work."*[6]

The Royal Family felt deeply for Victoria in this latest of a too heavy load of catastrophes that she had endured throughout her life. Uncle Arthur, the Duke of Connaught, and Victoria's remaining Uncle, wrote: *"I can hardly find words to express adequately to you how deeply I feel for you in this new great grief that has fallen upon you..."*[7]

The funeral took place in the little village of Bray. Georgie and Nada's home, Lynden Manor, was located there and the procession wended its way through the village to the small, unpretentious cemetery where Georgie would later be joined by Nada. Wreaths came from everywhere and the senders ran the gamut from the King and Queen to the actress Marlene Dietrich.

This latest sorrow served to temporarily break Victoria's spirit as the previous ones had not managed to do. Patricia Mountbatten later said that this was the only time that she had seen her grandmother cry. The day after the funeral, Victoria wrote to May. She thanked her for her sympathy and said: *"I am strong and my health is all right only my nerves are rather strained so that I can't control my feelings as well as I would."*[8] The Queen visited Victoria soon afterward. Though Victoria appreciated her family's sympathy, she was, in fact, never quite the same again. She remarked to Nona,

> *Thank goodness you will be spared the worst of all sorrows, even that of losing one's husband, which the suffering & death of Georgie is to me. When one is old, one can bear any one but that. I don't think I shall ever be my former self again.*[9]

In June, Victoria, with a heavy heart, once more began to take up her life. She continued her various and diverse reading, but this year, the subjects had a clear emphasis in the family tragedies and problems. She read, *The Woman who Rose Again* by Gleb Botkin and put in brackets after it, *"Story of the so-called Gr[an]d D[uchess] Anastasia,"* by Harriet Rathlef-Keifman, *La Fausse Anastasie* by Pierre Gilliard and Constantin Savech, *The Murder of the Romanovs* by Capt. Paul Bulygin, as well as *The Road to Tragedy* by Alexander Kerensky.[10] Hers was a mind continually active, and this no doubt helped her to cope with her immense sadness.

In the early summer, the rounds of visits started again. They were therapeutic and presented a return to a modicum of normal life, such as it could be for her. She wrote to her Aunt Louise, *"I am off tomorrow morning & as the wind has fallen should have a good crossing. I will write to you after my visit to Wolfsgarten & when I am with Irène."*[11] She met Irène at Wolfsgarten, a poignant visit at best, with memories and phantoms at every turn. Irène wrote about the visit:

> *It was such a comfort for me & Victoria on arriving here together yesterday for the first time in our dear old home since we lost so many of our loved ones. One has the feeling that dear Ernie & Onor must step in & be there & that they are only just by chance absent – one cannot realize it – & I often feel like in a dream. Peg and Lu are so sweet & kind, doing all they can that one shall not feel the sad change too much – he is quite wonderful, poor boy & Victoria too. We were at the Rosenhohe this morning – their graves are one big one –... It was very nice being a few days at Langenburg with Sandra, Ernie Hohenlohe & family, where there are so many remembrances of dear Grandmama & her Sister Feodora.*[12]

Victoria also wrote to her Aunt Louise about their stay, with details of the family members that remained, such as Lu and Peg, who were living at Wolfsgarten, with their niece, Johanna, in the nursery. It was inevitable, at this vulnerable time in Victoria's life, that nostalgia took over: *"My thoughts are often with you & in this dear old place now so empty & still I often think of those happy days of my youth, when you were here with us."*

She continued:

> *I spent a pleasant week at Langenburg with my granddaughter Margarita & with Sandra, who now has also had the sadness of losing her sister "Missie."* Irène spent a couple of days with me here & I leave to-night to join her at Hemmelmark ... from where I hope to go & visit my Louise & Gustaf, after they have got back to Sweden...*

However, she also wrote some good news, which would serve to elevate her mood:

> *I am glad to find that Ernie's son Lu is developing a real interest in the garden & grounds, which Ernie had done so much for with real taste & understanding, so that everything will be well looked after. Don & Cècile's little girl will be two in September & is a bright, healthy intelligent child. Her merry little ways brighten up this otherwise lonely place & thank goodness she is too young to know or feel her loss & is very happy with her Uncle & Aunt, who are quite devoted to her. I think Ernie would have been pleased to find his boy trying in every way to be worthy of his dear father...*[13]

From Wolfsgarten, Victoria joined Irène, who had returned to her home at Hemmelmarck. Writing to Peg, she thanked her for the visit, saying:

> *It was so nice being at Wolfsgarten and to feel I was welcome there, thanks to your natural kindness and thoughtfulness – It did me good to see how sensibly and bravely Lu is facing the loss of those he loved for I find it very hard to bear the loss of my Georgie on top of the other sorrows.*[14]

She wrote to Nada that Wolfsgarten, quite naturally, felt strangely empty and quiet, but that Lu and Peg were happy to have her and Lu looked *"decidedly less strained."*[15] It is interesting that just a couple of months later, Victoria felt impelled to write a postcard to her nephew and niece saying: *"Whatever befalls you will be both always in my thoughts and heart."*[16] Victoria was hardly being prescient, as the signs of war and upheaval became all too apparent to everyone as the thirties wore on.

By the end of the summer, Victoria was with Louise at Sofiero. She gardened with her daughter, which was always curative, and continued her correspondence with her friends and family. She confided in Nona, as she always did, mentioning Alice, who she felt at that point, was living a lonely life, separated from her husband and seeing little of her children. Indeed, Alice was either staying with family in England or living alone in a small flat in Athens.

Victoria returned to London in the fall to more sad news. Her Uncle Arthur of Connaught had lost his son, Prince Arthur** to cancer. She wrote feelingly to her Aunt Louise: *"I know how you will be grieving for Uncle Arthur's sorrow & long to see you again."*[17]

(*) *Queen Marie of Romania (October 29, 1875 – July 18, 1938). The indmitable "Missy" was finally felled by cancer, death bringing her much relief from the ill treatment her eldest son, King Carol II, inflicted on her.*
(**) *Prince Arthur of Connaught (January 13, 1883 – September 12, 1938). The Duke of Connaught, King Edward VII and the Duke of Edinburgh and Saxe-Coburg and Gotha all outlived their firstborn son.*

Victoria, however, distracted herself, doing what she did best, organizing people. In this case, she concentrated on Philip once again. He was finishing his time at Gordonstoun in preparation to enter the Royal Navy and exams were looming.

> *You will have heard from Mr. Hahn that it is advisable you should pass your exam in March & I trust you will feel that this is the best date under existing circumstances. As it means a good deal of hard work before & there is no time to waste, you will have, like many another young man in such times, to study a bit even during the Xmas holidays, & it will be easiest for you to do so in London.*[18]

She also wondered, in this letter, what tutors she should arrange for him and went on to agree with Mr. Hahn that March would be best for the exams. At that time, it would be easier for his Uncle Dickie to arrange a place in the Royal Navy. Alice was staying with her at the end of that year, and had taken a flat in Athens where she would return in January of 1939. Victoria also made arrangements for Philip to visit his mother:

> *I enclose your ticket for Dec 15th to here...The sleeper will cost 7/6 so I enclose a £1 note for it & for other small expenses....*

> *We won't discuss your "misdeeds," as I hope they won't occur again & they are passed* [sic] *& over.*[19]

One can only wonder at what schoolboy 'misdeeds' Philip's grandmother refers. However, it seems that Victoria was able, as an experienced mother of two boys, herself, to put these transgressions in perspective and to deal with them.

****

As the crucial year of 1939 was ushered in, Victoria was visiting the Duke of Connaught in France and remarked that she had seen Alice's estranged husband, Andrew, commenting that he was sticking to beer and a little white wine in moderation. Andrew, it seems, was living the typical exile's life on the Riviera with a mistress in one hand and a martini in the other. Victoria was, however, bound to Athens for Easter, hoping to see both Alice and Philip. This visit probably didn't occur because Victoria sprained her ankle at Cannes.

By April, she was back in Kensington Palace and in touch with her niece-in-law, Peg, with regard to some treatments that she hoped would be

> *a great success, but it may be some time before its effects show themselves...Much love to Lu who will be relieved that your treatment is over before he knew of it, though he will man-like probably reproach you for not telling him beforehand about it – I think you were wise however not to do so.*[20]

There is little doubt that this may refer to some sort of fertility treatments. Sadly, it was not to be Peg's fate to bear children, though apparently she did want them. She did however continue to care for her niece, Johanna, until her tragic death in June of that year.

Irène visited Victoria in May and the two of them visited Queen Mary at

Marlborough House. Since the Dowager Queen liked reminiscing about the past, these three ladies most certainly spent a great part of the visit talking about old times, as well as the dear ones from long ago. More momentous that summer, though obviously not known at the time, was the meeting of Philip with his cousin, Princess Elizabeth. The young man was at the Naval College at Dartmouth. The Princess and her family were on a cruise of the south coast on the *Victoria and Albert*. They made a private visit to the school that George VI had once attended as a young man. Philip was delegated to entertain Princesses Elizabeth and Margaret with ginger snaps and lemonade. He started leaping over the tennis net, which seemed to impress both little girls. They played croquet together and Philip had lunch on the yacht. The students then escorted the royal yacht out of harbor. The meeting was said to have made quite an impact on Princess Elizabeth.

As the summer drew to a close, Victoria became extremely introspective writing to Dickie about her faith and beliefs as though she knew that they would be tested once again. She clearly explained her position to her son:

I am not an atheist or theist, but a humble agnostic i.e. one who does not pretend to know anything beyond this finite life & world, but has an instinctive hope that I am not merely a body but a spark of that something which unknowable to us is what lies at the root of my innermost being & the world our minds can grasp. With this I am content...We who come from an old stock of a privileged family, that has not had to worry over material existence, have inherited that sense of duty towards our fellow men, those especially whose nation we belong to, & who look to us instinctively for example & guidance. I know that you feel this way too, more than ever in times like these.

Let us live or die honourable.

I am proud, with the old feelings of our ancestors that you my son, once more are called to such high service. My love for you & my pride in you are too deep for selfish worries or repining –[21]

As September 1939 came around, and Hitler marched into Poland marking the beginning of the so-called 'Phony War', not only did Victoria examine her faith, but the recollections of the first Great War, as well, came very strongly back to mind. She wrote feelingly to the Grand Duchess Xenia:

I am thinking so much & lovingly of you, to whom this new War under such altered circumstances will bring back so many recollections...

I should much have liked to go & see you, but I am looking after this place & my granddaughters as well as 24 evacuated school children & their 2 teachers, which are lodged in the servants quarters here. Edwina is doing many necessary jobs in London & is living in my apartment at Kens[ington] Palace as Dickie was worried at the idea of her living in her exposed flat in Brook House. I was in London a few days ago to see how my poor aunts are getting on & will try & do so weekly.

Sometimes it seems to me as if it were but yesterday that we were living in the same circumstances & I try to make that past experience of use now.

Alice & Philip are together in Athens, it will be a comfort to her to have him there. Louise, thank goodness, is in a completely neutral country & may be able perhaps to hear from time to time how Alice's daughters & Irène are keeping. In the Great War Daisy was able to do that too. If I can be of any help to you & your family please always count on me.[22]

Philip, who had been visiting his mother at her flat at 8 rue Coumbari, Athens, returned to London at the end of September. But of course the 'Phony War' had already begun by then, and everything was becoming chaotic. Alice complained that letters from England weren't arriving and of course, Victoria could no longer write to her granddaughters. She told Philip:

I can't write to the sisters, but Aunt Louise has been able to & sends them my love. She can do the same for you if you ask her to & can also let them know that you are well. I think often of you dear boy, & am sorry if I spoke rather sharply to you on the telephone, worry & anxiety upsets one sometimes. ... I go to London once a week to look after my affairs & see Aunt Edwina & my Aunt Louise.[23]

Victoria's Louise was now, as Victoria told the Grand Duchess Xenia, serving the same role that Daisy, Crown Princess Margaret of Sweden, had served in the First World War – a go-between for the relatives on warring sides who wished to keep in touch. It was especially difficult for Victoria's nephew, Lu of Hesse, who, of course, had married a British girl. Victoria often wrote to Lady Isabelle Geddes, Peg's mother, anxious to transmit any information she had concerning Peg. Louise had given her a letter from Irène, who stated that, *"Peg is marvelously brave, her commonsense and her kind heart and feeling come to the fore more than ever — I cannot tell you how much I admire her."*[24] She later wrote further to Lady Geddes, possibly as a reassurance, that: *"I would like to remark that the Hessians amongst whom Peg lives, have never been like the Prussians and have remained attached to our family and have evidently included Peg in their affection, thanks to her character."*[25] And finally, and most importantly, Victoria told Lady Geddes that, *"Peg writes that Lu is so touchingly good and such a comfort, they seem the most devoted couple and I am sure she is the greatest standby to him."*[26]

In a letter to Cousin May, Victoria told her that Edwina was moving all her possessions to Broadlands. Edwina moved into Kensington Palace with her mother-in-law at the beginning of the war since it was safer there than her home. The two women got along well. In fact, Victoria approved strongly of Edwina's war work and wrote to her: *"You have grown as dear to me as if you were my own daughter by birth & I am proud of the way in which you are facing the duties & difficulties of the war & its possible consequences."*[27]

For Britain, it was a long, hard, travail, especially when they stood alone against the Nazis from 1939 to nearly 1942. The King George VI and Queen Elizabeth proved to have a tremendous amount of mettle. There was much appreciative talk about the Queen, gaily clad in her best dresses, matching coats, and hats in dusty blues and pinks, going to the devastated East End which had been bombed out in the blitz and visiting the people. They were extremely delighted to see her, highly attracted by her beaming countenance, and seeming to know how to say the right thing at the right time. When Buckingham Palace was hit by bombs, she smiled calmly, and cheerfully said that since they had been bombed, she could now look the East End in the face. Many thought it was a good thing that King George's brother had abdicated, and that these two were far more appropriate monarchs for the times.

Victoria spent her time visiting about and actually got herself a small car. Sometimes she left London and went down to Bray to look after the garden at Lynden Manor, Georgie and Nada's home. She would often have Tatiana, their daughter, and Tatiana's lady companion for company. On that particular visit she also observed to her son Dickie that Philip was bored at Dartmouth and that Tatiana was extremely backward. Tatiana was in fact, mentally challenged and lived her entire life, very quietly, outside the public eye. Victoria was contemplative that sad autumn that signaled another war. She observed to her confidant, Queen Mary that as a result of the war the 'Bolsheviks' will be dominant.[28] She would remember this when the so-called 'Iron Curtain' fell across Europe after the war.

As 1939 came to a close, another sad death occurred. In December, Princess Louise, Duchess of Argyll, died at Kensington Palace. The Aunt who had been a favorite of Victoria's and had given her the beloved Kent House on the Isle of Wight was now gone. She wrote: *"When I pass Aunt Louise's door without going in, I feel I miss her affectionate pleasure at seeing me very much."*[29] Yet another of the old 'Royal Mob', now gone and Victoria would continue to miss her. She and Nada attended the funeral at St. George's Chapel.

As the shooting war finally got started in 1940, Victoria was persuaded to go to Broadlands, Edwina's home, where she would be safe. However, she managed to go back and forth quite often to Kensington Palace. A widow for over twenty years, it was difficult for her to give up her independence and move in with the family. Eventually, though, good sense prevailed and she spent a good deal of her time in the country. She filled in some of the time in the ensuing years working on her unpublished recollections. She, in fact, dictated them to her friend, Baroness Buxhoeveden, who helped her to give them shape. She was, however, never very happy with them and told Dickie that *"Isa B. is now here with me & we have been working again on my "Recollections," if you realised how much they bore me, you would be grateful to her keeping me up to the mark."*[30] Had they not bored her, and it was not an affectation that they did, they would most certainly have been published, and possibly more interesting than they turned out to be.

The rest of her family, however, was intimately involved with war work as well as her son, Dickie, and grandson, Philip in the Royal Navy. Victoria wrote her hopeful observations to her friends.

I still feel convinced that the Germans can't last out as long as we and that their spirits may break up unexpectedly, more so now that their idol is in command of his army and any failures of his may have a bad impression for him on the 'home front'.[31]

In this, Victoria, for once, wasn't entirely correct. However, her estimation of Winston Churchill, who had been at the Admiralty with Prince Louis, seemed more on the mark,

Everybody is full of admiration for Mr. Chamberlain's fine & noble behaviour – that he was perhaps too just & too dignified to sway the masses in wartime is an experience not new in history. Winston Churchill has, from all I hear from the Admiralty, ripened in character from what he was 25 years ago – with his abilities, dash & powers of eloquence he may make the right sort of Prime Minister in war time, even Lloyd George showed up well during the last one, so one must hope for the best.[32]

...and her estimation of England's chances, after Dunkirk:

I am almost relieved that now the French can't fight any longer, we shall no longer be drained of troops, and ammunition, etc. but can keep these at home. A campaign against an Island Power is none so easy to carry out as an attack on a continental country. You have to cross the sea by air and ships to get at us and our Navy and airforce are better than the enemy's.[33]

But, politics aside, Victoria missed her family, spread out as it was in Europe, some, of course, on the wrong side. She wrote to Philip:

Since the fall of the Netherlands & Belgium Aunt Louise & I can no longer write to each other, except by chance & I have had no letter from her for a long time. Mama has written a couple of times & 2 days ago I received a letter from her as recent as June 21st in which she asks me to forward a copy of Dolla's letter to her about Berthold having been wounded.... Mama says she is well & your sisters too....A bomb fell at Broadlands just beyond the kitchen gardens, but only damaged the outer wall....Meanwhile the girls have just been sent on a visit to friends in America.[34]

That indeed had been the case. Dickie and Edwina had sent Patricia and Pamela to America. Dickie had been concerned because their great-grandfather, Sir Ernest Cassel, was Jewish. Mountbatten was criticized for the move, people pointing out that the King and Queen had not, and indeed, would not send the princesses away. Nevertheless, the two girls joined a group of evacuee schoolchildren being sent to the States in July of 1940, Patricia Mountbatten continues, saying that they had

no idea when, or whether, we would ever be able to return home. We sailed in the American ship Washington's last crossing with many American families.

Our mother came over to the US on a wartime lecture tour for Red Cross and St. John in late 1941 and took Pamela home with her. I stayed on till my Graduation (from Miss Hewitt's classes in NYC) in June 1942 and flew back with a plane load of GIs, to join the Women's Royal Naval Service.[35]

When Patricia returned to England, Victoria noted to Nona Crichton, that she was unchanged by the experience.[36]

Victoria never became downhearted or discouraged. Like her grandmother, it was not in her nature. She wrote to Lady Geddes during the Nazi successes of Spring 1941, "*When I recall the critical and gloomy periods of the last war, when the enemy seemed so successful, I feel confident that this present anxious time will not cast us down too much and that he will breakdown ultimately as he did then.*"[37]

In addition to spending time in Broadlands, Victoria spent much time with Cousin May at Badminton. The two had lovely talks, and reminisced about the old days. The Dowager Queen wrote to her brother, Alexander, "*Victoria Milford Haven is staying with me this week, very pleasant and agreeable, & we have long talks about everything, & family affairs as of course she gets news of her people through Louise of Sweden.*"[38]

Victoria, herself, reported to the King on her 'doings' with his mother.

I have just come here from a six day's stay at Badminton, where I found your mother in very good health. She helps clearing up the dead wood in the big avenue, as the ground is to be put under the plough. We also visited a couple of factories in Bath.[39]

The main thrust, however, of their time together was reminiscing about olden times. As contemporaries, they had known all the same people and had witnessed together over fifty years of royal events, scandal, and family matters. However, that did not mean that they weren't very much aware of and living in the present as well as interested in all of the new and serious events of the war. Victoria told May,

> *As I increase in age & the circle of my contemporaries grows smaller, it is a real pleasure to me to talk over past days & acquaintances with them. You not only share these recollections with me but have also the rather rare gift of taking interest in present & future development of the world & people's trend of thought, without the strong bias against inevitable change, which so often clouds older folks judgment. I have always found more understanding of these problems amongst those who like you have had a broad outlook on life, than amongst people who have a class outlook on life.*[40]

May echoed these sentiments when writing to her brother Alexander: "*I have Victoria...this week & we are having some good talks, on all kinds of subjects, about old days etc. She has seen A[un]t B[eatrice] lately who she says is most alive & alert – as to brain, though feeble in body...*"[41]

That spring, Victoria heard of a death out of the very distant past. In May, Madame de Kolemine died at Hotel des Trois Couronnes, Vevey, Switzerland.* She had been the woman who Victoria's father had precipitously married when Victoria had married Louis, and just as precipitously the marriage had been annulled at the insistence of Queen Victoria. No doubt it all seemed very long ago and in a radically different world.

During the fall, Philip stayed with his grandmother, who happened to be at Kensington Palace, while doing some courses. Philip had "*circulated pretty freely among other members of the family, in particular to [his] ... sisters,*"[42] but had always had short visits with her either on the way to school or for his holidays. He thought her a very pivotal character in his life and observed this about her:

> *She always wore ankle-length, and usually black, dresses. She smoked a good deal and as she never carried a bag, she kept her heavy silver cigarette-case, lighter and cigarette holders in a pocket at the bottom of her petticoat. There were no 'filter-tips' in her day, but she obviously appreciated that the 'raw' smoke was dirty as she had a number of glass cigarette-holders into which her maid inserted a bit of cotton-wool. When the cotton-wool became stained by the smoke, she would discard it and start on a clean one. At the end of the day her maid would then clean out the dirty cotton-wool and insert clean bits.*[43]

Victoria's unique smoking ritual was well-known in the family and described often. However, she never quit the habit she picked up from her cousin Willy, who had incidentally died in exile in June 1941.

When Philip arrived at the Palace, Victoria wrote to her cousin, George, that he had arrived safely from Greece and would certainly inform the King himself. In addition

---

(*) *Madame de Kolemine was born in Bucharest, Romania, on November 15, 1852.*

to that, the young man wanted to *"thank you for allowing him to continue his service in your navy, which he is so proud & keen to do."*[44] Philip went to visit the Royal Family at Windsor during this time, and Victoria wrote another letter to King George, thanking him for his hospitality and telling him how much Philip enjoyed himself and was glad that they liked her grandson. She also penned a description of Philip to her dear friend Nona Kerr Crichton: *"He has broadened out & his likeness to his father, in face, is getting very pronounced. He looks quite the man & is very independent & glad to be back."*[45]

Family sorrows continued through the war when Victoria's Uncle Arthur of Connaught died January 16, 1942, and more tragically, the young Duke of Kent was killed in August 25, 1942. Victoria had just gone to the christening of the Duke's younger son, Prince Michael and had stood as his godmother.

The sad bane of Victoria's existence as she entered her eightieth year, however, was her problems with circulation and the chilblains from which she suffered since childhood. However, now she complained and apologized in her letters that her handwriting was getting shaky due to this condition. In a letter to May, she grumbled a little about the affliction on her fingers and toes, though a new treatment seemed to improve her circulation. Nevertheless, she retained her dry sense of humor and commented that after her birthday in 1943, the Court Circular seemed to be on a countdown from then on.

That summer, Dickie was made Supreme Allied Commander of Southeast Asia. It was an honor, no doubt, that Victoria could have foregone. She was later extremely upset when Dickie became the last Viceroy of India. She was sure that whatever went wrong, Dickie would ultimately be blamed. There was also some family gossip and scandal, though Victoria never subscribed to innuendo about her family. She and her sisters had learned from "Madgie" Hardcastle never to gossip and Victoria certainly had no desire to start now. She did, however, complain to Dickie about Lady Iris Mountbatten, daughter of her nephew Drino Carisbrooke and granddaughter of her Aunt Beatrice. The young woman was a lady who, *"I have never managed to like, is getting herself more talked about than ever...."*[46*]

Victoria, thankfully, was occasionally able to hear news about her family in the Axis countries. She told May that correspondence with Louise was difficult at the moment; however, she had heard recently from her daughter and that *"Irène is well & has been to Wolfsgarten...."*[47] Later, the news wasn't as good. Telling May that her chilblains make it difficult for her to write letters, she continued:

> You will be sorry to hear that my granddaughter Tiny's husband (Sophie), Mossy's son Christopher, has been killed in a long-distance flight.** You will sympathize with poor Mossy going through your own most sad experience now. This is the 3d son she has lost by war, the two eldest in the last great war & her favourite in this war.***
>
> I feel sure Tiny's sisters will manage to go & see her – it was a happy marriage & she is expecting a baby in Feb. next.[48]

In January of 1944 more interesting news came down the 'pipeline' from Germany.

(*) *Lady Iris Mountbatten was married and divorced three times.*
(**) *Princess Sophie of Greece remarried Prince Georg Wilhelm of Hanover in 1946. He was the second son of the Duke and Duchess of Brünswick and Lüneburg, as well as an older brother of Queen Frederika of Greece.*
(***) *Prince Friedrich Wilhelm of Hesse was killed on September 12/13, 1916; Prince Maximlian of Hesse was killed October 13, 1914; Prince Christoph of Hesse was killed on October 7, 1943.*

They [Lu and Peg] were packing up their flat at Potsdam and both now moving for good to Wolfsgarten. My daughter says too that she has heard that all Princes of former reigning houses and the members of prominent houses are no more at the front – I can't fathom the reason, evidently a political one, for this removal, but anyhow it is comforting to know that Peg and Lu will be living together at home now and in much less danger than before.[49]

This of course alludes to the edict removing the old aristocracy from Hitler's army.

That summer, while Victoria stayed at Kensington Palace, she wrote to Nona about the air raids. *"I am careful & keep as sheltered as I can in my inner corridor chiefly when the guns begin to go & I don't go further than across to my garden when the sirens go."*[50] In order to continue to ensure Victoria's safety, she was urged to go to Windsor for the duration and her daughter-in-law, Edwina, arranged the move. The best part of that time was that she became better acquainted with both Princess Elizabeth and Princess Margaret. Victoria told Nona that

we take our meals together otherwise I am free to do what I like. Princess Elizabeth does host at meals, when her parents are away – when they are here we generally lunch amongst ourselves only. These young girls are charmingly brought up, not shy & quite natural. The younger does not come to dinner as a rule yet....The elder is the more attractive to me.[51]

Victoria continued to be the 'gasbag' that her grandmother had called her and talked ceaselessly. The Princesses however profited from this endless chatter since she talked a great deal about her family and their history. Princess Elizabeth, in particular, had a special interest in the family and loved listening to all of Victoria's stories. The young Princess, like many others in Victoria's family, always noted that her mind was as sharp as a 'crackerjack'. All in all, she enjoyed her stay as she had *"not lived in the castle for years and enjoy going about the grounds. The alterations are real improvements."*[52] As she had been much of her life, Victoria was never interested in fashion or appearance; she seemed to wear the same hairstyle and, especially after Louis' death, dressed constantly in black. One of her cousins, Princess Alice, Countess of Athlone, went so far as to say she looked like a *"rag-bag."*

The year 1944 saw some further sad and significant deaths in Victoria's family. In October, the last of Queen Victoria's children and Victoria's close friend, aunt and sister-in-law, Beatrice, died at Brantridge Park in Sussex. She told her granddaughter: *"She was only 6 years older than I & we had many recollections of our youth in common. Though she became my sister-in-law...I always thought of her as my Aunt."*[53] Several months later in December, Prince Andrew of Greece died of a heart attack at Hotel Metropole in Monte Carlo. He and Alice had been separated for many years, and not seen each other during the war – nevertheless it was another painful break with the past. Theirs had, after all, been one of those 'Weddings of the Decade' back in 1903, and one of the last times that the Romanovs had joined in family festivities. Dickie and Alice notified Philip who was at that time, serving on the *HMS Whelp*.

After the liberation of Athens in October 1944 and the entrance of the Allies by the end of the year, Alice was able to make a surprise return to England in early 1945. She spent her sixtieth birthday with Victoria at Broadlands. She returned to Athens, however, in March of that year. In a letter to Lady Geddes, Victoria remarked that Alice had been with her for two weeks, and that she was now *"safe back at Athens, it was a great pleasure having a visit from her after not having seen her since 1939."* Later on in the letter, she commented that *"Peg wrote too that Wolfsgarten was filled "to last cupboard" by refugees, friends and relations mostly."*[54] Indeed, Wolfsgarten had become a sort of refuge for the aforementioned friends and family. No one was turned away though the couple lived in constant fear of the Gestapo.

As the war finally wound down, news from the 'other side' was more forthcoming. Irène's son, Toddy died of a hemorrhage at Tützing, Bavaria since there was no means of blood transfusions, and possibly because the Allies denied it to him. Though this was sad news, Victoria was worried about her own son and grandsons, as well as her nephew, Lu, and all of her granddaughters and families in Germany. She wrote to May,

> *I have heard from one of her brothers, who has seen them, that Peg & Lu are all right at Wolfsgarten & Tiny & her children are still at Friedrichshof, though no longer in the main building, which is occupied by the Americans – they are badly off for food as they have no farm & Lu proposes taking in the four eldest ones, he [is] getting his food from his Kranichstein farm – Tiny & the youngest will remain with Mossy who has been very ill & is still weak & helpless. Louise has telegraphed that she hopes to be able to come to me at the end of next month.*[55]

Victoria was eighty-two years old and began the process of withdrawing and disconnecting from the world. She, in fact, often joked that she would wake up in the morning and look about her thinking, still here?! As if to punctuate the process, she did not attend the VE day service at St. Paul's and would not travel again to Germany.

Chapter XVI

May 1945 – September 1950

During the summer, Victoria began to hear more about her relations in Germany, as well as having some communication from Irène. Since the Neues Palais in Darmstadt was bombed and completely destroyed during the war, Victoria worried about many of the possessions of the Hessians, and most importantly the letters, photographs, and documents stored in the archives. As news slowly began to trickle in of her German family, she was gratified to hear that a visitor there had been *"successful in retrieving Queen Victoria's letters etc."*[1] With the Neues Palais gone, the Heiligenberg lost to her a long time ago, Seeheim in disrepair, and Wolfsgarten being the only Hessian residence intact after the war, Victoria surely felt a great nostalgia for the places of her youth, now living only in her memory. Characteristically, however, she interested herself with affairs in the new Germany, divided as it was between the Allies. She wrote to Lady Geddes that she felt that leadership could come from some of the former ruling families. However, she was positive that *"such a movement must come of itself, not imposed by the conquerors."*[2]

Alice and Louise could now visit back and forth once again and there was much discussion about Philip's future. Dickie, who had returned from South East Asia in 1946, was interested in taking part in these deliberations. As well, Victoria began traveling and paying some visits again, for example, to Louise in Sweden. However, she would never again be as active as she had been and was certainly of an age to stay quietly at home. However, that did not keep her from being involved in all that went on, nor did she for a moment stop thinking and working out things as she had been doing continually from a young age. She was philosophical as the year 1945 closed, writing to Dickie *"I take life as it comes & have always found it easy to adapt myself to circumstances as by nature I don't cling to old ways & habits & happiness does not consist for me in having a thousand little things of no real importance in life. The older I get the less my everyday needs & desires become."*[3]

Luckily, bad as the war had been, it had not devastated her family in the way that the Great War had. Outside of the death of her granddaughter Sophie's husband, Prince Christoph, her immediate family suffered no casualties. Even though Hitler had rejected the German aristocracy in the last years of the war, Victoria had to write letters and avowals to clear Lu's name. She wrote a statement vouching for his character and then sent it to King George for his comments.

> *Thank you most gratefully for so promptly returning my proposed declaration that my poor nephew Lu was not over here in 1946 [sic] to make propaganda for the Nazis, as it seems some German people are pretending now.. And above all your kind letter to me on the subject.*[4]

The family was also occupied in settling Prince Andrew's estate. Eventually, Philip would go to the South of France to sort out his father's affairs.

Irène was anxious to see her last living sister and tried to obtain permission to go to Sweden where Victoria would be visiting. She wrote to May about her difficulties:

I am in a fix as I had hoped to be able to visit Louise in Sweden accompanied by Barbara* – so as to see Victoria, & my Grandson before he goes to Costa Rica leaving on August 28th by sea – he has been staying in Switzerland since 1938. It seems that I cannot attain a permit from the British occupation army here in Kiel unless you kindly showed your interest in this case for our meeting to take place. The fact is that I have urgent family matters pertaining to inheritance to settle which Alfred** must submit to Sigismund [Bobby] his father – & also certain things to settle with Victoria which both I cannot postpone.[5]

Unfortunately, she was not able to get permission, though May tried to intercede. It would be some time before the German relatives would be able to freely visit with their 'Allied' counterparts. However, Victoria thanked May for the effort, saying:

Thank you so much for your kind letter & for having enquired why Irène could not receive a visa – Of course it would have been nice for us if we could have met once more, but perhaps we may have a chance to do so next year…Olga*** of Russia came over from Denmark to see me, for 2 days. She is a dear affectionate soul, full of energy at home where she works really too hard for her health and she suffers now from a strained heart in consequence… Algy & Alice**** were very well & cheerful, when they spent a week here, I am looking forward to finding them established at Kens[ington] Palace when I get back…[6]

Irène was more or less stuck now at Hemmelmarck, since she was not free to travel. She told May that

[h]ere the British occupation, which was in the main house, has left – I go on living in the servants wing – & the Red Cross society I have offered to take over the former, as a home for old homeless nurses & such as are in need of recuperation, which seems to answer the purpose very well & are settling into…. Life is full of sadness but I like to think of old days when we were one autumn together with dear Grandmama in Balmoral especially.[7]

Like many of her generation, Irène, too, liked to think about those old and golden days before war, loss, and heartache had changed her world.

Victoria, however, was never one to dwell, though she continued to miss her grandmother every day of her life. She was ever forward thinking possibly because she had more family around her than Irène, who was alone except for her granddaughter, Barbara, her grandson, Alfred, having left Europe for Costa Rica. Patricia became engaged to be married in the summer of 1947 to Captain Lord Brabourne of the Coldstream Guards, and in October, the couple was married at Romsey Abbey in the village of Romsey near Broadlands. The wedding took place in the presence of the King and Queen as well as the Princesses Elizabeth and Margaret, who were bridesmaids. Victoria, Alice, and Philip

---

(*) *Princess Barbara of Prussia (1920-1994) – Bobby's daughter. She married in 1954, Duke Christian Ludwig of Mecklenburg-Schwerin (1912-1996), the second son and heir to the last Grand Duke of Mecklenburg-Schwerin. Barbara and Christian Ludwig had two daughters: Donata and Edwina. After her grandmother's death, Barbara inherited Hemmelmark. With her husband's help, they ran the estate for several decades. Later, part of the Hemmelmark property was sold to a private buyer, while Barbara's descendants continue owning parts of it.*
(**) *Prince Alfred of Prussia, Bobby's son (1924-2013).*
(***) *Grand Duchess Olga Alexandrovna (1882-1960), Nicholas II's youngest sister.*
(****) *May's brother Alexander, 1st Earl of Athlone and his wife, Princess Alice of Albany.*

attended as well. It was said to be the first time that Elizabeth and Philip were photographed together.

Dickie was striving towards the pinnacle of the Royal Navy as the war ended. He continued to be Supreme Commander in South East Asia, and as such was responsible as he put it, for one hundred and twenty eight million people. The decisions he made during that period after he accepted the Japanese surrender in Singapore were, he said, dictated by history, and by Victoria's excellent advice:

My mother said, 'Don't worry about what people think now. Don't ever work for popularity. Above all, don't care what the newspapers say. What is important is that your decisions should be clear and stand up to history. So all you've got to think about is whether your children and grandchildren will think you've done well.'[8]

Not only was Victoria prescient, like her grandmother, but her advice was, as ever, sound. Many today would be well-served by such counsel. Dickie came home a hero and was now on his way to becoming First Sea Lord, the title his father tragically had to give up in 1914. It was a deep and personal ambition that would come to fruition in 1955.

In 1947, he and Edwina went to India as its last viceregal couple. It was flattering for Dickie to have the responsibility of what would prove to be an extremely difficult 'handover', but Victoria was not the least gratified for her son. She, in fact, once again objected, thinking, as she had been conditioned to do, that if it all went wrong, they would blame him. This is hardly surprising considering what had happened to Prince Louis in 1914. She was tremendously suspicious of the intentions of politicians, and felt that they had ruined her husband. She feared that they would use Dickie as a scapegoat since *"Politicians are incorrigible."*[9] Patricia Mountbatten says that this was the first time she saw her grandmother swear. Luckily it went well enough under very harrowing circumstances.

Another more positive development was Alice's continued good mental health. She had successfully combated her psychological and emotional problems, and wanted to found a nursing order in Greece as her Aunt Ella had done so many years before in Russia. It was not a completely successful venture and Alice never actually became a nun, though she always appeared in the habit.* She spent the Second World War in Athens working as a lay sister and incidentally bravely rescuing a Jewish family by hiding them in her apartment. Her lifelong deafness came in very handily when the Gestapo would try to question her. She would pretend not to understand though she could lip-read in five languages. They would just dismiss her as a crazy old nun. Nevertheless, she was hardly without her wits and is recognized today by Yad Va'Shem as a Righteous Gentile. Not only that, but she had been able, in a normal manner, to recover from the harrowing deaths of her daughter, Cecile, and Don, as well as Sophie's husband, and her own estranged husband. She spent most of her time in Athens, but would come to England to care for her mother who was becoming increasingly arthritic and fragile.

Meanwhile, the plans for Philip were coming to fruition. He had taken the name of Mountbatten, though that had never been his mother or father's name. Princess Alice had, of course, been a Battenberg until she married Andrew. He renounced his Greek titles and became a naturalized British subject and so Prince Philip of Greece and Denmark became

---

(*) Perhaps it was just as well. Victoria remarked, "Whoever heard of a nun who smoked and played canasta." (Lady Mountbatten to author, April 25, 2003)

Lieutenant Philip Mountbatten, RN. Victoria felt that this would be the best thing for her grandson and would give him a firm basis for his life, as well as a fixed career. It seemed in this, that he was going the way of his grandfather. There had been hints all along, and comments from many members of the family, of another reason for the naturalization. The Duchess of Kent thought it a good thing as it would be an asset for other matters.[10]

Early in 1944, Victoria wrote to Dickie that as Philip *"has not touched on the subject you spoke about to me with reference to his future, I also refrain from doing so."*[11] Later that year, Alice wrote to Philip on his birthday and mentioned that she has heard he had been to Coppins for Easter *"paid an interesting visit as well as lunching with a certain young lady & her parents before you left."*[12] That young lady was, of course, Princess Elizabeth.

The King and Queen gave their consent to the engagement in January of that year; however, it remained a secret until the summer. In July, Buckingham Palace officially announced the engagement of Philip to Princess Elizabeth. Philip stayed at Kensington Palace that summer along with Alice. Victoria was getting ready for the wedding by having the drawing room of her apartments painted, and since the family was frequently there, the excitement was intense. Alice wrote to Dickie, who continued in India, that Victoria was *"delighted as she is very fond of Lilibet & likes her character very much."*[13] However, there was one snag – the German sisters could not be invited. It was obviously still impolitic to invite great numbers of any German Royal Family – even sisters. There was much, though, to rejoice. Victoria with her sense of history and family was overjoyed about so many things. She wrote to May:

> I am touched & grateful to you for sending me your Victoria & Albert order for use on the wedding-day of our grandchildren....How well I remember my Alice's pride at being one of your bridesmaids & now my granddaughter Pamela is to be one of the bridesmaids to your granddaughter.[14]

The wedding took place November 20, 1947 at Westminster Abbey and Victoria was one of the proud signers of the marriage certificate along with Nada, Edwina, Dickie, Alice and Lady Patricia Ramsay, formerly Princess Patricia of Connaught. Philip, who wore his grandfather's, Prince Louis, sword for the ceremony, probably felt slightly let down that his sisters could not be there. However, the King created him Duke of Edinburgh, and a host of other titles just before the wedding.

The festivities were considered relatively austere because of the post-war rationing. Indeed, the material for Princess Elizabeth's dress of pearl satin, with clouds of tulle, seed pearls, and crystal, with a fifteen-foot long train and designed by Norman Hartnell, had all been bought with ration coupons. The Princess received thousands of presents, which were all laid out at St. James Palace.

Victoria was now in her late eighties, and did little traveling. Mostly it was just back and forth from Kensington Palace to Broadlands. She was lucky that outside of the childhood illnesses of scarlet fever and diphtheria and later, the bout of typhoid from which she suffered when a young woman, she was never seriously ill. She had an incredible constitution, though she continued to have circulatory problems and suffer with arthritis. She was exceedingly fit for a woman of her age, and walked every day with a firm stride, but affects of chain-smoking and the frailties of old age were decidedly setting in.

As her long life crept to its close, she undoubtedly felt as though she had a foot in two worlds. With her friend May, whom she considered among other things, her grandmotherly colleague,[15] and the few others still alive, she reminisced about the old days: the 'Royal Mob'*, taking sepia brownie pictures of one another, sailing on large yachts, walking through the countryside of Germany or Russia, hunting for mushrooms, attending Queen Victoria for tea, or sneaking cigarettes, showing themselves at some ceremony or another, looking regal, but always complaining and gossiping about one another.

And then there was the much less colorful and different world of the present. Dickie was back in the Royal Navy, having returned from India in the spring of 1948. Irène was still alive but Victoria no longer visited Germany. The two wars had the inevitable effect of estranging, at least a little, the sisters, even though they were the last of their immediate family's generation. That did not mean that they did not keep in touch, but it was more sporadic than before.

As the year progressed, Victoria continued to slow down considerably. There was no specific illness, but was weakening. There were colds, and problems with circulation, as well as the constant pain she suffered with her chilblains – nothing major, but annoyances, nonetheless. Just before the birth of Prince Charles she wrote a letter to May thanking her for *"your note & your kind thought of sending me some of your excellent nourishing food to help me pick up quickly after the stupid cold I have suffered from."*[16] The Dowager Queen was proving to be the loving friend of Victoria's old age. May also consistently sent Victoria very welcome checks. It was a consideration of which most people knew nothing.

On November 14, Princess Elizabeth gave birth to Prince Charles Philip Arthur George at Buckingham Palace, Philip's firstborn and Victoria's great-grandson. Charles was named for King Haakon of Norway, whose original name, before he went to Norway to be King, had been Charles.[17] Victoria must have been thrilled to hold this baby who would one day be King of England. She attended the christening ceremony December 15, 1948. It was probably her last major family occasion. She wore grey, pearls, and a black hat. The infant was christened by the Archbishop of Canterbury, wearing the royal christening robe of white silk and Honiton lace that had been used for Queen Victoria's children and subsequent progeny. His godparents were the King, May, Princess Margaret, the King of Norway, Prince George of Greece, Patricia Brabourne, Princess Elizabeth's maternal great-Uncle, David Bowes-Lyon, and Victoria. According to the Archbishop, the baby was *"as quiet as a mouse' as he was bathed in water specially brought from the River Jordan, a royal tradition dating back to the Crusades."*[18]

Charles' biographer Anthony Holden made the observation that:

> *...the room contained four grand-daughters of Queen Victoria – the Dowager Marchioness of Milford Haven, Princess Marie Louise, Princess Alice, Countess of Althone, and Lady Patricia Ramsay – all of whom had themselves worn the same christening robes.*[19]

There is a photograph of the occasion, perhaps the last official one of Victoria, with the baby Prince's sponsors. Victoria is sitting on one side of Princess Elizabeth, while May is seated on the other. It is a nice symmetry.

Irène, of course, was not there; however May did not forget her and sent her photographs of the newborn and his parents. She thanked May warmly saying: *"I have to thank you too for a delightful photo of Elisabeth [sic], Philip & their sweet Baby Charles, that*

(*) Now, once again, sadly dwindled with the death of Princess Helena Victoria, Aunt Helena's eldest daughter, "Thora," as she was called within the family circle, died in London on Masrch 13, 1948.

212

you sent me..., he looks such an adorable child!" and went on to remember *"Fancy – one Xmas I spent with Harry at Hong Kong & dear Grandmama had managed to send each of us an Xmas card – arriving on the day itself with such kind words. It was 1898 & I treasure it still."*[20]

Certainly the christening day was full of remembrances of their dear Grandmother, but for Victoria, the day also carried other meaning as well. She undoubtedly experienced some great satisfaction that this great-grandson might someday be King of England. With the prejudice that Prince Louis had experienced during his life and the petty annoyances from relations, such as Cousin Willy and Uncle Sasha of Russia about Louis' less than perfect pedigree, the position of this child would have been vindication indeed.

****

Victoria's last few years were quiet. She and Irène did not visit, though they did correspond. She, herself, was just as irascible and energetic as was possible for her to be. She continued to talk unceasingly, and loved answering the phone. Her grandson commented on her loquaciousness saying that *"[c]onversation with her brother and others of her generation was pretty competitive."*[21] She was inexhaustible in her habit of smoking and when her doctors advised her to quit or at least to halve her daily intake, she did so, cutting her cigarettes in half, and smoking as much as ever.

Her last letters to Queen Mary and Dickie were in May of 1950, as her health deteriorated causing real concern to her children. As the summer came, Victoria was suffering from bronchitis and she was endlessly frustrated by waking up every morning. Louise told May's brother, Alexander, who in turn told May that *"dear Victoria is not easy to nurse because she wants to die!"*[22] As a matter of fact, she was quite adamant about wanting to die at home, in Kensington Palace, and she by no means wanted to linger – as the summer wore on, life for her seemed to go on and on. It didn't help that people who had come to say goodbye had to make second visits. *"She would wake up in the morning and say: 'Am I still here? I'm not supposed to be here.'"*[23]

A great event in the summer of 1950 was that Princess Elizabeth had her second child, Princess Anne, on August 16. There was general rejoicing and Victoria was gratified that another great-grandchild was born. During that last summer, there were times when Victoria 'picked up' a little, however, those times were temporary, and she simply declined. In August she had a heart attack and the bronchitis from which she often suffered got much worse. Indeed, by September the case was looking hopeless. Though he didn't want to distress anyone, Dickie, in a pragmatic way his mother would have endorsed, began to make the necessary arrangements.

On the morning of September 24, 1950, Victoria, Princess of Hesse and by Rhine, Princess Louis of Battenberg, the Dowager Marchioness of Milford Haven, died peacefully at Kensington Palace, at the age of eighty-seven. Her remaining children were with her. Dickie remarked in his diary that she looked very sweet at the end and that it was sad, but beautiful.

Epilogue

September 1950 – November 1953

Victoria left a letter for her family in which she expressed her deep regard for them. She continued,

> *The bitterest grief in my life has been the loss of Georgie. You will miss me I know, but let it be a comfort to you to realize that the best part of my life & on the whole it has been a happy one, was ended when your dear father died & that I am ready & willing to enter into my rest at any time now.*[1]

On September 28 there was a small private service at the Chapel Royal. This was only for closest relatives, friends, such as the Crichtons, Baroness von Buxhoeveden, and some of Victoria's household, including her devoted lady's maid of nearly fifty years, Miss Pye, or as Prince Philip called her, the Pye-crust. Though Irène was not able to attend she wrote to May:

> *I am deeply touched by your kind sympathy at the loss of our dear Victoria we shall miss so terribly. Thank God that you still have Algy & Alice of your generation. You cannot imagine what a comfort it was to Victoria – all your kindness to her – of which she so often told me & was such a comfort to her – such a dear link with old times & the happy past – it is sad when one grows so lonely in age, even when all the many young generations are so kind to one. How dear of Bertie suggesting that a Destroyer should take the coffin over to Cowes – so that her remains can be placed by Ludwig's – her Louis. – For you it also needs a brave heart – that you have ever shown in these especially difficult times – God be with you dear May –*

> *Affectionate love to you, Irene.*[2]

Victoria lay at the Chapel Royal at St. James Palace while the King decreed family mourning. She was subsequently conveyed from there to the Isle Wight where she was buried alongside Prince Louis at St. Mildred's Church in Whippingham.

A chapel devoted to the Battenberg family is contained inside of St Mildred's. The sarcophagi of Prince and Princess Henry of Battenberg rest there, and along the walls are many interesting commemorative plaques and items associated with the family. Those for the children of Prince and Princess Louis Battenberg are on one end: Princess Alice of Greece, Queen Louise of Sweden, Prince George, Second Marquess of Milford Haven, and the Earl Mountbatten of Burma. Outside in the little churchyard stand the graves of Prince and Princess Louis. There is a large cross surrounded by shrubbery, and some tall trees in the background. The view overlooks the River Medina.

It was most appropriate that Princess Victoria was there in the Isle of Wight, where she had had a home, Kent House, and, of course, where she had visited the Queen at Osborne House on so many occasions. It was also a place with many naval associations and Dickie remarked in his diary that she would have been happy to feel that the navy had buried her.[3]

Victoria was eulogized in *The Times* of London as a calm presence and a woman of a retiring nature. Her family, possibly, might not have agreed with that last assessment. The papers no doubt thought this because, unlike her more glamorous sisters, she led such a private life. Had she not been often seen in the Court Circulars, she might have been the perfect Victorian lady who was only in the papers at her birth, marriage, and death. However, she was also commended for being constantly helpful to charities and other worthy causes. She was the honorary President of National Society for Cancer Relief, President of the Ladies Naval Luncheon Club, and Vice-Patron of the Central Committee of the Royal Naval Friendly Union of Sailors' Wives.

Irène wrote to Dickie that the fact *"that I could not see her once more is a great grief to me. ... Mama's courage & loving heart were wonderful & her loving advice I always had from her, in so many ways."*[4] It was unfortunate that the war and its aftermath kept Victoria and Irène from meeting again. However, it may have been just as well, as with so many bitter events to divide them, their relationship would never have been the same.

Accolades came from other relatives as well. Victoria's niece-in-law, Lady Irene Carrisbrooke, who was married to her Aunt Beatrice's only surviving son, Alexander ("Drino"), wrote to Dickie that his mother gave *"always such wonderful sane advice, & had one of those rare things, an out-look on life which discarded the unnecessary things (which so many cling to) & kept her eyes on what really mattered."*[5] Harold Wernher, Nada's brother-in-law wrote to Dickie, *"Without doubt she was the most outstanding woman I have ever met. She did not grow mentally old, but remained alert and up to date in a changing world."*[6] He also remarked that she was a woman who had much sadness in her life.

Her nephew Lu, gave an interesting, loving, and yet extremely honest assessment of her character. He wrote to Dickie that he was struck again and again at her

> *greatness...her fanatical intellectual honesty and her very loving understanding for anything human. There was absolutely nothing bogus and nothing hypocritical about her, a very rare thing, I have found, amongst people of her generation. It is very sad to think that our world will now have to do without her astringent criticism and always loving, though not always forgiving understanding.*[7]

Old friends weighed in, though not many of them remained. Louise wrote to Lady Drury, who had worked with Victoria in the Royal Naval Friendly Union of Sailors' Wives. In responding to her letter of sympathy, Louise wrote that *"the kind thoughts of an old friend of our dear mother really has meant much to us.... You were too one of her few old friends left, starting with those happy times in Malta...."* She also expressed how tired and weary Victoria was of this life though her brain was *"as active as ever...."*[8]

On October 24, at the decree of the King, there was a memorial service for Victoria. It was attended by the King and Queen, as well as members of their family. The Mountbattens, of course, attended as well as Lady Patricia Ramsay, Drino, Peg and Lu, the Badens, the Hohenlohe-Lagenburgs and Wernhers. As well, there were representatives from Greek and Swedish delegations, and the faithful friends, the Baroness von Buxhoeveden, and the Crichtons. Alice and Louise were unable to attend since both of them had already returned to their respective homes.

Dickie wrote his mother's epitaph:

Then come what will and come what may!
As long as thou dost live, 'tis day.
And if the world through we must roam,
where ere thou art, there is my home
I see thy face so dear to me,
Shades of the future I do not see.

Victoria's death was truly the end of an era. There were few of the forty-two grandchildren of Queen Victoria still alive: Irène, Patricia Ramsay, Alice Althlone, and several others, but perhaps, none had been as close to their grandmother and understood her quite so well, as had Victoria. Being one of the last of her generation, she had always endeavored to live her life up to her grandmother's standards, using everything she had learned from the Queen as a guide. Paramount to her, however, was that she always did her duty; she was completely honest and constantly sought out the truth along with a keen sense of honor and loyalty.

****

Irène lived on at Hemmelmarck quietly for several more years, devoting herself largely to good works. She was Honorary Chairman of the German Red Cross, and founded the Heinrich Children's Hospital in Kiel. After the war she gave up living in the big house and *"lived modestly and worked unremittingly until her death"* in a small cottage on the estate.[9] She still kept in touch with relatives in England after Victoria's death and wrote to May on the occasion of her eighty-fifth birthday nostalgically,

It is such a pleasure to know how fond my mother was of your dear Parents & of us being taken to visit your grandmother...Many instances are impressed on my memory of long ago – which crop up more & more now as one grows older – & are quite fresh in ones memory....It is such a comfort to know you are there still – that ones thoughts can recall you in Marlborough house, where we last met, my dear Sister Victoria accompanying me to you.[10]

She died on November 11, 1953 with her granddaughter and heir, Barbara at her side. Louise went to the funeral at Eckernförde, along with hundreds of other mourners.

****

Now, at last, their respective roles in history played out, some basic themes in the lives of the four Hessian Princesses emerge. Alix and Ella, the wives of autocratic men of a fallen empire, were very much nineteenth century women. Both were, though most particularly Alix, grounded in the traditions of absolute monarchy, lavish pageantry, the mysteries of religion, and the prescribed roles of a divinely appointed Imperial Family. Victoria and Irène, possibly because of their longevity, though most probably not in Victoria's case, fell squarely into the twentieth century. They might, in fact, be seen as metaphors for that chaotic period. Irène, in some ways self-deluding, was the royal princess to the end as her family quietly slipped into obscurity. Victoria, however, was the matriarch of the aristocratic

Mountbatten clan. They went on to become a most successful and modern family.

In the end, the four women, imbued from birth in a world view that is almost inconceivable today, fashioned their lives according to these now arcane constructs and consequently, met their inevitable fates.

The Grand Dukes of Hesse and by Rhine

Ludwig II = Wilhelmine of Baden
1777-1848   1788-1836

Ludwig III
1806-1877
=Mathilde
of Bavaria
1813-1862

Karl = Elisabeth of Prussia
1809-1877   1815-1885

Alexander = Julie v. Hauke
1823-1888   1825-1895

See Tree on Page 222

Marie
1824-1880
= Alexander II
of Russia
1818-1881

Alexander III
1845-1894
= Dagmar
of Denmark
1847-1928

Ludwig IV
1837-1892
= Alice of Great Britain
1843-1878

Heinrich
1838-1900
1)= Caroline Willich gen von Poellnitz
1848-1879
2)= Emilie Hrzic de Topuska
(1868-1961)

Anna
1843-1865
= Friedrich Franz II
of Mecklenburg-Schwerin
1823-1883

Wilhelm
1845-1900
= Josephine
Bender
1857-1942

Counts v. Nidda and v. Dornberg

von Lichtenberg descendants

Victoria
1863-1950
= Louis of
Battenberg
1854-1921

Elisabeth = Serge
1864-1918   1857-1905

Irène
1866-1953
= Henry of Prussia
1862-1929

Ernst Ludwig (1868-1937)
1)= Victoria Melita
of Edinburgh (1876-1936)
2)= Eleonor
of Solms-Hohensolms-Lich
1871-1937

Frederick
1870-1873

Marie
1874-1878

Alix = Nicholas II
1872-1918   1868-1918

Alice
1885-1969
= Andrew of Greece
1882-1944

See Tree on Page 221

Waldemar
1889-1945
= Calixta
of Lippe
1895-1982

Sigismund
1896-1978
= Charlotte Agnes
of Saxe-Altenburg
1899-1989

Heinrich
1900-1904

Elisabeth
1895-1903

1 son, 1 daughter

Olga
1895-1918

Tatiana
1897-1918

Maria
1899-1918

Anastasia
1901-1918

Alexis
1904-1918

Cecile = George Donatus
1911-1937   1906-1937

Margaret Geddes = Ludwig
1913-1997   1908-1968

Ludwig
1931-1937

Alexander
1933-1937

Johanna
1936-1939

EUROHISTORY.COM

UK and Hessian Genealogical Connections *

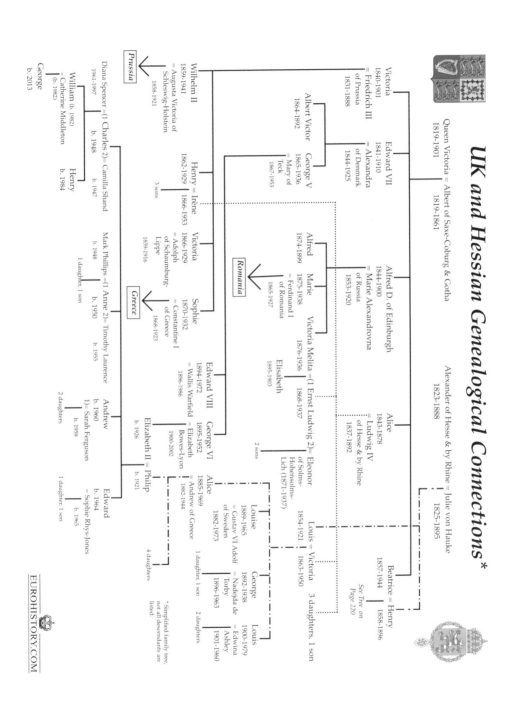

Queen Victoria = Albert of Saxe-Coburg & Gotha
1819-1901   1819-1861

Alexander of Hesse & by Rhine = Julie von Hauke
1823-1888   1825-1895

Victoria
1840-1901
= Friedrich III
of Prussia
1831-1888

Edward VII
1841-1910
= Alexandra
of Denmark
1844-1925

Alfred D. of Edinburgh
1844-1900
= Marie Alexandrovna
of Russia
1853-1920

Alice
1843-1878
= Ludwig IV
of Hesse & by Rhine
1837-1892

Beatrice = Henry
1857-1944   1858-1896

See Tree on
Page 220

Prussia

Wilhelm II
1859-1941
= Augusta Victoria of
Schleswig-Holstein
1858-1921

Albert Victor
1864-1892

George V
1865-1936
= Mary of
Teck
1867-1953

Henry = Irène
1862-1929   1866-1953

Victoria
1866-1929
= Adolph
of Schaumburg-
Lippe
1859-1916

Alfred
1874-1899

Marie
1875-1938
= Ferdinand I
of Romania
1865-1927

Victoria Melita =(1 Ernst Ludwig 2)= Eleonor
1876-1936   1868-1937   of Solms-
                           Hohensolms-
Elisabeth   Lich (1871-1937)
1895-1903

Louis = Victoria   3 daughters, 1 son
1854-1921   1863-1950

3 sons

Sophie
1870-1932
= Constantine I
of Greece
1868-1923

Edward VIII
1894-1972
= Wallis Warfield
1896-1986

George VI
1895-1952
= Elizabeth
Bowes-Lyon
1900-2002

2 sons

Alice
1885-1969
= Andrew of Greece
1882-1944

Louise
1889-1965
= Gustav VI Adolf
of Sweden
1882-1973

George
1892-1938
= Nadejda de
Torby
1896-1963

Louis
1900-1979
= Edwina
Ashley
1901-1960

Romania

Greece

Diana Spencer =(1 Charles 2)= Camilla Shand
1961-1997   b. 1948   b. 1947

Mark Phillips =(1 Anne 2)= Timothy Laurence
b. 1948   b. 1950   b. 1955

Andrew
b. 1960
1)= Sarah Ferguson
b. 1959

Elizabeth II = Philip
b. 1926   b. 1921

Edward
b. 1964
= Sophie Rhys-Jones
b. 1965

1 daughter, 1 son

2 daughters

4 daughters

William (b. 1982)
= Catherine Middleton
(b. 1982)

Henry
b. 1984

2 daughters

1 daughter, 1 son

1 daughter, 1 son

George
b. 2013

* Simplified family tree,
not all descendants are
listed.

The Princely House of Battenberg

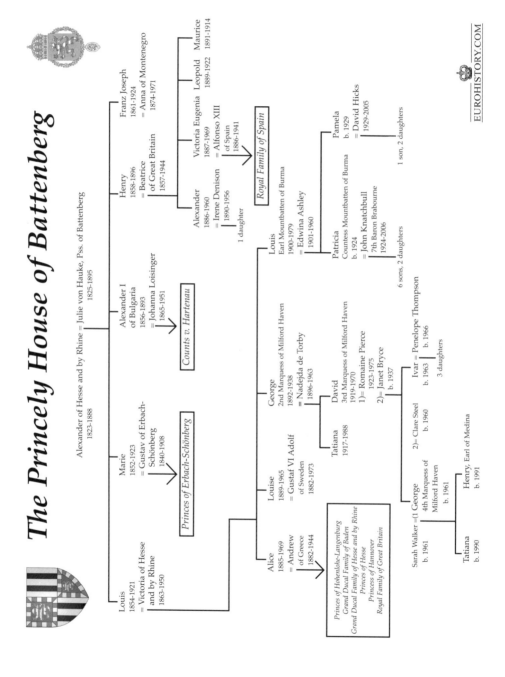

Alexander of Hesse and by Rhine = Julie von Hauke, Pss. of Battenberg
1823-1888 1825-1895

Louis
1854-1921
= Victoria of Hesse and by Rhine
1863-1950

Marie
1852-1923
= Gustav of Erbach-Schönberg
1840-1908

Princes of Erbach-Schönberg

Alexander I of Bulgaria
1856-1893
= Johanna Loisinger
1865-1951

Counts v. Hartenau

Henry
1858-1896
= Beatrice of Great Britain
1857-1944

Alexander
1886-1960
= Irene Denison
1890-1956

1 daughter

Victoria Eugenia
1887-1969
= Alfonso XIII of Spain
1886-1941

Royal Family of Spain

Leopold
1889-1922

Maurice
1891-1914

Franz Joseph
1861-1924
= Anna of Montenegro
1874-1971

Alice
1885-1969
= Andrew of Greece
1882-1944

Louise
1889-1965
= Gustaf VI Adolf of Sweden
1882-1973

George
2nd Marquess of Milford Haven
1892-1938
= Nadejda de Torby
1896-1963

Louis
Earl Mountbatten of Burma
1900-1979
= Edwina Ashley
1901-1960

Tatiana
1917-1988

David
3rd Marquess of Milford Haven
1919-1970
1)= Romaine Pierce
1923-1975
2)= Janet Bryce
b. 1937

Patricia
Countess Mountbatten of Burma
b. 1924
= John Knatchbull
7th Baron Brabourne
1924-2006

6 sons, 2 daughters

Pamela
b. 1929
= David Hicks
1929-2005

1 son, 2 daughters

Sarah Walker =(1 George
b. 1961   4th Marquess of
            Milford Haven
            b. 1961

Ivar = Penelope Thompson
b. 1963   b. 1966

3 daughters

2)= Clare Steel
    b. 1960

Tatiana
b. 1990

Henry, Earl of Medina
b. 1991

Princes of Hohenlohe-Langenburg
Grand Ducal Family of Baden
Grand Ducal Family of Hesse and by Rhine
Princes of Hesse
Princess of Hanover
Royal Family of Great Britain

The Descendants of Andrew and Alice of Greece

Louis, 1st Marquess of Milford Haven = Victoria of Hesse and by Rhine
1854-1921 | 1863-1950

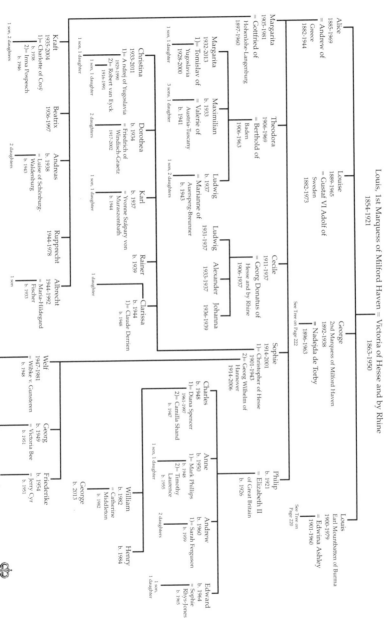

Alice
1885-1969
= Andrew of Greece
1882-1944

Louise
1889-1965
= Gustaf VI Adolf of Sweden
1882-1973

George
2nd Marquess of Milford Haven
1892-1938
= Nadejda de Torby
1896-1963

See Tree on Page 222

Louis
Earl Mountbatten of Burma
1900-1979
= Edwina Ashley
1901-1960

See Tree on Page 220

Margarita
1905-1981
= Gottfried of Hohenlohe-Langenburg
1897-1960

Theodora
1906-1969
= Berthold of Baden
1906-1963

Cecile
1911-1937
= Georg Donatus of Hesse and by Rhine
1906-1937

Sophie
1914-2001
1)= Christopher of Hesse
1901-1943
2)= Georg Wilhelm of Hannover
1914-2006

Philip
b. 1921
= Elizabeth II of Great Britain
b. 1926

Kraft
1935-2004
1)= Charlotte of Croÿ
b. 1938
2)= Irma Poespesch
b. 1946

Beatrix
1936-1997

Andreas
b. 1938
= Luise of Schönburg-Waldenburg
b. 1943

Rupprecht
1944-1978

Albrecht
1944-1992
= Maria-Hildegard Fischer
b. 1953

Margarita
1932-2013
1)= Tomislav of Yugoslavia
1928-2000
2)= Robert van Eyck
b. 1916-1991

Maximilian
b. 1933
= Valerie of Austria-Tuscany
b. 1941

Ludwig
b. 1937
= Marianne of Auersperg-Breuner
b. 1943

Ludwig
1931-1937

Alexander
1933-1937

Johanna
1936-1939

Christina
1933-2011
1)= A Andrej of Yugoslavia
1929-1990
2)= Friedrich of Windisch-Graetz
1917-2002

Dorothea
b. 1934
= Friedrich of Windisch-Graetz

Karl
b. 1937
= Yvonne Szápary von Muraszombáth
b. 1944

Rainer
b. 1939

Clarissa
b. 1944
1)= Claude Derrien
b. 1948

Welf
1947-1981
1)= Wibke v. Gunsteren
b. 1948

Charles
b. 1948
1)= Diana Spencer
1961-1997
2)= Camilla Shand
b. 1947

Anne
b. 1950
1)= Mark Phillips
b. 1948
2)= Timothy Laurence
b. 1955

Andrew
b. 1960
1)= Sarah Ferguson
b. 1959

Edward
b. 1964
= Sophie Rhys-Jones
b. 1965

Georg
b. 1949
= Victoria Bee
b. 1951

Friederike
b. 1954
= Jerry Cyr
b. 1951

George
b. 2013

William
b. 1982
= Catherine Middleton
b. 1982

Henry
b. 1984

1 son, 2 daughters

1 son, 2 daughters

1 son, 1 daughter

1 son, 1 daughter

3 sons, 1 daughter

1 son, 2 daughters

2 daughters

1 son, 1 daughter

1 daughter

1 daughter

2 daughters

2 daughters

1 son

1 daughter

2 daughters

1 son, 1 daughter

1 son, 1 daughter

Appendix A

Victoria's poem for "Frittie."

1874 May 29 Death has been here and
borne away
Dear Fritzie from our side
So pale upon the bed he
lay
When we stood at his side

A lovely angel carried him
Up into yon bright heaven
To heaven where there is
no sin
And sins are all forgiven

It was very hard to part with one
Whom we all love so dearly
How very, very fast he could run
And prattled each world nearly

Oh, weep not mother I beseach
thee
For Fritzie is in heaven
In heaven where angels sing
with glee
And sins are all forgiven

Victoria.

End Notes

Archive Sources and Some Abbreviations

BA – Broadlands Archives.
Grand Duchess Xenia Archive.
Hemmelmarck Archives.
HI Hoover Institute Archives, Collection Title: M. Giers, Box Number 39, Folder ID: 12.
HS - Family Archives, Darmstadt OR Hessisches Staatarchiv Darmstadt Section D 22, 24, 26, (Grand Ducal Family Archives).
RA – Royal Archives, Windsor Castle.
RAM – Royal Archives Madrid.
SA – Southampton Archives, Hartley Library, the University of Southampton.
AF – Empress Alexandra Feodorovna ("Alix")
EF – Grand Duchess Serge Alexandrovich ("Ella")
EFP – Empress Friedrich Wilhelm of Prussia
EL – Grand Duke Ernst Ludwig of Hesse and by Rhine ("Ernie")
GDA – Grand Duchess Alice of Hesse and by Rhine
GDE – Grand Duchess Eleonore of Hesse and by Rhine ("Onor")
MB – The Earl Mountbatten of Burma ("Dickie")
NK – Nona Kerr
PI – Princess Henry of Prussia (Irène)
QV – Queen Victoria
VMH – Victoria Milford Haven (Princess Victoria of Hesse and by Rhine, Princess Louis Battenberg)

Prologue and Chapter One

1. Invitation courtesy of Argyll Etkin Limited.
2. Christopher Hibbert, ed., Queen Victoria in Her Letters and Journals (New York: Viking, 1985), 175.
3. Victoria Milford Haven, Recollections 1863-1914 (Darmstadt: ms. not published Eingang 4. XII 1969. Hess. Staatsarchiv D 24 64/1), 1, hereafter "Rec."
4. RA VIC/ Z 15/8.
5. April 18, 1863, RA VIC/ Add U 32/12.
6. Hibbert, 175.
7. E. F. Benson, Queen Victoria's Daughters (New York, London: D. Appleton-Century Company Incorporated, 1938), 58.
8. Nina Epton, Victoria and her Daughters (New York: W.W. Norton & Company, Inc., 1971), 90.
9. Benson, 62.
10. Epton, 98.
11. Hector Bolitho, ed., Letters of Queen Victoria from the Archives of the House of Brandenburg-Prussia, trans. by Mrs. J. Pudney and Lord Sudley (New Haven: Yale University Press, 1938), 125.
12. George Earle Buckle, ed., Letters of Queen Victoria: A Selection From Her Majesty's Correspondence and Journal Between the Years 1862 and 1878, 2 vols. (New York: Longmans, Green & Company, 1926) vol. 1 (Extract from the Queen's Journal, Osborne, July 1, 1862), 40.
13. Ibid.
14. Greg King, "The Hessian Royal Family," Atlantis Magazine, vol. 2, no. 2, 7-25.
15. Rec., 58. Latin translation from: Ronald Allison & Sarah Riddell, eds., Royal Encyclopedia (Macmillian Press, 1991).
16. Ibid., 17.
17. Meriel Buchanan, Ambassador's Daughter (London: Cassell & Company Ltd., 1958), 15.
18. Idem, Diplomacy in Foreign Courts (New York: J. H. Sears and Company, Inc., 1928), 18.
19. Ibid.
20. Idem, Queen Victoria's Relations (London: Cassell & Company Ltd., 1954), 49.
21. Princess Marie Zu Erbach-Schönberg (Princess of Battenberg), Reminiscences (London: George Allen & Unwin Ltd. Reprinted by Royalty Digest, Ticehurst In Sussex, 1996), 25-6.
22. Buchanan, Relations, 50.
23. Ibid.
24. Buchanan, Diplomacy, 19.
25. MB to NK, Dartmouth, November 7, 1916, SA MB1/A2.
26. Prince Louis of Battenberg, Bachelor Recollections of Louis Prince of Battenberg Marquess of Milford Haven 1854-1884.... Written for his wife and children (Southampton: Unpublished in typed ms form. Southampton Archives, Hartley Library), SA MB 6/M/27, 7.
27. RA VIC/ QVJ: 27th April, 1863.

Chapter Two

1. GDA to QV, May 23, 1863 Darmstadt. HRH Princess Helena of Great Britain and Ireland (comp.), Alice Grand Duchess of Hesse Princess of Great Britain and Ireland: Biographical Sketch and Letters with Portraits (New York: G.P. Putnam's Sons, 1884), 47.
2. GDA to QV, June 27, 1863, Alice, 50.
3. Douglas Liversidge, The Mountbattens: From Battenberg to Windsor (London: Arthur Barker Limited, 1978), 18.
4. Count Egon Corti, The Downfall of Three Dynasties, trans. by L. Marie Sieveking and Ian F. D. Morrow. (New York: Books For Libraries Press, 1970), 63-4.
5. Roger Fulford (ed.) Your Dear Letter: Private Correspondence of Queen Victoria and the Crown Princess of Prussia 1865-1871 (New York: Charles Scribner's Sons, 1971), 27.
6. GDA to QV, Alice, Seeheim, June 15, 1865,101.
7. Gerard Noel, Princess Alice: Queen Victoria's Forgotten Daughter (Wilby, Norwich: Michael Russell Ltd., 1974), 195.
8. Alice, 65.
9. Ibid.
10. GDA to QV, Kranichstein, July 10, 1865 Alice, 103.
11 . Epton, 111-114.
12 .David Duff, Hessian Tapestry: The Hesse Family and British Royalty (London: David & Charles, 1979), 120.
13. Princess Marie of Erbach-Schönberg, 25-6.
14. Hajo Holborn, A History of Modern Germany (Princeton, New Jersey: Princeton University Press, 1969), 186.
15. Your Dear Letter, 82-3.
16 . Alice, 142.
17 . RA VIC/QVJ: 23rd August 1866.
18 . Rec., 23.
19. Alice, 276-7.
20. QV to VMH, August 22, 1883, RA VIC/Z 88/12.
21. Your Dear Letter, 121.
22. Ibid., 123.
23. EMP to QV April 22, 1868, Your Dear Letter, 185.
24. QV to EMP, Windsor, June 27, 1868, Ibid., 197.
25. QV to EMP, November 6, 1867, Ibid., 158.
26. GDA to QV, Darmstadt, April 5, 1869, Alice, 213.
27. John Van der Kiste and Bee Jordaan, Dearest Affie...: Alfred, Duke of Edinburgh Queen Victoria's Second Son (Stroud: Alan Sutton, 1984), 50.
28. Prince Louis of Battenberg, 19.
29. Rec., 6.
30. GDA to QV, October 24, 1867, Alice, 186.
31. GDA to QV, Alice, 240.
32. Rec., 5.
33. Ibid., 30.
34. Ibid., 31.
35. Ibid.
36. Ibid., 35.
37. Princess Marie Louise, My Memories of Six Reigns (London: Evans Brothers Limited, 1957), 60-1.
38. Rec., 46-7.
39. Ibid., 8.
40 . George Earle Buckle, ed., Letters of Queen Victoria, vol. 2, QV to EMP, July20, 1870.
41. RA VIC/Z 78/26 and 30, April 11 and May 20, 1871.
42. Rec., 39-40.
43. Alice, 280.
44. VMH, to QV Kranichstein, September 29, [1872], RA VIC/Z 78/60
45. Buchanan, Diplomacy, 20.
46. Richard Hough, Advice to My Grand-daughter Letters from Queen Victoria to Princess Victoria of Hesse (New York: Simon and Schuster, 1975), 3.
47. GDA to QV, Alice 321.
48. VMH to QV, April 7, 1874, RA VIC/Z 78/103
49. Ibid.
50. GDA to QV, Alice, 320.
51. HS Abt. D 24 Nr. 26/2
52. Ibid.
53. Bolitho, QV to Empress Augusta of Prussia, Osborne, April 14, 1875, 205.
54. Ibid.
55. Ibid., QV to Empress Augusta, Balmoral, May 25, 1875, 208.
56. VMH to GDA, June 11, 1876, HS Abt. D 24 Nr. 26/2 1876.
57. Ernst Ludwig, Grossherzog of Hesse and bei Rhein. Erinnertes. Aufzeichnungen des letzten Grossherzogs Ernst Ludwig von Hessen und bei Rhein (Darmstadt: Roether, 1983), 58.
58. GDA to QV, Darmstadt, November 26, 1876, Alice, 348.
59. VMH to QV, June 15, 1877, RA VIC/Z 79/74.

60. Marion Wynn, "Eastbourne Remembers Princess Alice Grand Duchess Louis of Hesse" Royalty Digest, Volume XII, no. 1, July 2002, 8.
61. Hough, Richard, Louis and Victoria: The First Mountbattens (London: Hutchinson & Co, 1974), 29-30.
62. Benson, 161.
63. Marion Wynn, "Eastbourne Remembers Princess Alice Grand Duchess Louis of Hesse" Royalty Digest, Volume XII, no. 1, July 2002, 9.
64. George Earle Buckle, ed., Letters of Queen Victoria, vol. 2, Balmoral, November 13, 1878, Balmoral, QV's journal, 646.
65. The Times of London, December 12, 1878.
66. George Earle Buckle, ed., Letters of Queen Victoria, vol. 2, Balmoral, November, 16, 1878, QV's journal, 646-7.
67. PI to EL, November 9, 1878, HS Abt. D 24 Nr. 36/1A.
68. RA VIC/Z 86/1..
69. George Earle Buckle, ed., Letters of Queen Victoria, vol. 2, Windsor, December, 14, 1878, QV's journal, 654.
70. Ibid., 655.

Chapter Three

1. QV to VMH, December 29, 1878, RA VIC/Z 86/12.
2. VMH to QV, December 16, 1878, RA VIC/Z 86/2.
3. EF to QV, December 16, 1878, RA VIC/Z 86/3.
4. Alice, 206.
5. EF to QV December 23, 1878. RA VIC/Z 86/7.
6. BA S 405.
7. Rec., 50.
8. PI to QV, December 22, 1883 RA VIC/Z 88/22.
9. Greg King, "The Hessian Royal Family," Atlantis Magazine, Vol. 2 No. 2, 50.
10. Princess Marie Louise, My Memories of Six Reigns, 60-1.
11. Buchanan, Diplomacy, 26.
12. Ibid.
13. Rec., 54-5.
14. Ibid., 61-2.
15. VMH to QV, January 14, 1879, RA VIC/Z 86/22.
16. Rec., 51.
17. Ibid.
18. VMH to QV, Darmstadt, March 2, 1879, RA VIC/Z 86/24.
19. VMH to QV, April 26, 1879, RA VIC/Z 86/41.
20. Prince Leopold to PI, July 9, 1879, HS Abt. D 24 Nr. 65/2.
21. VMH to QV, May 17, 1879, RA VIC/Z 86/47.
22. VMH to QV, March 13, 1880, RA VIC/Z 86/109.
23. September, 9, 1879, RA VIC/Z 86/71.
24. VMH to QV, Darmstadt, November 6, 1880, RA VIC/Z 87/5.
25. VMH to QV, July 6, 1879, RA VIC/Z 86/56.
26. EF to QV, September 19, 1879, RA VIC/Z 86/74.
27. Hough, Advice, 15, Windsor Castle, July 4, 1879.
28. VMH to QV, August 1, 1879, RA VIC/Z 86/63.
29. Erinnertes, 77.
30. Ibid.
31. Hough, Advice, 19, Balmoral Castle, September 23, 1879.
32. VMH to QV, October 3, 1879, RA VIC/Z 86/77.
33. VMH to QV, November 15, 1879, RA VIC/Z 86/87.
34. Ibid.
35. Hough, Advice, 21, Windsor Castle, December 12, 1879, Windsor Castle.
36. RA VIC/QVJ: 31st March, 1880.
37. Ibid.
38. Hough, Advice, 23, Villa Hohenlohe, Baden Baden, April 4, 1880.
39. Ibid., 26, Osborne, August 4, 1880.
40. VMH to QV, December 4, 1880, RA VIC/Z 87/9.
41. Ibid.
42. Hough, Advice, 29, Windsor Castle, December 8, 1880.
43. VMH to QV, Darmstadt, December 12, 1880, RA VIC/Z 87/12.
44. VMH to EL, Balmoral, June 12, 1880, HS Abt. D 24 Nr. 35/1a.
45. Hough, Advice, 28-9, Balmoral, October 26, 1880.
46. VMH to QV, Brussels, July 15, 1881, RA VIC/Z 87/42.
47. October 19, 1880, RA VIC/Z 80/95.
48. VMH to QV, Darmstadt, November 6, 1880, RA VIC/Z 87/5.
49. VMH to QV, January 15, 1881, RA VIC/Z 87/20.
50. PI to QV, February 11, 1881, RA VIC/Z 87/24.
51. RA VIC/Z 87/29.

52. EF to QV, March 23, 1881, RA VIC/Z 87/30.
53. VMH to EL, June 3, 1881, HS Abt. D 24 Nr. 35/1a.
54. Rec., 63.
55. Rec., 43.
56. BA S 405.
57. Hough, Advice, 33, Balmoral, August 27, 1881.
58. VMH to QV, January 14, 1882, RA VIC/Z 87/ 78.
59. Roger Fulford, ed. Beloved Mama: Private Corresondence of Queen Victoria and the German Crown Princess 1878 – 1885 (London: Evans Brothers Limited: London, 1981), 111, QV to EMP Windsor Castle, November 26, 1881.
60. VMH to Prince Leopold, Waldeiningen, November 21, 1881 November, RA VIC/Add A 30/440.
61. QV to Prince George, later King George the V, May 31, 1882, RA VIC/AA 10/11.
61. PI to EL, Florence, October 7, 1882, HS Abt. D 24 Nr. 36/1a.
62. Rec., 69-70.
63. VMH to QV, November 27, 1882, RA VIC/Z 87/118.
64. Hough, Advice, 42-3, Osborne, January 1, 1883.
65. VMH to QV, January 9, 1883, RA VIC/Z 87/130.
66. Rec., 65.
67. Hough, Advice, 44-5, Buckingham Palace, March 7, 1883.
68. VMH to QV, April 26, 1883, RA VIC/Z 87/141.
69. VMH to unknown [QV?], September 6, 1883, RA VIC/ H 27/16 1883.
70. VMH to QV, December 13, 1882, RA VIC/Z 87/121.
71. Rec., 72.
72. VMH to QV, Mary 23, 1883, RA VIC/Z 88/4.
73. L&V, 111.
74. Liversidge, The Mountbattens, 62.
75. PI to QV, Houlgate, Maison de Beauvan, July 12, 1883, RA VIC/Z 81/85.
76. Erinnertes, 76.
77. Jerrold M. Packard, Victoria's Daughters (New York: St. Martins Press, 1998), 165.
78. Arthur Ponsonby, Henry Ponsonby: Queen Victoria's Private Secretary: His life from his Letters (London: The Macmillan Company, 1944), 300.
79. Hough, Advice, 48, QV to VMH, Balmoral, June 19, 1883.
80. Ibid., 59, QV to VMH, Osborne, January 21, 1884.
81. Bolitho, 249, QV to Empress Augusta, Osborne, July 27, 1883.
82. Prince Arthur to QV, Bagshot Park, June, 24, 1883, RA VIC/Add A 15/4014.
83. Hough, Advice, 49, Osborne, July 29, 1883.
84. Prince Louis of Battenberg, 309.
85. VMH to QV, August 17, 1883, RA VIC/Z 88/8.
86. QV to VMH, Osborne, August 22, 1883, RA VIC/Z 88/12.
87. Hough, Advice, 54, Balmoral, September 11, 1883.
88. Ibid., 56-57, Balmoral, October, 21, 1883.
89. Ibid.
90. VMH to QV, December 29, 1883, RA VIC/Z/ 88/30.
91. EF to QV, March 1, 1884, RA VIC/Z 88/35.
92. PI to QV, March 1, 1884, RA VIC/Z 88/36.
93. VMH to QV, Maison Beauvau, Houlgate, July 14, 1883, RA VIC/Z 88/7.
94. Hough, Advice, 54, Balmoral, September 11, 1883.
95. VMH to QV, Darmstadt, March 29, 1884, RA VIC/R 12/47.

Chapter Four

1. Ponsonby, 301.
2. Ibid.
3. Hough, Advice, 63, New Palace, Darmstadt, while the Queen was staying there.
4. Prince Louis of Battenberg, 90.
5. VMH to QV, March 12, 1884, RA VIC/Z 88/37.
6. EF to QV, March 15, 1884, RA VIC/Z 88/38.
7. The Times of London, May 1, 1884.
8. Michaela Reid, Ask Sir James: Sir James Reid, Personal Physician to Queen Victoria and Physician-in-Ordinary To Three Monarchs (London: Hodder & Stoughton, 1987), 63-4.
9. RA/VIC/QVJ: 30th April 1884.
10. Ibid.
11. The Times of London, May 1, 1884.
12. Ibid.
13. RA VIC/QVJ: 30th April 1884.
14. Ibid.
15. The Times of London, May 1, 1884.
16. Ibid.

17. RA VIC/QVJ: 30th April, 1884.

18. L&V, 122.

19. VMH to Grand Duke Ludwig, Sennicotts, July 3, 1884, HS Abt. D 24 Nr.11/6 246-49.

20. Rec., 78.

21. Mark Kerr, Prince Louis of Battenberg: Admiral of the Fleet (London: Longmans, Green and Co., 1934), 109-110.

22. RA VIC/ QVJ: 2nd May 1884.

23. EF to QV, Sennicotts, May 22, 1884, RA VIC/Z 88/45.

24. Baroness Sophie von Buxhoeveden, The Life and Tragedy of Alexandra Feodorovna Empress of Russia (London: Longmans, Green and Co., 1930. Reprinted by Royalty Digest, Ticehurst, 1996), 18.

25. May 26, 1884, HS Abt. D 24 Nr. 35/1a.

26. Ibid.

27. EF to QV, Darmstadt, May 31, 1884. RA VIC /Z 88/47.

28. EF to QV, May 24, 1884 RA VIC/ Z 88/46.

29. Rec., 82.

30. Marie, Queen of Romania, The Story of My Life, vol.1, (London: Cassell and Company, Ltd. 1934), 94.

31. Ibid.

32. BA S 372.

33. E. M. Almedingen, An Unbroken Unity (London: The Bodley Head Ltd., 1964, reprinted by Pavlovsk Press), 23.

34. Rec., 83.

35. L&V, 128. Louis later said he was glad he was in England where such pettiness did not exist.

36. VMH to Grand Duke Ludwig, the Royal Yacht Osborne, June 23, 1884, HS Abt. D 24 Nr. 11/6.

37. Hough, Advice, 67, Balmoral Castle, September 29, 1884.

38. Philip Ziegler, Mountbatten: Including His Years as The Last Viceroy of India (New York: Perennial Library; Harper & Row, Publishers, 1985) 24.

39. Princess Marie of Erbach-Schönberg, 183.

40. Prince Louis to Hon. Francis Spring-Rice, a shipmate, June 23, 1885, Kerr, 109-10.

41. VMH to EL, Sennicotts, October 13, 1884, HS Abt. D 24 Nr.35/1b.

42. VMH to EL, Kent House, December 23, 1884, HS Abt. D 24 Nr.35/1.

43. January 23, 1885, HS Abt. D 24 Nr.35/1b.

44. VMH to Grand Duke Ludwig, Sennicotts, July 3, 1884, HS Abt. D 24 Nr.11/6 246-249.

45. Ibid.

46. L&V, 129.

47. Elizabeth Longford, Queen Victoria: Born to Succeed (New York: Harper & Row, 1964), 479.

48. VMH to Grand Duke Ludwig, Kent House, January 3, 1885, HS Abt. Dr 24 Nr. 11/6.

49. VMH to EL, Kent House, January 9, 1885, HS Abt. D 24 Nr.35/1b.

50. PI to QV, February 20, 1885, RA VIC/Z 88/68.

51. RA VIC/QVJ: 25th February 1885.

52. Ibid.

53. PI to QV, February 28, 1885, RA VIC/Z 88/69.

54. VMH to EL, Windsor, March 15, 1885, Abt D 24 Nr.35/1b.

55. SA MB1/T95.

Chapter Five

1. Hough, Advice, 73, QV to VMH, Maison Mottet, Aix Les Bains. April 3, 1885.

2. BA S 372 VMH to QV, August 22 1885.

3. VMH to Grand Duke Ludwig, Windsor Castle, March 21, 1885, HS Abt. D 24 Nr. 11/6 357-60.

4. Ibid.

5. The Times of London, April 27, 1885.

6. PI to QV, Nov 28, 1885, RA VIC /Z 88/89.

7. PI to QV, March 19, 1886, RA VIC /Z 89/10.

8. VMH to EL, Sennicotts, June 23, 1885, HS Abt. D 24 Nr. 35/1b.

9. EL to VMH, Seeheim, June 12, 1885, HS Abt. D 24 Nr. 35/3.

10. VMH to Grand Duke Ludwig, Kent House, January 3, 1885. HS Abt. D 24 Nr. 11/6.

11. Princess Marie of Erbach-Schönberg, 217.

12. Ibid., 218.

13. Christopher Hibbert, Queen Victoria in Her Letters and Journals (Stroud: Sutton Publishing, 2001), 271.

14. Hough, Advice, 76, QV to VMH August 21, 1885.

15. VMH to EL, Darmstadt, September 8, 1885, HS Abt. D 24 Nr. 35/1.

16. Rec., 66-7.

17. VMH to the Prince of Wales, Wolfsgarten, August 26, 1886, RA VIC/T 9/76.

18. VMH to the Prince of Wales, Darmstadt, August 30, 1886, Bertie RA VIC/T 9/79.

19. George Earle Buckle, ed., Letters of Queen Victoria Third Series: A Selection From Her Majesty's Correspondence and Journal Between the Years 1886 and 1901, vol.1, (New York: Longmans, Green & Company, 1930), footnote 205.

20. Ibid., Prince Louis to QV, Jugenheim, September 9, 1886, 205.

21. VMH to Grand Duke Ludwig, Heiligenberg, September 9, 1886, HS Abt. D 24 Nr. 11/6 439-442.

22. BA S 405.

23. PI to QV, September18, 1886, RA VIC /Z 88/120.
24. VMH to Grand Duke Ludwig, Heiligenberg, September 11, 1886. HS Abt. D 24 11/6 443-6.
25. Ibid.
26. George Earle Buckle, ed., Letters of Queen Victoria Third Series Prince Louis to QV, Heiligenberg, September 24, 1886, 214.
27. Rec., 89.
28. VMH to EL, November 25, 1886, HS Abt. D 24 Nr. 35/1b.
29. PI to QV Neues Palais, Darmstadt, December 25, 1886, RA VIC/ Z 89/5.
30. QV to VMH, Windsor, February 20, 1886, BA S 405.
31. QV to VMH, Osborne, Feb 2, 1887, BA S 372.
32. Hough, Advice, 88, Osborne.
33. EL to VMH, Crown Prince's Palace, Berlin, March 26, 1887, HS Abt. D 24 Nr. 35/3.
34. VMH to QV, Darmstadt, April 6, 1887, BA S 372.
35. PI to QV, March 19, 1887, RA VIC /Z 89/10.
36. PI to QV, March 24, 1887, RA VIC /Z 89/11.
37. PI to QV April 6th, 1887, RA VIC /Z 89/13.
38. Lance Salway, Queen Victoria's Grandchildren (Oxford: Signpost Books, Ltd, 1991), 20.
39. Hough, Advice, 89, Windsor , March 2, 1887.
40. Christopher Hibbert, ed., Queen Victoria in Her Letters and Journals (New York: Viking,1985), QV to VMH, March 2, 1887, 301.
41. PI to QV, May 20, 1887, RA VIC /Z 89/17.
42. Prince Alfred of Edinburgh to QV, Naples, June 4, 1887, RA VIC /Z 189/48.
43. QV to VMH, Balmoral, June 10, 1887, BA S 405.
44. George Earle Buckle, ed., Letters of Queen Victoria Third Series, QV's Journal, Buckingham Palace, 320.
45. Theo Aronson, Grandmama of Europe: The Crowned Descendants of Queen Victoria (London: Cassell& Company Ltd., 1973, Reprinted by Royalty Digest, Ticehurst, 1998), 3.
46. L&V, 160.
47. The Times of London, Letter to editor from A. Cooper Key, August 4, 1887.
48. VMH to EL, San Antonio, November 16, 1887, HS Abt. D 24 Nr. 35/1.
49. Rec., 100.
50. Hough, Advice, Osborne, January 2, 1888.
51. Rec., 108.
52. SA MB 11/1/1.
53. VMH to EL, Malta, December 26, 1887, HS Abt. D 24 35/1.
54. PI to QV, December 3, 1887, RA VIC /Z 89/32.
55. Christopher Hibbert, Queen Victoria in Her Letters and Journals (Stroud: Sutton Publishing, 2001), 308.
56. John Van der Kiste, Dearest Vicky, Darling Fritz (Stroud: Sutton, 2001), 204.
57. VMH to EL, March 12, 1888, HS Abt. D 24 Nr. 35/1.
58. BA S 372.
59. Rec., 112.
60. Agatha Ramm, ed. Beloved and Darling Child: Last Letters Between Queen Victoria and Her Eldest Daughter 1886 - 1901 (Stroud: Alan Sutton, 1990), 71-2, QV to EFP, May 21, 1888.
61. The Times of London, February 25, 1889, from a dispatch from Vienna dated February 24.
62. VMH to Grand Duke Ludwig, Darmstadt, February 25, 1889. HS Abt. D 24 Nr. 11/7.
63. BA S 373.
64. VMH to Grand Duke Ludwig, Darmstadt, February 25, 1889 HS Abt. D 24 Nr. 11/7.
65. George Earle Buckle, ed., Letters of Queen Victoria Third Series, vol.1, Buckingham Palace, February 25, 1889, 469-70.
66. Ibid., Count von Hartenau to QV, April 6, 1889.
67. Rec., 151.

Chapter Six

1. Hugo Vickers, Alice: Princess Andrew of Greece (London: Hamish Hamilton, 2000), 125 VMH to QV.
2. PI to QV, January 7, 1888, RA VIC /Z 89/40.
3. PI to QV, Berlin, March 2, 1888, RA VIC /Z 89/43.
4. Illustrated News of London, June 2, 1888.
5. John Van der Kiste, Dearest Vicky, Darling Fritz, 226.
6. Wilhelm II, My Early Life, trans. from the German, (New York: George H. Doran Company, 1926), 302.
7. PI to Louis, July 8, 1888, SA MB1/T76.
8. VMH to the Marquess of Lorne, Wolfsgarten, July 19, 1888, RA VIC/Add A 17/1904.
9. QV to VMH, Windsor, July 4, 1888, BA S 405.
10. Hough, Advice, 94, Balmoral, June 14, 1888.
11. PI to QV, Darmstadt, March 19, 1890, RA QV /Z 91/37.
12. Lubov Millar, Grand Duchess Elizabeth of Russia: New Martyr of the Communist Yoke (Richfield Springs, New York: Nikodemos Orthodox Publication Society, 1991), 53.
13. VMH to QV, Darmstadt, December 22, 1888, BA S 372.
14. EF to Prince Louis of Battenberg, 1889, no date, SA MB1/T95.
15. Hough, Advice, 98-9, Windsor, February 20, 1889.

16. PI to QV, Kiel, February 2, 1889, RA VIC /Z 91/19.
17. Rec., 119.
18. Prince Henry of Prussia to QV, Kiel, March 24, 1889, RA VIC /Z 91/22.
19. VMH to Grand Duke Ludwig, Heiligenberg, June 29, 1889, HS Abt. D 24 Nr. 11/7.
20. Hough, Advice, 100, Pavilion La Rochefoucauld, Biarritz, March 31, 1889.
21. Rec., 122.
22. Christopher Hibbert, ed., Queen Victoria in Her Letters and Journals (New York: Viking, 1985), 317, QV to VMH, October 30, 1889.
23. PI to QV, Kiel, June 17, 1889, RA VIC /Z 91/26.
24. Ibid.
25. Christopher Hibbert, ed., Queen Victoria in Her Letters and Journals, QV to VMH, October, 30, 1889.
26. VMH to QV, November 14, 1889, BA S 373.
27. Hough, Advice, 106, Windsor, July 15, 1890.
28. VMH to QV, Heiligenberg, July 18, 1890, BA S 373.
29. PI to QV, August 25, 1890, RA QV /Z 91/45.
30. PI to QV, Kiel, April 11, 1891, RA QV /Z 91/52.
31. PI to EL, Kiel, January 18, 1891, HS Abt. D 24 Nr. 36/2B.
32. L&V, 168.
33. Chirstopher Hibbert, 318, QV to VMH, December 29, 1890.
34. Hough, Advice, 111, September 18, 1891.
35. QV, September 18, 1891, BA S 405.
36. Christopher Hibbert, ed., Queen Victoria in Her Letters and Journals (Stroud: Sutton Publishing, 2001), 319, QV to Lord George Hamilton, First Lord of the Admiralty, September 5, 1891.
37. RA VIC /Z 93/60.
38. AF to QV, Darmstadt, December 12, 1891, RA VIC /Z 90/17.
39. VMH to QV, Malta, December 10, 1891, RA VIC /Z 475/117.
40. Christopher Hibbert, ed., Queen Victoria in Her Letters and Journals (Stroud: Sutton Publishing, 2001), 322, QV to VMH.
41. Ibid.
42. Ibid.
43. VMH to QV, December 1, 1891, HS Abt. D 24 Nr. 35/3.
44. AF to QV, Darmstadt, January 16, 1892, RA VIC /Z 93/75.
45. PI to QV, Kiel, January 20, 1892, RA VIC /Z 93/110.
46. PI to QV, March 11, 1892, RA VIC /Z 174/9.
47. AF to QV, April 3, 1892, RA VIC /Z 174/33.
48. George Earle Buckle, ed., Letters of Queen Victoria Third Series, vol. 2, 105, QV's journal, Osborne.
49. Margit Fjellman, Louise Mountbatten, Queen of Sweden (London: George Allen and Unwin Ltd., 1968), 33.
50. PI to QV April 3, 1892, RA VIC /Z 174/32.
51. George Earle Buckle, ed., Letters of Queen Victoria, Third Series, vol. 2, 111-2, QV's journal, Neues Palais, Darmstadt.
52. Margit Fjellman, 33.
53. Ibid.
54. AF to QV, Darmstadt, May 9, 1892, RA VIC /Z 174/39.
55. VMH to QV, Heiligenberg, May 21, 1892, BA S 373.
56. QV to VMH, Balmoral, June 2, 1892, BA S 405.
57. AF to QV, June 9, 1892, RA VIC /Z 90/25.
58. RA GVD/ 1st October 1892.
59. VMH to QV, November 24, 1892, RA VIC /Z 90/33.

Chapter Seven

1. QV to VMH, Osborne, January 1, 1893, BA S 405.
2. VMH to EL, London, March 29, 1893, HS Abt. D 24 Nr. 35/1.
3. VMH to EL, Windsor, May 13, 1893, HS Abt. D 24 Nr. 35/2.
4. VMH to QV, Heiligenberg, August 30, 1893, BA S 373.
5. QV to VMH, September 24, 1893, BA S 405.
6. VMH to EL, London, October 24, 1893, HS Abt. D 24 Nr. 35/2.
7. Ibid.
8. George Earle Buckle, ed., Letters of Queen Victoria Third Series, vol. 2, QV's journal.
9. EF to Prince Louis of Battenberg, Moscow, November 8/20, 1893, SA MB1/T95.
10. PI to QV, December 10, 1893, RA VIC /Z 91/90.
11. VMH to QV, November 28, 1893, RA VIC /H 36/118.
12. AF to QV, December 26, 1893, RA VIC /Z 90/66.
13. VMH to EL, Osborne, December 29, 1893, HS Abt. D 24 Nr. 35/2.
14. VMH to EL, January 15, 1894, HS Abt. D24 Nr. 35/2.
15. George Earle Buckle, ed., Letters of QueenVictoria Third Series, vol.2, 394, QV's journal.
16. Ibid., 395, QV's journal.
17. Ibid., QV's journal, 394-5.
18. Marion Wynn, "'Princess Alix was Always Extremely Homely': Visit To Harrogate, 1894," Royalty Digest, vol.XI, no.2, August

1999, 51-4.
19. VMH to QV, Harrogate, June 6, 1894, BA S 373.
20. VMH to QV, Walton, May 23, 1894, BA S 373.
21. AF to QV, Harrogate, June 9, 1894, RA VIC /Z 90/74.
22. Christopher Hibbert, Queen Victoria in Her Letters and Journals (Stroud: Sutton, 2001), 329, QV to VMH, October 21, 1894.
23. Rec., 155.
24. George Earle Buckle, Ed., Letters…, 418, QV's journal.
25. PI to QV, Darmstadt, RA VIC /Z 90/108.
26. The Times of London, October 25, 1894.
27. Baroness Sophie von Buxhoeveden, The Life and Tragedy of Alexandra Feodorovna Empress of Russia, 44.
28. SA MB1/T95.
29. VMH to EL, Malta, March 7, 1895, HS Abt. D 24 Nr. 35/2.
30. Hough, Advice, 130, Grand Hotel Chimiez, Nice, March 31, 1895.
31. Meriel Buchanan, Queen Victoria's Relations (London: Cassell & Company Ltd., 1954), 33.
32. AF to Prince Louis of Battenberg, September 11/24, 1895, SA MB1/T95.
33. Infanta Eulalia to King Carlos of Portugal, Paris, January 5, 1896, RAM.
34. Hough, Advice, 135, February 22, 1896.
35. Christopher Hibbert, Queen Victoria in Her Letters and Journals (Stroud: Sutton, 2001), 331.
36. Sir Frederick Ponsonby, ed., Letters of the Empress Frederick (London: Macmillan and Co., 1929), 238.
37. VMH to QV, Moscow, May 20, 1896, BA S 374.
38. RA VIC/Z 160/2.
39. Ibid.
40. Rec., 168.
41. Ibid., 170.
42. Hough, Advice, Balmoral, June 1, 1896.
43. George Earle Buckle, ed., Letters of Queen Victoria Third Series, vol. 3, 48, Cypher Telegram, Queen Victoria to Sir Nicholas O'Conor, British Ambassador in St. Petersburg, Balmoral, June 4, 1896.

Chapter Eight

1. Rec., 176.
2. PI to EL , Kiel, January 27 1897, HS Abt. D24 Nr. 36/3A.
3. Agatha Ramm, ed., Beloved and Darling Child: Last Letters Between Queen Victoria and Her Eldest Daughter 1886 – 1901 (Stroud: Alan Sutton, 1990), 201-2, QV to EFP, Excelsior Hotel Regina, Cimiez, March 31, 1897.
4. VMH to QV, Malta, April 16, 1897, BA S 374.
5. VMH to EL, Malta, April 24, 1897, HS Abt. D 24 Nr. 35/2.
6. Rec., 180.
7. VMH to NK, August 7, 1900, BA S 383.
8. George Earle Buckle, ed., Letters of Queen Victoria Third Series, vol. 3, 174, QV's journal.
9. Christopher Hibbert, ed., Queen Victoria in Her Letters and Journals (Stroud: Sutton Publishing, 2001), 335.
10. PI to EL, Windsor, May 7, 1898, HS Abt. D 24 Nr. 36/3B.
11. John C.G. Rohl, Wilhelm II: the Kaiser's Personal Monarchy, 1888-1900 (Cambridge: Cambridge University Press, 2004), 630.
12. Greg King, "The Russian Church of St. Mary Magdalene in Darmstadt," Atlantis Magazine, vol. 2, no. 2, 60.
13. EL to VMH, Coburg, Winter 1899, HS Abt. D 24 Nr. 35/3.
14. PI to EL, Kiel, HS Abt. D 24 Nr. 36/3B.
15. EL to VMH, December 31, 1900, HS Abt. D 24 Nr. 35/3.
16. Last letter from QV to VMH, August 9, 1900, BA S 405.
17. Rec., 196.
18. Rec., 198.
19. Rec., 205.
20. Baroness Sophie Buxhoeveden, The Life and Tragedy of Alexandra Feodorovna Empress of Russia, 90, AF to VMH, January 28, 1901.
21. The New York Times, February 3, 1901.
22. Ibid.
23. Ibid.

Chapter Nine

1. PI to the Infanta Eulalia, Kiel, August 19, 1901, RAM.
2. EL to VMH, Neues Palais, November 10, 1901, HS Abt. D 24 Nr. 35/3.
3. Rec., 212.
4. Charlotte Zeepvat, "Alix and Gretchen," Royalty Digest, Volume XIII, no. 8, February 2004, 226-231.
5. EL to VMH, Darmstadt, March 16, 1902, HS Abt. D 24 Nr. 35/3.
6. VMH to NK, Heiligenberg, July 23, 1902, BA S 383.
7. Ibid.
8. David Duff, Hessian Tapestry: The Hesse Family and British Royalty (London: David & Charles, 1979), 292.

9. EL, to VMH, Darmstadt, May 29, 1903, HS Abt. D 24 Nr. 35/3.
10. Rec., 218.
11. Grand Duchess Marie Pavlovna of Russia, Education of a Princess, 50.
12. Prince Louis of Battenberg to Princess Louise of Battenberg, June 9, 1903, SA MB1/T90.
13. Princess Marie of Erbach-Schönberg, 293-4.
14. Ibid.
15. VMH to NK, August 9, 1903, BA S 383.
16. Rec., 226.
17. VMH to NK, November 23, 1903. BA S 383.
18. VMH to EL, Cadogan Square, December 13, 1903, HS Abt. D 24 Nr. 35/2.
19. PI to EL, December 30, 1903, HS Abt. D 24 Nr. 36/3B.
20. EL to VMH, Darmstadt, February 10, 1904, HS Abt. D 24 N4. 35/3.
21. PI to EL, March 8, 1904, HS Abt. D 24 36/3B.
22. PI to the Infanta Eulalia, Kiel, March 15, 1904, RAM.
23. Rec., 233.
24. Rec., 230.
25. For My Grandchildren: Some Reminiscences of Her Royal Highness Princess Alice, Countess of Athlone, 18.
26. The Times of London, January 16, 1905.
27. E.A. Brayley Hodgetts, The Court of Russia in the Nineteenth Century, vol.2 (New York: Charles Scribner's Sons, 1908) 231-3.
28. Rec., 235.
29. Rec., 236.
30. Princess Marie of Erbach-Schönberg, 303.
31. Rec., 236.
32. VMH to NK, March 2, 1905, BA S 383.

Chapter Ten

1. VMH to GDE, Darmstadt, May 5, 1905, HS Abt. D 24 NR. 45/1.
2. Princess Louise to Prince Louis of Battenberg, June 17, 1905, BA S 261.
3. Rec., 243.
4. VMH to GDE, Heiligenberg, October 16 1905, HS Abt. D 24 Nr. 45/1.
5. The Times of London, November 2, 1905.
6. L&V, 229.
7. VMH to MB, January 9, 1944, BA S 362.
8. The Times of London, November 6, 1905.
9. Princess Marie of Erbach-Schönberg, April 27, 1906, 304-5.
10. Rec., 247.
11. VMH to GDE, Illyinskoje, July 27, 1906, HS Abt. D 24 Nr. 45/1.
12. VMH to GDE, Illyinskoje, August 17, 1906, HS Abt. D24 Nr. 45/1.
13. VMH to NK, October 19, 1906, BA S 383.
14. Rec., 237.
15. Princess Marie of Erbach-Schönberg, 374.
16, Rec., 263-4.
17. VMH to GDE, Malta, March 16, 1908, HS Abt. D 24 Nr. 45/1.
18. Rec., 273-4.
19. Ibid., 276.
20. Ibid., 268.
21. Ibid., 271.
22. Ibid., 280.
23. VMH to Queen Mary, May 8, 1910, RA GV/CC 45/324.
24. EL to VMH, June 29, 1910, HS Abt. D 24 Nr. 45/1.
25. Greg King, "Requiem: The Russian Imperial Family's Last Visit to Darmstadt, 1910," Atlantis Magazine, Vol. 2 No.2, 104-113.
26. VMH to GDE, Peterhof, 1911 (?), HS Abt. D 24 Nr. 45/1.
27. Rec., 284.
28. Ibid., 285.
29. Janet Morgan, Edwina Mountbatten: A Life of Her Own (New York: Charles Scribner's Sons, 1991), 100.
30. Rec., 288.
31. VMH to EL, Mall House, December 26, 1912, HS Abt. D 24 Nr. 45/1.
32. David Duff, Hessian Tapestry, 294.
33. Ibid., 295.
34. Ibid.
35. http://www.telegraph.co.uk/history/world-war-one/10991582/Revealed-how-King-George-V-demanded-Britain-enter-the-First-World-War.html
36. The Times of London, February 27, 1913.

Chapter Eleven

1. "Historians say so: The years between 1910 and 1915 were the pleasantest this country [the United States] has ever known." From: Remember When by Allen Churchill.
2. Rec., 294.
3. Ibid., 292.
4. VMH to NK, September 6, 1913, BA S 383.
5. VMH to Princess Louise, Duchess of Argyll, Mon Repos, June 22, 1914, RA VIC/Add 17/1200.
6. VMH to EL, June 1914, HS Abt. D 24 Nr. 45/2
7. Ibid.
8. Princess Marie of Erbach-Schönberg, 375.
9. Rec., 298.
10. Ibid., 299-300.
11. Ibid., 305.
12. Ibid., 307.
13. Ibid., 308.
14. E.M Almedingen, An Unbroken Unity (London: The Bodley Head Ltd., 1964, reprinted by Pavlovsk Press), 86, AF to VMH.
15. VMH to NK, Mall House, October 30, 1914, BA S 384.
16. The Times of London, Letter by Lord Shelborne, October 31, 1914.
17. Ibid. Letter by John Hay, same date.
18. Buxhoeveden, The Life and Tragedy of Alexandra Feodorovna, 198, AF to VMH.
19. Louis to NK, Kent House, November 20, 1914, SA MB1/T72.
20. VMH to NK, March 4, 1915, BA S 385.
21. Crown Princess Margaret of Sweden to EL, October 24, 1915, HS Abt. D 24 Nr. 45/2.
22. VMH to NK, May 12, 1915, BA S 385.
23. VMH to NK, Kent House, August 22, 1915, BA S 386.
24. Margit Fjellman, Louise Mountbatten, Queen of Sweden, 39.
25. Christina Croft, Ella: Grand Duchess Elisabeth Feodorovna (California: Kensington House Books, California, 2005), 125.
26. SA MB1/Y10
27. VMH to NK, April 13, 1916, BA S 385.
28. VMH to King George V of England, April 16, 1916 RA GV/ AA 43/259.
29. Joseph T. Fuhrmann, ed., The Complete Wartime Correspondence of Tsar Nicholas II and the Empress Alexandra: April 1914 – March 1917 (Connecticut: Greenwood Press, 1999), 445, AF to Nicky, Tsarskoe Selo, April 8/20, 1916.
30. Prince Louis of Battenberg to Princess Louise, May 27, 1916, SA MB1/T90.
31. VMH to MB, June 26, 1916, BA S 368.
32. MB to NK, Dartmouth, November 7, 1916, SA MB1/A2.
33. Christina Croft, Ella: Grand Duchess Elisabeth Feodorovna, 138.
34. RA PS/GV Q 722/36.
35. VMH to NK, January 3, 1917, BA S 387.
36. VMH to NK, January 9, 1917, BA S 387.
37. RA GV Diary: 15th March, 1917.
38. VMH to NK, Kensington Palace, March 18, 1917, BA S 387.
39. VMH to NK, April 6, 1917, BA S 387.
40. Prince Louis of Battenberg to Princess Louise, May 17, 1917, SA MB1/T90.
41. Brian Connell, Manifest Destiny: A Study in Five Profiles of the Rise and Influence of the Mountbatten Family (London: Cassell and Company, Ltd., 1953), 50.
42. VMH to NK, June 7, 1917, BA S 387.
43. Prince Louis of Battenberg to Princess Louise, June 6, 1917, SA MB1/T90.
44. Kerr, 264.
45. VMH to Thomas Whittmore, August 9, 1918, BA S 368.
46. VMH to King George V of England, August 10, 1918, RA GV/AA 43/283.
47. Telegram from the D.M.I to General Poole, Archangel, August 9, 1918, RA PS/GV M/1344A/20.
48. Princess Marie Louise, My Memories of Six Reigns, 186.
49. Ibid.
50. Ibid., 187.
51. VMH to NK, Kent House, September 3, 1918, BA S 387.
52. VMH to King George V of England, Kent House, September 3, 1918, RA GV/AA 43/284.
53. VMH to Thomas Whittmore, September 14, 1918, BS 371.
54. VMH to King George V of England, Kent House, September 22, 1918, RA GV/AA 43/285.

Chapter Twelve

1. VMH to King George V, Kent House, September 22, 1918, RA GV/AA 43/285.
2. VMH to NK, Broadlands, November 9, 1918, BA S 387.
3. VMH to NK, Kent House, February 6, 1919, BA S 388.
4. VMH to King Alfonso XIII of Spain, Sept. 22, 1918, Madrid Archives.
5. The Times of London, Oct 22, 1937, Grand Duke of Hesse; Bravery in Face of the Revolutionary Mob, from a correspondent.

6. The Times of London, November 25, 1918.
7. Prince Louis of Battenberg to Princess Louise, May 19, 1919, SA MB1/T90.
8. VMH to NK, Kent House, May 22, 1919, BA S 388.
9. Douglas Liversidge, The Mountbattens: From Battenberg to Windsor (London: Arthur Barker Limited, 1978), 102.
10. VMH to GDE, Mall House, December 19, 1913, HS Abt. D 24 Nr. 45/2.
11. Hugo Vickers, Alice: Princess Andrew of Greece, 116-17, 127-130.
12. VMH to EL, Hotel Bellevue, Thurn, Switzerland, August 8, 1919, HS Abt. D 24 Nr. 35/2.
13. VMH to EL, December 31, 1920, HS Abt. D 24 Nr. 35/2.
14. PI to VMH, June 14, 1922, Hemmelmarck Archives.
15. VMH to GDE September 22, 1920, HS Abt. D 24 Nr. 45/2.
16. VMH to NK, Vulpera, Switzerland, August 13, 1919, BA S 388.
17. VMH to NK, April 6, 1919, BA S 388.
18. VMH to EL, Southampton, October 7, 1919, HS Abt. D 24 Nr. 35/2.
19. Unpublished Diaries of Grand Duke Dmitri Pavlovich London, January, 30, 1919, Houghton Library, Harvard University.
20. Kenneth Rose, King George V (London: PAPERMAC a division of Macmillan Publishers Limited, 1984), 229.
21. VMH to NK, Hotel Royal, Rome, January 8, 1920, BA S 389.
22. Ibid.
23. Hoover Institute Archives, Collection Title: M. Giers, Box Number 39, Folder ID: 12.
24. VMH to EL, December 31, 1921. HS Abt. D 24 Nr. 35/2.
25. Hoover Institute Archives, Collection Title: M. Giers, Box Number 39, Folder ID: 12. VMH to M. de Gries, Fishponds, September 20, 1920.
26. VMH to GDE, Fishponds, December 19, 1920, HS Abt. D 24 Nr. 45/2.
27. Hemmelmarck Archives.
28. PI to VMH, Hemmelmarck, November 1, 1920, Hemmelmarck Archives.
29. PI to VMH, Hemmelmarck, December 22, 1920, Hemmelmarck Archives.
30. VMH to EL, Port Said, January 27, 1921, HS Abt. D 24 Nr. 35/2.
31. Kerr, 262.
32. VMH to NK, Jerusalem, February 7, 1921, BA S 389.
33. PI to VMH, Hemmelmarck, February 13, 1921, Hemmelmarck Archives.
34. PI to VMH, Hemmelmarck, February 14, 1921, Hemmelmarck Archives.
35. VMH to EL, Hotel Royal, Rome, February 21, 1921, HS Abt. D 24 Nr. 35/2.
36. Ibid.
37. VMH to George Milford Haven, Fishponds, April 24, 1921, SA MB1/Y27.
38. VMH to NK, Corfu, March 20, 1921, BA S 389.
39. The Rt. Honourable Lord Lee of Fareham, First Lord of the Admiralty, to Lord Stamfordham, August 8, 1921, SA MB1/T39 (386).

Chapter Thirteen

1. VMH to King George V, September 15, 1921, RA GV/ AA 43/325.
2. Ibid.
3. VMH to Queen Mary, September 15, 1921, RA GV/CC 45/602.
4. VMH to King George V, Fishponds, September 22, 1921, RA GV/ AA 43/326.
5. VMH to Queen Mary, Fishponds, September 26, 1921, RA GV/CC 45/605.
6. RA GV/AA 43/327
7. VMH to King George V, October 24, 1921, RA GV/AA 43/328.
8. EL to VMH, Wofsgarten, September 24, 1921, HS Abt. D 24 Nr. 35/4.
9. VMH to EL, Fishponds, November 29, 1921, HS Abt. D 24 Nr. 35/2.
10. VMH to MB, Malta, April 15, 1935, BA S 361.
11. VMH to George Milford Haven, July 3, 1934, SA MB1/Y27.
12. VMH to NK, February 20, 1922, BA S 389.
13. Ibid.
14. VMH to King George V, February 23, 1922, RA GV/AA 43/331.
15. VMH to George Milford Haven, March 27, 1922, SA MB1/Y27.
16. VMH to George Milford Haven, April 24, 1922, SA MB1/Y27.
17. EL to VMH, Darmstadt, April 5, 1922, HS Abt. D 24 Nr. 35/4.
18. VMH to George Milford Haven, May 7, 1922, SA MB1/Y27.
19. Ibid.
20. VMH to NK, September 10, 1922, BA S 389.
21. Robert Golden, "Going to the Chapel," Majesty Magazine, Vol. 25, no.7, 29-30.
22. Queen Mary to VMH, Buckingham Palace, June 23, 1922, BA S 347.
23. King George V to VMH, Buckingham Palace, June 24, 1922, BA S 347. The expression "Aunt Heap" has been attributed to David, the Prince of Wales (Edward VIII) but he may have been paraphrasing or repeating remarks of Prince Arthur of Connaught. At the time no. 7 KP was offered to VMH there were three of her aunts in residence: Louise, Beatrice and Helen Albany. Robert Golden, email, September 23, 2005.
24. EL to VMH, Wolfsgarten, August 28, 1922, HS Abt. D 24 Nr. 35/4.
25. Janet Morgan, Edwina Mountbatten: A Life of Her Own, 444.

26. Hugo Vickers, Alice: Princess Andrew of Greece, 161-171 for details.
27. VMH to Lord Stamfordham, Kensington Palace, December 4, 1922, RA PS/GV/M 1823/48.
28. VMH to Lord Stamfordham, Kensington Palace, December 7, 1922, RA PS/GV/ M 1823/54.
29. RA Queen Mary's Diary, 5th November, 1922.
30. VMH to EL, December 26, 1922 HS Abt. D 24 Nr. 35/2.
31. Ibid.
32. The Times of London, July 3, 1923.
33. Margit Fjellman, Louise Mountbatten, Queen of Sweden, 94.
34. The Times of London, July 3, 1923.
35. VMH to King George V, June 26, 1923, RA GV/ AA 43/349.
36. EL to VMH, Darmstadt, June 30, 1923, HS Abt. D 24 Nr. 35/4.
37. VMH to George Milford Haven, July 31, 1923, SA MB1/Y27.
38. Margit Fjellman, Louise Mountbatten, Queen of Sweden, 99.
39. The Times of London, December 10, 1923.
40. Email, Lady Mountbatten to author, September 16, 2004.
41. EL to VMH April 3, 1924, HS Abt. D 24 Nr. 35/4.
42. VMH to George Milford Haven, August 4, 1924, SA MB1/Y27.
43. VMH to King George V, January 14, 1925, RA GV/ AA 43/233.
44. Ibid.
45. King George V to VMH, January 15, 1925, BA S 367.
46. Greg King and Penny Wilson, The Fate of the Romanovs, see 68-69, 141-143, 505.
47. Email, Philip Goodman on behalf of Sonia Goodman, daughter of Countess Marika Kleinmichel, to author, January 1, 2006.
48. EL to VMH, Darmstadt, November 27, 1925, HS Abt. D 24 Nr. 35/4.
49. VMH to Sir Austen Chamberlain, August 4, 1926, RA PS/GV/M 2062/21.
50. Foreign Office to VMH, August 17, 1926, RA PS/GV/M 2062/23.
51. EL to VMH, Darmstadt, December 2, 1928, HS Abt. D 24 Nr. 35/4.
52. The Times of London April 22, 1929.

Chapter Fourteen

1. E.F. Benson, Queen Victoria's Daughters, 29.
2. VMH to EL, St. Cloud, January 31, 1930, HS Abt. D 24 Nr. 35/2.
3. VMH to Princess Cecile, Continental Hotel Berlin, February 13, 1930, HS Abt. D 24 Nr. 73/6.
4. The Times of London, February 4, 1931.
5. VMH to EL, Kensington Palace, May 19, 1930, HS Abt. D 24 Nr. 35/2.
6. VMH to Princess Cecile, Kensington Palace, October 31, 1931, HS Abt. D 24 Nr. 73/6.
7. VMH to Princess Cecile, Kensington Palace, November 11, 1931, HS Abt. D 24 Nr. 73/6.
8. VMH to MB, Stockholm, April 11, 1933, BA S 360.
9. Email, Lady Mountbatten to author, September 16, 2004.
10. Questions answered by letter, HRH, The Duke of Edinburgh to author, July 22, 2003.
11. Email, Lady Mountbatten to author, January 31, 2006.
12. VMH to Princess Cecile, Lynden Manor, wrote November 27, 1932, HS Abt. D 24 Nr. 73/6.
13. The Times of London, July 26, 1932.
14. VMH to MB, Kensington Palace, June 18, 1933 BA S 360.
15. VMH to MB, June 21, 1934, BA S 361.
16. The Times of London, October 12, 1934, Books of the Week Prince Louis of Battenberg, Admiral Mark Kerr's Biography.
17. VMH to Princess Cecile, Kensington Palace, May 27, 1933, HS Abt. D 24 Nr. 73/6.
18. SA MB 11/1/4.
19. VMH to Princess Cecile, Kensington Palace, October 18, 1933, HS Abt. D 24 73/6.
20. VMH to MB, Kensington Palace, November 13, 1933, BA S 360.
21. Arturo Beéche, Interview with Prince Alfred of Prussia, ERHJ, Issue X, March-April 1999, 5.
22. VMH to George Milford Haven, July 3, 1934, SA MB1/Y27.
23. VMH to Princess Cecile, Kensington Palace, October 29, 1934, HS Abt. D 24 Nr. 73/6.
24. VMH to Princess Cecile, Kensington Palace, November 5, 1934, HS Abt. D 24 Nr. 73/6.
25. VMH to MB, November 22, 1934, BA S 361.
26. VMH to Queen Mary, May 1, 1935 RA GV/CC 45/957.
27. Ian Vorres, The Last Grand Duchess (Canada: Key Porter Books, 2001), 192.
28. VMH to NK, Wolfsgarten, May 7, 1935, BA S 391.
29. VMH to MB, Sofiero, June 16, 1935, BA S 361.
30. VMH to Princess Cecile, Carisbrooke Castle, August 18, 1935, HS Abt. D 24 Nr. 73/6.
31. VMH to Princess Cecile, Kensington Palace, May 15, 1936, HS Abt. D 24 Nr. 73/6.
32. VMH to Prince Philip, Kensington Palace, October 17, 1935, BA S 356.
33. VMH to MB, Kensington Palace, January 12, 1936.
34. VMH to Prince Philip, Rosneath, October 13, 1936, BA S 356.
35. VMH to Prince Philip, Kensington Palace, October 28, 1936, BA S 356.
36. VMH to EL, Kensington Palace, December 21, 1936, HS Abt. D 24 Nr. 35/2.

37. VMH to Princess Cecile, Kensingon Palace, February 9, 1937, HS Abt. D 24 Nr. 73/6.
38. VMH to MB, Cologne, April 2, 1937.
39. VMH to Princess Cecile, Adsdean, June 20, 1937, HS Abt. D 24 Nr. 73/6.
40. PI to EL, July 17, 1937, HS Abt. D 24 Nr. 36 3/D.
41. VMH to NK, Wolfsgarten, September 12, 1937, BA S 392.
42. The Times of London, October 11, 1937.
43. VMH to May, October 13, 1937, RA GV/CC 45/1111.
44. VMH to Prince Philip, Kensington Palace, October 29, 1937, BA S 356.
45. VMH to Prince Philip, Kensington Palace, November 15, 1937, BA S 356.
46. Janet Morgan, Edwina Mountbatten: A Life of Her Own, 259.
47. Queen Mary to VMH, November 21, 1937, BA S 368.

Chapter Fifteen

1. VMH to MB, January 27, 1938, BA S 357.
2. VMH to Prince Philip, Kensington Palace, March 7, 1938, BA S 356.
3. VMH to Prince Philip, Kensington Palace, March 31, 1938, BA S 356.
4. L&V, 360.
5. Mountbatten: Eighty Years in Pictures, 127.
6. Email Lady Mountbatten to author, January 26, 2006.
7. Duke of Connaught to VMH, April 8, 1938, BA S 368.
8. VMH to Queen Mary, April 14, 1938, May RA GV/CC 45/1149.
9. VMH to NK, Sofiero, August 28 1938, BA S 392.
10. SA MB 11/1/4
11. VMH to Princess Louise, [early July, 1938], RA VIC/Add A 17/1675.
12. Irène to Princess Louise, July 12, 1938, RA VIC /Add A/17/ 1679.
13. VMH to Princess Louise, Wolfsgarten, July 19, 1938, RA VIC/Add A 17/1680.
14. VMH to Princess Margaret of Hesse and by Rhine, Hemmelmarck, July 22, 1938, HS Abt. D 26 Nr. 78/9.
15. VMH to Nada Milford Haven, July 27, 1938 SA MB1/Y27.
16. Postcard VMH to Prince and Princess Ludwig of Hesse and by Rhine, Chichester, September 26, 1938 HS Abt. D 26 Nr. 78/9.
17. VMH to Princess Louise, September 17, 1938, RA VIC/Add A 17/1686.
18. VMH to Prince Philip, Adsdean, November 26, 1938, BA S 356.
19. VMH to Prince Philip, Kensington Palace, December 10, 1938, BA S 356.
20. VMH to Princess Margaret of Hesse and by Rhine, Kensington Palace, April 28, 1939, HS Abt. D 26 Nr. 78/9.
21. VMH to MB, Adsdean, August 28, 1939, BA S 361.
22. VMH to Grand Duchess Xenia, Adsdean, September 8, 1939, the Grand Duchess Xenia Archive.
23. VMH to Prince Philip, Lynden Manor, October 19, 1939, BA S356.
24. VMH to Lady Isabelle Geddes, Lynden Manor, October 27, 1939, HS Abt. D 24 Nr. 103/5.
25. VMH to Lady Isabelle Geddes, Lynden Manor, November 28, 1939, HS Abt. D 24 Nr. 103/5.
26. VMH to Lady Isabelle Geddes, Broadlands, August 28, 1944, HS Abt. D 24 Nr. 103/5.
27. VMH to Edwina Mountbatten, Kensington Palace, March 9, 1940, BA S 358.
28. VMH to Queen Mary, Lynden Manor, October 31, 1939, RA GV/CC 45/1206.
29. L&V, 375.
30. VMH to MB, September 20, 1941, BA S 361.
31. VMH to Lady Isabelle Geddes, Kensington Palace, May 11, 1940, HS Abt. D 24 Nr. 103/5.
32. VMH to NK, Kensington Palace, May 11, 1940, BA S 392.
33. VMH to Lady Isabelle Geddes, Kensington Palace, June 18, 1940, HS Abt. D 24 Nr. 103/5.
34. VMH to Prince Philip, Greywood, Borley, Hants, July 4, 1940, BA S 356.
35. Email, Lady Mountbatten to author, February 7, 2006.
36. July 8, 1942, BA S347.
37. VMH to Lady Isabelle Geddes, Broadlands, April 22, 1941, HS Abt. D 24 Nr. 103/5.
38. Queen Mary to the Earl of Athlone, Badminton, January 17, 1941, RA GV/ CC 53/819.
39. VMH to King George VI of England, Kensington Palace, September 2, 1941, RA VI/PRIV/01 /12/1.
40. VMH to Queen Mary, June 12, 1942, RA GV/CC 45/1329.
41. The Earl of Athlone to Queen Mary, June 10, 1942, RA GV/CC 53/1035.
42. Questions answered by letter, HRH, The Duke of Edinburgh to author, July 22, 2003.
43. Ibid.
44. VMH to King George VI, Kensington Palace, September 2, 1941, RA GVI/PRIV/01 /12/1.
45. VMH to NK, Kensington Palace, September 10, 1941, BA S 392.
46. VMH to MB, October 28, 1943, BA S 361.
47. VMH to Queen Mary, Kensington Palace, June 24, 1943, RA GV/CC 45/1355.
48. VMH to Queen Mary, Kensington Palace, October 16, 1943, RA GV/CC 45/1359.
49. VMH to Lady Isabelle Geddes, Kensington Palace, January 20, 1944, HS Abt. D 24 Nr. 103/5.
50. VMH to NK, Kensington Palace, June 19, 1944, BA S 392.
51. VMH to NK, Windsor Castle, June 30, 1944, BA S 392.
52. Janet Morgan, Edwina Mountbatten: A Life of Her Own, 322.

53. L&V, 383.
54. VMH to Lady Isabelle Geddes, Broadlands, April 9 1945, HS Abt. D 24 Nr. 103/5.
55. VMH to Queen Mary, Kensington Palace, May 10, 1945, RA GV/CC 45/1415.

Chapter Sixteen

1. VMH to Sir Owen, August 10, 1945, RA/ VIC/Add A 1/20.
2. VMH to Lady Geddes, Broadlands, September 4, 1945. HS Abt. D 24 Nr. 103/5.
3. VMH to MB, December 31, 1945, BA S 362.
4. VMH to King George VI, Kensington Palace, July 5, 1946, RA GVI/PRIV 01/12/5.
5. PI to Queen Mary, Hemmelmarck, July 15, 1946, RA GV/CC 46/486.
6. VMH to Queen Mary, Sofiero, September 2, 1946, RA GV/CC 45/1468.
7. PI to Queen Mary, Hemmelmarck, October 18, 1946, RA GV/ CC 45/1474.
8. Richard Hough, Mountbatten: A Biography (New York: Random House: New York, 1981), 213.
9. Douglas Liversidge, The Mountbattens: From Battenberg to Windsor, 124.
10. Hugo Vickers, Alice: Princess Andrew of Greece, 319.
11. VMH to MB, Kensington Palace, February 4, 1944, BA S 362.
12. Hugo Vickers, Alice: Princess Andrew of Greece, 319.
13. Ibid., 324.
14. VMH to Queen Mary, Kensington Palace, November 15, RA GV/CC 45/1541.
15. VMH to Queen Mary, Kensington Palace, December 17, 1947, RA GV/CC 45/ 1555.
16. VMH to Queen Mary, Kensington Palace, October 10, 1948, RA GV/CC 45/1606.
17. The Times of London, December 15, 1948.
18. Anthony Holden, Charles, Prince of Wales (London: Weidenfeld & Nicolson, 1979), 54-55.
19. Ibid.
20. PI to Queen Mary, Hemmelmarck, January 4, 1950, RA GV/CC 45/1657.
21. Questions answered by letter, HRH, The Duke of Edinburgh to author, July 22, 2003.
22. Earl of Athlone to Queen Mary, September 14, 1950, RA GV/CC 53/1534.
23. Mountbatten: Eighty Years in Pictures, 191.

Epilogue

1. Hugo Vickers, Alice: Princess Andrew of Greece, 339-40.
2. PI to Queen Mary, September 28, 1950, RA GV/CC 45/1686.
3. Philip Ziegler, Mountbatten: Including His Years as The Last Viceroy of India, 507.
4. PI to MB, September 24, 1950, BA S 354.
5. Lady Irene Carrisbrooke to MB, September, 1950, BA S 354.
6. Harold Wernher to MB, September 24, 1950, BA S 354.
7. Prince Ludwig of Hesse and by Rhine to MB, September 30, 1950, BA S 354.
8. Queen Louise of Sweden to Lady Drury, dated Oct 2, 1950, courtesy of Argyll Etkin Limited.
9. The Times of London, November 12, 1953.
10. PI to Queen Mary, May 26, 1952, RA GV/CC 45/1801.

Bibliography

Archives

Family Archives, Darmstadt OR Hessisches Staatarchiv Darmstadt Section D 22, 24, 26, (Grand Ducal Family Archives).
Broadlands Archives
Grand Duchess Xenia Archive
Hemmelmarck Archives
Hoover Institute Archives, Collection Title: M. Giers, Box Number 39, Folder ID: 12.
Royal Archives
Royal Archives Madrid
Southampton Archives, Hartley Library

Memoirs

Alice, Princess, Countess of Athlone. *For My Grandchildren: Some Reminiscences of Her Royal Highness Princess Alice, Countess of Athlone.* Evan Brothers Limited: London, 1966.
Dmitri Pavlovich,Grand Duke. *Unpublished Diaries of Grand Duke Dmitri Pavlovich.* Houghton Library, Harvard.
Ernst Ludwig, Grand Duke of Hesse and by Rhine. *Erinnertes. Aufzeichnungen des letzten Grossherzogs Ernst Ludwig von Hessen und bei Rhein.* Darmstadt: Roether, 1983
Helena, Princess of Great Britain and Ireland. *Alice Grand Duchess of Hesse Princess of Great Britain and Ireland: Biographical Sketch and Letters with Portraits.* G.P. Putnam's Sons: New York, 1884.
Louis, Prince of Battenberg. *Bachelor Recollections of Louis Prince of Battenberg, Marquess of Milford Haven 1854 – 1884.* Written for his wife and children. Unpublished in typed ms form. MB6/M/27 Southampton Archives, Hartley Library.
Marie Pavlovna, Grand Duchess. *Education of a Princess.* New York: Viking Press, 1931.
Marie, Princess of Erbach-Schönberg, Princess of Battenberg. *Reminiscences.* London: George Allen & Unwin Ltd., 1925. Reprinted by Royalty Digest, Ticehurst, 1996.
Marie Louise, Princess. *My Memories of Six Reigns.* Evans Brothers Limited: London, 1957.
Marie, Queen of Romania. *The Story of My Life. Vol.1.* Cassell and Company, Ltd.: London, Toronto, Melbourne,Sydney, 1934.
The Earl Mountbatten of Burma. *Mountbatten: Eighty Years in Pictures.* A Studio Book, The Viking Press: New York, 1979.
Victoria, Princess of Hesse and by Rhine, Princess Louis of Battenberg, Marchioness of Milford Haven. *Recollections 1863-1914.* Unpublished in typed ms form. Eingang 4. XII 1969. Hess. Staatsarchiv Darmstadt D 24 64/1.
William II, Ex-Emperor of Germany. *My Early Life.* New York: George H. Doran Company on Murray Hill, 1926.

Books

Almedingen, E. M. *An Unbroken Unity.* London: The Bodley Head Ltd., 1964. Reprinted by Pavlovsk Press.
Aronson, Theo. *"Grandmama of Europe" The Crowned Descendants of Queen Victoria.* London: Cassell & Company Ltd., 1973. Reprinted by Royalty Digest, Ticehurst, 1998.
Beéche, Arturo, ed. *The Grand Dukes.* California: Kensington House Books, 2010 – "Few perhaps

cherish his memory, but I do," by Ilana D. Miller.

Benson, E. F. *Queen Victoria's Daughters*. New York: D. Appleton-Century Company Incorporated, 1938.

Bolitho, Hector, ed. *Letters of Queen Victoria from the Archives of the House of Brandenburg-Prussia*. Translated by Mrs. J. Pudney and Lord Sudley. New Haven: Yale University Press, 1938.

Buchanan, Meriel. *Ambassador's Daughter*. London: Cassell & Company Ltd., 1958.

_____. *Diplomacy in Foreign Courts*. New York: J. H. Sears and Company, Inc., 1928.

_____. *Queen Victoria's Relations*. London: Cassell & Company Ltd., 1954.

Buckle, George Earle, ed. *Letters of Queen Victoria: A Selection From Her Majesty's Correspondence and Journal Between the Years 1862 and 1878*. Vol. 1 and 2. New York: Longmans, Green & Company, 1926.

_____. *Letters of Queen Victoria Third Series: A Selection From Her Majesty's Correspondence and Journal Between the Years 1886 and 1901*. In Three Volumes, Vol.1 1886-1890. New York: Longmans, Green & Company, 1930.

_____. *Letters of Queen Victoria Third Series: A Selection From Her Majesty's Correspondence and Journal Between the Years 1886 and 1901*. In Three Volumes, Vol. II 1891-95. New York: Longmans, Green & Company, 1931.

_____. Letters of Queen Victoria *Third Series: A Selection From Her Majesty's Correspondence and Journal Between the Years 1886 and 1901*. In Three Volumes, Vol. III 1896-1901. New York: Longmans, Green & Company, 1932.

Buxhoeveden, Baroness Sophie. *The Life and Tragedy of Alexandra Feodorovna Empress of Russia*. London: Longmans, Green and Co., 1930. Reprinted by Royalty Digest, Ticehurst, 1996.

Chavchavadze, David. *The Grand Dukes*. New York: Atlantic International Publications, 1990.

Connell, Brian. *Manifest Destiny: A study in five profiles of the rise and influence of the Mountbatten family*. London: Cassell and Company, Ltd., 1953.

Cookridge, E.H. *From Battenberg to Mountbatten*. London: Arthur Barker Limited, 1966.

Corti, Count Egon. *The Downfall of Three Dynasties*. (trans. by L. Marie Sieveking and Ian F. D. Morrow.) New York: Books For Libraries Press, 1970.

Croft, Christina. *Ella: Grand Duchess Elisabeth Feodorovna*. California: Kensington House Books, 2005.

Duff, David. *Hessian Tapestry: The Hesse Family and British Royalty*. London: David & Charles, 1979.

Epton, Nina. *Victoria and her Daughters*. New York: W.W. Norton & Company, Inc., 1971.

Fjellman, Margit. *Louise Mountbatten, Queen of Sweden*. London: George Allen and Unwin Ltd., 1968.

Fulford, Roger, ed. *Beloved Mama: Private Corresondence of Queen Victoria and the German Crown Princess 1878 - 1885*. London: Evans Brothers Limited, 1981.

_____. *Your Dear Letter: Private Correspondence of Queen Victoria and the Crown Princess of Prussia 1865-1871*. New York: Charles Scribner's Sons, 1971.

Fuhrmann, Joseph T. *The Complete Wartime Correspondence of Tsar Nicholas II and the Empress Alexandra: April 1914 – March 1917*. Connecticut, London: Documentary Reference Collections, Greenwood Press, 1999.

Hibbert, Christopher, ed. *Queen Victoria in Her Letters and Journals*. New York: Viking, 1985.

Hodgetts, E.A. Brayley. *The Court of Russia in the Nineteenth Century. Vol. 2*. New York: Charles Scribner's Sons, 1908.

Holborn, Hajo. *A History of Modern Germany*. Princeton, New Jersey: Princeton University Press, 1969.

Holden, Anthony. *Charles, Prince of Wales*. London: Weidenfeld & Nicolson, 1979.

Hough, Richard, ed. *Advice to My Grand-daughter: Letters from Queen Victoria to Princess Victoria of Hesse*. New York: Simon and Schuster, 1975.

_____. *Louis and Victoria: The First Mountbattens*. London: Hutchinson & Co, 1974.

_____. *Mountbatten: A Biography*. New York: Random House, 1981.

Kerr, Mark. *Prince Louis of Battenberg: Admiral of the Fleet*. London: Longmans, Green and Co., 1934.

King, Greg, and Penny Wilson. *The Fate of the Romanovs*. New Jersey: John Wiley & Sons, Inc., 2003.

Liversidge, Douglas. *The Mountbattens: From Battenberg to Windsor*. London: Arthur Barker Limited, 1978.

Longford, Elizabeth. *Queen Victoria: Born to Succeed*. New York: Harper & Row, 1964.

Millar, Lubov. *Grand Duchess Elizabeth of Russia: New Martyr of the Communist Yoke*. New York: Nikodemos Orthodox Publication Society, 1991.

Morgan, Janet. *Edwina Mountbatten: A Life of Her Own*. New York: Charles Scribner's Sons, 1991.

Noel, Gerard. *Princess Alice: Queen Victoria's Forgotten Daughter*. Norwich: Michael Russell Ltd., 1974.

Packard, Jerrold M. *Victoria's Daughters*. New York: St. Martins Press, 1998

Pakula, Hannah. *An Uncommon Woman: The Empress Frederick*. New York: Simon & Schuster, 1995.

Ponsonby, Arthur. *Henry Ponsonby: Queen Victoria's Private Secretary: His life from his letters*. London: The Macmillan Company: London, 1942.

Ponsonby, Frederick, ed. *Letters of the Empress Frederick*. London: Macmillan and Co., Limited, 1929.
_____. *Recollections of Three Reigns*. New York: E.P. Dutton and Co., Inc., 1952.

Ramm, Agatha, ed. *Beloved and Darling Child: Last Letters Between Queen Victoria and Her Eldest Daughter 1886-1901. In completion of the five volumes edited by the late Roger Fulford. Stroud:* Alan Sutton, 1990.

Reid, Michaela. *Ask Sir James: Sir James Reid, Personal Physician to Queen Victoria and Physician-in-Ordinary To Three Monarchs*. London: Hodder & Stoughton, 1987.

Rohl, John C. G. *Wilhelm II: the Kaiser's Personal Monarchy, 1888-1900*. Cambridge: Cambridge University Press, 2004.

Rose, Kenneth. *King George V*. London: PAPERMAC a division of Macmillan Publishers Limited, 1984.

Salway, Lance. *Queen Victoria's Grandchildren*. Oxford: Signpost Books, Ltd, 1991.

Van der Kiste, John. *Dearest Vicky, Darling Fritz*. Stroud: Sutton, 2001.
_____. *Princess Victoria Melita: Grand Duchess Cyril of Russia: 1876-1936*. Stroud: Sutton, 1994.

Van der Kiste, John, and Bee Jordaan. *Dearest Affie: Alfred, Duke of Edinburgh Queen Victoria's Second Son*. Stroud: Alan Sutton, 1984.

Vickers, Hugo. *Alice: Princess Andrew of Greece*. London: Hamish Hamilton, 2000.

Viroubova, Anna. *Memories of the Russian Court*. New York: The Macmillan Company, 1923.

Vorres, Ian. *The Last Grand Duchess*. Canada: Key Porter Books, 2001.

Ziegler, Philip. *Mountbatten: Including His Years as The Last Viceroy of India*. New York: Perennial Library; Harper & Row, Publishers, 1985.

Newspapers

Illustrated News of London
The Times of London

Magazines

Atlantis Magazine –
King, Greg. "The Hessian Royal Family." Vol. 2 No. 2, pp.7-25.
_____. "The Russian Church of St. Mary Magdalene in Darmstadt." Vol. 2 No. 2,
_____. "Requiems: The Russian Imperial Family's Last Visit to Darmstadt, 1910." Vol. 2 No. 2, pp.104-113.

European Royal History Journal (Eurohistory) –
Beéche, Arturo. "An Interview with Prince Alfred of Prussia," Issue X, March/April 1999, 3-6.
Miller, Ilana D. "A Family Chapel: The Battenberg Chapel." Issue XLIII, Volume 8.1, February 2005, 19-20.
_____. "The marriage of Prince Louis' parents had been a very romantic affair." Issue XXXVIII,

Volume 7.2, April 2004, 25-8.

Majesty Magazine –
Golden, Robert. "Going to the Chapel", Vol. 25, no.7, pp.29-30.

Royalty Digest –
Wynn, Marion. "Eastbourne Remembers Princess Alice Grand Duchess Louis of Hesse", pp.8-11. RD, Volume XII, no. 1, July 2002.
Zeepvat, Charlotte, "Alix and Gretchen", 226-231. RD, Volume XIII, no. 8, February 2004.

Index

The Coburgs of Europe

A royal biography of the Saxe-Coburg & Gotha dynasty and all its branches in Great Britain, Belgium, Portugal, Bulgaria and Coburg.

Queen Victoria and the Prince Consort were both Coburgs and they feature prominently in the storyline of each of the dynasty's branches.

It includes more than 500 photos of the various Coburg branches.

The price of this hardback book is: USA price: $48.95 + shipping ($8 in the USA – $24.00 overseas). WE SHIP WORLDWIDE!

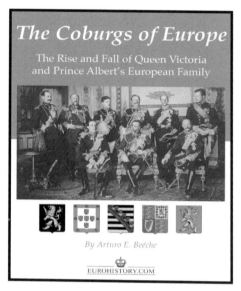

To order by phone: (510) 236-1730 or email: books@eurohistory.com

---

Russia and Europe – Dynastic Ties

Authored by Galina Korneva and Tatiana Cheboksarova, it includes nearly 600 photos, an overwhelming majority among them collected from the main archives of Russia and several European countries. The moment captured by these original photos is able, often times, to tell the reader far more about the unique world of royalty and aristocracy than countless pages of text. The authors also relied on important information obtained from Russian and foreign periodicals, memoirs and scientific literature. The English-language version of this book was expanded with contributions written by Arturo Beéche, founder and publisher of Eurohistory.

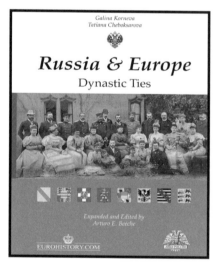

The price of this hardback book is: USA price: $49.95 + shipping ($8 in the USA – $24.00 overseas). WE SHIP WORLDWIDE!

To order by phone: (510) 236-1730 or email: books@eurohistory.com

Dear Ellen

Royal Europe Through the Photo Albums of Grand Duchess Helen Vladimirovna of Russia

With special access to the Grand Duchess' private photo albums, as well as images from the Eurohistory Archive and the private collections of the grand duchess' descendants, the author built a photographic journey covering the lives of Helen and her husband, Prince Nicholas of Greece, and their descendants. Hardbound, glossy paper and contains more than 350 unique photographs, as well a massive several family tree showing Helen and Nicholas in the context of both their families.

The book sells for $43.95 plus shipping ($8.00 in the USA – $24.00 overseas).

Royal Gatherings

Who is in the Picture? – Volume I

Inspired by a very popular feature inside the pages of EUROHISTORY, Ilana D. Miller and Arturo E. Beéche wrote a book on royal gatherings that happened between 1859-1914. Spanning many of Europe's royal families, Royal Gatherings tells the story behind 38 group photos of royals from King Francesco II of the Two Sicilies, to the wedding of Prince Heinrich of Prussia, and the Assassination of Archduke Franz Ferdinand of Austria.

Royal Gatherings' 176 pages are filled with more than 250 unique photographs, most of them from the Eurohistory Archive and some from private royal collections.

The book sells for $43.95 plus shipping ($8.00 in the USA – $24.00 overseas). Order by Phone: 510-236-1730 or email at: books@eurohistory.com

The Grand Dukes

Sons and Grandsons of Russia's Tsars

Included in this unique work, the First Volume in a two-volume series, are biographies of Russian grand dukes who were sons of Tsars or Claimants. These grand dukes came from the senior lines of the Russian Imperial Family at the time of the Revolution in 1917. The book is illustrated with exquisite and rare photographs of these intriguing men, their families and descendants. It also includes several family trees. The chapters were authored by some of today's most recognized authors and scholars on the Romanov Dynasty.

The Other Grand Dukes

Sons and Grandsons of Russia's Grand Dukes

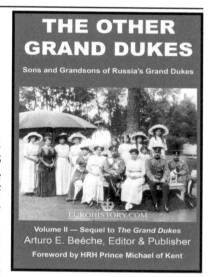

Included in this unique work, the Second Volume in a two-volume series, are 18 biographies of Russian grand dukes. These grand dukes came from the junior lines of the Russian Imperial Family at the time of the Revolution in 1917: Vladimirovichi, Konstantinovichi, Nikolaevichi and Mikhailovichi. The book is illustrated with exquisite and rare photographs of these intriguing men, their families and descendants. It also includes several family trees. The chapters were authored by some of today's most recognized authors and scholars on the Romanov Dynasty. Foreword by Prince Michael of Kent.

The Grand Duchesses

Included in this unique work, are 26 biographies of Romanov women, along with exquisite and rare photographs — many of them from the private collections of Russia's Imperial Family.

The book also includes eight family trees, 36 glossy pages of beautiful photos of these women and their families — 73 photos in total, as well as contributions from many of today's most distinguished royalty authors.

The price of this paperback book is: USA price: $43.95 plus $8 shipping and handling. International shipping and handling: $24.00 – WE SHIP WORLDWIDE! To order by phone: (510) 236-1730 or email: books@eurohistory.com

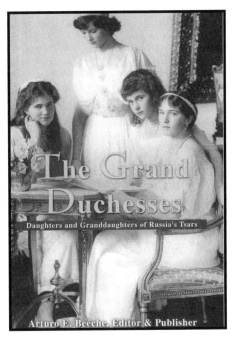

Daughters and Granddaughters of Russia's Tsars

Arturo E. Beéche, Editor & Publisher

Gilded Prism

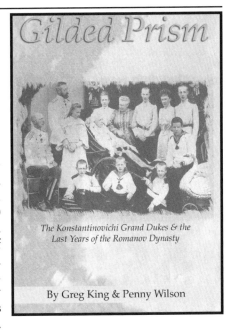

Eurohistory is proud to present to you *GILDED PRISM:* The Konstantinovichi Grand Dukes and the Last Years of the Romanov Dynasty, by renowned royalty authors Greg King and Penny Wilson.

It brings to life the story of the Konstantinovich line of the Russian Imperial Family, beginning with Grand Duke Konstantin Nicholaevich (1827-1892) and following the lives of his six children (Nicholas Konstantinovich, Queen Olga of Greece, Vera of Württemberg, Konstantin Konstantinovich (the famed poet KR), Dimitri Konstantinovich and Vyacheslav Konstantinovich) and many of this grandchildren and great-grandchildren. 238 pages, 3 photo sections!

The Konstantinovichi Grand Dukes & the Last Years of the Romanov Dynasty

By Greg King & Penny Wilson

The book sells for $43.95 plus shipping ($8.00 in the USA – $24.00 overseas).

The Royal Hellenic Dynasty

This is the English-language version of Elleniki Dynazteia published in 2003. The book made an indelible impression on collectors of royal books back then. Due to its widespread acclaim, Eurohistory negotiated for the publication of the book in English as: The Royal Hellenic Dynasty, a book filled with more than 160 photographs of the Greek royal family from between 1863-1950. The Royal Hellenic Dynasty draws an exquisite selection of photos from the private collection of Mrs. Eleni Helmis-Markesinis. The captions were written by Prince Michael of Greece and translated by him and Arturo Beéche, Eurohistory's founder. The book is in the usual coffee-table format, hardback with dustjacket and printed in glossy paper.

Price: $29.95, plus shipping ($8 shipping and handling in the USA. International shipping and handling available for $24).

APAPA

King Christian IX of Denmark and His Descendants

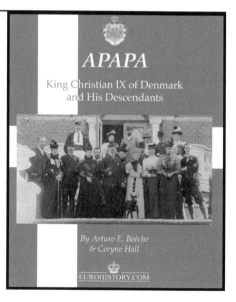

The history of King Christian IX of Denmark, the Father-in-law of Europe, and his descendants. Covering the last 150 years of the royal and imperial houses of: Denmark, Norway, Great Britain, Greece, Romania, Russia, Hanover, Baden, Mecklenburg-Schwerin and many other related dynasties and princely houses.

The authors have handsomely documented their writings with nearly 450 exquisite and rare photos of King Christian IX and his wife Louise and their descendants.

USA price: $48.95 plus shipping ($8.00 in the USA – $24.00 overseas).